Food, Wine, and Culture in California

San Francisco State University
Department of Hospitality and Tourism Management
HTM 421 – Food, Wine, and Culture in California

Taken From:

The Essentials of Wine: with Food Pairing Techniques
by John P. Laloganes

Food Around the World: A Cultural Perspective, Second Edition
by Margaret McWilliams

Custom Publishing

New York   Boston   San Francisco
London   Toronto   Sydney   Tokyo   Singapore   Madrid
Mexico City   Munich   Paris   Cape Town   Hong Kong   Montreal

Cover Art: Courtesy of PhotoDisc/Getty Images

Taken from:

The Essentials of Wine: with Food Pairing Techniques
by John P. Laloganes
Copyright © 2010 by Pearson Education, Inc.
Published by Prentice Hall
Upper Saddle River, New Jersey 07458

Food Around the World: A Cultural Perspective, Second Edition
by Margaret McWilliams
Copyright © 2007, 2003 by Pearson Education, Inc.
Published by Prentice Hall
Upper Saddle River, New Jersey 07458

This special edition published in cooperation with Pearson Custom Publishing.

All trademarks, service marks, registered trademarks, and registered service marks are the property of their respective owners and are used herein for identification purposes only.

Printed in the United States of America

10 9 8 7 6 5 4 3 2

2009800028

WH

Pearson
Custom Publishing
is a division of

www.pearsonhighered.com

ISBN 10: 0-558-36941-3
ISBN 13: 978-0-558-36941-5

Contents

Taken from *Food Around the World: A Cultural Perspective,* Second Edition, by Margaret McWilliams

Taken from *The Essentials of Wine: with Food Pairing Techniques*, by John P. Laloganes

Acknowledgments   xiii

Web Resources   xiv

Chapter 2   Wine Tasting   27

Chapter 3   Viticulture and Enology   41

Unit 2   Wine And Food Compatibility

Unit 3   Wines of The New World

Chapter 7   Wines of the United States and Canada   145

Chapter 8   Other New World Wine Countries   159

Unit 5   Other Types of Wine

Food Around the World

Margaret McWilliams, PhD.

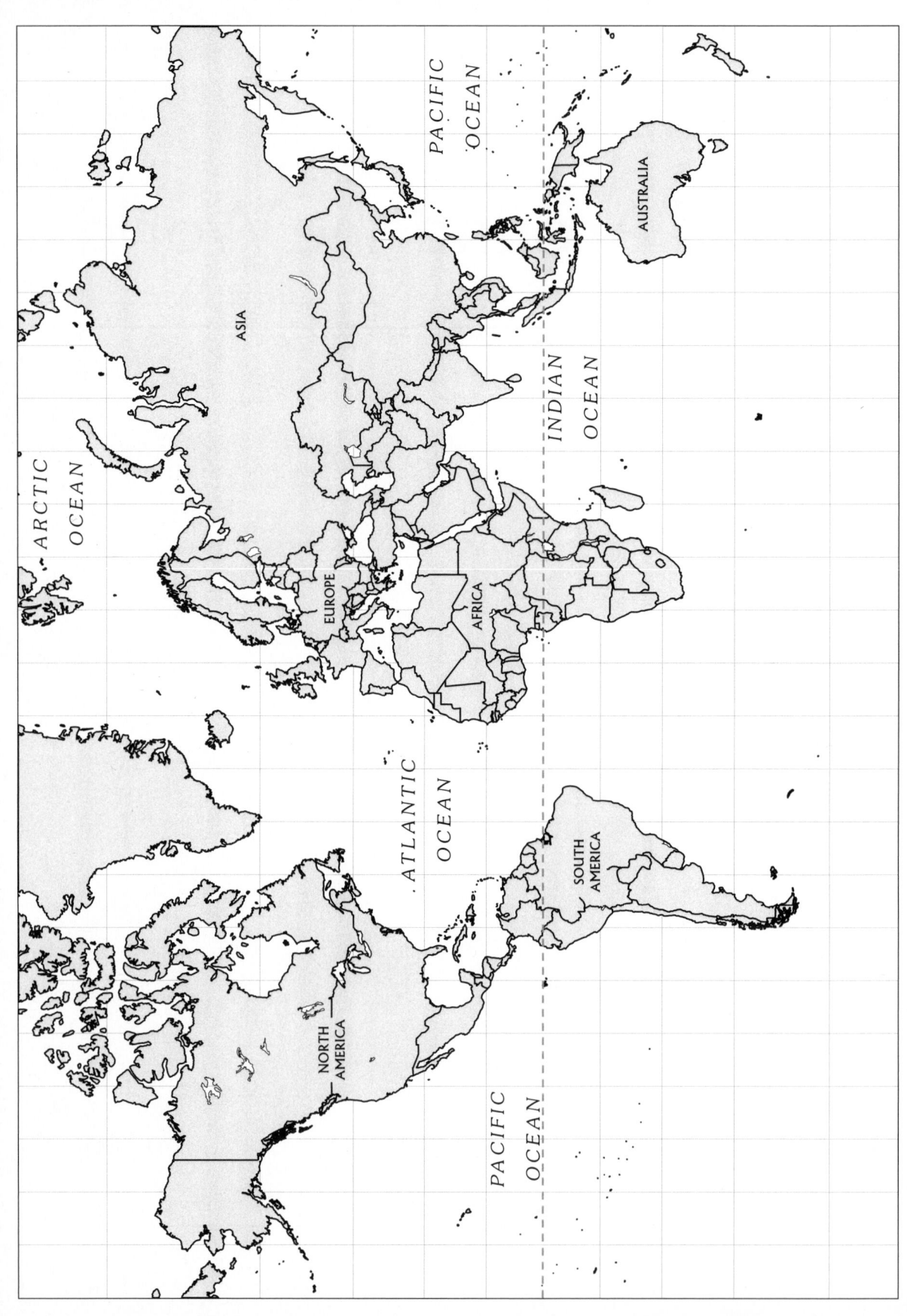

Part

I

Influences on Food Around the World

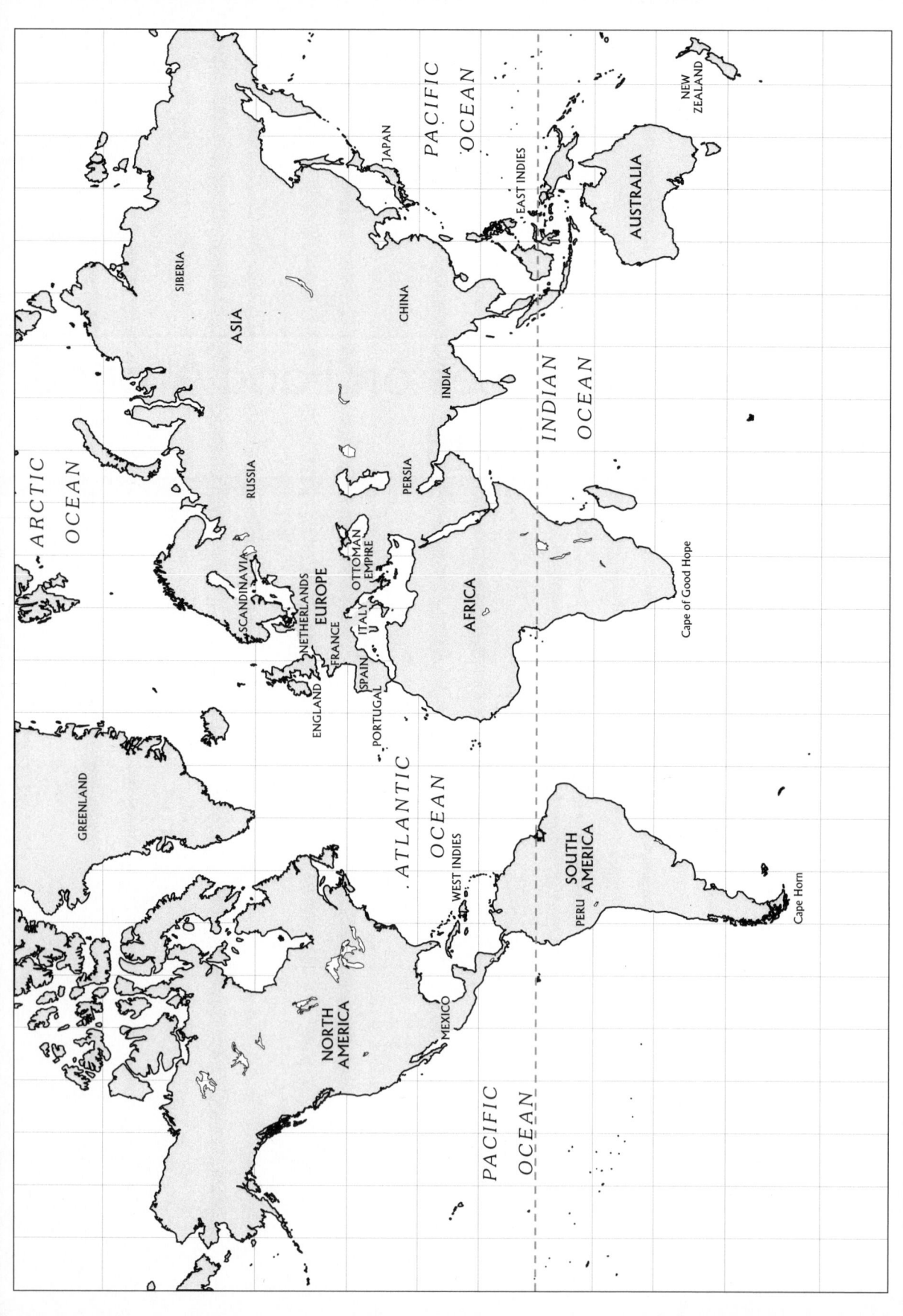

1 Introduction

Have you ever wondered why you eat the foods you do or why certain foods are your favorites? If you compare your food choices and preferences with those of other students, you may find some major differences. Most people enjoy eating, but what they choose varies widely, whether they are living in this country or some other part of the world. The reasons for these differences can be traced to many factors including place of birth, cultural heritage, individual preferences, and income.

This book examines cuisines in countries and regions around the world and focuses on the geographic, cultural, and historic influences that shaped these food patterns. The geographic origins of foods determined the diets of early people because they had to survive on whatever they could find to eat in their immediate environment. Development of farming practices (crops and domesticated animals) over many centuries resulted in a more reliable food supply. As foods became cultivated and plentiful, various cultures evolved in distant places, and special food patterns and preferences began to play an important role in celebrations and religions, as well as in daily living.

Travel, conquests, and migrations gradually expanded human knowledge and experiences. Exciting tales of such travelers as Marco Polo introduced ideas and evidence of different cultures from distant places. Discoveries included new foods, some of which could be traded and transported to other people and places. Even today, the global economy is continuing to expand knowledge of food from other cultures as new foods from afar appear in our markets and on menus.

Food Origins

Early Food Habits

Early people's food habits derived strictly from what was available in the near environment. Hunter-gatherers were restricted to the particular plants and prey indigenous to where they lived. Survival was the driving force that determined what was eaten. Archaeologists have been able to identify some of the foods eaten by the people who lived at the sites being studied, although many food samples have been destroyed by time (Figure 1.1).

Geographic features of their immediate environment determined significantly what foods were available to early people. If they were living in an area next to an ocean, the possibility of food from the sea was a nourishing, if challenging, prospect. Similarly, some people were fortunate enough to live near a lake or a stream where they could catch fish to eat. Civilizations with access to either fresh or salt water fishing developed dietary patterns in which fish played a very prominent role. Evidence of shellfish being used as human food as far back as 127,000 years ago has been found in southern Africa. Some early cave paintings indicate that hunting was another way of acquiring food (Figure 1.2).

Agricultural Developments

Civilizations that flourished in temperate river valleys were able to grow wheat or other cereal and vegetable crops. They also were able to domesticate animals, which were allowed to graze or were fed portions of the crops reserved for that purpose. Central Europeans developed this type of agriculture, and their dietary patterns took on quite a different character from the Japanese and others around the world living near the sea.

Around 12,000 BCE, people in Upper Egypt and Nubia were using grindstones to make flour from wild grasses (Chart 1). In Palestine, wild **emmer** (wheat) was being harvested by 10,000 BCE, and **einkorn** (a type of wheat) was eaten in Syria by 9000 BCE. Wheat, barley, and pulses (legumes) were cultivated around Jericho and in the favorable locales from Syria to Mesopotamia and Egypt by 8000 BCE. Sheep were domesticated to add to the diet in this region (Table 1.1). Before 7000 BCE, goats and pigs were domesticated as sources of meat from Anatolia (now southern Turkey) as far east as Pakistan.

Barley became a food crop in India, and farming was developing in the region between the Indus River and the Baluchistan Hills around 7000 BCE. **Taro**

In Leviticus, Chapter 11, permission for eating some insects is stated: "Even these of them ye may eat; the locust after his kind, and the beetle after his kind, and the grasshopper after his kind." Even today, various insects are popular as food among people in some parts of the world, sometimes being fried or roasted to add flavor.

Emmer—An early type of wheat farmed in Palestine by 10,000 BCE.

Einkorn—A type of wheat grown in Syria around 9000 BCE.

Barley—Cereal grain suitable for human and animal diets.

Taro—Starchy root vegetable that thrives in tropical climates.

Figure 1.1 The immediate environment was early man's only source of food.

Figure 1.2 Painting from the wall of a cave in southern Libya depicts scenes of hunting.

Table 1.1   Foods by Hemisphere of Origin

Eastern Hemisphere	Western Hemisphere
Cereals	
Barley	Amaranth
Buckwheat	Corn
Rice	Quinoa
Rye	Wild rice
Wheat	
Vegetables	
Beet	Peppers
Broccoli	Pumpkin
Cabbage	Squashes
Carrot	Tomato
Cauliflower	Beans
Onion	Dry legumes
Pea	Peanuts
Soybean	Potato
Fruits	
Banana	Avocado
Breadfruit	Blue-, straw-, raspberries
Cherry	Cherimoya
Kiwi	Grapefruit
Citrus	Papaya
Mango	Passion fruit
Pear	Pineapple
	Plum
Other	
Almond	Arrowroot
Cashew	Chocolate
Dairy	Tea
Eggs	Macadamia nuts
Mushrooms	Pecans
Spices	
Sugarcane	

Chart I   Time Line—Food

12,000 BCE	Flour from wild grasses—Egypt
10,000 BCE	Emmer (type of wheat)—Palestine
9000 BCE	Einkhorn (type of wheat)—Syria
8000 BCE	Wheat, barley, pulses (legumes)—Syria, Mesopotamia, Egypt
	Sheep domesticated—Middle East
7000 BCE	Goats and pigs domesticated—Turkey to Pakistan
	Barley—India
	Taro—New Guinea
	Fermented beverage—China
6500 BCE	Goats and sheep domesticated, cereals—Balkans
6200 BCE	Farming—Western Europe, Mediterranean lands
6000 BCE	Farming—Mesopotamia, China
	Potatoes—Peru
5000 BCE	Wet rice farming—Eastern China
	Maize—Mexico
	Irrigation—Mesopotamia
4500 BCE	Cattle used for plowing—lower Danube
3500 BCE	Cattle used for plowing and milk, sheep for wool—Europe
3000 BCE	Millet—Korea
500 BCE	Wet rice farming—Japan
300 BCE	Rice traded from China to Mediterranean and North Africa
200 BCE	Water buffalo used as draft animals—Southeast Asia
1493 CE	Maize transported to Spain from Mexico
1500 CE	Tomatoes and sweet potatoes traded from Central America
1520 CE	Chocolate from New World to Europe
1522 CE	Spices from Southeast Asia brought to Europe (Magellan's ship)
1600 CE	Potatoes traded from South America to Europe, Africa, and India
1850 CE	Palm oil traded from Africa to North and South America and Southeast Asia

Manioc—Inclusive name for group of related tropical plants native to the Western Hemisphere that had fleshy roots rich in starch.

was a cultivated crop in New Guinea by 7000 BCE, approximately the same time **manioc** was being grown in the upper region of the Amazon in South America.

Domestication of goats and sheep and the raising of cereal crops had spread into the Balkans from Anatolia by approximately 6500 BCE. By 6000 BCE, farming was established in central Mesopotamia and China, and Peruvians in South America were raising potatoes. Around 6200 BCE, farming was extending into Western Europe and along the Mediterranean Sea, but use of cattle for plowing did not begin until around 4500 BCE near the lower Danube. Use of animals for milk and wool did not occur in Europe until about 3500 BCE, at which time the plow was introduced in western and northern areas of Europe.

Around 5000 BCE, wet rice farming was being carried on in eastern China, maize was being cultivated in Mexico, and irrigation was being developed as an aid to farming in Mesopotamia. Millet began to be cultivated in Korea about 3000 BCE. Wet rice farming was not begun in Japan until 500 BCE. Water buffalo began to be used as draft animals in Southeast Asia in approximately 200 BCE.

Influences Determining Diets

Geography

Topography was a geographic dimension that influenced agricultural land use. Mountainous regions were inhospitable settings for early people. The rugged terrain made agriculture virtually impossible, and the extreme cold due to the high elevations added to the hazards of attempting to live in the upper elevations of the Alps, the Hindu Kush, and the Himalayas.

Lower valleys in the mountains could be used for grazing animals in the summer, but the mountains were not the regions where early civilizations developed. Extremely steep slopes were appropriate only for raising goats or perhaps sheep. On the other hand, gently rolling or flat lands were well suited to growing a variety of crops. Some regions required labor-intensive terracing for crops or animal husbandry efforts to produce food.

The land available for habitation by people on the earth was limited. About 80 percent of the world was covered by oceans. Mountain ranges restricted use of large parts of Asia and South America plus many regions in Europe and North America.

Civilizations based on farming in early times were established where the land was fertile enough for good crops to be raised. The region in Mesopotamia where early civilization and agriculture flourished in the valleys of the Tigris and Euphrates rivers was dubbed the "Fertile Crescent" by historians, a name clearly reflecting the importance of rich farmland with water and weather suited to raising crops to eat.

Environmental Factors

Water   Several environmental factors determined the feasibility of early farmers growing a crop in a particular location. Adequate moisture, but not too much, was vital to a crop. In contrast to Mesopotamia's favorable weather, the climate of approximately the northern half of Asia was not only dry and arid, but also severely cold in winter due to its northern latitude and some high elevations. Northern China was dry, but southern China had a wet, tropical climate. Northern Africa had a very hot, dry climate, with the Sahara Desert occupying a huge area where crops could not be grown (Figure 1.3). Western Asia was rather desert-like, especially the Arabian Peninsula and portions of the western interior. Europe and the eastern half of North America had moderate climates more amenable to a wider variety of agricultural products than could be produced in desert lands.

Figure 1.3 The Sahara Desert that covers a large area of North Africa is unsuited for growing crops because of the intense heat and lack of water.

Farmers today are still battling the problems of drought and temperatures that kill their crops. Africa has regions (e.g., Niger, Malawi, Zambia, and Zimbabwe) that are affected particularly hard by weather problems. Millions have died and many more will die in famines caused by crop failures. Natural disasters (earthquakes and floods) create serious food shortages that lead to many deaths unless food aid reaches survivors. Political corruption and problems with food distribution in times of famine are other factors that compound the deaths.

Natural rainfall has been adequate for growing many crops around the world, and this reliance on nature influenced the early crops that were raised in various regions. For instance, rice was the staple grain for centuries in the monsoonal areas of the world, from India to Japan, while wheat was the favored grain crop in farm areas that received moderate amounts of rain.

Early people living in rice-growing areas did not eat wheat because it did not grow well in such wet conditions. It did thrive in Europe, Asia, and the northern part of China, where it was the staple cereal in the diet. These contrasts illustrate how rainfall influenced the diets of people long ago in different regions, particularly before trade developed between regions.

In some parts of the world, rainfall was adequate most seasons for early people to raise a crop while in more arid regions, irrigation was required for crops to flourish. This necessitated building a functional irrigation system with an adequate supply of water if farmers were to be successful (Figure 1.4). In other regions of the world, early farmers faced failure of crops when they were inundated with rainfall to the point where fields were flooded and crops were washed away.

The need to control water for crops has been addressed for centuries in various parts of the world. Long ago, farmers terraced the steep hillsides of Bali to create rice paddies that have been maintained and utilized for centuries (Figure 1.5). In much of Southeast Asia, water is directed into and out of rice paddies as is necessary to plant and eventually harvest rice in the paddies throughout the year.

Irrigation systems were developed in Mesopotamia around 5000 BCE so crops could be watered using water from the Tigris and Euphrates as necessary, regardless of droughts. Much later in Europe, the Romans engineered and constructed aqueducts to transport water long distances to meet the needs of people and agriculture in parts of the Roman Empire where the local water supply was inadequate.

Growing Conditions   Temperature was a key determinant of crop successes. An early illustration of this geographic factor is that oranges and dates (Figure 1.6) were successful crops in the warm climates at the eastern end of the Mediter-

Figure 1.4 Although Egypt is situated in the Sahara Desert, irrigation using waters from the Nile River has made it possible for farmers to raise crops in the Nile Valley for thousands of years. (Photo courtesy of Ruth MacFarlane.)

Figure 1.5 People have built and maintained elaborate terraces so they could control the water needed to raise rice successfully on the steep hills of Bali.

ranean Sea, but they were unknown to the Norsemen, whose climate was far too severe for citrus and dates to survive. Similarly, the tropical fruits of Southeast Asia could not withstand the cold winters in Beijing, China.

The length of the growing season (the number of days at temperatures warm enough for active growth) also determined whether or not a crop could be grown in a particular location. For example, corn requires a growing season of at least 140 days to mature. Countries at very high or very low latitudes did not have enough warm days for corn to mature. Vegetables requiring a comparatively short growing season to reach maturity could be grown in such northern latitudes as Alaska with surprising results because of almost continuous daylight in the height of summer.

Successes in raising livestock and crops supported earth's early population growth in places where climate and terrain were favorable (Figure 1.7a, b). Lives of these early people were gradually evolving beyond the basic pursuit of food for mere survival. In fact, evidence suggests that a fermented beverage was produced in northern China around 7000 BCE, which is far earlier than a similar drink from 5400 BCE that was found in Iran.

Trade   At several points around the world, pockets of rather sophisticated cultures emerged. These civilizations began to create riches that sometimes resulted in the exchange of goods. Trade routes such as the Silk Route across Asia were developed over land; sea captains ventured around Africa to destinations in the Indian Ocean. As a result, food and other goods were carried to and from new

Figure 1.6 Date palms thrive at oases in North Africa, providing a food that can easily be dried and stored safely in the hot climate there.

Figure 1.7a Nomads on the plains in Iran still herd goats, a heritage that began many centuries ago.

Figure 1.7b Rainfall in Baja, California barely supports enough plant growth to feed a few cattle. (Photo courtesy of Jim Bull.)

markets, thus adding some variety to foods and flavors enjoyed by people over vast distances.

Sometimes envious and aggressive leaders mounted military attacks to plunder such territories and to build empires at the expense of the conquered. Selected illustrations of these developments that ultimately led to today's expanded food experiences are presented in the next section.

A Capsule of Cultures and Conquests

Early Cultural Sites

Egypt is likely to be the first early culture that comes to mind (Figure 1.8), for the dramatic temples and pyramids built by early Egyptians more than 4,000 years ago remain as testimonials to these people (Chart 2). They controlled land along the eastern end of the Mediterranean Sea and the northeastern corner of Africa as far south as the Sudan before they began to be conquered by various invaders.

The lands to the north of the Persian Gulf also fostered the development of cultures. Sumerians came south from Persia around 2000 BCE. Their contemporaries, the Hittites, who were flourishing in the Anatolian region that is now Asian Turkey, conquered Sumeria's Babylon and ruled Syria as well for four centuries, until 1200 BCE. Assyrians, the next group to conquer the region, ruled until the Persians took Nineveh in 612 BCE.

Meanwhile, Chinese culture was developing and flourishing on the eastern edge of Asia as early as 1800 BCE during the Shang dynasty. In contrast to the history of many other parts of the world, China has continued over many centuries as its own political unit, except for the Mongol incursion from 1280 CE to about 1350 CE. The ruling sequence after the Shang period included the Chou, Ch'in, Han, Sung, Ming, and Ch'ing dynasties.

In the western hemisphere, enduring evidence of the early culture of the Olmecs, who lived along the Gulf of Mexico in what is now Mexico and in Central America, dates from 1200 BCE for almost 1,000 years. They peacefully coexisted near Oaxaca with the Zapotecs, who also left enduring ruins as evidence of their culture around 500 BCE.

Figure 1.8 This giant stone sculpture of Rameses II is but one of several statues in his honor that can still be seen today at Luxor Temple on the east bank of the Nile in Luxor, Egypt.

Conquests and Empires

Achaemenid Empire— Empire that extended from the eastern end of the Mediterranean eastward to central Asia, then southward to northern India and the Persian Gulf (also called the Persian Empire); conquered in 331 BCE by Alexander the Great.

Cultural centers developed at various points around the world during the two millennia prior to the birth of Christ, but these tended to be isolated from each other. However, geographical barriers eventually began to be breeched, and knowledge of other groups led to the desire for conquest and possible riches. When conquerors established themselves by settling among the conquered for extended periods, considerable sharing of such aspects as foods and arts of both cultures resulted in lasting changes, many of which are still evident today.

The Achaemenid Empire   The Persians conquered a vast empire by the 6th century BCE. The **Achaemenid Empire,** also called the Persian Empire, included

Chart 2   Time Line—Cultures

3000 BCE	Egypt
2000 BCE	Sumerians (Persia)
2000 BCE–1200 BCE	Hittites (Turkey, Babylon, Syria)
1800 BCE–1280 CE	Chinese dynasties (China)
?–1625 BCE	Minoan (Crete in Mediterranean Sea)
1500 BCE–1100 BCE	Myceneans (Greek Peloponnesus, Crete, Sicily, Troy)
1200 BCE–612 BCE	Assyrians (Turkey, Babylon, Syria)
700 BCE–300 BCE	Greeks (Greece, Mediterranean lands to Spain, Asia to India)
612 BCE–331 BCE	Achaemenid Empire (Persians)—Middle East
350 BCE–1200 CE	Mayan Empire (Yucatan to Guatemala)
?BCE–284 CE	Roman Empire (Rome, Tunisia, Levant, Europe, England)
284 CE–493 CE	Western Roman Empire (Rome and Europe)
284 CE–1453 CE	Eastern Roman Empire (Constantinople to the Adriatic)
1206 CE–1405 CE	Mongols (Middle East, Central Asia, China, Eastern Europe)
1300 CE–1533 CE	Incas (Peru and bordering regions)
1345 CE–1519 CE	Aztecs (Mexico to Guatemala)

present-day Turkey, the Levant (eastern end of the Mediterranean Sea), Armenia, eastward in Asia beyond the Caspian Sea and Samarkand, southward over the Hindu Kush Mountains of Afghanistan to the Indus River in India, then westward to the Persian Gulf and Mesopotamia. Particularly prominent among the various rulers of the Achaemenid Empire were Cyrus, Darius, and Xerxes. The ruins of the great palace at Persepolis in Iran still reveal some of the artistic glory of the Persian Empire, which finally was ended by Alexander the Great in 331 BCE (Figure 1.9 and Figure C50, p. C17).

Minoans—Mediterranean people who developed a prosperous, artistic civilization on Crete that was ended by a tidal wave in 1625 BCE.

Early Mediterranean Cultures The **Minoan** civilization on the island of Crete flourished in its Mediterranean location because of the favorable environment for farming and safety from attacks of other peoples. Art was developed and appreciated, as can be seen in the frescoes from the ruins of King Knossus' palace (Figure 1.10, Figures C59 and C60, p. C20). The bounty of their food supply is evident from the huge amphorae for storing olive oil and wine that were found at the palace. This culturally advanced early civilization was destroyed dramatically by the enormous tidal wave in the eastern end of the Mediterranean Sea that was generated following the gigantic volcanic eruption on Thera (today's Greek island of Santorini) in 1625 BCE.

Myceneans—Civilization centered on the Greek Peloponnesus that controlled Crete and other Mediterranean islands.

As a result of the abrupt end to the Minoan civilization, the **Myceneans** on the Greek Peloponnesus were able to establish control over Crete, and they extended their control to Sicily, Sardinia, and Troy at the eastern end of the Mediterranean. They even ranged as far north as the Baltic Sea and westward to Britain. Mycenean control of the region lasted four centuries (from about 1500 BCE to 1100 BCE). Agamemnon was the most prominent ruler of this vast trading empire (Figure 1.11). A period of strife dominated the region that is now Greece for almost 800 years after the fall of the Myceneans.

Hellenistic Greece—Ancient Greek civilization that reached its peak of political dominance and cultural influence from about 323 BCE to 27 BCE.

Hellenistic Greece (Classical Greece) began to emerge by 323 BCE as a civilization characterized by remarkable achievements in philosophy, mathematics, and the arts. The artistic creations of the Greeks of this era are among the leading cultural gifts to the world that are still prized today. These include the Acropolis in Athens (with its dramatic Parthenon [Figure C.34, p. C12], Erechtheum, and the Theatre of Dionysus) and Ephesus and Priene in Turkey, as well as numerous beautiful marble sculptures and vases.

Dining was an important aspect of life for wealthier Greeks of this era. Servants prepared and served meals to masters and their male guests who reclined on couches in the male dining room. Women ate separately from the men. Meals

Figure 1.9 Persians created lovely bas reliefs that decorated the palace at Persepolis in Iran.

Figure 1.10 King Knossus's palace (partially reconstructed) and a colorful mosaic illustrate the highly developed Minoan culture that once developed on Crete in the Mediterranean Sea.

featured breads and cake (made with wheat and barley), local fruits such as figs and grapes, vegetables, and perhaps seafood and cheese prepared from goat's milk, as well as wine from local grapes. Olives were important in Greek meals served as an accompaniment or used as an ingredient in various recipes. They also were pressed for their oil, which was used extensively in preparing foods.

Greeks extended their influence westward over the entire northern shores of the Mediterranean Sea to the eastern part of Spain and eastward along the Turkish shores of the Black Sea. The Macedonian military leader Alexander the Great was able to extend the conquests to central Asia by such feats as defeating the Persians at Persepolis (Figure C.50, p. C17) and then marching to Afghanistan and on southward to northern India before his death in 323 BCE at the age of 33.

Roman Empire—Vast empire based in Rome that gradually was formed to cover much of the areas along the Mediterranean coast into Turkey, France, and England.

The **Roman Empire** began in Italy but gained immense dimensions as its leaders sent legions to various points, starting with lands bordering the Mediterranean Sea. Romans fought three Punic Wars against Carthage in Tunisia from 264 BCE to 146 BCE to gain control not only of Carthage itself (Figure C.86, p. C29), but also of its territories (Sicily, Corsica, Sardinia, the Balearics, and Spain). Later conquests included the Dalmatian coast of the Adriatic Sea, the western part of Anatolia (part of Turkey in Asia Minor), land along the Black Sea, the Levant (from Syria almost to the Red Sea), and finally France and England.

Figure 1.11 The Lions' Gate decorates the entrance to the crumbled remains of Agamemnon's Palace on the Peloponnesus south of Athens, Greece.

Among the significant contributions of the Romans to their provinces were law and government, roads, aqueducts, and baths. Romans also brought their food patterns with them as their empire extended across Europe and into Africa and Asia. Greek foods and dining practices had been assimilated and further elaborated by the Roman aristocracy. When the Roman legions conquered and occupied new lands, they also introduced their cuisine featuring heavy spices, thick sauces, and wine. Such fare could be enjoyed in the provinces because the roads built by the Romans and their subjects made it possible to transport spices and some food from great distances.

The enormity of the Roman Empire made it difficult to defend from the warlike tribes threatening the borders. Emperor Diocletian (Figure 1.12) split the territories in 284 CE to establish the Eastern Roman Empire with its headquarters in Byzantium (subsequently renamed Constantinople by its emperor Constantine). This part of the Roman Empire lasted until 1453 CE when the Ottoman Turks conquered it. The Western Roman Empire was overrun by northern barbarians, thus ending that part of the Roman Empire in 493 CE. Over the course of the centuries that Rome dominated its vast empire, it was ruled by many different emperors; Julius Caesar is perhaps the best known.

Mongol Empire—Barbaric, short-lived empire ranging southward from central Asia and westward to threaten even Vienna in Europe.

The **Mongol Empire** presents a sharp contrast to the ways of the Roman Empire. It lasted for only 200 years (1206 to 1405 CE), beginning under Genghis Khan. He united very fierce warriors from the various tribes of Mongolia and central Asia, who breeched the Great Wall (Figure C.161, p. C54) and invaded China in 1211 CE. He also sent troops westward toward northern Tibet and on to encircle the Caspian Sea and penetrate Kashmir and northern India. One of the consequences of the westward push beyond the Caspian Sea was the acquisition of many Turkish-speaking people, which ultimately led to the demise of the Seljuk sultanate in Turkey and the establishment of the Ottoman Empire there.

The food habits of the Mongols were drastically different from those of the Greeks and Romans. The harsh climate and living conditions of the Mongol's native lands fostered a diet based heavily on meats from both wild and domesticated animals. Meat might be dried for later use, but much of it was consumed fresh after either being fried or boiled. Grain was also available and frequently was made into noodles. Vegetables and fruits were rare. Meals were far less elaborate in the Mongol than in the Roman Empire and were a means of survival rather than an entertainment.

One of the consequences of the Mongol Empire was a weakening of Christianity, which had been fairly strong in Constantinople, and tremendous gain in support of Islam, as well as some strengthening of Buddhism (in the Far East only). Even after Genghis Khan died in 1227 CE, Mongol hordes attacked Russia

Figure 1.12 Diocletian, an Emperor of the Roman Empire, built his palace on the Dalmatian Coast in Split, Croatia, during his reign and retired there in 295 CE.

Figure 1.13 Shah Jahan built the Taj Mahal near Agra, India, but later his son imprisoned him in the Red Fort in a chamber where he could see the Taj in the distance above the river.

in 1237 CE and then went on to conquer Poland and Hungary in 1241 CE. Fortunately for Europe, the Great Khan Ogedei, the Mongol leader, died, and so did the Mongol threat to Europe. However, Mongols held control in Russia until the last ruler, Tamerlane, died in 1405 CE.

Babur, a descendant of Tamerlane, provided an interesting footnote to the Mongol Empire. He invaded India in 1526 CE to begin the Mughal Empire, which extended eastward from the Arabian Sea well into Afghanistan and included all of Kashmir, southward along the Indian side of the Himalayas, and a long coastline of the Bay of Bengal before turning westward to the Arabian Sea just north of Bombay. Akbar, the grandson of Babur, fostered the unique artistic style that blended Persian and Indian influences. The Taj Mahal (Figure 1.13. and Figures C.111 and C.112, pp. C37 and 38), built by Shah Jahan, is the architectural masterpiece of the Mughal Empire, which ended in 1707 CE.

Western Empires   Three empires (Mayan, Incan, and Aztec) were dominant in different areas of the Americas, the earliest of these being the Mayan Empire (350 BCE to about 1200 CE). Remains of this culture still stand on the Yucatan Peninsula of Mexico (Figure C.191, p. C64) and in the jungle lowlands of Guatemala. The Incan Empire was the leading civilization in the mountains of Peru (Figure C.177, p. C59) and beyond in South America from about 1300 CE until Pizarro arrived from Spain, conquering the Incas and seizing Cuzco in 1533. The Aztecs gained control of land near today's Mexico City when they arrived in 1345 CE and built their capital, Teochitlan. By the time Spain's Cortez arrived in 1519, they ruled the land from the Gulf of Mexico to the Pacific and from central Mexico to Guatemala, land that immediately became Spain's.

Emerging Trade Routes

The growth of trade was a natural result of the conquests mentioned above, as well as many others around the world (Table 1.2). Wheat was one of the early items traded from the Fertile Crescent of Mesopotamia, for this was a crop that could be transported long distances to such places as Europe, Scandinavia, and the British Isles without spoiling. By the end of the 15th and beginning of the 16th centuries, wheat had even been carried to the Caribbean and Argentina. Spanish conquerors and friars aided in the introduction of wheat to North America.

Maize was developed in Central and South America, and then it was introduced to Europe when the Spanish expedition returned to Spain in 1493, carrying some maize from Mexico. A century later, maize from South America was

Table 1.2 Food Origins and Trade

Food	Origin	Trade Destinations
Cabbage	Europe	North America
Cacao	Latin America	Europe
Coffee	East Africa	Europe, Africa, SE Asia
Maize	Latin America	Europe, Africa, India
Onions	Europe	North America
Palm oil	West Africa	Americas, SE Asia
Potato	South America	Europe, Africa, India
Rice	China	India, SE Asia, Mediterranean
Spices	SE Asia	Europe
Sweet potato	Central America	Europe
Sunflower	Central America	Europe
Tea	Northern China	Westward to Europe
Tomato	Central America	Europe, North America
Wheat	Mesopotamia	Europe, North America

introduced to West Africa. European voyagers in the 16th century not only transported maize to Europe, but also carried Mexican maize to eastern South America and on to part of India and northeastern China. Rice originated in China, spread to India, and then was carried by traders to the Fertile Crescent and throughout the Mediterranean and North Africa by about 300 BCE.

Central America was the origin of the tomato and sweet potato. From there, they were introduced to Europe in the very late 15th and early 16th centuries. South America and Central America added chiles to the world's larder.

Europe provided not only onions and cabbage, but also tomatoes to North America in the 19th century (long after tomatoes had ventured to Europe from Central America). Potatoes went from western South America throughout Europe and to eastern Africa and India by the 17th century.

Coffee appears to have originated in eastern Africa. Its acceptance spread rapidly to Amsterdam and all along the routes of the Dutch traders around Africa and to Southeast Asia. Tea originated in northern China and then spread rapidly all along the trade routes back to Europe. Cocoa is the only popular beverage that originated in the New World. The wonderful discovery of chocolate was carried in about 1520 CE to a very appreciative audience in Europe.

Another gift of the New World to Europe was the sunflower with its excellent oil. Palm oil had its origins in the western part of Africa around the Niger River. From there, its use spread to both Americas and Southeast Asia in the 19th century. Much of the production of palm oil for the world is centered now in Malaysia, where it is an agricultural commodity of considerable importance.

Spices offered very early traders two particularly outstanding characteristics that spurred the spice trade: long shelf life and high market value per volume. Various spices were known and highly prized from China all the way to Rome and beyond long before the time of Christ. Traders carried their valuable cargoes thousands of miles, often under extremely difficult conditions. Despite these long ocean voyages, the spices from Southeast Asia brought such high prices when they finally reached their markets that many traders became very wealthy. It is said that the spices carried back in the hold of Magellan's only ship that returned from his three-year voyage of 1519 to 1522 returned sufficient money to pay for the entire expedition.

Traders from various European nations plied the seas between Indonesia and Europe, bringing home fortunes in spices. The exciting flavors were appreciated not only for their uniquely pleasing variety, but also for their ability to help disguise off flavors in the era when refrigeration was not available to extend the

Actions of traders in centuries past are still influencing trade practices today. Early entrepreneurs who bought cloves in Indonesia in the early days devised a plan to shorten the length of the voyage. Their solution was to carry clove seedlings to Madagascar and grow clove trees there off the eastern coast of Africa, a point much closer to Europe and with a climate that suited the trees. Cloves from Madagascar have held a strong position in the spice trade for many years, although governmental regulations and trade barriers impact the current rivalry between Indonesia and Madagascar.

useful life of foods. A further subtle message conveyed by the use of spices was that the household was wealthy and could afford such luxuries.

Changes in food habits and diets occurred gradually as a consequence of conquests and trade, but improvements in transportation since the time of the early empires have accelerated this trend. Over the centuries since these early days of exploration, trading has expanded greatly. Food from all over the world is shipped to distant ports to add variety to people's meals. Thanks to refrigerated and frozen containers, perishable foods can be transported by air, sea, and land so that they arrive at markets in excellent condition. Although some of the food may be grown locally, people choose diets today that are only partially determined by climate, geography, and growing conditions. A very broad array of foods is available if people can afford and wish to buy products from other parts of the country and the world.

Summary

The diets of people very long ago were determined by food they could obtain by fishing, hunting, or gathering plant foods. Early foods native to different parts of the world included emmer, einkorn, barley, pulses, taro, and manioc. Agriculture developed gradually in temperate areas near rivers; animals also were domesticated. Factors influencing the foods that were being produced in various regions included geography and such environmental factors as water and growing conditions.

As food production became adequate to meet the needs of groups of people living fairly close together, some groups developed cultures that were so advanced that they created some buildings and art that can still be seen today. Among the early cultures were those found in Egypt, Persia (Hittite, Sumerians, and Assyrians), China, and Central America (Olmec and Zapotec). Conquests by warring on other people resulted in the establishment of the Achaemenid (Persian) Empire. Early Mediterranean cultures included the Minoans on Crete (ended when the volcano on Thera [Santorini] erupted) and the Myceneans and the Greeks, whose best-known conqueror was Alexander the Great. The Roman Empire extended over much of Europe, the north of Africa, and into the Middle East. Mongols followed briefly toward Europe but remained a comparatively short time, and little of their presence remains today. In the western hemisphere, the three key empires were the Mayan, Incan, and Aztec.

Food patterns were influenced significantly by trade routes that developed as conquests and exploration increased knowledge of other parts of the world. Foods that had originated in the western hemisphere sometimes were carried to very distant places, including the eastern hemisphere. Similarly, foods originally found in the eastern hemisphere were transported to the west.

Today shipping has evolved so that food can be marketed anywhere in the world, depending on demand and people's ability to purchase food from other regions. Diets no longer are dependent on only the local food supply.

Selected Sites

www.foodhistorynews.com—Magazine about food history.

www.arts.adelaide.edu.au/centrefooddrink/html—Australian site with articles on food and drink by members of the Research Centre for the History of Food and Drink.

http://dmoz.org/Home/Cooking/World_Cuisines/Historic/—Many different articles on food history.

www.cliffordawright.com/history/—Articles on food history in various regions of Europe, Middle East, and Africa.

www.kitchenproject.com/history/—Breadth of material on food history.

www.foodmuseum.com—Articles on food origins.

http://www.foodtimeline.org/foodfaq3.html—Timelines on food history and recipe development.

Study Questions

1. What geographic characteristics were found in the Fertile Crescent that were favorable to the development of an agrarian society?
2. Why is development of a culture dependent on the food supply?
3. Identify 10 of your favorite foods and the part of the world where each probably originated.
4. Where did the food that you ate yesterday come from? As much as possible, indicate where each ingredient probably was produced.
5. Why was rice the staple cereal in Japan? Why was wheat the traditional grain in Central Europe?
6. Briefly describe each of the following empires: Western Roman, Mughal, Persian, Mycenean.
7. Why were food patterns influenced by empire builders?
8. Compare the food patterns of citizens of the Roman Empire with those of the Mongol Empire and discuss the reasons for the differences.

Bibliography

Barraclough, G., ed. 1998. *Harper Collins Atlas of World History.* 2nd rev. ed. Border Press. Ann Arbor, MI.

Batmanglij, N.K. 2000. *New Food of Life: Ancient Persian and Modern Iranian Cooking and Ceremonies.* Mage. Washington, DC.

Billings, J. and P.W. Sherman. 1998. Antimicrobial functions of spices. Why some like it hot. *Quarterly Review of Biology 73:* 3–49.

Brander, B. 1966. *River Nile.* National Geographic Society. Washington, DC.

Civitello, L. 2003. *Cuisine and Culture: History, Food, and People.* Wiley. New York.

Davidson, A. 1999. *Oxford Companion to Food.* Oxford University Press. Oxford, U.K.

Dunn, R.E. 1986. *Adventures of Ibn Battuta, a Muslim Traveler of the Fourteenth Century.* University of California Press. Berkeley.

Fletcher, N. 2004. *Charlemagne's Tablecloth.* St. Martin's Press. London, England.

Grew, R. 1999. *Food in Global History.* Westview Press. Boulder, CO.

Grun, B. 1991. *Timetables of History.* 3rd ed. Simon and Schuster/Touchstone Books. New York.

Harper Collins. 1997. *Past Worlds: Atlas of Archaeology.* Border Press. Ann Arbor, MI.

Huot, J.L. 1965. *Archaeology Mundi: Persia I.* World Publishing. Cleveland, OH.

Kiple, K.F., ed. 2000. *Cambridge World History of Food.* Cambridge, U.K.

Lapidus, I.M. 2002. *History of Islamic Societies.* Cambridge University Press. Cambridge, UK.

Pan American. 1978. *World Guide.* McGraw-Hill. New York.

Pearcy, G.E. 1980. *World Food Scene.* Plycon Press. Redondo Beach, CA.

Pomeranz, K. and S. Topik, eds. 1999. *World That Trade Created: Culture, Society and the World Economy 1400 to Present.* M.E. Sharpe. Armonk, New York.

Shahbazi, A.S. 1976. *Persepolis Illustrated.* Institute of Achaemenid Research. Persepolis, Iran.

Tannahill, R.T. 1995. *Food in History.* Three Rivers Press. New York.

Toussaint-Samat, M.T. 1994. *History of Food.* Blackwell Publishing Ltd. Oxford, U.K.

Ward, S., C. Clifton, and J. Stacey. 1997. *Gourmet Atlas.* Macmillan. New York.

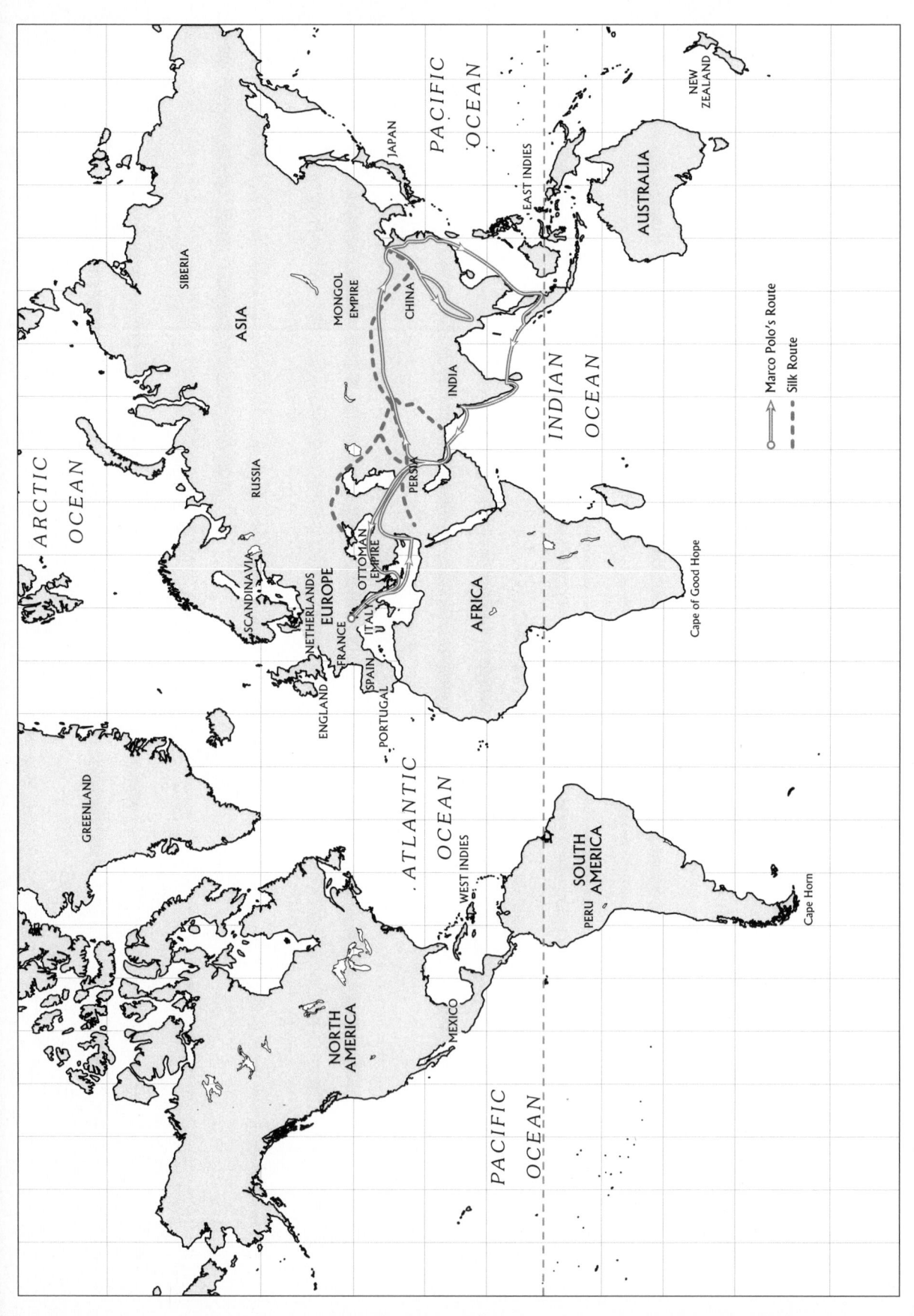

2 Cultural Parameters

Five words—"You eat what you are" and "You are what you eat"—placed in two different sequences provide an intriguing introduction to this chapter. The first statement shows an appreciation of some of the cultural factors that shape food choices and preferences. The second is a pragmatic way of relating physical outcome to a lifetime of eating (nutrition). If food is thought of only as the means of getting the nutrients needed for life, the important subtleties that influence what people actually eat will be missed.

Take a moment to think about the way you eat: how many meals, foods you usually like to eat at each meal during a day, dishes served at family gatherings on special holidays, and your favorite foods. Then consider why you have these food preferences and dietary pattern. In other words, describe what influenced what you eat. These thoughts set the stage for reading this chapter.

Culture refers to the way of life of a people. Customs, habits, language, knowledge, housing, tools, and the arts all contribute to the uniqueness of a culture.

Components of Culture

Culture—Way of life of a group of people (what they create, do, and think).

Culture is a somewhat nebulous concept because a wide variety of characteristics may all contribute to a complex picture. Customary beliefs, social forms, and material traits of a racial, religious, or social group are some of the characteristics contributing to the description of a culture. *Ethnicity* is the affiliation with a race, people, or cultural group. Culture and ethnicity are essential foundations of the study of food and people. Knowledge of the major cultures around the world and appreciation of the cultural richness that is a part of their food patterns not only add pleasure to our lives, but also strengthen the ability of food professionals to work effectively with people from cultures other than their own.

Country of Birth

To an extent, the country where a person is born and resides shapes the food patterns of the individual and families. The geographic realities of climate and terrain suitable for productive agriculture define the local foods that may be available (Figure 2.1). Other resources of the country will influence whether or not manufacturing and business and other commercial endeavors generate a vigorous economy. In countries where all is favorable, an abundant and varied food supply can be obtained by virtually all people in that country. In less favored locales, food may be in very short supply and unavailable in adequate amounts. In other words, the economy and the agricultural conditions combine within a country to define one of the parameters of the nation's food culture.

Housing

Housing is another dimension of a person's culture. People in some cultural groups live in elegant, single-family dwellings; some live in cottages; others live in apartments or condominiums. The roof may be anything from a leaky thatch (Figure 2.2) to an orderly fireproof tile. Some people have a bedroom for each person, while others live in a one-room house in which the entire family must eat and sleep. The kitchens range from spotless and completely equipped with every appliance to those in which refrigeration is unavailable or extremely limited in space, a situation that imposes serious problems of food safety and necessitates daily shopping. A family of a cultural group often lives in housing that is similar to the others in the group.

Language

Language is a key component of culture because it provides a means of sharing thoughts, ideas, and information (Figure 2.3). Accurate, meaningful communication is important in families, communities, nations, and the world. The fact that many international airports around the world require pilots to use English to communicate with the tower illustrates the importance of language as a common denominator in business. Even with the same language, word definitions may differ by country (e.g., *biscuit* in England means a different food than in the United States). Similarly, people in the same cultural group need to be able to understand what is being said in personal conversations.

Figure 2.1 Several different fruits and vegetables grown locally are brought to the outdoor market in Mandalay, Myanmar (Burma).

Figure 2.2 This thatched house is on the bank of the River Kwai in rural Kanchanaburi, Thailand.

Figure 2.3 The Rosetta Stone, dating from 196 BCE, provided a communication key to ancient Egypt once the three scripts and two languages were translated by Champollion in 1822.

A national language helps to define what a nation is culturally. Even within a country speaking the same language, confusion may exist due to differences in dialects and accents. An illustration of such communication difficulties can be found in China with its numerous dialects. Mandarin is the dialect that often serves as the communication interface for people who use different dialects in their daily lives.

Lifestyle

Lifestyle adds to a cultural identification. Certain national habits of living help to define a culture. An example of this is the very late dinner hour (10 P.M. or later) in Spain and in countries that were former Spanish colonies. This tradition developed because the intense heat of mid-day was made more tolerable by taking a siesta and then continuing business in the late afternoon, thus pushing dinner to a late hour. In contrast, Americans tend to try to push as much work into the day as possible. Although these examples are generalizations, many people can relate to such cultural influences.

Food habits are shaped, at least in part, by lifestyle. For example, families with children make decisions about where their young children are cared for, and by whom. Are parents with their children most of the day, or are they away from home for long hours while working many miles away? Mode of transportation—trishaws, buses, bicycles, cars, trains, or foot—shapes lifestyle. Other aspects of lifestyle are food habits. Do families eat all meals together at home, or do they eat in some other setting for one or more meals daily? Who prepares these meals? These are some of the practical questions regarding lifestyle that help to develop some understanding of a specific cultural group.

The Arts

One of the important threads that tends to identify a culture and to continue to hold its members together as a group is that of art. Styles of art vary over the ages and around the world, yet most cultural groups have an artistic heritage that they feel to be their own (Figure 2.4). In fact, paintings, sculptures, mosaics, bas-reliefs, and other forms of art provide a somewhat historic documentation of the earlier

Figure 2.4 Lively, whimsical figures and masks are characteristic of the graceful art of Thailand.

people who helped to define the group's artistic culture. These visual works sometimes depict foods and/or dining scenes that convey a cultural message. For instance, Pieter Brueghel's *Peasant Wedding* depicts a wonderful Dutch wedding feast in the mid-16th century; Renoir's *Luncheon of the Boating Party* reveals a completely different cultural scene in France in the late 19th century.

Music and dance are other art forms that communicate directly to individuals and draw them toward the local culture. Performances of *Swan Lake* ballet (by Tschaikovsky, a famous Russian composer) and the Barong dance (traditional presentation in Bali) are representative of the cultural heritage from Russia and Bali (Figure 2.5).

Musical examples also abound. Sibelius's *Finlandia* is an orchestral work that creates pride in their heritage among Finnish people while also providing an appreciation of Finland to all people who hear this rich and very strong composition. Austria is noted for its music, which ranges from the numerous works of Salzburg's Wolfgang Amadeus Mozart to the lilting Viennese waltzes of Johan Strauss. The United States boasts such composers as Aaron Copland (works include *Appalachian Spring* and *Rodeo*), John Williams (*Star Wars*), and Stephen Foster (composer of "Swanee River" and other songs of the South). Some American

Figure 2.5 Musicians in Bali play gamelans for folk dancers and to entertain listeners.

songs such as "Rum and Coca Cola," "Short'ning Bread," and "Shoo Fly Pie and Apple Pan Dowdy" are musical reminders of some cultural foods in the South.

Literature

An enduring part of a nation's culture is the literature written by its people. William Shakespeare remains revered among British authors long after his death. Charles Dickens brought the food tradition of an English Christmas to life for all to share in his classic "A Christmas Carol." Victor Hugo, who wrote his masterpiece *Les Miserables* in the 19th century, occupies an important place among French writers. Henry Wadsworth Longfellow is the beloved American poet who wrote "Paul Revere's Ride." Carl Sandburg brought the drama of aspects of food production in early 20th-century America to life in his poetry. These are but a few examples of the contributions writers have made to the culture of their land.

Storytelling is another aspect of culture; although similar to literature, stories are embedded in the culture by being passed from person to person rather than being preserved in printed form. This is an art form in many places in Africa, particularly in the western and central regions. Legends have been told from generation to generation in many countries, and some of these have evolved into print. German fairy tales are an example of this type of literature.

Architecture

Public architecture affords additional insights into a culture. Recent excavations in Egypt have revealed two bakeries that were used to feed the workers building the pyramids more than 4000 years ago. In homes of the elite that have been unearthed in Pompeii, the *triclinium* (formal dining room) had benches for reclining around three sides of the room. In Russia, the survival of the Summer Palace and the Hermitage, as well as other grand buildings from the Tsarist era, provides mute testimony to the appreciation that the citizens of Leningrad (now St. Petersburg, once again) held for their cultural heritage even through the Revolution and eventual break up of the Soviet Union.

In the United Kingdom, the stern and imposing palaces and castles are proudly viewed as the cultural heritage of the country. The strength and independent nature of earlier citizenry were clearly expressed in the castles that were built and defended to keep invaders from their stark and windswept coastland. Cooking for all the people in the castle was done over open fires in huge fireplaces, and the privileged residents of the castle dined in the great hall.

All around the world architectural sites continue to reveal the beauty and strength of earlier cultures. The Parthenon on the Acropolis in Athens, with its open and inviting style, is an enduring reflection of the early Greeks. Karnak Temple near Luxor, Egypt, affords a glimpse of yet a different ancient culture that is an important part of a nation's culture almost five millennia later.

The famed Taj Mahal in Agra, India, is a dazzlingly lovely and graceful tribute to Shah Jahan's dead wife, its intricate inlaid designs of semiprecious stones attesting to the highly developed skills of the craftsmen and artists in India. Deeply carved bas-reliefs adorning the long walls of the huge Angkor Wat complex in Cambodia (Figure 2.6) add a different artistic dimension to the cultural context of architecture. The Forbidden City, with its temples and mazes of buildings and rooms within its encompassing walls, affords a remarkable look at the cultural heritage of both Beijing residents and all people of China.

These glimpses of the importance of the arts in creating emotions and feelings are presented to help you begin to think about similar artistic works that help to define your cultural inheritance.

Figure 2.6 Bas-reliefs at Angkor Wat reveal the remarkable artistry of the Khmer artists in northern Cambodia in the 12th century.

Additional Dimensions of Culture

Other defining aspects of cultural groups are their food traditions, national histories, and religions (see Chapter 3). When people live within a region that constitutes a nation or possibly just a portion of a nation, common experiences related to government of the land and beliefs and values can either unite people or create civil unrest and even wars. From such influences, cultural identity and groupings often result, and these groups continue for many centuries when governments are stable.

Immigration

Nations with a history that included empire building often have a mixture of cultures that is evident today. In the United Kingdom, for example, many immigrants from Pakistan or other distant parts of the realm have settled in England, thus permanently altering the homogeneity of earlier years. Similarly, France now has many residents from its earlier territory in North Africa. Even in these countries with strong national identities, the addition of significant numbers of immigrants from other cultures has altered elements of the national image permanently.

Terrible wars in past years caused many people to flee their countries to avoid persecution and probable death. These political refugees often have sought asylum and new beginnings in countries quite distant from their country of origin. An illustration is provided by the very large influx of Vietnamese, Cambodians, and Laotians (Hmong) into the United States as the Viet Nam War was ending. Their arrival in their new country brought awareness of cultures into focus, both for the new arrivals and for Americans. At first, refugees were settled all around the country in an attempt to provide community support for some individuals and families in numerous towns. Gradually, these new immigrants began to gravitate in the new country to regions where others from their own culture were already beginning to gather. The result is a few very large pockets (e.g., "Little Saigon" in Orange County, California) of residents formerly from Southeast Asia.

The hope for a better life is the reason many people choose to immigrate to the United States. Examples over the years include the Pilgrims (seeking religious freedom), the Irish in the mid-19th century (escaping the Potato Famine), students pursuing higher education, and workers looking for higher-paying jobs to support their families.

Immigrants from other cultures often tend to settle together because of strong cultural ties. Evidence of the importance of their former culture is retained in their daily lives. For example, they often speak to each other in their native language and shop where they can get food ingredients for making their native dishes. Such tangible reminders of their cultural heritage provide support and a feeling of belonging.

Thus, the cultural fabric of nations with significant immigrant populations is becoming a patchwork quilt with a piece of this culture and a piece of that one scattered in various places. However, the overall culture of a nation ties the country into a multicultural whole. The United States, a nation with a significant amount of heterogeneity since its colonial beginnings, is a living example of cultural identities being retained while being united into a single nation.

Religion is a particularly strong factor in cultural identity. Sharing common beliefs and practices that are central to a particular religion creates common threads that bind people together into a culture. By the same token, the fact that people practicing a different religion do not have the same beliefs and customs serves to separate the followers of each major religion into isolated groups or into groups who respect each other, but who are not as close between as within religious groups. Even though groups are defined, knowledge and appreciation of various religions can do much to reduce possible tensions and enrich the fabric of our American culture.

Special Messages of Food

Salt

Food sometimes carries special meanings beyond simply providing nutrients. The subtle messages conveyed by a particular food may be a nonverbal exchange between people at a meal or a social occasion. Certain foods may be absolutely essential on a particular occasion. For example, matzo (unleavened bread) must be served for Jewish Passover. Bread or wafers and wine or grape juice served at Communion are symbols of Christ's body for Christians.

Special green tea prepared in the Japanese tea ceremony conveys total welcome and hospitality to guests. Wassail is a traditional Christmas beverage in the United Kingdom that is served to welcome guests during the holidays. The specific foods and traditions vary greatly around the world. Some of these will be discussed in later chapters in this book. However, the importance of salt is sufficiently universal to all people that it warrants some attention here.

Salt, a simple yet essential part of the diet for people and animals, has been valued throughout the world for many centuries (Figure 2.7). The Romans were well aware of the importance of salt for their troops in their military conquests as they carved out their vast empire. Caesar's armies had persons responsible for making salt (by boiling down brine) for the troops. In remote Tibet during the time of Marco Polo (around 1300 CE), salt cakes served as the currency. The remains of Mayan salt-production facilities that have been excavated recently just off the coast of Belize provide evidence that salt was an important trade commodity in the Mayan Empire of Central America.

Chinese Emperor Yu, in 2200 BCE, attempted to control and tax salt in his domain. Throughout the centuries, taxes on salt have punctuated numerous political upheavals, including the French Revolution. Even in the 20th century, England's tax on salt in India and its ban on personal harvesting of salt from the sea triggered Mahatma Ghandi's famous 200-mile protest march to the sea in 1930.

Figure 2.7 In Thailand, seawater is directed into shallow paddies and then evaporated until salt crystals form to produce salt for market. (Photo courtesy of Bill Malcolm.)

The universality of the importance attached to salt can be seen in various religious and cultural traditions of the past. Catholic priests used to place a little salt on the baby's tongue during baptismal rites so the baby would "receive the salt of wisdom." Early Jewish rites required that salt be a part of their offerings. Both Jews and Christians had a tradition of rubbing salt on infants to ensure a long life. Friendship between Arabs was sealed with the expression "There is salt between us." This meant that they would not do harm to each other when they had shared salt. The negative predictions of bad luck from spilled salt are immortalized in Leonardo's *The Last Supper* in which the salt is spilled by Judas.

Eggs

Another food that has been a symbol over many centuries and in different cultures is the egg. Since pagan times, eggs have conveyed special meaning to people. Pagans considered the egg to be a symbol of fertility and renewal of life. The shell represented earth, the membrane was air, the white was water, and the yolk was fire.

In China, eggs colored red are presented at parties announcing a baby's birth. Sometimes two hard-cooked eggs are used to symbolize birth of a girl and a single egg represents a boy. Mayans also endowed eggs with special powers, albeit very different from the symbolism of fertility. Apparently, evil spells could be broken by a medicine man with a special ceremony. He would wave an egg in front of the face of the afflicted person several times and then break the egg before burying it to break the spell.

Christians have traditionally associated eggs with Easter celebrations. Eggs are used symbolically to represent the resurrection of Christ. Hard-cooked eggs are often colored and used in Easter egg hunts in many Christian cultures. Various branches of the Eastern Orthodox Church decorate eggs very elaborately (often just the shell after the interior has been blown out). Many of the traditional symbols applied to the eggs convey particular meaning. Ukraine and other Eastern European countries are noted for their decoration of Easter eggs (Figure 2.8).

Czar Alexander III commissioned the artist Fabergé to make a very special jeweled egg for him to give to his wife, Czarina Maria, in 1884. This Easter gift was such a success that Fabergé eggs were made even after Alexander's death until 56 eggs had been made. These eggs now are admired more for their beauty than for their religious significance and sometimes are shown in special exhibits in museums.

Figure 2.8 Decorative designs are carefully painted on eggs in Romania and other countries in preparation for the celebration of Easter in Eastern Orthodox churches and homes.

Summary

Some of the key components of culture are discussed in this chapter. These include beliefs, social forms, and material traits of a racial, religious, or social group. Geography of the region where a person is born and lives is of great importance, and so is the economic strength of that nation and of the individual families. Housing has a tangible influence on lifestyles, as do the choices about working. Both of these factors certainly influence food patterns. Language, lifestyle, art, music, dance, literature, and architecture also make significant contributions to cultural identity. World history and religions are other key components defining cultural groups.

America today is made up of a kaleidoscope of immigrants from virtually all parts of the world. Regardless of how long ago immigrants first came to America, they or their descendants have stories of remembrances or at least some knowledge of their country of origin. Appreciation of this heritage helps bind people of similar backgrounds into cultural groups that reinforce the customs and traditions to maintain a richness of memories and experiences in the next generation. Often these traditions are shared with others in the community. Such sharing increases understanding and appreciation of the wonderful diversity that is becoming America.

Food conveys special symbolism in different cultures. Salt and eggs provide two examples of how food assumes significance in different cultures apart from merely serving as something to eat.

Selected Sites

www.glossika.com—Site with information on Chinese (including dialects) and other languages.

www.indo.com/culture/barong.html—Story of an important cultural dance on Bali in Indonesia.

www.tech.mit.edu/Shakespeare—Complete works of Shakespeare.

www.online-literature.com/victor_hugo—Biography and works of Victor Hugo.

http://eclecticesoterica.com/longfellow.html—Collection of Longfellow's poems.

www.timsheppard.co.uk/story/dir/traditions/Africa.html—Tradition of storytelling in Africa.

www.fln.vcu.edu./grimm/grimm_menu.html—Grimm Brothers' fairy tales in German and English.

www.touregypt.net/karnak—Information on the Temple of Karnak.

www.taj-mahal.net—Video tour of the Taj Mahal.

www.greatbuildings.com/buildings/The_Parthenon.html—Information about the Parthenon and the Acropolis.

www.angkorwat.org—Information and pictures of Angkor Wat and nearby historic sites.

www.chinavista.com/beijing/gugong/!start.html—Virtual tour of the Forbidden City in Beijing, China.

www.searac.org/vietref.html—Information on immigration program for refugees from Southeast Asia.

http://eggs-files.tripod.com/pysanky_4.html—Traditions of Ukrainian Easter eggs.

http://archive.1september.ru/eng/2003/14/2.htm—History of eggs in cultures.

www.kresy.co.uk/easter_food.html—Symbolism of eggs and other foods for Easter in Poland.

http://ourladyprairie.home.mchsi.com/Ossymbl.html—Symbolism of designs on Ukrainian Easter eggs.

http://users.vnet.net/schulman/Faberge/eggs.html—Description of the Fabergé eggs for the Czars of Russia.

Study Questions

1. What are the characteristics that describe the cultural group with which you identify most closely?
2. What are some of your food preferences and patterns? Did any of these gain this status with you because of your cultural group (or groups)? If so, explain the foods you have identified in terms of your cultural identity.
3. Using a recent newspaper, describe a current example of how some aspect of culture (as described in this chapter) is influencing the food intake of the people involved.

Bibliography

Armstrong, R.G. 1964. *Sisters Under the Sari.* Iowa State University Press. Ames, IA.

Barer-Stein, T. 1979. *You Eat What You Are.* McClelland and Stewart. Toronto, Canada.

Batmanglij, N.K. 2000. *New Food of Life: Ancient Persian and Modern Iranian Cooking and Ceremonies.* Mage. Washington, DC.

Brown, L.K. and K. Mussell. 1984. *Ethnic and Regional Foodways in the United States.* University of Tennessee Press. Knoxville, TN.

Bryant, C.A., et al. 2004. *The Cultural Feast: Introduction to Food and Society.* 2nd ed. Wadsworth. Belmont, CA.

Katz, S.H. 2003. *Encyclopedia of Food and Culture.* Charles Scribner's Sons. New York.

Geisler, E.M. 1998. *Pocket Guide to Cultural Assessment.* Mosby. St. Louis.

Kurlansky, M. 2002. *Salt.* Walker and Co. New York.

Le Couteur, P. and J. Burreson. 2004. *Napoleon's Buttons.* Jeremy P. Tarcher/Penguin. New York.

Lowenburg, M.E., et al. 1974. *Food and Man.* Wiley. New York.

McIntosh, E.N. 1995. *American Food Habits in Historical Perspective.* Praeger. Westport, CT.

Norris, R.E. and L.L. Haring. 1980. *Political Geography.* Charles E. Merrill Publishing Co. Columbus, OH.

Scarre. C. and B.M. Fagan. 2003. *Ancient Civilizations.* 2nd ed. Prentice Hall. Upper Saddle River, NJ.

Stoddard, R.H., B.W. Blouet, and D.J. Wishart. 1986. *Human Geography: People, Places, and Cultures.* Prentice Hall. Englewood Cliffs, NJ.

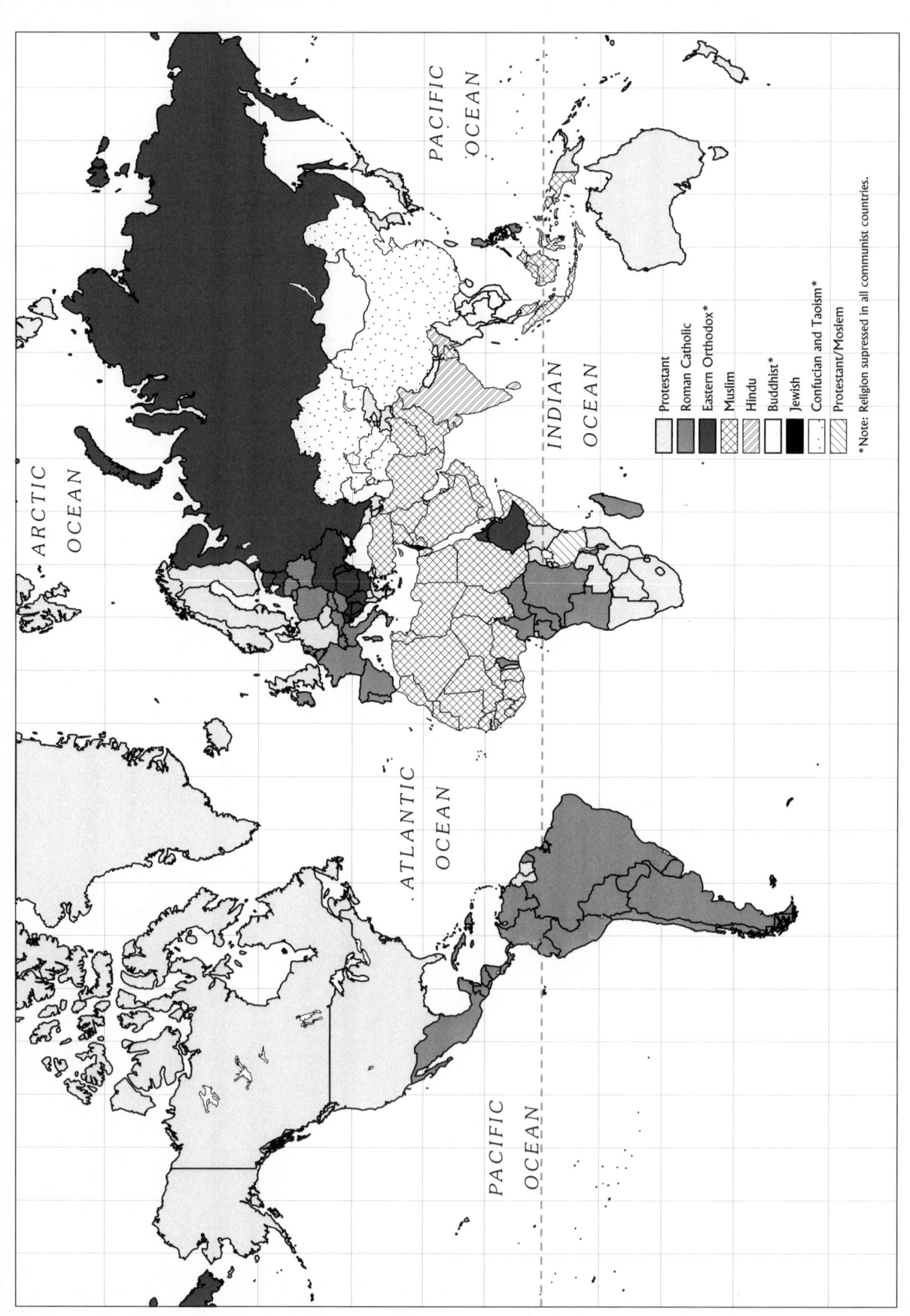

ARCTIC OCEAN

PACIFIC OCEAN

PACIFIC OCEAN

ATLANTIC OCEAN

INDIAN OCEAN

Protestant

Roman Catholic

Eastern Orthodox*

Muslim

Hindu

Buddhist*

Jewish

Confucian and Taoism*

Protestant/Moslem

*Note: Religion supressed in all communist countries.

3 Religions

Beliefs in a god (or gods) have shaped behaviors and cultural patterns of people around the world since very early times. The beliefs and the deities differed quite considerably. Sumerians worshiped Mother Goddess Innin and her son Tammuz around 3000 BCE. Isis and Osiris were important as an Egyptian goddess and god, respectively, around 2500 BCE, approximately the time when Minoans were viewing the snake and bull as religious symbols. Early Greeks had a pantheon of gods and goddesses, including Zeus, Poseidon, Athena, Aphrodite, and many more during the millennium preceding the birth of Christ.

During the intervening centuries, different religions have emerged as dominant in today's world. Christianity includes Protestant, Roman Catholic, and Eastern Orthodox, which together comprise the largest religious group. Islam is the second most numerous when the Sunni, Shiah, and other branches are counted. Hindu believers are the third in terms of numbers, although they are clustered primarily in India and Nepal. Buddhism also has many followers (somewhat more than half as many as Hinduism). Confucianism has many followers in the Far East; in the same region, Shintoism and Taoism also are found but with smaller groups of followers. Judaism is a religion with far fewer followers than the other major religions but with a very significant influence in today's world.

In the United States, significant changes in religious preferences have been taking place even since 1970, due in part to the large numbers of immigrants from many parts of the world who brought their religions with them. The practice of these religions attracted attention and heightened interest in learning about these different approaches to spirituality. Converts to these different religions and immigrants who already practiced the predominant religion of their cultures account for an increasing religious diversity, which adds to the breadth of cultures in America (Table 3.1).

All of these religions are of considerable importance in influencing not only spiritual beliefs of people, but also their value systems and their cultural behaviors,

Table 3.1 Estimates of Religious Affiliations in the United States in 1970 and 2000

Religion	1970 (millions)	2000 (millions)
Protestants	70.7	88.8
Roman Catholics	48.4	61.8
Jews	6.7	5.5
Muslims	0.8	4.0
Buddhists	0.2	2.0
Hindus	0.1	0.95
Sikhs	0.001	0.22

Adapted from *Encyclopedia Britannica Book of the Year.* 1998. Association of Statisticians of American Religious Bodies.

which may include dietary practices. This chapter provides a review of the major religions of the world. It offers background information about each of these religions but not an in-depth philosophical examination. These glimpses will add insight into the dietary patterns found in the countries and regions where each of these religions holds considerable influence.

Hinduism

Overview

Manu—Source of Hindu laws on living and ancestor of Hindus; progenitor of the human race and source of Vedas.

Vedas—Four volumes of the collective wisdom on how Hindus must live.

Hinduism probably is the oldest continuing religion in the world, with its roots going back to about 2000 BCE. India and Nepal are the primary countries where Hinduism is found. A distinctive aspect of this religion is that it is not based on the life or teachings of a single person or on the worship of a single god (Figure 3.1). Hindus believe in reincarnation and that the spirit is reborn in another form in a seemingly eternal cycle in pursuit of spiritual perfection. **Manu** was the name for the progenitor of the human race and the source of the Vedas. The **Vedas** are four volumes, which are the collective statements on how Hindus must live.

Figure 3.1 Hindu temples, such as this one in Sri Lanka, are elaborately decorated with images of the various gods.

Prominent Gods

Although there are many gods and goddesses in Hinduism, three are dominant: Vishnu and Shiva, the two of prominence today, and Brahma. The belief is that Brahma was responsible for creating the present world and that Shiva will destroy it after about 425,000 years so that **Brahma** can make the world again. In short, Brahma is the creator god of the triad of Hindu gods. In contrast, **Vishnu** is the preserver god, and **Shiva** (or Siva) is the destructive god of Hinduism.

Beliefs

Hinduism is a religion with definite emphasis on mysticism and on becoming free of desires—in short, living an ascetic existence and rising above desires of the flesh. Hindus believe that some people, designated as **avatars,** are incarnations of deities here on earth. Ramakrishna, a prominent Hindu saint, is viewed as an avatar of Shiva. Hindu worship includes chanting of incantations, or **mantras.** The sound involved is **om** (pronounced with a long *o* and extended *m* sound). With extended chanting, a religious energy presumably is generated. Another prayer form is the chanting of "The Thousand Names of Sivasahastranaman (Shiva)."

Caste System

Inherent in Hinduism is the caste system, which divides people socially into classes that are required to maintain distinct divisions and privileges (or lack of privileges) associated with each specific caste level. **Brahmans** are the highest of the castes, and the **untouchables** are the lowest. The Brahmans were the priests and teachers and were viewed as being derived from the mouth of Brahma, the universal spirit. Next is the caste called **Kshatriyas,** thought to be from the arms of Brahma and designated as the warriors and rulers.

Vaisyas, the farmers and businesspeople, were from the thighs. Brahma's feet were the caste of menial workers, the **Sudras.** Believers in Hinduism were born into the caste of their ancestors. Anybody who was not born as a Brahman, a Kshatriyas, a Vaisyas, or a Sudras was deemed unworthy and was designated as an untouchable. Indian law prohibits designation as "untouchable," but discrimination still may occur.

Hindus may wear a **talik** on the forehead between the two eyebrows. This mark may indicate caste, or it may indicate the god that is being worshiped or other special religious meaning. It is applied in this location because this is where the body is thought to emanate energy.

Reincarnation

Fundamental to Hinduism is the lack of upward mobility through the good deeds one might do during life. However, such deeds are believed to be able to exert influence on the soul in which a person is reborn in the next life. The way a person lives is the responsibility of the individual. The fact that status in rebirth is the direct result of the acts in the previous life is a powerful motivation to live according to Hindu beliefs. The new form of the soul in the next life can be far lower than in the present life, or it can be better. The whole purpose is to constantly strive to reach the universal spirit during some future rebirth. The deeds performed in all previous lives determine the nature of a person's next existence; this force is called **karma.**

Respect for Life

All life, whether human or animal, is highly respected by Hindus and is believed to be sacred, because part of the spirit of Brahma is thought to be a part of any living thing. An extension of this belief is that one's ancestor might actually be the

---

Brahma—Creator god in Hindu religion.

Vishnu—Preserver god in Hindu religion.

Shiva—Destructive Hindu god, also called Siva.

Avatar—Person so saintly that he is thought to be an incarnation of a deity.

Mantra—Hindu incantation.

Om—Sound chanted repeatedly by Hindus for long periods to generate religious energy.

Brahmans—Highest caste in Hinduism; priests and teachers.

Untouchable—Person unworthy of belonging to a caste.

Kshatriyas—Second caste in Hinduism; warriors and rulers.

Vaisyas—Third level Hindu caste; farmers and businesspeople.

Sudras—Lowest Hindu caste; menial workers.

Talik—The colored mark (often red) that many Hindus wear on the forehead between the eyebrows.

Karma—Force generated by actions in a Hindu's life that will determine what the next life will be.

spirit of the life that is taken if something is killed. Cows occupy a particularly revered niche because they are thought by Hindus to have been created by Brahma at the same time that people were created. This reverence for **sacred cows** is still seen in India, where they are allowed to wander freely on any street, road, or land they wish.

Sacred cow—Wandering cow where Hindus live; protected from harm because of respect for life.

Holidays

Some of their numerous gods and goddess are prominent in Hindu holidays at various times throughout the year (Figure C.152, p. C51). **Krishna,** worshiped as the eighth incarnation of the god Vishnu, is a figure celebrated as Janmashtami or Gokul Ashtami on the occasion marking his birthday. This unusual celebration features pots of milk curds hung very high so that they can be reached only by boys or men forming a human pyramid topped by someone swinging a stick to break the pots.

Krishna—God celebrated as the eighth incarnation of Vishnu.

Kama, the Hindu god of love, and Krishna are honored at Holi, a light-hearted celebration in which brightly colored powdered dyes are thrown at others as men play pranks and dance around.

Kama—Hindu god of love.

On a more somber note, the festival called Dussara is a time of pageantry to honor Devi, the goddess who is Shiva's wife. This celebration continues for 10 days.

One of the more unusual gods is Ganesha, who is easily recognized because of the happy elephant head and the rotund human belly of his figure. His birthday is celebrated with the holiday Ganesha Chaturthi. Not surprisingly, quantities of food offerings (milk, fruit, and puddings) are featured at this three-day holiday.

Brahmans get new clothing and give away their old sacred clothing as a part of their celebration of Rakhi Purnima to honor Shiva (who has three eyes). The coconut, with its three eyes, is traditional for this celebration, and it is broken at a shrine as part of the festivities.

Rama Navami is another holiday featuring coconuts. In this celebration, a coconut is placed in a cradle to represent the birth of Rama, the seventh incarnation of Vishnu. Dancing and entertainment are featured at this particularly important festival.

Divali is the joyous celebration of the new year. Even fireworks are included. The greeting for the occasion is "A happy Divali and a prosperous new year!"

Hinduism has had many rituals in years past, although today some have been eliminated either by law or by practice. An example is sati, which occurred occasionally in centuries past when a widow would throw herself on her dead husband's funeral pyre and die in self-immolation. Sati was outlawed over 100 years ago. Furthermore, Hindu widows now are allowed to marry again. The class of untouchables also has been eliminated.

Underlying some rituals is the notion of purity and pollution. The ritual of bathing is dictated by the need for purity and the elimination of pollution. Since human wastes are all considered pollution, there are various rituals that are to be followed when coping with these sources of pollution. *Dharma* is a term that encompasses the rituals of daily life. These include rituals for praying, which Brahmans are to do three times daily.

When a child is born, the house must be purified, and the newborn's horoscope must be determined. On the sixth or twelfth day, the baby is named, and the occasion is marked by feeding the baby its first solid food. Ear-piercing may also be done then or at some later time. The child's head may be shaved at the age of one to thank the Deva for safeguarding the child through infancy.

Weddings are of greatest ritual importance, and every Hindu is expected to marry, because it is a religious duty. The religious debt to the couple's ancestors is paid by having children. The rituals associated with the marriage may take more than a week and involve such acts as the couple walking seven times around the sacred fire.

Funerals are needed to empower the departing spirit to leave the present world and to take care of the pollution that is associated with death. The funeral pyre is lighted by the oldest son of the departed (Figure C.115, p. C39). The mourning period, which lasts 10 or 11 days after the cremation, is marked by various rituals that restrict what the relatives can do during that time. The ending ritual involves offerings of balls of rice or barley and some milk. These offerings are also presented annually from then on. This ritual is intended to help the departed get a new spiritual body.

Worship can be done as temple worship (Figure 3.2), home worship, or in congregational worship. Priests are responsible for conducting the rituals associated with the god and goddesses of the particular temple. The ceremonies are marked by a variety of practices, including food and flower offerings, ringing of bells, prayers, music, and possibly other practices. Each household also maintains an area for worship, which may include images, yantras (geometric designs), and offerings, all of which are kept in a state of purity. Pilgrimages are undertaken to such holy sites as Banaras in the hope of achieving a spiritual experience. These efforts often are well arranged and may include religious fairs.

Food Practices

Puja—Hindu worship ritual that begins with seating, cleansing, and dressing a deity. Food is offered to the god and then some is eaten by the worshiper.

Food is offered at a shrine as a part of **puja,** a ritual that is conducted at the shrine in a home or temple (Figure 3.3). The ritual begins in front of the altar with the deity being offered a seat. Ritual washing of its feet, bathing and dressing the figure of the deity, and then adding garlands of flowers follow. Incense is burned, and a lighted lamp is waved in front of the deity. The worshiper bows and offers the deity water and then fruit and cooked food, which have been placed on the altar. Finally, the worshiper eats a bit of the food,

The high respect for life means that many Hindus are vegetarians. Since the cow is considered to be sacred, beef is not eaten by Hindus. Not surprisingly, Brahmans are the caste most likely to forgo eating meats and eggs, which potentially represent life. Castes below that of Brahman do not eat beef but do eat other meats. However, chickens and pigs, viewed as unclean because they may scavenge for food, also may be avoided. Fish seem to be more acceptable than other flesh foods. Animals that are to be killed for food can be killed by people who are in the Kshatriyas caste, for they are designated as the leaders and soldiers.

Figure 3.2 On this festival day in Bali, Indonesia, Hindus bring specially prepared food to the temple to be blessed before eating it at home.

Figure 3.3 Beautifully arranged trays of fruit are stacked high and balanced on the heads of these Hindu women as they participate in a festival in Bali, Indonesia.

Pakka—Hindu word for food containing ghee; offered to gods and then high-ranking guests.

Ghee—Clarified butter made by boiling butter to evaporate the water and precipitate the milk solids before filtering to clarify it.

Kacca—Hindu term for level of food just below pakka but made without ghee.

Good sanitation underlies activities in a Brahman kitchen, for this is considered a holy place. The cook must have a ritual bath before cooking. Lower castes should not prepare the food, but they can give uncooked foods or those cooked in ghee, or clarified butter, to Brahmans. All Brahmans eating the food also need to bathe the entire body and dress in clean clothes. The foods they eat are designated as **pakka,** the foods offered to the gods and then to guests of high rank. All pakka foods contain **ghee.** The next level of food is designated as **kacca** and does not contain ghee, which makes the products, such as bread, drier. If any kacca is left over, it is designated as jutha (garbage). Jutha is suitable for animals, lower castes, or untouchables. Only wives or others of lower status are allowed to scrape kacca from plates.

Brahmans tend to avoid garlic and onions to avoid association with lesser classes. Avoidance of alcohol by Brahmans is required to avoid any possible loss of self-control. Lower Hindu castes, however, are allowed to drink alcohol.

Fasting may be done at various times of the year, particularly in the higher castes. Celestial events (e.g., summer and winter solstice, an eclipse, new and full moon) can mark a day of fasting. Special days, such as the anniversary of the death of a parent, may be fasting days to honor the memory of the person.

Recipes

Jeera Rice (Serves 3)

1 c Basmati rice
1½ tbsp ghee (or clarified butter)
1 tsp each cumin and black cumin seeds (or 2 teaspoons cumin)
1 bay leaf
1 cinnamon stick (2″)
¼ tsp ground cloves
2 tbsp cashews
2 c water
½ tsp salt (or to taste)

1. Wash rice and soak in water to cover for 30 minutes; drain.
2. Heat ghee, spices, and cashews in a 2-quart saucepan, stirring constantly until nuts are pleasingly brown.
3. Stir in the drained rice until it is coated with the ghee mixture.
4. Add water and salt; cover pan and heat to a boil before lowering heat to simmer.
5. Simmer until water is gone and holes are seen on the surface of the rice.
6. Fluff with a fork and serve.

Palak Paneer (Cottage Cheese and Spinach Curry) (Serves 3)

1 tbsp ghee or clarified butter
2 tbsp chopped onion
1 bunch spinach
2 tbsp chopped carrot
1 tbsp chopped tomato
½ tsp ground cumin
¼ tsp ground turmeric
1 tsp garam masala
1 tsp cream

1 c paneer pieces or large curd cottage cheese

1. Heat ghee and sauté onion.
2. Add spinach and carrot; stir while heating until wilted and tender.
3. Stir in tomato, spices, and cream and continue heating for 5 minutes.
4. Stir in paneer and simmer 10 minutes; stir occasionally.

Aloo Ka Bharta (Potatoes and Chilies) (Serves 3)

4 potatoes
2 onions, chopped
1 4-oz can diced green chilies
½ tsp salt
½ tsp chili powder

2 tbsp chopped coriander leaves

1. Pare and boil potatoes; drain and mash briefly.
2. Stir in remaining ingredients.

Buddhism

History

Buddha—Religious name of Siddhartha Gautama, founder of Buddhism.

Buddhism is the religion of vast numbers throughout Southeast Asia, including Taiwan, Vietnam, Cambodia, Laos, Bhutan, Nepal, Tibet, China, Japan, Myanmar (Burma), Thailand, and Sri Lanka. This far-reaching religion began in northeastern India in about 530 BCE and was based on the teachings of Siddhartha Gautama, who became known as **Buddha** (Figure 3.4).

Figure 3.4 A very tall standing Buddha quietly reminds Buddhists of their faith as they pass this statue in Colombo, Sri Lanka.

During his lifetime, Buddha renounced his worldly position and spent six years searching for the truth. His "enlightenment" occurred while he was sitting under the bodhi tree, where he reached *Nirvana* and all worldly desires disappeared. The religion that flowed from his teachings represented a departure or reformation movement from the Hindu roots of India. This was a religion that spread successfully over vast regions but did not replace Hinduism among most Indians. Asoka, the strong Mauryan ruler of India, was converted to Buddhism and did much to spread Buddhism to China, Japan, Korea, and beyond.

Although Buddha is central to the Buddhist religion and is important for his teachings, he is not worshipped as a god. Buddhism has no gods and thus is quite different from Hinduism (Figure C.158, p. C53). Also, there is no caste system. The ultimate goal of Buddhism is to reach **Nirvana,** a process that could involve countless rebirths.

Nirvana—The ultimate state in Buddhism—enlightenment; free of pain, care, and desire.

Foundations

The basic teachings, called the Four Noble Truths, are these:

1. Existence is suffering.
2. The origin of human suffering is craving pleasure, possessions, or cessation of pain.
3. Craving is cured by detachment from oneself and from all things.
4. Detachment is achieved by following the Eight-Fold Path:
   a. Right conduct
   b. Right effort
   c. Right intentions
   d. Right livelihood
   e. Right meditation
   f. Right mindfulness
   g. Right speech
   h. Right viewpoint

The code of conduct, called the dasa-sila or Ten Precepts, includes the following:

1. Thou shalt not take another's life.
2. Thou shalt not take that which is not given.
3. Thou shalt not engage in sexual misconduct. (Monks are to be celibate, and others are not to be adulterous.)
4. Thou shalt not engage in false speech.
5. Thou shalt not use intoxicants.
6. Thou shalt not eat after midday.
7. Thou shalt shun worldly amusements.
8. Thou shalt not adorn with ornaments or perfume.
9. Thou shalt not sleep on high or luxurious beds.
10. Thou shalt not accept gold or silver.

The mantra (chant) is repeated three times: "I take refuge in the Buddha. I take refuge in the teachings. I take refuge in the community."

Mahayana—Mystical form of Buddhism practiced in Tibet, Mongolia, and the Himalayas.

Theravada—Buddhism sect practiced in Southeast Asia in which monks carry begging bowls in the mornings.

Buddhism in Practice

Buddhism is broadly divided into three sects: eastern (Japan, Korea, and China) (Figure C.167 and C.168, p. C56), northern or **Mahayana** (Tibet, Mongolia, and the Himalayas), and southern or **Theravada** (Thailand, Myanmar, Sri Lanka, Cambodia, and Laos). The Theravada in Southeast Asia (Figure 3.5) developed as a monastic sect. The Mahayana (Figure 3.6) in the north developed a somewhat

Figure 3.5 This Buddhist temple in Luang Prabang, Laos, is Theravada, the sect that dominates in Southeast Asia.

Bodhisattva—Semidivine, mystical being incorporated in Mahayana Buddhism.

more mystical approach and included **bodhisattvas** (supernatural, semidivine beings who helped people achieve Nirvana). The Dalai Lama is considered to be the reincarnation of Bodhisattva of Mercy, Avalokitesvara.

In Thailand and the other countries where Theravada Buddhists worship, it is a common sight to see monks strolling about during the mornings with a beggar's bowl (usually brass). This enables the woman of a house to fill or add to the bowl with food she has prepared (Figure C.133, p. C45). Her generous act allows her to gain merit (**kutho**) and, of course, enables the monk to eat during the day until midday, after which he is not to eat.

Kutho—Kind or generous act that brings merit to help strive toward Nirvana.

All Buddhist males following the practices of the Theravada sect are expected to become monks, although their "careers" as monks may be as short as only a few days (Figure 3.7, Figure C.129, p. C43). The monasteries provide education for boys who remain in their group, and the boys provide help to the older monks and to the monastery.

Stupa—Hemispherical mound within a central decoration, which serves as a shrine for Buddhists.

Buddhism has resulted in the creation of innumerable statues of Buddha in different positions—sitting (Figure 3.8), standing, and reclining. Another feature of Buddhism is the construction of **stupas,** which are hemispherical mounds with

Figure 3.6 The Norbulinka Monastery outside Lhasa, Tibet, is Mahayana, the sect of the northern Buddhists.

Figure 3.7 This young boy who lives in Mandalay, Myanmar, is becoming a monk as family and friends join in this important ritual.

Figure 3.8 This sitting Buddha smiles at the partially reconstructed ruins of a Theravada Buddhist temple in Sukhothai, Thailand's early capital in the north.

Pagoda—Shrine of several stories where Buddhists worship.

Chorten—Tibetan (Buddhist) monument, often with some gold or silver gilding.

a central mast or decorative feature (Figure C.116, p. C39). **Pagodas** of various designs and with several stories also serve as shrines for Buddhists. Relics of religious significance may be found in these stupas (Figure 3.8) and pagodas (Figure 3.9): a tooth from Buddha, an alms bowl he used, or an object that symbolizes Buddha, for example.

In Tibet a special type of stupa called a **chorten** is built to house religious relics or to honor a special figure, such as a deceased Dalai Lama. Prayer wheels and prayer flags are other familiar aspects of Buddhist worship in Tibet, Nepal, and Bhutan. By whirling the prayer wheels, Buddhists send their prayers. Prayer flags strung along ropes and tied against the strong breezes of the Himalayas are an efficient way for Buddhists to pray (Figure 3.10).

In Tibet, China, and Japan, as well as in much of Southeast Asia, Buddhism has been influenced by wars and politics (Figure 3.11). However, Buddhism is

Figure 3.9 The Bodnath stupa near Katmandu, Nepal, is a destination for not only Mahayana sect Buddhists, but also for some Hindus.

Figure 3.10 Buddhist prayer flags flap prayers skyward as the wind whips them in the high Himalayas near Lhasa, Tibet.

practiced in all of these places today in whatever form it has evolved to in the various cultures. One of the enduring attributes of Buddhism over the centuries has been its flexibility to adapt to change and to the needs of its followers, regardless of the sect.

Festivals

Buddhist festivals are calculated according to lunar months, with the full moon being especially important. Festivals of agricultural significance are found in many places where Buddhism is practiced. Festivals of lights typically celebrate the full moon and Buddha's first sermon, as well as the sending out of the first Buddhist missionaries.

Figure 3.11 Two giant Buddhas stood recessed in their caves from the time they were created in the 3rd century CE near Bamian, Afghanistan, until the Muslim Taliban leaders ordered them destroyed in 2001.

Circumambulate—Process of prostrating and praying repeatedly while encircling a Buddhist temple once or many times.

Local pilgrimages are taken by individual Buddhists, such as can be seen in Lhasa, Tibet, as pilgrims prostrate themselves repeatedly on the road surrounding the Jogkhang Temple as they painfully **circumambulate** this most honored temple clockwise.

Food Practices

Because of the respect for life, Buddhists may abstain from eating meat and fish. However, these foods are not strictly forbidden, and many dishes do contain some meat or fish. If meat is eaten, it should not be meat from an animal that the Buddhist has killed. Rice is the staple of the diet. Moderation in eating is encouraged, and some fasting may be done occasionally.

Monks are likely to be more restricted in their dietary practices than other Buddhists. They may avoid eating meats and fish. They do not eat anything solid after noon. Fasting for the entire day is expected on the new moon and the full moon each month.

Recipes

Yoh Mari (Festival Steamed Dumplings) (Serves 5)

Dough:
  2 c rice flour
  1 c boiling water
Filling:
  ¾ c sesame seeds
  3 tbsp shredded coconut
  ¾ c jaggery (or brown sugar)
  1 tbsp water (or enough to make very thick sauce)

1. Stir rice flour while adding boiling water and moistening all of the flour. Cover and let rest.
2. Roast sesame seeds in a dry pan until slightly browned.
3. Grind seeds to a fine powder in a blender before adding coconut and grinding again.
4. Transfer to a mixing bowl and add jaggery before stirring in just enough water to make a paste.
5. Work the rice flour dough into a long log before cutting the log into 15 pieces.
6. Roll each piece between your hands to make a ball.
7. With a small spoon, shape a well in the ball, and fill it with 2 teaspoons of filling.
8. Work the filled ball so that the filling is enclosed and sealed within the ball.
9. Place on a steamer tray after shaping into a fish or other creative shape. Leave at least half an inch between dumplings because they swell during steaming.
10. Steam for 12 minutes.

Dal Bhat (Lentil Soup) (Serves 4)

1 c lentils
½ tsp salt
3 c water
2 tsp grated fresh ginger root
1 tbsp canned diced green chilies
1 tsp peanut oil
¼ tsp cumin seeds
½ tsp 5-spice powder (or curry powder)
4 sprigs of cilantro

1. Simmer lentils in salted water until soft (20 minutes).
2. Purée lentils with the ginger and chilies.
3. Heat oil and cumin in a frying pan until seeds pop.
4. Add lentil mixture and 5-spice powder to the frying pan and heat while stirring for 4 minutes.
5. Serve garnished with cilantro.

Potato Curry (Serves 4)

4 c potatoes (e.g., Red Triumph), cut in large cubes
1½ tbsp peanut oil
1 medium onion, chopped
1 tbsp grated ginger root
2 garlic cloves, minced
¼ tsp fenugreek
1 tsp curry powder
½ tsp powdered cumin
¼ tsp turmeric
2 c water

4 sprigs coriander

1. Boil potatoes until barely soft. Drain.
2. In a large saucepan, heat oil and sauté onion, ginger root, and garlic until barely browned.
3. Add seasonings and water to the saucepan and simmer 30 minutes, covered.
4. Add the potatoes and continue cooking until potatoes are tender. Add more water, if needed.
5. Serve garnished with coriander.

Confucianism and Taoism

Confucianism

Religion in China for the majority of the people is a blend of Confucianism, Taoism, and Buddhism. Confucianism underlies the morality and behavior of people, including rites of passage. Taoism provides for the needs and healing of the sick and is a basis for regulating festivals. Buddhism is the source of compassion in life and salvation after life. The three together provide for all aspects of life, both during and after.

Confucianism can be traced back to six centuries BCE. Confucianism evolved into a school collected into the Four Books and Five Classics. The founder of Confucianism was a 6th century BCE man named **Confucius**, or K'ung Fu-tzu (Master Kung). He taught that the way to live was by correct ethical conduct, which would allow one to achieve ideal harmony with the "way of Heaven" and make one become more than human.

Actually, Confucianism presents ways to live one's life, but it is not a religion. It does not include worship of a god. Respect for parents and loyalty to the government are precepts of Confucianism. There also is emphasis on continuing in the type of social order in which a person is born and striving toward loving, kindly relationships with family and friends.

Followers of Confucianism have many guidelines for living. From Confucianism come the norms for behaviors, which embrace (1) respect, (2) family love, (3) benevolence toward strangers, and (4) loyalty to the state. However, Confucius surprisingly did not define guidelines or prohibitions on eating.

Confucius—Chinese philosopher (551–479 BCE) whose teachings form the basis of Confucianism.

Taoism

Taoism was founded slightly later than Confucianism and was based on teachings from Chuang-Tzu and Lao-Tzu in the 6th century BCE. The goal of Taoism was to achieve a passionless oneness with the divine Absolute, a process that encouraged a passive approach to living one's life and a peaceful acceptance while awaiting death. Retreat into meditation and nature or into a life as a monk or isolated person allowed for connecting with the ways of nature. Thrift, humility, simplicity, patience, contentment, and harmony are the basic principles of Taoism.

Contributions from Taoism in current Chinese religions stem from the cosmic concept that Tao gave birth to the primordial breath (the One), which birthed yin and yang (the Two), which gave birth to water, earth, and heaven (the Three), which birthed the myriad creatures. This becomes a never-ending cycle in Taoism as the myriad creatures return to Tao. The concept of cosmos can be summarized

Yang—In taoism, the term for heaven.

Yin—In taoism, the term for the underworld and its nine stages.

in terms of yin and yang. Pure **yang** is heaven, the visible world of life is both yang and yin, and the underworld (in nine stages) is pure **yin.** The soul is believed to sink into the domain of pure yin for a period following death, where it can ultimately be freed to ascend to heaven.

Rituals and Food

Unlike Hinduism and Buddhism, Confucianism and Taoism do not provide guidelines for daily eating. However, many traditions and rituals have developed in China over the centuries during which the culture has been evolving. Several of these include food traditions that are based predominantly on a vegetarian diet. Soy products, whole grains, vegetables, nuts, seeds, herbs, (sometimes medicinal herbs), and tea are the main components, and meats, dairy, and additives are usually avoided.

Marriage   Traditional marriage rituals begin with a three-day period when the characters representing the year, month, day, and hour of birth of both the prospective bride and groom are placed on the family altar in the bride's family home. If all goes well in that household during those three days, invitations are sent for the wedding. A special procession is the means for transporting the bride's vanity box and dowry to the household of the groom and his family, where he opens the vanity box (symbolizing sincere love) and the dowry is counted.

The groom matches the value of the dowry in such items as jewelry or clothing for the bride. The groom then must go to his bride's home and take her back to his home, which she enters by stepping over a cooking pot, a saddle, and an apple. At the reception following the marriage ceremony, the bride and groom make a small rice wine toast before proceeding with toasts (tea) at each of the tables of guests at their wedding dinner. The next morning the bride serves breakfast to her new in-laws, including dried dates and seeds to signify many children as a gift from the bride; then they serve her breakfast. Finally, she is a guest in her own parents' home on the third day.

Pregnancy   Rituals are important in the Chinese religious culture. For example, pregnant women are excused from a variety of chores that might impose undue physical or psychological pressures. They also are expected to be fed a diet rich in protein and vitamins by other family members for one month following delivery. Gifts that might include eggs and rice or other special healthy foods to symbolize good health and prosperity are given in the first, fourth, and twelfth month after birth. The new mother's family is expected to give all of the clothing and diapers at these times too.

Death   A death in the family also invokes religious rituals, beginning with wailing at the moment of death, followed by removal of jewelry and fine clothes as mourning begins. White-paper-wrapped money or other talismans are placed as a cover over the body as symbols of protection from harm and of purification for the deceased. Money gifts and condolences are given to help the family with the funeral. The burning of a paper house with its furnishings, symbolic clothes, and paper money combines appreciation of the merits of living and prayers for eternal salvation for the dead. A willow branch to represent the deceased is a part of the family's procession with the coffin to the grave, and it then is carried to the family altar at home to put the soul into the memorial tablet. Special liturgies are to be performed by the deceased's minister 7, 9, and 49 days after the burial as well as on the first and third anniversaries of the death.

Festivals   Some festivals have food traditions as a part of the celebration. The Lunar New Year (festival of spring) is celebrated by a big gathering of family from all over to share a banquet. To celebrate the family's ancestors, five or seven sets of chopsticks, bowls of cooked rice, wine, and tea are placed at the family altar. The family members then share a huge banquet (16 or 24 courses): three or five kinds of cooked meat, noodles, bean curd, vegetable dishes, cake, sweets, dried fruit, and fish. The celebration includes gifts and cash in a red envelope for children. Women don flowers in their hair, and fireworks add to the festivities, which include visits to friends, to shrines, and to churches.

The third day of the third lunar month is a festival day for cleaning graves and a family picnic. Rice cakes are eaten for the festival on the fifth day of the fifth lunar month (the first day of summer), and dragon boat races are held where possible. The 15th day of the seventh month is the all souls' day festival, which is the occasion for another large family banquet. Fresh fruits and round mooncakes are the traditional fare for the harvest festival on the 15th day of the eighth lunar month.

Shintoism

Kami—The supernatural form of a deceased ancestor.

Shinto was the religion of early Japan and still is in practice today (Figure 3.12, Figure C.174, p. C58), as is Buddhism and sometimes blends of religions. Ancestors are revered in Shinto; each ancestor is assumed to become a **kami,** or supernatural being, following death, and as such remains as a life within the family. Kami can be either good or evil, depending upon the life the person led on earth.

Among the patron saints in Shinto is a dwarf named Okuninushi, or Master of the Great Land, who is the saint of rice wine brewing. The Emperor of Japan is the person who symbolically shares new rice and rice wine with Shinto deities, according to a very careful ritual, and by doing so assumes his own divinity. Some Japanese homes still maintain two altars: a kami altar for life and its activities and a Buddha altar for death and ancestral veneration. Both altars are maintained with fresh food and drink at the start of each day.

Festivals

Festivals highlight the religious calendar in Japan at various times of year. The three-day New Year celebration is marked by thoroughly cleaning house and yard and paying all debts, as well as by visits to elderly relatives, teachers, and others. If a family member has died during the year, the family does not celebrate, but it does send cards to friends, asking them not to send New Year's greetings

Figure 3.12 A Shinto shrine in Kyoto, Japan.

this time. The Bon festival is held in the summer, at which time many return to the family home to honor their ancestors who are on their ancestral tablet.

Family graves are cleaned and freshened on the occasion of the spring and autumnal equinoxes, and a family picnic is held at the graves. Children are taken to their Shinto shrine to be presented to the kami at the end of the first month of life and again at ages three and seven if a girl and at age five if a boy. These rituals are conducted to place each child under the divine care of the kami. Religious rites associated with death tend to follow Buddhist traditions.

Judaism

Torah—Five books of the Old Testament that are the foundation of Judaism.

Talmud—Authoritative body of Jewish tradition.

Maimonides—Spanish Jew who wrote the law code of Judaism in the 12th century.

Diaspora—Settling of Jews outside of Palestine.

The history of Judaism traces back to ancient Hebrews who developed their religion based on their belief in one God, who was revealed to them, the Chosen People. The **Torah** (Pentateuch, or first five books of the Old Testament of the Bible) provided the foundation to which were added the Neviim (the Prophets) and Ketuvim (writings) to ultimately compose a 24-book Hebrew Bible. The **Talmud** contains extensive oral teachings and many other important interpretations of the Jewish faith. **Maimonides,** a Spanish Jew who lived from 1135 to 1204, authored the Mishneh Torah, which provided the great law code of Judaism (Figure 3.13).

The stories of early Judaism are those of the books of Genesis, Exodus, Leviticus, Numbers, and Deuteronomy and of such powerful figures as Abraham (patriarch and founder of the Hebrews) and Moses (Hebrew prophet who led the Israelites out of Egypt). Although Judaism was centered in Judea (Figure C.53, p. C18), history has chronicled the Jewish **diaspora** to far-flung regions over a period of centuries. The conquest of Babylonia and the destruction of the First Temple in Jerusalem resulted in Jews being exiled to Babylon.

Invasion of Judea by the Romans in 63 BCE started another dark period for the Jews, a time in which the Temple was again destroyed (70 CE). The brave rebels who had fled to Masada (overlooking the Dead Sea) all died dramatically in 73 CE. Jews gained some prominence in Rome because of their cultural and economic abilities, talents that they revealed wherever they settled.

Figure 3.13 This statue of Maimonides, the noted Jewish philosopher and physician, stands in a small square in Cordoba, Spain, where he was born.

Sephardic Jews—Jews in Spain and Portugal.

Ashkenazi Jews—Jews living in northern Europe and Russia.

Rosh Hashanah—Celebration of the Jewish New Year.

Shofar—Hollowed out ram's horn blown in the synagogue during Rosh Hashanah to call man to be aware of his shortcomings and to emphasize that God is the divine king.

Yom Kippur—Day of Atonement; celebration 10 days after Rosh Hashanah.

Sukkot—Nine-day Festival of Tabernacles; celebrated five days after Yom Kippur.

Hanukkah—Feast of Lights in memory of the rededication of the Second Temple and the miracle of the oil lighting the lamp for eight days in 165 BCE; also spelled *Chanukah*.

Menorah—Jewish candelabra designed to hold four candles in a row on each side of a central holder that is slightly higher than the other eight holders; one additional candle is lighted each day of the eight days of Hanukkah.

Purim—Celebration of the rescue of Jews from under the Persian ruler Haman.

Pesach—Eight-day celebration marking the escape of the Israelites from Egypt; also called *Passover*.

Shavuot—Celebration of Moses receiving the Ten Commandments in the Sinai; Pentecost.

Shabbat—Weekly religious observance from sundown Friday until darkness falls on Saturday.

Bar Mitzvah—Celebration of maturity at which a boy reads from the Torah in the synagogue at age 13.

Bat Mitzvah—Celebration of a girl reaching maturity (age 12).

Eventually, Jews were living in much of Europe. In Spain they played very significant roles in commerce and the economy. However, the adoption of Christianity in the Roman Empire in the 4th century CE caused increasing isolation for Jews throughout the Empire. The conquest of Spain by Muslims in 711 CE gave considerable acceptance and recognition to the Jews there, but they were expelled when the Moors were driven out of Spain and the Catholic monarchs, Ferdinand and Isabella, ruled in 1492.

The Jews who lived in Spain and Portugal were identified as **Sephardic Jews,** and those who were situated in northern Europe and toward Russia were called **Ashkenazi Jews.** Sephardic Jews were treated with some degree of tolerance by people in the Muslim world, but the Ashkenazi Jews suffered extreme persecution in many cases. These two divisions have some differences, but they both believe in the foundations of Judaism.

Religious Celebrations

The Jewish ritual calendar has 12 lunar months, which requires leap months to accommodate the 11 days that would be missing to keep in step with the agricultural seasons. On this calendar, **Rosh Hashanah** (the New Year) occurs in late September or early October (2005 was 5766 on the Jewish calendar). The **shofar** (a hollowed out ram's horn) traditionally is blown in the synagogue during Rosh Hashanah (Table 3.2). Ten days later is **Yom Kippur** (the Day of Atonement). Five days after Yom Kippur is **Sukkot** (the Festival of Tabernacles), which is a nine-day event.

About two months later, **Hanukkah** (Festival of Lights) is celebrated for eight days in remembrance of the miracle that oil found in the temple after the defeat of the Greeks (who had conquered the Jewish homeland and repressed religion) continued to burn in the temple lamps for eight days. Celebration of this festival includes lighting one more candle on the **menorah** each of the eight days. Asarah Be-Tevet (the 10th of the month of Tevet) is a fast day.

The 14th day of the Jewish month of Adar is **Purim,** a festival based on the book of Esther (from the Bible). **Pesach** (Passover) is an eight-day celebration that is held in the spring. **Shavuot** (Festival of Pentecost) is held seven weeks after the second day of Passover. A three-week period of mourning begins five weeks after Shavuot with a daytime fast (Shivah Asar Be-Tammuz) and ends with a 25-hour fast (Tisha Be-Av). There also are minor festivals at the beginning of each lunar month (Rosh Codesh). **Shabbat** is celebrated each week, beginning at sunset on Friday and ending when it is dark on Saturday (Figure 3.14).

Traditions

In Judaism, traditions are very important on special occasions and in daily living. Children born of a Jewish mother are considered to be Jews; the father does not have to be Jewish, although a Jewish father is preferred. If a male baby is born, circumcision is done on the eighth day to symbolize the baby's entry into the covenant God made with Abraham and his descendants; a feast celebrates this event.

Careful and thorough instruction in Hebrew and in the translations of parts of the Torah and prayers continues for both boys and girls until they reach maturity (12 for girls and 13 for boys), at which time their maturity is celebrated by the **Bar Mitzvah** for boys and **Bat Mitzvah** for girls. At a Bar Mitzvah, a boy will read from the Torah in the synagogue, and a very elaborate family party, which also includes friends, will be held. Bat Mitzvah celebrations usually are somewhat less elaborate (and may not occur in Orthodox families).

Marriage in Judaism is extremely important, for the family occupies a central position in the religion. The ceremony is held under a canopy, sometimes in the synagogue (unless the marriage is with a non-Jewish person) and occasionally

Table 3.2 Jewish Holidays: Their Timing, Significance, and Mode of Celebration

Holiday	Timing	Significance	Mode of Celebration
Rosh Hashanah (New Year)	2 days; late September or October	New Year; divine judgment (fate of world for next year determined).	Shofar blown 100 times to symbolize awareness of shortcomings and repentance. Sweet foods on first day symbolize good year to come; fast on second day remembering tragic event in past.
Yom Kippur (Day of Atonement)	10 days after Rosh Hashanah	Seek atonement from God for past sins.	Fast day (25 hours beginning at dusk). Mostly spent in the synagogue in worship. No leather shoes are worn.
Sukkot (Tabernacles)	9 days; begins 5 days after Yom Kippur	Commemorates flight from Egypt.	Ritual of Tabernacles: taking of palm branch, willows, myrtle, and a citrus shaken together during prayers. No work is done on first two days or on last day. End yearly cycle of Torah readings and begin reading Genesis again. Singing, dancing, and alcohol.
Hanukkah (Chanukah, Feast of Lights)	8 days; 2 months after Sukkot	Commemorates victory of Hasmonean priests over non-Jewish and rededication of second Temple in 165 BCE; Feast of Lights recalls Talmudic tale of 1 day's oil burning in Temple for 8 days.	One candle is lighted each day on the menorah (total of 8); fruits, nuts, and sweet treats are served; children receive small gifts of wrapped money. Star of David and gifts wrapped in blue and white paper are prominent during the celebration.
Asarah Be-Tevet	10th day of Tevet	Remembers tragic event.	Fast day.
Purim	14th day of Adar	Commemorates rescue of Jews from Persia and its leader Haman (as told in book of Esther).	Elaborate, dressy day with gifts, a big feast in afternoon, and much alcohol.
Pesach (Passover)	8 days; 1 month after Purim	Commemorates the Passover and Exodus of Israelites from Egypt. Very important family holiday.	Complete cleaning of house, removal of all leaven. Seder (ritual meal) and the story of the Exodus the first night; 4 cups of wine are drunk; bitter herbs and unleavened bread are ritual foods.
Shavuot (Pentecost)	7 weeks following Passover	Festival of Pentecost; celebrates time when Moses received the Ten Commandments on Mt. Sinai.	Study the Torah all night.
Shabbat (Sabbath)	Begins every Friday at sunset; ends Saturday at dark.	Sabbath, or seventh day; day of rest and worship.	Mother lights candles before Shabbat begins, father blesses children for reciting kiddush and says blessing over two loaves of challah (special bread); hymns sung at the three Shabbat meals; Shabbat ends with prayer over wine, incense, and lighted candle.

outdoors (the preference of some Ashkenazi Jews). A ritualistic service often is presented by the rabbi and the synagogue cantor and includes the traditional breaking of a glass, symbolizing the poignancy of the great joy of the wedding with the tragedy of the destruction of Jerusalem.

Funerals for Jewish people also involve many traditions. The burial needs to be done immediately or just as soon as possible after death, and a little dirt from Israel is thrown on the coffin before it is lowered into consecrated ground in a Jewish cemetery. Official mourning is done by the next of kin for a week and in-

Figure 3.14 Challah is the bread traditionally served by Jews for Shabbat.

cludes sitting on low stools, not wearing leather shoes, and praying with people who come to comfort them.

Worship in the synagogue is shorter during the week than on Saturdays, but there are prayers for morning, afternoon, and evening; worshipers face Jerusalem and the Ark of the synagogue where the Torah is placed. Saturday morning services may last as long as three hours and include more reading from the Torah, prayers, and chanting.

Orthodox services are conducted by men, with the women attendees seated in a special gallery, whereas Reform and Conservative services, if held in a temple rather than a synagogue, have combined seating and participation in the service. Orthodox and Conservative Jewish men wear the **yarmulke** (type of skullcap) in the synagogue, and Orthodox men wear it at all times to show respect and reverence to God. Orthodox married women also cover their hair, at least in the synagogue.

Yarmulke—Skullcap worn by Jewish men.

In Orthodox homes, strict practices are followed. The men may choose to wear the black hats and long black coats that have so long been a traditional garment. Another traditional male garment is a four-cornered vest with strings fastened to each corner, which is a version of the prayer shawl used for morning prayers

Among Jewish people in the United States today, the differences in traditions and approaches to Judaism are creating potentially sharp divisions within the faith. A 1997 survey among Jewish households throughout metropolitan Los Angeles found that 4.3 percent of those surveyed were Orthodox, 28.2 percent were Conservative, 39.9 percent were Reform, and 2 percent were Reconstructionist. A 2001 census of U.S. synagogues reported 3,727 synagogues, of which 40 percent were Orthodox, 26 percent were Reform, and 23 percent were Conservative. The number of members was not included in the study. The trend since 1979 has been a reduction in the numbers of both Orthodox and Conservative with an increase in Reform and Reconstructionists.

Food Practices

Kashruth—Requirements outlining the preparation and types of food that Orthodox and other Jews may eat.

Kosher—Ritually prepared and approved for consumption.

Kashruth spells out kosher requirements for Orthodox Jews and others wishing to have the purity connoted by selecting foods designated officially as **kosher.** In the Orthodox kitchen, separate utensils and dishes must be used for meat and for dairy foods, and strict dietary laws (kashruth) are practiced. Kosher products in the market are designated with such markings as K.U. or COR, signs that indicate rabbinical approval.

Meats that can be eaten include only those from animals that chew their cud and have a cloven (split) hoof, and these must be slaughtered and bled according to kosher requirements, which includes slaughter by a butcher (shochet) who uses a very sharp knife (challef) following the prescribed kosher method. The meat is soaked in cold water and then salted with kosher (coarse) salt for an hour and allowed to drain on a slanted board to remove the blood. Finally, the meat is washed before it is considered fit for consumption.

The types of meat that can be eaten by people following kashruth include beef, sheep, goat, and deer. Fish with scales and fins are also approved, but mollusks and crustaceans are prohibited. Chickens and turkeys are approved, but ostrich is not.

These and other dietary laws are contained in Leviticus and Deuteronomy. The quote in Deuteronomy and in Exodus suggests that a kid should not be cooked in its mother's milk, which is the basis for waiting between one and six hours between eating meat and dairy products, the timing being quite variable among rabbis.

Hasidic Jews who trace their sect to 18th century Poland follow particularly strict kashruth rules, even requiring that such egg-containing products as egg noodles be prepared by a Hasidic because there is a very remote possibility that the egg might have a blood spot.

Food Traditions

Seder—Traditional celebration held on the second night of Passover.

Special foods are important in Jewish traditions. Although each family has special favorites, certain dishes are familiar in most homes, especially for holidays and feasts. Some of these are listed in Table 3.3. **Seder** is the traditional celebration that is held on the second night of Passover. The Seder plate (Figure 3.15) is featured before the meal and includes these symbols: maror (bitter herbs); karpas

Table 3.3 Selected Traditional Jewish Favorite Dishes

Dish	Description	Holiday
Latke	Fried potato pancake.	Hanukkah
Gefilte fish	Baked or stewed fish balls containing egg, bread, and seasonings.	Sabbath eve dinner
Matzo[a]	Unleavened flat bread made of flour and water and baked in a very hot oven.	Passover
Matzo meal	Coarsely ground matzo used in place of flour or bread crumbs during all of Passover.	Passover
Matzo farfel	Coarse pieces of matzo similar to flaked cereals; replaces noodles and pasta during Passover.	Passover
Matzo cereal	Used in place of cream of wheat and as a thickener in place of flour.	Passover
Hamantashen	Prune and poppy-seed-filled three-cornered cookies (eat Haman's hat).	Purim
Challah	Two circles or loaves baked for Sabbath, symbolizing double portion of manna provided by God on Fridays for Sabbath during 40 years in the wilderness.	Sabbath eve
Challah	Bread with birds or ladders to carry Rosh Hashanah prayers to heaven. With slice of apple and honey, gives wish for sweet new year.	Rosh Hashanah
Kreplach	Pasta-wrapped meat morsels (Jewish tortellini).	Meal before Yom Kippur fast
Honey cake	Spicy, sweet cake made with honey and perhaps dried fruit.	Rosh Hashanah or to break fast of Yom Kippur

[a] Matzo in various forms is used in preparing foods during Passover. Flour is not to be used (actually, no flour is in the house nor are any products made with regular flour in the house at that holiday).

Figure 3.15 The seder plate is arranged with maror (bitter herbs); karpas (vegetable); chazeret (bitter vegetable); charoset (apple, nut, wine, and spice mixture); zeroa (shank bone); and beitzah (egg).

(vegetable); chazeret (bitter vegetable); charoset (apple, nut, wine, and spice mixture); zeroa (shank bone); and beitzah (egg). Family and guests participate in the readings and ceremony preceding the Seder dinner.

Recipes

Gefilte Fish (Serves 4)

Balls:
  1 lb boneless white fish, ground
  1 onion, chopped
  2 carrots, grated
  2 eggs, beaten
  1 tsp salt
  1 tbsp sugar
  ½ tsp pepper
  ⅔ c matzo meal
Broth:
  1 carrot, sliced
  1 onion, chopped
  1 tbsp salt

3 tbsp sugar
½ tsp pepper
1 qt water

1. Combine ingredients for the balls and shape into balls, squeezing tightly.
2. Place ingredients for the broth in a large pan and heat to boiling.
3. Carefully add the balls; simmer for 2 hours, adding more water as needed to keep the balls immersed.
4. Cool before removing balls and refrigerating. Serve cold with horseradish.

Brisket for Hanukkah (Serves 8)

1 beef brisket (about 4 lbs)
½ tsp salt
1 tsp pepper
1½ tsp paprika
1 tbsp corn oil
1 onion, chopped
½ c sun-dried tomatoes
2 tbsp lemon juice
⅓ c catsup

⅓ c brown sugar

1. Sprinkle brisket with salt, pepper, and paprika before browning all sides in a Dutch oven.
2. Scatter onion and tomato over the meat.
3. Stir lemon juice, catsup, and brown sugar together before pouring over meat.
4. Cover and simmer for 3 hours until fork tender.

Chicken for Purim (Serves 4)

2 chicken breasts, split in half
1 onion, chopped
1 garlic clove, minced
½ c chopped prunes
½ c chopped apple
⅓ c chopped raisins
⅓ c chopped dried apricots
¾ tsp cinnamon
½ tsp pepper
¼ tsp salt

¼ tsp saffron
¼ tsp curry powder
1 lemon, thinly sliced

1. Mix the ingredients except the chicken and lemon.
2. Spread fruit-spice mixture over chicken, and garnish with the lemon slices.
3. Bake in 400°F oven for 40 minutes.

Borekas (Vegetable-Filled Pastries) (15 Pieces)

Dough:
  1½ c flour
  ¼ tsp salt
  ½ c shortening
  ¼ c water
Filling:
  1 tbsp oil
  1 onion, finely chopped
  1 10-oz package frozen spinach, thawed
    and drained very dry
  ¼ c chopped parsley
Glaze:
  1 egg
  1 tbsp water
  1 tbsp sesame seeds

1. Mix the flour and salt together.
2. Add the shortening and cut into pieces the size of rice grains.
3. Toss flour mixture with a fork while adding water by drops.
4. Stir flour mixture until it holds together. Cover and set aside while preparing filling.
5. Heat oil and sauté onion until golden.
6. In a blender, purée the onion and spinach.
7. Roll the dough into a thin sheet.
8. Cut dough into 15 circles 3 inches in diameter.
9. Place spoonful of filling on each round.
10. Fold dough over to make semicircles and seal by pressing edges continuously with a fork.
11. Transfer to a baking sheet before brushing surface with the egg and water glaze and sprinkling with sesame seeds.
12. Bake in a preheated oven at 400°F until golden brown (about 10 minutes).

Matzo Balls (12 balls)

1 c matzo meal
½ c water
1 c minced onion
1 tbsp corn oil
4 eggs
¼ tsp salt
¼ tsp pepper
¼ c chopped parsley
1 qt chicken broth

1. Soak matzo in water in a mixing bowl.
2. Sauté onion in oil until golden.
3. Beat eggs with seasonings and parsley.
4. Add the soaked matzo meal and onions; mix thoroughly.
5. Chill mixture at least an hour.
6. Roll into balls about an inch in diameter while heating a pan of chicken broth to boiling.
7. Add matzo balls and simmer until balls rise to the top (about 10 minutes). No peeking is allowed.

Carrots for Seder (Serves 4)

1 lb baby carrots
1 tbsp honey
¼ tsp salt
½ tsp grated ginger

1. Boil carrots in water to barely cover for 6 minutes. Drain.
2. Stir in the remaining ingredients.

Christianity

Christianity as a religion separate from Judaism developed in the early centuries following the death of Jesus. The Old Testament was accepted as a record of early important events, which is not surprising, since Jesus and his disciples were born as Jews and lived in that context during at least a part of their lives. However, the interpretation of Jesus on earth and thereafter provides the schism between Judaism and Christianity.

The name *Christian,* derived from the Greek *Cristos* (translation from the Hebrew word *Messiah*), was coined in about 35 CE in Syria to describe a group worshiping there. The New Testament, with its first four chapters attributed to the apostles Matthew, Mark, Luke, and John, and other books added later, provided the written foundation for the period that included Christ, and the combination of the Old and New Testaments became the Bible for Christians.

Although early believers in Christianity had been born as Jews, the religion fanned out from Jerusalem and attracted many converts who had never been Jews. Eventually, Christianity became widespread among Gentiles, and new traditions gradually evolved.

Hellenistic influences contributed to the developing religion, with a large role being played by the apostle Paul. Roman Emperor Constantine became a Christian, which led to a strong Christian influence in the Roman Empire for centuries, especially in the Eastern Roman Empire.

Eastern Orthodox Church—Church resulting when the Roman Catholic Church was split and the eastern part was no longer controlled from Rome.

The Roman Catholic Church was split permanently when the branch in Constantinople officially broke away in 1054 CE. The **Eastern Orthodox Church** (Figure 3.16), which also is referred to as the *Greek Orthodox* and the *Russian Orthodox Church,* is a version of Christianity in which icons are the tradition, and

Figure 3.16 This statue of a patriarch stands in front of a Greek Orthodox Church in Athens, Greece.

Jesus, the Divine Son, is the icon or image of what humans can aspire to be. The four patriarchates (Jerusalem, Antioch, Alexandria, and Constantinople) of Eastern Orthodoxy exist even today, although they are diminished in numbers of followers. Eastern Christianity also had an ancient group of churches that were termed *Oriental* and that remain today as the Coptic Orthodox Church (Egypt) and as the Church of Ethiopia and the Church of Armenia.

Roman Catholic Church— Western branch of the Christian faith that remained after the Eastern Orthodox Church split away.

The **Roman Catholic Church** was the branch of Christianity that developed in Roman times and remains today, with its headquarters at the Vatican and the Pope as its head. The sacraments of the Roman Catholic Church included the rites of baptism, confirmation, marriage, Eucharist, penance, anointing of the sick before death, and ordination. Latin became the language of the Roman Catholic Church and was spread throughout the western part of Europe (Figure 3.17, Figure C.22, p. C8) from Scandinavia to the Danube region despite the confusion of the Middle Ages. However, discontent with the religion was festering in the northern region of the European continent.

Martin Luther—German priest credited with creating the rift in the Roman Catholic Church that resulted in the Protestant movement.

October 31, 1517, was a historic day in Wittenberg, Germany, for it was there that **Martin Luther** (an ordained Roman Catholic priest) nailed to the cathedral doors his 95 theses enumerating objections to practices within the Roman Catholic Church. This posting sparked the break with Rome that resulted in the Protestant branch of Christianity and eventually its several independent groups around the western world, including Methodists, Presbyterians, Congregationalists, and many others (Figure 3.18).

Protestant churches used the language of the regions where they were practiced rather than the Latin of the Roman Catholic Church. The freedom of religious thought generated by the Protestant movement engendered the start of the rather wide range of church groups that are considered Christian now but are clearly neither Roman Catholic nor Orthodox. Despite the many differences among Christian groups, there is agreement that God is the Holy Father, the Spirit, and the Holy Ghost; that He made Heaven and Earth; that Jesus was God's only son and that Jesus rose from the dead. Baptism and communion (the ingestion of wine and bread, symbolizing the blood and body of Christ) are unifying rituals in Christianity.

Figure 3.17 The cathedral in Cologne, Germany, was built over a period of 600 years, starting in 1248 CE.

Figure 3.18 Protestant churches, such as this one on Cape Cod in Massachusetts, are divided into several denominations.

Sunday was the holy day in the Christian calendar because it was the first day of the week (Mark 16:2, which states that the resurrection occurred early in the morning of the first day of the week). This designation had the advantage of distinguishing the Christian holy day from the Jewish Sabbath, which was on Saturday.

Religious Holidays

Religious holidays for Christians focus particularly around Christ's death and birth. Christians dwelt more on the event of death and the hereafter than did Jews, so it is not surprising that the events around Christ's death were honored before traditions arose around his birth. Easter was established as the Sunday following the first full moon after the vernal equinox, falling between March 22 and April 25. The Eastern Orthodox Church observes its Easter only after the Jewish Passover, which can represent a delay of a month from the Easter celebration of other Christian churches.

Coincidental with the selection of the date for Easter was the pagan celebration of Eastre, the fertility goddess of spring. The tradition of the Easter bunny for Christian children may have sprung from the acknowledged fertility of hares. Another Easter pagan ritual was the sacrificing of a horned bull, which led to the practice of tracing the pattern of the crossed horns into the top of bread, probably the forerunner of Easter's traditional fare of hot cross buns.

The observance of Lent for 40 days prior to Easter evolved as a time to contemplate and consider one's life and behaviors. The precedent for the 40-day period may have been Jesus' fast for 40 days after he was baptized, or it may refer to the time Moses and Elias spent wandering in the wilderness, or it may even symbolize the 40 years the Jews wandered in search of the Promised Land. The first day of Lent is Ash Wednesday, a time when a smudge of ash in the shape of a cross is marked on the forehead, the ash preferably being from the palm leaves kept from the previous Easter's Palm Sunday celebration.

The actual week of Easter is a seven-day event, beginning with Palm Sunday, commemorating Christ's triumphant entry into Jerusalem. Holy Monday of that week is in recognition of Jesus' chasing the money lenders from the Temple. Holy Tuesday honors Christ's speaking to his disciples on the Mount of Olives outside Jerusalem, and it recognizes the plotting of the Pharisees to trap Jesus. Holy Wednesday is in recognition of Judas' agreeing to betray Christ for 30 pieces of silver. Maundy Thursday is marked as the Last Supper, at which Christ washed his disciples' feet, emphasized brotherly love, and initiated the sacrament of the Eucharist (communion). On Good Friday the march to the cross and the Crucifixion are remembered. The especially sober period is the three hours from noon until 3 P.M. when Christ was on the cross. Holy Saturday is the eve of Christ's Ascension into Heaven, which is celebrated with Easter sunrise services by many Christian churches today.

December 25 is celebrated as the birth of Christ by all Christians, despite the fact that his real birth date is far from certain. In the 4th century, this date was picked because it coincided with a pagan celebration, which allowed Christians to celebrate without too much attention. Christmas became a firm tradition on December 25 in 337 when Emperor Constantine was baptized, an act that symbolized that Christianity was the state religion.

The period from November 30 until Christmas Eve has been designated as Advent, a time for spiritually preparing for the wondrous gift of Christ to all Christians. January 6 is celebrated as the Epiphany because three major events in Christ's life occurred on that date: the visit of the Magi at his manger in Bethlehem following his birth, his baptism at the River Jordan, and the miracle at Cana when Christ changed water to wine at a marriage feast.

Food Practices

Eucharist—Religious service in which a wafer represents the body of Jesus and wine his blood; also called *communion.*

Eucharist (communion) uses food symbolically for Christians. In this most religious ceremony, a wafer or bread is placed on the tongue (or in the hand) to represent the body of Jesus, and wine is drunk symbolizing his blood. Communion is held only at religious services and is not a part of worship in the home.

The apostle Paul is credited with freeing Christians from the dietary laws practiced by the Jews, which thus served as a means of distancing the new Christian religion from its Jewish origins. In fact, the symbolic drinking of wine as a representation of the blood of Christ clearly was a great departure from the strong avoidance of blood proscribed in the Jewish dietary laws.

The prohibition of meat on Fridays apparently was an economic measure that derived from shortages in England during the reign of King Edward VI. The practice not only relieved shortages of meat a bit, but also bolstered the sale of fish, an industry that needed a boost. Meat has been returned to the tables of Roman Catholics since the 1960s by the decree of then Pope John XXIII.

Lent is the 40-day period from Ash Wednesday to Easter. During Lent, some Christians decide to forgo eating some specific food as a personal sacrifice during this most significant period. Part of the Easter celebration for many Christians includes a big meal, which often features lamb, symbolic of the Lamb of God.

Paska—Easter bread traditional in Eastern celebrations; usually dough is braided and decorated before baking in round pan.

Paska is a special Easter bread that is prominent in the Eastern Orthodox Church celebration. The name of this bread reflects the fact that Jesus was crucified during the Jewish Passover, but Paska is a sweet, yeast-leavened bread quite different from the unleavened matzo eaten during the Jewish Passover that symbolizes the exodus from Egypt.

Eggs, considered to be a symbol of the Resurrection of Christ, usually are decorated and featured by Christians throughout North America and northern Europe; Eastern Orthodox Christians transform egg shells with particularly elaborate decorations after they blow out the interior. Another tradition in eastern Europe is to have women bring their baskets containing food for the Easter dinner to church so that the priest can bless them.

Recipe

Paska (Eastern European Easter Bread) (2 loaves)

1 package active dry yeast
¼ c lukewarm water
¼ c sugar
1 tsp salt
¼ c melted butter
¾ c scalded milk
2 eggs
about 5 c flour

1. Soften yeast in lukewarm water.
2. Meanwhile, scald milk and pour over sugar, salt, and butter in a large mixing bowl.
3. Beat eggs before stirring into the milk mixture.
4. Check that milk mixture has cooled to lukewarm and then stir in about ¼ cup of the flour before stirring in the softened yeast/water mixture.
5. Add another cup of the flour and beat.
6. Gradually stir in enough flour to make a dough firm enough that it can be kneaded easily.
7. Knead the dough on a floured board until blisters start to develop under the surface.
8. Lightly coat the dough with a few drops of oil, cover, and let rest in a warm place until doubled in volume.
9. Punch the dough down. Divide into 6 pieces and roll each into long dough ropes.
10. Braid 3 of the ropes in a greased deep round pan to make a circular loaf. Repeat with the 3 remaining ropes in a second pan. (An optional technique is to braid 2 ropes and reserve the third one to shape into a crucifix on top of the loaf.)
11. Brush surface of the loaf with egg yolk and then let dough double in volume in a warm place.
12. Bake loaves at 350°F for 40 minutes until done and the crust is a pleasing brown.
13. Remove from pans immediately.

Islam (Muslim)

Prophet Muhammad—Arab man who founded Islam in the 7th century.

The youngest of the major religions of the world is Islam, the religion spawned on the Arabian Peninsula by the **Prophet Muhammad** in about 622 CE. Muhammad apparently led a somewhat unremarkable life from his birth in around 570 CE until he was 40, the time when he began seeing visions and revelations and started preaching about them in Mecca, the town where he lived.

Muhammad's protests against worshiping various gods at the stone shrine (Ka'ba) in the center of Mecca resulted in his being banished from Mecca, and he lost the protection of his clan, the Hashim. He and his followers were allowed to settle a little less than 300 miles north of Mecca in a town now called Medina, meaning the city of the Prophet. Muhammad and his group gained such strength and support between 622 and 630 that Mecca surrendered to them in 630 without a fight, and he continued to lead his movement until his death in 632 CE.

Islam spread very rapidly into many parts of the known world. The Arabs conquered the Fertile Crescent, Iran, and Egypt by the end of the 7th century and built the Dome of the Rock in Jerusalem starting in 691 CE on the site where Muhammad is said to have ascended to heaven. In 711 they invaded Spain and went to the Indus River in India. People quickly converted to Islam, and large portions of this vast region remain in the Muslim realm to this day.

Foundations of Islam

Koran—Writings from Allah given to Muhammad by Angel Gabriel to define the spiritual life for Muslims.

The **Koran** is the book containing the writings that Muhammad is believed to have received from Allah through the Angel Gabriel. Muslims are guided by the Koran with its 114 writings (some brief, some long) that are called *suras*. Considerable study and debate have been carried on over the centuries involving the interpretation and the contradictions that occur between the Koran and the hadith, which discusses the Prophet and daily life (in many volumes). The combination defines not only the spiritual life but also the practical daily life for all practicing Muslims.

The religion's basis is the **Five Pillars of Islam,** consisting of the Shahada (creed), Salat (prayers), Saum (fasting), Zukat (purifying tax), and Hajj (pilgrimage to Mecca).

Five Pillars of Islam— Requirements of Islam: Shahada (creed), Salat (prayers), Saum (fasting), Zukat (purifying tax), and Hajj (pilgrimage to Mecca).

Shahada (creed) The **Shahada** or confession consists of two statements from different places in the Koran: "There is no god but God (Allah)"; and "Muhammad is the Messenger of God."

Shahada—One of Five Pillars; chanting of creed, "There is no god but God; Muhamad is the messenger of God."

Salat (prayers) Performance of the **Salat** has evolved over the centuries from the two times indicated in the Koran to the present practice of five times daily: at sunrise, midday, mid-afternoon, sunset, and evening, the times when the muezzin (usually now a recording of the crier) chants out the call to prayer from the minaret of the mosque (Figure 3.19).

Salat—Muslim daily prayer according to the Five Pillars.

Before going into the mosque, Muslims are required to achieve purity by washing according to a defined ritual in the place provided for this in the courtyard of the mosque. Inside the mosque, worshipers pray facing Mecca with all of the other worshipers and are led by the imam in a carefully structured communal prayer service that involves changes in position, including prostration, semikneeling, prostration again, standing, kneeling, and sitting at various points in the prayer.

Mosque—Place of worship for Muslims; contains a mihrab pointing to Mecca, a minbar atop a staircase for delivering the Friday sermon and daily prayers, and at least one minaret.

Fridays are the holy day in Islam, and the noon Salat on Friday is extended into a special worship service. The original selection of Friday as the holy day apparently was made because that was the day for the weekly market in Muhammad's town of Medina, which made it possible for many people to attend. It also had the advantage of distinguishing the Muslim holy day from the Jewish choice of Saturday and the Christian selection of Sunday. The service, like the Salat during the week, is held in a mosque.

Mihrab—Niche in an interior wall of a mosque indicating the direction of Mecca for worshipers during Salat.

Minbar—Staircase topped with a pulpit in a mosque.

Mosques have a niche (**mihrab**) in the interior wall, indicating the direction of Mecca (Figure 3.20). The **minbar,** an ornate pulpit atop a straight staircase, is

Figure 3.19 Muslims are called to prayer by a summons coming from the minaret of a mosque, such as this one in Port Said, Egypt.

Figure 3.20 The mihrab is the niche in a mosque indicating the direction of Mecca so worshipers can direct their prayers there.

Khatib—Person who reads the Friday sermon.

Minaret—Tower of a mosque from which people are called to prayer.

Muezzin—Person who calls Muslims to prayers five times daily.

Saum—Ritual of fasting.

Ramadan—One-month period of fasting from sunrise to sunset each year; one of the Pillars of Islam.

the place where the Friday sermon is read by the **khatib** and daily prayers are led by the imam in the mosque (Figure 3.21). The floor of the large interior room of a mosque is carpeted, and no seats are placed anywhere, which leaves all of the floor available for the many men praying together. Women are allowed in galleries around the side of the main room. Distinctive features of the exterior of a mosque include one or more **minarets,** or towers, for the **muezzin** to call people to prayer and the fountain or pool in the courtyard for ablutions.

Saum   **Saum** is the Pillar that is observed during the ninth month of the Muslim lunar calendar, when the 30-day fast of **Ramadan** takes place. At this time, adult Muslims are expected to fast from just before sunrise until sunset. The fast requires abstaining from all food and drink during that period, as well as from smoking, intentional vomiting, and sex.

Figure 3.21 The minbar is the pulpit atop the staircase that is used for Friday worship in Muslim mosques.

Travelers, sick people, and women who are menstruating are excused from fasting but are required to make up the day(s) immediately following the celebration that ends Ramadan. Children are not expected to participate in fasting.

Since the lunar calendar causes Ramadan to occur at different times of year, the temperatures in the very hot climates may make the fast of Ramadan extremely difficult when it falls in summer. Even when the weather cooperates, this long period of fasting places considerable physical strain on many people, although a few seem to welcome the opportunity to lose a few pounds while pondering religious truths. The end of Ramadan brings the very joyous celebration of **Id al-Fitr** (Feast of the Breaking of the Fast), a three-day holiday highlighting wonderful food, new clothes, and family visits.

Zukat The giving of alms, the **Zukat,** was originally a means of sharing one's blessings with the less fortunate. It evolved into taxes collected by the nations in which the Muslims lived and eliminated the voluntary aspect of giving. Now Zukat is sometimes provided as an optional giving in addition to the required governmental taxes.

Hajj The **Hajj** is the last of the Five Pillars and often is the event of a lifetime for a Muslim if the trip is financially and physically possible. The final parts of the Hajj can be done only on certain days in the 12th lunar month. The two parts of the pilgrimage can be completed in two segments or in a continuous effort. The pilgrim is to wear a white garment, and visit the mosque in Mecca as soon as ablutions are finished.

Pilgrims must circumambulate around the **Ka'ba,** and hair is either shaved off or trimmed. Official ceremonies are held on the seventh and eighth days, and a sermon is given on the ninth day while the pilgrims stand on the hillside in the hot sun, listening for many hours. The tenth day there is a ritual throwing of stones at a pillar representing Satan, followed by ritual slaughtering of many animals in preparation for the Feast of the Sacrifice, which remembers Abraham's willingness to sacrifice for God. Three more days of celebration are held in Mecca before pilgrims begin to disperse for a visit to Medina and the long journey home.

In recent years there have been such crowds making the Hajj that people have been killed when stampedelike situations erupted. The small area around the sacred Ka'ba and the mosque in Mecca creates what sometimes can become fatal congestion.

Roles of Islamic Men

In the Islamic world, men are to provide for their wives and children and to protect them, a traditional situation that has tended to curtail opportunities for women that are assumed to be their rights in other countries. Theoretically, Muslim men are able to have four wives as long as they treat them all equally. However, this is not the general practice today.

Women's Roles

Islamic women often have lived in **purdah** (isolated from public view) and spent much of their days at home caring for their families. They have traditionally dressed according to the **hijab** (dress code for Muslim women designed to create a curtain of modesty) generally followed in their country. In Afghanistan, the Taliban required women to wear the **burqa** (head to toe covering consisting of a loose, long robe and a head covering with a thick veil and only a rather narrow slit to look outward. In Iraq, Iran, and some other Muslim countries, women wear a **chador** composed of an **abaya** (loose, long cloak) and a head scarf or covering that may or may not veil the face. Usually these garments are black, although exceptions are seen in some areas.

Id al-Fitr—Three-day holiday celebrating the end of Ramadan, the month of fasting.

Zukat—Purifying tax; one of Five Pillars.

Hajj—Pilgrimage to Mecca; one of Five Pillars.

Ka'ba—Black stone cube with a meteorite in its wall; shrine in the center of Mecca that pilgrims circumambulate as part of the hajj.

Purdah—Seclusion of women in some Islamic regions.

Hijab—Dress code for Muslim women; varies somewhat in various countries and regions.

Burqa—Loose, long robe covering the body to the toes and a head covering with a thick veil and a narrow slit; form of hijab worn by Muslim women in Afghanistan.

Chador—Long, loose cloak and head covering (sometimes veiled) worn by Muslim women in Muslim countries (e.g., Iraq and Iran).

Abaya—Long, loose cloak worn by many Muslim women.

In the 1980s, many Muslim women were no longer wearing garments that covered their faces and hid their bodies, and they were often found in the workplace alongside men who were not their relatives. This situation caused sufficient consternation that a more fundamental approach toward Muslim women is being put into play in many places throughout the Muslim world now. In fact, some young women are actively seeking to resume the more traditional Muslim lifestyle.

Architectural Heritage

Among the remarkable buildings constructed by the Muslims are the great Mosque of Damascus (705 CE), the Great Mosque at Cordova in Spain (785–987 CE), the Alhambra (Figure C.25, p. C9) in Granada, Spain (1333–1391 CE), the Mosque of Suleyman the Magnificent in Istanbul (1550–1560 CE), and the Taj Mahal in Agra, India (built by the Mughal Emperor Shah Jahan from 1632 to 1652 CE).

Historical Perspectives

European Crusaders mounted vigorous attacks on the Muslims in the Levant (Figure C.47, p. C16) and captured Jerusalem from them in 1099 CE only to lose the city to Saladin (who had been ruling from Cairo while Jerusalem was in Christian hands) in 1187. The Mamluks, who ruled in Egypt from 1254 to 1517, captured Tripoli from the Crusaders in 1289.

The Moors (Muslims from North Africa) were forced out of Spain in 1492. Istanbul was controlled by the Ottomans from 1453 until Ataturk's successful overthrow in 1922. Pakistan was formed as a Muslim country in 1947 at the time of the British partition of India. Muslim is the principal religion in many nations in the Middle East, North Africa, Central Asia, and some areas in Southeast Asia.

Muslim Calendar

Muslim calligraphy is done using a pen made from a reed that has been buried in manure for four years to achieve the desired red color, ink made from ground soot, and paper dyed with tea and coated with egg white to make it easier to correct mistakes. These practices stem from the 7th century.

The Muslim calendar is a lunar calendar with only 354 days in a year, and it starts at a different year in history than the Gregorian calendar that is used by most countries. Year 1 was 622 CE. The year 2006 on the Gregorian calendar corresponds approximately to the Muslim year 1427. Since the Islamic calendar has 12 lunar months and no extra days, the seasonal timing for various Muslim holidays shifts over time.

Dietary Laws

The dietary laws for Muslims were developed by Muhammad and served partly to differentiate Muslims from those who practiced other religions, particularly Jews and Christians. The rules were quite simple:

1. Do not eat the flesh of carrion (animals found dead).
2. Do not consume blood in any form.
3. Stay away from all swine.
4. Do not eat food that has been given as an offering to idols.
5. Do not drink anything that has the power to inebriate.

Islamic Sects

Shiite—Muslim sect that comprises a majority in Iran, Iraq, Bahrain, and Azerbaijan.

Sunni—Muslim sect that comprises a majority in some Middle Eastern countries.

Within Islam there are different groups, including the **Shiite,** the **Sunni,** and the Sufis, with each of these plus others being split into still more clusters. Shiite is a large majority sect of Islam with much of its religious activities centered in Iran.

In addition to Iran, other countries with a Shiite majority include Iraq, Bahrain, and Azerbaijan. Sunni is the majority sect in Jordan, Saudi Arabia, Egypt, Afghanistan, Turkey, United Arab Emirates, Pakistan, Syria, Yemen, and Kuwait. Sufi, another sect of Muslims, are noted for their use of music and dance in their religious observances; the Whirling Dervishes of Kona, Turkey, are examples.

Seventh Day Adventist

Seventh Day Adventist— Religious sect rooted in Protestantism and with a carefully defined behavior code.

Seventh Day Adventist is a group that had its origin in the United States in the mid-1800s when one of its founders, Ellen Harmon White, reported having visions and wrote about these visions and dreams for 70 years. Basically, this religion has roots in Protestantism, but it adds to this foundation the expectation of a second coming of Christ. The lifestyle espoused by Seventh Day Adventists included establishing the seventh day of the week, Saturday, as the holy day, with meal preparation and dish-washing chores being done either on the day before or the day following, thus leaving Saturday entirely free for dedication to their religion. The behavior code is based strongly on the Ten Commandments.

The dietary code of the Seventh Day Adventists is of particular interest in this chapter because of its thoroughness and its dedication to consuming a totally healthful vegetarian diet. This specific interest has led to considerable research that has added to the knowledge regarding this type of diet.

Simplicity of foods is one of the basic premises on which Adventists have based their lacto-ovo-vegetarian diets. However, some followers have been more restrictive and have opted to eliminate eggs or milk (or both) from their diets, changes that greatly complicate the achievement of an adequate diet for people. Emphasis for protein sources is placed heavily on a variety of legumes, with nuts, cereals, eggs, and milk rounding out the protein requirement.

Olive oil is recommended in place of animal fats, and whole-grain cereals are preferred over refined products. Alcohol, tobacco, tea, and coffee are prohibited because of their negative effects on health.

Summary

Major religions have shaped the cultures and food practices of people around the world for many, many centuries (Table 3.4). These include Hinduism, Buddhism, Confucianism, Taoism, Shintoism, Judaism, Christianity, and Islam.

Hinduism is the oldest religion and includes the worship of several gods, notably Vishnu, Shiva, and Brahma, as well as the concept of castes. Hindus believe in repeated reincarnation. They frequently are vegetarians, a reflection of their reverence for life, and they also avoid alcohol. India is home to the majority of Hindus, although followers can be found in the United States and other parts of the world, too.

Buddhism is a religion based on the Four Noble Truths and a carefully defined code of conduct. Among the directions for living are the avoidance of alcohol and, if a monk, not eating after midday. Animals are not to be killed to become a source of food, although eating meat is approved if the animal was not killed specifically to feed the person who might eat it. Buddhism is the major religion in the Himalayan countries and other places in Southeast Asia. In China, Confucianism and Taoism are blended with Buddhism, while in Japan Shintoism is blended with Buddhism.

Table 3.4   Food Guidelines in Selected Religions

Religion	Restricted Foods	Other Food Practices
Hinduism	Beef because sacred; may avoid pigs and chickens because not clean Brahmans avoid alcohol	Ritual bath before cooking in Brahman kitchen Brahman food contains ghee; no ghee for lower castes Brahmans avoid garlic, onions Food offerings at temples
Buddhism	Meats, but can eat if killed by non-Buddhist	May eat fish Monks beg and eat only until noon Avoid overeating
Confucianism, Taoism		Diet rich in protein, vitamins in pregnancy until 30 days after birth Eggs and rice for health and wealth Rice wine wedding toasts Food for ancestors on family altar
Shintoism		Altars in home with daily food, drink
Judaism	Pork, ostrich, mollusks, crustaceans	May eat beef, sheep, goat chicken, turkey, fish Separate dishes for meat/dairy (Orthodox) Kosher products for Orthodox
Christianity		Wafer and wine for Communion
Islam	Pork, alcohol	Fasting during Ramadan
Seventh Day Adventist	Meat, alcohol	Most are ovo-lacto-vegetarians Usually avoid animal fats

Judaism is a religion based on the Torah (particularly Genesis, Exodus, Leviticus, Numbers, and Deuteronomy) and the Talmud. This religion spread widely and contributed to the cultures of many different people scattered throughout Europe, Asia, and Africa prior to and after Christ. There are varying traditions, depending on the particular Jewish sect. However, the key holy traditions for all sects include Rosh Hashanah, Yom Kippur, and Passover. Kosher food is required among Orthodox Jews with the added stipulation that separate utensils and dishes must be maintained for meat dishes and dairy products. Pork is not a part of Jewish menus because it is from an animal that has a cloven hoof but does not chew its cud.

Christianity also utilizes the Old Testament, but it adds to this the New Testament and a belief that Jesus was the son of God, which is in direct contrast to the Jewish interpretation of Jesus. The Roman Catholic Church was prominent in Europe, and the Eastern Orthodox Church represented Christianity in Greece and farther east. Protestantism split from the Roman Catholic Church. Catholics in years past have avoided eating meat on Fridays, but this is no longer required.

Islam is the youngest of the major religions, the product of the teachings of Muhammad, an Arabian prophet who lived in the 7th century. This religion is prominent among Arab populations but also is the religion of many other people around the world today. Its foundation is the Five Pillars of Islam: Shahada, Salat, Saum, Zukat, and Hajj. Saum requires fasting, and Ramadan, the ninth lunar month, is a 30-day fasting period, which places strong demands on followers, particularly when this fast occurs in the heat of summer. The Five Pillars and all aspects of the lives of Muslims are described in the Koran and the hadith. Food prohibitions include avoiding eating swine, the flesh of carrion, blood in any form, food previously offered to gods, and alcohol.

The Seventh Day Adventist religion is included in this chapter because of its dietary dictates, which are based on vegetarianism (usually lacto-ovo), whole-grain cereals, and legumes. Alcohol, tea, coffee, and tobacco are prohibited.

Selected Sites

http://www.gadnet.com/fooodx.html—Many Indian recipes.

www.penzeys.com—Source of Indian spices.

www.food-india.com—Information on Indian ingredients and recipes.

www.asiarecipe.com—Glossary of terms and recipes.

www.everythingjewish.com—Extensive information about Judaism.

www.holidays.net/passover/seder2.htm—Discussion of the celebration of Passover and the Seder.

www.jewish-food.org—Web site for numerous Jewish foods.

http://islam.about.com/blintroc.htm—Information about Five Pillars of Islam.

www.religioustolerance.org/var_rel.htm—Background information on several different religions.

www.adherents.com/Religions_By_Adherents.html—Census data on religions around the world.

Study Questions

1. Give a brief description of each of the following religions: (a) Hinduism, (b) Buddhism, (c) Judaism, (d) Christianity, and (e) Islam.
2. Which three major religions view Jerusalem as a very important city for their faith, and why does each religion attach this importance?
3. Compare the dietary laws and food practices of the religions discussed in this chapter.

Bibliography

Barer-Stein, T. 1999. *You Eat What You Are.* 2nd ed. Firefly Books, Ltd. Ontario, Canada.

Confucius. 1960. *Four Books and Five Classics.* Hong Kong University Press.

Cousins, L.S. 1997. Buddhism. In J.R. Hinnells, ed. *A New Handbook of Living Religions.* Penguin. London, England.

Goldman, A.L. 2000. *Being Jewish.* Simon and Schuster. New York.

Hinnells, J.R., ed. 1997. *A New Handbook of Living Religions.* Penguin. London, England.

Hussaini, M.M. 1993. *Islamic Dietary Concepts and Practices.* Islamic Food and Nutrition Council of America. Bedford Park, IL.

Jackson, M.A. 2000. Getting religion—For your products, that is. *Food Tech. 54*(7): 60.

Kilara, A. and K.K. Iya. 1992. Food Practices of the Hindu. *Food Technol. 46:* 94-104.

Lowenberg, M., E.N. Todhunter, E.D. Wilson, J.R. Savage, and J.L. Lubawski. 1974. *Food and Man.* 2nd ed. Wiley. New York.

Marcus, A.D. 2000. *The View from Nebo: How Archaeology Is Rewriting the Bible and Reshaping the Middle East.* Little, Brown. Boston.

Mbiti, J.S. 1970. *African Religions and Philosophy.* Doubleday Anchor. Garden City, NY.

Morgan, K.W. 1953. *Religion of the Hindus.* Ronald. New York.

Panati, C. 1996. *Sacred Origins of Profound Things.* Penguin. London, England.

Regenstein, J.M. and C.E. Regenstein. 1992. Kosher food market in the 1990s—Legal view. *Food Technol. 46:* 122–124.

Simoons, F.F. 1994. *Eat Not This Flesh.* 2nd ed. University of Wisconsin Press. Madison.

Unterman, A. 1997. Judaism. In J.R. Hinnells, ed. *A New Handbook of Living Religions.* Penguin. London, England.

Walls, A. 1997. Christianity. In J.R. Hinnells, ed. *A New Handbook of Living Religions*. Penguin. London, England.

Weightman, S. 1997. Hinduism. In J.R. Hinnells, ed. *A New Handbook of Living Religions*. Penguin. London, England.

Welch, A.T. 1997. Islam. In J.R. Hinnells, ed. *A New Handbook of Living Religions*. Penguin. London, England.

Part VII

America's Food Scene Today

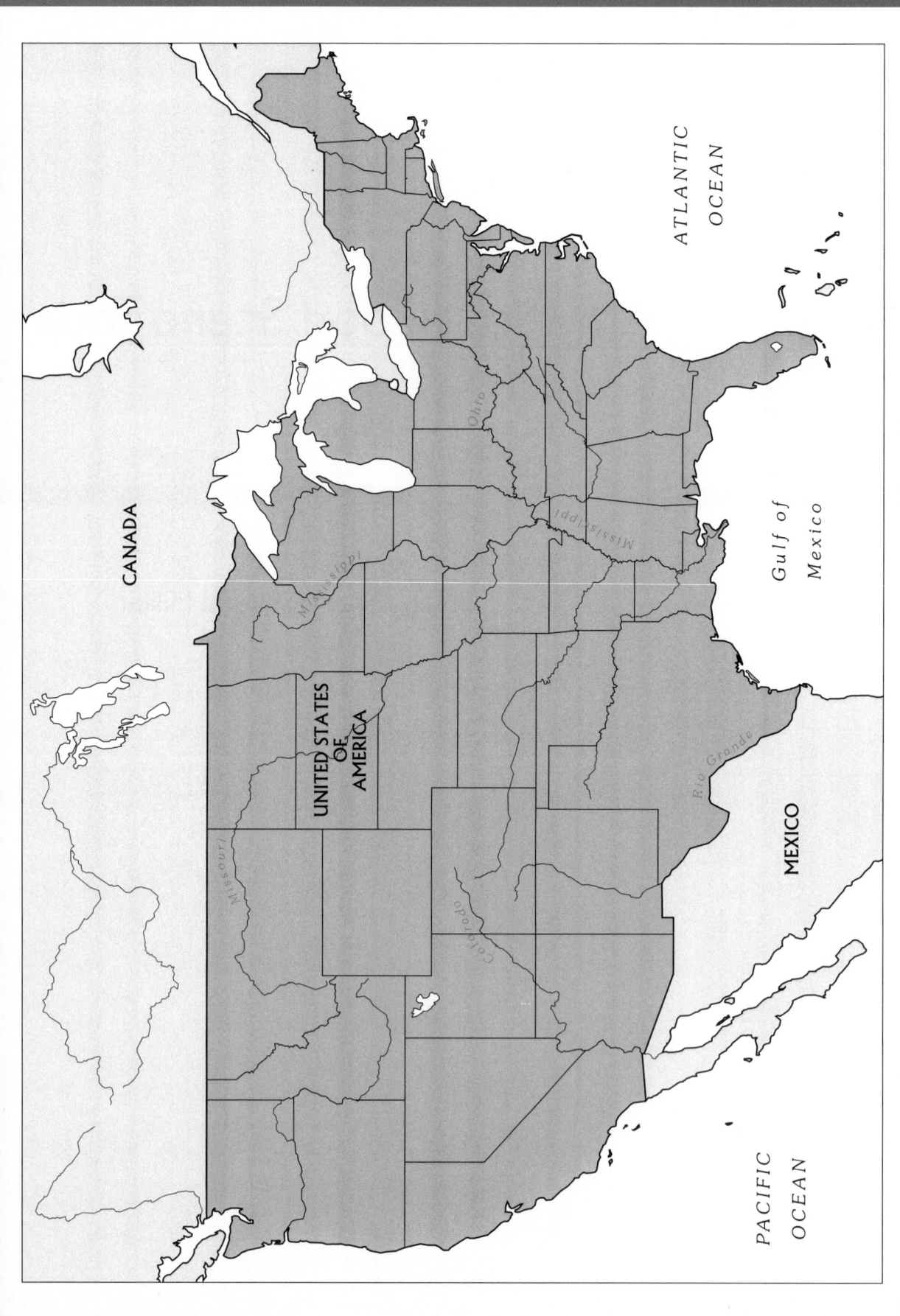

23 United States

Traditional Regional Foods

Around the United States, food specialties have helped to define the food patterns of different regions. Probably the first area that comes to mind is the Northeast because that is where American History as a subject in school usually begins. Other major regions in terms of food patterns are the South, the Midwest, the Southwest, and the West.

The foods that characterize each region reflect the heritage of the people who established it. The food traditions that have been studied in previous chapters often contributed to the foods that developed into a cuisine characterizing each region, depending on the local traditions or the country of origin of the immigrants.

Northeastern Traditions

Native American Indians contributed to the dietary practices that the Pilgrims and other early settlers brought to the Northeast. Indians added wild turkey to the menus as well as corn, cranberries, and maple syrup. In addition, lobsters and clams were available. These early settlers cooked meats and vegetables in plain dishes typical of English cuisine. Special dishes that reflect the Northeast are Indian pudding, Boston brown bread, and Boston clam chowder.

Southern Cuisine

Settlers arrived from England along the Atlantic coast, but other significant groups shaping food in the South came from Africa (usually as slaves), France via Canada and the Caribbean, and Spain (via the Caribbean). Southern cooks combined familiar cultural dishes with such available foods as okra, greens, pork, and cornmeal. The result was that Southern cooking traditionally produced such specialties as deep-fat fried chicken, ham and red-eye gravy, biscuits, bacon, salt pork and beans, greens, and Hoppin' John (rice and black-eyed peas).

In southern Louisiana, two distinctive styles of cooking developed in the late 18th century as a result of immigrant groups arriving in that area. The Acadian French came from Nova Scotia and settled in the bayous and rural areas where they established **Cajun** cooking. This style can be described as simple cooking usually done in a single pot and often laced with fiery pepper. Examples of Cajun dishes that are famous include gumbo and jambalaya.

Creole is the other unique cuisine; it developed in New Orleans and other urban centers in southern Louisiana. Wonderful spices brought by immigrants from the Caribbean blended with the French, African, and Spanish cuisines of other immigrants over two centuries ago to create Creole dishes, such as shrimp Creole.

Cajun—Style of one-pot cooking developed in southern Louisiana based on combining fish or meat, local vegetables, and rice.

Creole—Flavorful cuisine of New Orleans and southern Louisiana that integrates spices from the Caribbean with cuisines brought by French, Spanish, and African immigrants.

Midwest Fare

British, Scandinavian, German, and some Italian immigrants frequently settled in the Midwest as the country was developing, and typical meals reflect their ethic of hard work and plenty of good, simple food. Chicken that is usually fried in some butter, mashed potatoes and gravy, corn on the cob, and apple pie immediately come to mind when one thinks about traditional foods in the Midwest. Excellent cheeses, sausages, and beers are available, due particularly to the Scandinavian and German settlers. Italians added pizza and some of their sauces and pastas to the mix.

Southwestern Food

In terms of real time, the Southwest cuisine developed before that in the Northeast because of the push of the Spaniards northward through Mexico. Some Spanish influences on Mexican food are seen in Southwestern foods (e.g., enchiladas, burritos, tacos). Beef in the form of steaks or shredded is used in traditional Southwest dishes, which is not surprising in view of the ranching that is typical in this part of the country. Guacamole, salsa (ranging from mild to killing hot), pinto beans, and tortillas are very much part of the food scene.

Western Dishes

Fusion is a word that may best embody the range of dishes typical of the West. This descriptor fits because cuisines from all around the world have migrated to this part of the nation. That cultural input has been combined with the wide array of produce that can be grown in California and some other parts of the West. The result is that no single picture emerges. The Chinese influenced food when they were brought to the area to help build the railroads. Although Mexican and Spanish influences were already defining the cuisine, Chinese ingredients began to be used in some dishes. Subsequently, many immigrants brought aspects of such unique cuisines as those from India and Vietnam. Creative cooks have blurred many of the lines between these cuisines to the point where *fusion* indeed describes food in the West.

Special foods in the West include Dungeness crab, clams, calamari, and many other ocean fish. The Northwest is known not only for its salmon, but also its excellent raspberries, other berries, and apples. California grows a wide range of produce, particularly strawberries, avocadoes, broccoli, artichokes, asparagus, and tree fruits. Nuts and rice are other foods grown in significant quantities for use in the West and the rest of the nation, too.

Recipes

Boston Clam Chowder (Northeastern) (Serves 4)

1 strip bacon, chopped
1 large onion, chopped
1 stalk celery, diced
1 garlic clove, minced
1 tbsp butter
½ tsp dried thyme
½ tsp dried basil
1½ tbsp flour
½ tsp salt
1 c bottled clam juice
1¼ c milk
2 medium Red Triumph potatoes, boiled and diced
1 6½-oz can clams

1. Sauté bacon, onion, celery, and garlic in butter over low heat, but avoid browning.
2. Stir in spices and flour; stir in clam juice gradually to make a smooth slurry before finally stirring in the milk.
3. Heat to boiling while stirring continuously to avoid lumps.
4. Add potatoes and clams (including their juice), and stir before simmering covered for 5 to 10 minutes.

Hoppin' John (Southern) (Serves 3)

1 onion, chopped
2 tsp bacon drippings
¾ c cooked ham, chopped
1 can (about 16 oz) black-eyed peas
¼ tsp cayenne pepper
2 c cooked rice

1. Sauté onion in bacon drippings.
2. Add the ham, black-eyed peas, and cayenne; stir before covering and simmering 5 to 10 minutes.
3. Add the rice and stir while heating to serving temperature.

Fried Chicken (Midwestern) (Serves 4)

1 frying chicken or 4 pieces chicken parts
½ c milk
1 c butter
½ c flour
1 tsp season salt
½ tsp ground pepper

1. Soak chicken in milk while preheating oven to 400°F.

2. Put butter in a baking dish that will hold chicken pieces in a single layer; place in oven to heat and melt the butter.
3. Put flour and seasonings in a 1-quart plastic bag and mix before adding chicken pieces and coating each with the mixture.
4. Remove baking dish from oven, and arrange chicken pieces with the skin side down in the butter.
5. Bake for 20 minutes; turn each piece over and return to the oven to bake 20 more minutes.

Sopaipillas (Southwestern) (Serves 6)

2 c flour
1½ tsp baking powder
½ tsp salt
2 tbsp shortening
¾ c water
Oil for deep-fat frying

1. Stir the flour, baking powder, and salt together.
2. Add the shortening and cut it in with a pastry blender until the size of rice grains.
3. Add water and stir with a fork until the dough is all moistened and holds together.
4. Turn out onto a floured bread board, flour fingers, and knead the dough by folding over, rotating, and pressing lightly with the fingertips; continue folding, rotating, and pressing about 9 times or until the dough is cohesive. Wrap in plastic wrap and refrigerate at least 30 minutes.
5. Preheat oil to 375°F, starting heating after dough has been chilling 20 minutes.
6. Divide the dough into 2 pieces. Add flour to the board and then roll one of the pieces into a thin rectangle. Cut into 3″ squares. Repeat with the second piece of dough.
7. Carefully place squares in the hot oil, frying very few at a time so the oil stays hot enough. Use tongs to turn them over once so that both sides brown nicely.
8. Remove from oil with tongs and drain on paper toweling.
9. Serve hot with honey available to drizzle into the center after diners bite off a corner and reveal the cavity in the middle.

California Salad Toss (Western) (Serves 4)

1 head Bibb lettuce, torn into pieces
8 leaves red leaf lettuce, torn into pieces
8 arugula leaves
2 green onions, thinly sliced
4 radishes, sliced
1 carrot, sliced
1 stalk celery, diced
1 small jar marinated artichoke hearts
½ c alfalfa sprouts
½ c Chinese snow pea pods
2 tbsp diced red pepper
⅓ c crumbled feta cheese

Salt
Coarsely ground black pepper
3 tbsp olive oil
1 tbsp balsamic vinegar

1. Spin the washed lettuce pieces in a salad spinner; place all ingredients except the oil and vinegar in a large salad bowl.
2. When ready to serve, toss the salad with the oil and vinegar. (NOTE: The oil and vinegar cruets can be placed on the table for each person to add to the salad, as desired.)

The Changing Scene

Just as the immigrants shaped the traditional foods in various parts of the United States in earlier times, the influx of immigrants today is altering the types of food eaten in different regions of the country. Many large U.S. cities today have enclaves of the various ethnic groups that compose our rich cultural mix. The foods in the markets and the dishes that are prepared most frequently reflect the cultural heritage and dietary patterns of specific cultural groups rather than simply the region of the country where the people live.

Due to increased mobility of the population and the diverse, large numbers of immigrants, regional food patterns are much less clear than they once were. Instead, the palate of food choices is broadening in many markets, particularly in urban settings, because of the increasing cultural milieu. Food traditions brought by immigrants when they came to this country provide comfort and pleasure in their new lives. They also have broadened the dining experiences of many others.

Evolving Demographics

Changes in population size and demographics are discussed in this section to highlight the reasons why our menus are increasingly reflecting of the way people choose to eat all around the world.

European Immigration

The United States is a nation that has always admitted immigrants from other parts of the world to start new lives here. Dreams of better lives as a result of increased riches, freedom, and escape from political risks are just some of the many factors that have motivated people to immigrate to America. Many immigrants in the 19th century were from Europe (Table 23.1), with Great Britain, Ireland, and Germany contributing a little less than half a million people to the American influx between 1830 and 1860, according to Rischin 1989.

These three countries plus Scandinavia were the source of about 10 million more new arrivals in the second wave of immigration that occurred between 1860 and 1890 (Figure 23.1). The third wave (between 1890 and 1930) brought a different mixture of Europeans from Greece, Austria-Hungary, Italy, Poland, Russia, Portugal, and Spain. The numbers during this third European immigrant wave totaled another 22 million. These waves of emigration from Europe resulted in a population that was predominantly white, and had some commonalities as well as many differences. The focus for these immigrants was on fitting in by learning English and working to support their families.

African Immigrants

This European heritage presents only part of the picture, for workers from other parts of the world became part of the nation's population as this fledgling country developed agriculturally and industrially in the 18th and 19th centuries. African slaves were reluctant immigrants exploited by southern plantation owners to develop their lands and fortunes. This chapter in American history remains a legacy still being resolved as African-Americans seek better lives for themselves and their families today.

Asian Immigrants

Asians also entered this country as strong workers to aid in building railroads and performing other work required to develop the American West in the 19th century. The majority of these workers came from China (Figure 23.2), and many stayed in this country after their original tasks were finished. Subse-

Table 23.1   Origins of U.S. Legal Immigrants from 1820 to 1976

Region of Origin	Approximate Percent of Total Immigrants					
	1820–60	1861–1900	1901–30	1931–60	1961–70	1971–76
Northern and western Europe	95	68	23	41	17	7
Canada	3	7	11	21	12	4
Southern and eastern Europe	—	22	58	17	15	13
Asia	—	2	3	5	13	32
Latin America	—	—	5	15	39	41
Other	2	1	—	1	3	3

Adapted from data from Population Reference Bureau.

Figure 23.1 This church on Cape Cod in Massachusetts is representative of the religion familiar to Americans whose heritage was often rooted in Protestant parts of Europe.

quently, wars at various places around the world have triggered immigration from Asia and other regions. The influx of Vietnamese resulting from American involvement in the Vietnam War created a significant presence that is evident today (approximately 225,000 people from there as of 2002). Political ties with the Philippines created the opportunity for many Filipinos to immigrate into the United States.

Current Immigrants

Economic opportunity clearly is a strong factor motivating immigration to the United States, even in the face of legal limits on the numbers admitted annually. Illegal border crossings and smuggling via land, sea, and air currently are taxing

Figure 23.2 Buddhism was brought to the United States by early Chinese immigrants and then expanded as other immigrants from Asian countries followed.

Table 23.2   Immigration Trends in the United States from 1981–2002*

Country of Origin	Total, 1981–1990	Total, 1991–2000	2002[†]
Europe	705,600	1,311,400	174,200
Mexico	1,653,300	2,251,400	219,380
India	261,900	383,300	71,105
China	388,800	424,600	61,282
Philippines	495,300	505,600	51,308
Vietnam	401,400	421,100	33,627
El Salvador	214,600	217,400	31,168
Cuba	159,200	180,900	28,272
Bosnia/Herzogovina	Not available	39,100	25,373

*Data from U.S. Census, 2000.
[†]The figures are for one year only; other columns are for 10 years.

U.S. Immigration and Naturalization Service— Federal agency responsible for enforcing immigration and naturalization regulations and laws.

the **U.S. Immigration and Naturalization Service**'s resources as an attempt is made to control immigration.

The trends in sources of immigrants over the years are presented in Table 23.2. Clearly, the demographics in the United States are changing significantly as a result of the decline in immigration from Europe and the dramatic increases from Asia and Latin America (Figure 23.3). These data reflect legal immigration and ignore the significant numbers who enter unauthorized (Table 23.3), particularly along the southwestern border that stretches from Texas to California. Of the total unauthorized immigrants in 2000, 68.7 percent were from Mexico and the next most numerous were from El Salvador (2.7 percent).

Figures on immigration changes represent only a partial picture because births and deaths in the resident population also contribute to demographic changes. Data from the U.S. Bureau of the Census (Table 23.4) indicate the changes in the racial mix. A significant increase in the percentage of Hispanics is occurring and is predicted to continue, while the percentage of Caucasians is decreasing. Other minorities are also increasing, but at a significantly slower rate than Hispanics.

Figure 23.3 Sikhs, many of whom are immigrants from India, celebrate their religion in Los Angeles on a day of worship and a parade for Sikhs from as far away as San Francisco.

Table 23.3   Unauthorized immigration estimates*

State	1990	2000	Percent in 2000[†]	2004[‡]
Total United States	3,500,000	7,000,000	2.5	10,300,000
California	1,476,000	2,209,000	6.5	2,400,000
Texas	438,000	1,041,000	5.0	1,4000,00
New York	357,000	489,000	2.6	650,000
Illinois	194,000	432,000	3.5	400,000
Florida	239,000	337,000	2.1	850,000
Arizona	88,000	283,000	5.5	200,000–250,000
Georgia	34,000	228,000	2.8	500,000
North Carolina	26,000	206,000	2.6	300,000
Colorado	31,000	144,000	3.3	200,000–250,000

* Data from U.S. Immigration and Naturalization Service.
[†] Percentage of total population living in the state in 2000.
[‡] Adapted from Passell, J.S. 2005. *Unauthorized Migrants: Numbers and Characteristics.* Pew Hispanic Center. Washington, D.C.

The overall changes are occurring somewhat differently within the various states (Tables 23.5 and 23.6). In 2002, California was the state receiving the most legal immigrants (Figure 23.3), followed by New York, Florida, Texas, Illinois, and Georgia, in descending order. The influx of undocumented immigrants (Table 23.3) adds to the impact of immigration on many of the same states. The striking increases in the Latino and Asian populations in California are partially the result of geography (a long border with Mexico and a logical entry point for arriving Asian immigrants).

Nationwide, the numbers of Asians and Latinos have increased significantly, although African-Americans remain the largest minority group. The figures are quite remarkable and clearly indicate that the United States is undergoing significant demographic changes that are creating an evolving pattern affecting almost all aspects of people's lives, including their diets and the foods available to them. Although these states are encountering the changes accompanying increased cultural diversity significantly now, most states are noticing similar, but smaller, shifts in demographics.

Immigrant Adjustments

"Little Saigon" is the local designation for part of Westminster, Orange County, in southern California (Figure 23.4). This name is a proud indication that the area is the focal point for the largest Vietnamese American community in the United States (approximately 200,000 in southern California). Vietnamese political refugees arriving at the peak of migration in 1975, when Saigon fell, were distributed quite broadly around the nation.

The cultural isolation this approach to resettlement created was too painful for many of the new immigrants. They moved a second time to cluster in cultural

Table 23.4   Racial Mix of U.S. Population*

Race	Percent in 2000	Percent in 2003	Percent predicted in 2050
White alone	75.1	66.8	50
Black alone	12.3	12.8	15
Hispanic	12.5	13.7	24
Asian	3.6	4.1	8
American Indian	0.9	1.0	2

* From U.S. Bureau of the Census figures (exceeds 100 percent) due to rounding of figures.

Table 23.5   Racial Distribution in the United States in 2000*

Foreign Born (percent)	States
>15	California, Florida, Hawaii, Nevada, New York
10–14.9	Arizona, Connecticut, Illinois, Massachusetts, Rhode Island, Texas
5–9.9	Alabama, Alaska, Colorado, Idaho, Kansas, Michigan, Minnesota, New Mexico, North Carolina, Oregon, Utah, West Virginia
<5	Arkansas, Georgia, Indiana, Iowa, Kentucky, Louisiana, Maine, Missouri, Montana, Nebraska, New Hampshire, North Dakota, Ohio, Oklahoma, Pennsylvania, South Carolina, Tennessee, Vermont, West Virginia, Wisconsin

*U.S. Census 2000.

enclaves along the eastern seaboard from Boston to Washington, the Gulf Coast from Texas to Mississippi, the Pacific Northwest, San Jose and the Silicon Valley in California's Bay Area, and southern California's Orange and San Diego counties.

The consequence of such population movements has been a growing appreciation of the culture, including the cuisine, of the Vietnamese, as they have brought demand for the unique food ingredients that help to define Vietnamese food and have held their festivals and celebrations, not only for themselves, but also for their new neighbors in their new land.

This broadening of cultural awareness and understanding of new food patterns is occurring in many parts of the country and for other immigrant ethnic groups, as well as for the Vietnamese. The specific cultural and ethnic groups differ with the particular region or location within the country, but tremendous opportunities for becoming acquainted with new foods and other cultural components are widely available and continue to increase as more immigrants arrive and are assimilated (Figure 23.5).

Restaurants and ethnic markets are wonderful places to gain knowledge and to experience foods that may be quite new to you. The potential may be more varied in an urban rather than a rural setting. For instance, among the ethnic neighborhoods scattered around the Los Angeles area now are German, Chinese, Latino, Korean, African-American, East Indian, Vietnamese, Japanese, and Thai. This list does not include the many other small spots where special ethnic markets and restaurants are clustered and shoppers can experience foods from the Middle East, Greece, Italy, and just about any other place you wish to name.

Table 23.6   Legal Immigration in United States and Selected States in 2002 (U.S. Census data, 2004)

Country	U.S.	California	New York	Florida	Texas	Illinois	New Jersey
Total	1,063,733	291,216	114,827	90,819	88,365	47,235	57,721
Mexico	219,380	105,699	2,250	3,822	44,694	11,461	1,209
India	71,105	18,265	4,728	1,652	4,294	5,197	9,683
China	61,282	19,494	9,872	1,022	2,561	2,768	2,966
Philippines	51,308	21,971	2,319	1,897	2,258	2,451	3,111
Vietnam	33,627	13,126	760	887	3,704	594	557
El Salvador	31,168	13,497	5,123	665	3,289	266	933
Cuba	28,272	548	449	22,262	87	128	1,274
Bosnia/Herzegovina	25,373	901	2,074	1,926	293	1,483	211

Figure 23.4 This large shopping mall in Westminster ("Little Saigon") attracts Vietnamese immigrants from all of Southern California; it provides wonderful flavors of their original country.

Ethnic Celebrations

Special holiday celebrations (Figure 23.6) of ethnic groups also draw attention to the increasing cultural richness in America. Iranians now living in Southern California (estimated to be about 600,000 in the region in 2000) mark their new year (coincident with the beginning of spring, the vernal equinox) with a 13-day celebration that includes prayer, purification and rejuvenation of the spirit, gift giving, and feasting, and culminates in a huge gathering at a public park to mark the end of the celebration.

Kwanzaa—African-American holiday lasting a week at the end of the year to celebrate African-American heritage.

Cinco de Mayo—Celebration on May 5 honoring Mexican defeat of the French in 1862 at Puebla; celebrations in the United States also recognize the Mexican Americans living in this country.

Kwanzaa is an African-American holiday (December 26 to January 1) celebrated in Los Angeles since 1966, an event that was inspired by Maulana Ron Karenga, who was at that time chair of the Black Studies Department at California State University, Long Beach. This celebration of African-American heritage has spread to various points in the United States and abroad to include parts of West Africa. It is estimated that 20 million people enjoy this tradition annually, despite its recent founding.

Cinco de Mayo, which is celebrated on May 5 in many locales with a significant presence of Mexican Americans, is yet another highly visible holiday celebration that emphasizes the importance of our nation's ever-broadening cultural heritage.

Figure 23.5 This beautiful Hindu temple in Southern California is a place of worship and comfort for many Hindus from India now living in the United States.

Figure 23.6 Float in a holiday parade commemorates the vision of Our Lady of Guadeloupe, an important celebration for Hispanic Catholics in East Los Angeles.

Immigrants from around the world have brought their religions with them, resulting in construction of places of worship quite different from the traditional churches and synagogues that dominated much of the United States until just the past few years. Religious structures in the United States now include Hindu shrines, Buddhist temples, and mosques, as well as Christian and Jewish places of worship. In 2000, Ramadan, Christmas, and Hanukkah happened to fall at approximately the same time. Public displays celebrating these three major religious events (Figures 23.7, 23.8, and 23.9) occurred together at a major intersection in Mission Viejo, California, clearly showing the evolving demographic shifts occurring in the United States today.

Religion

Religion is another increasingly diverse part of the nation's rich mixture of beliefs, traditions, and cultures. Christianity has been a prominent religion in the United States since its founding as colonies. Various Protestant faiths and Catholicism continue to draw large numbers of followers throughout the nation. Other faiths that have been practiced here for many years include Seventh Day Adventists and Jesus Christ of Latter Day Saints.

Eastern religions are becoming increasingly prominent in various communities around the United States today. Islamic mosques, Buddhist shrines and Hindu temples, now are available to worshipers, with the temples being considerably more numerous than the shrines.

Jewish synagogues and temples are concentrated in New York, Los Angeles, Miami, Ft. Lauderdale, and Chicago (in descending number of worshipers). Surprisingly, the Jewish population in the United States in 1997 exceeded that in Israel.

Smaller groups also add to the religious scene; for example, the Ethiopian Christian Church. Eastern Orthodox churches also often add their celebrations to the cultural mix.

Muslim presence in America can be seen anywhere from the mosque on a Navajo Indian reservation in New Mexico to those in cities. Worshipers originate from many parts of the globe (particularly from Southeast Asia) and various races (African-Americans, represent more than 40 percent of this presence).

Figure 23.7 Jewish street corner display in celebration of Hanukkah in Mission Viejo, California.

Figure 23.8 Manger scene is displayed at Christmas in Mission Viejo, California.

Figure 23.9 Giant photograph of a mosque is displayed in Mission Viejo, California, to celebrate the Muslim observance of Ramadan.

New Foods in the Marketplace

Depending on where you live, you may find some unfamiliar food items in your local markets and restaurants. Their presence is a clear indication of the evolving cultural blend in your neighborhood. A spirit of adventure will be helpful as you reach out for new food experiences. A basic ingredient guide may help you translate and enjoy your cultural food experiments. The listings in Tables 23.7 through 23.15 indicate the familiar food categories into which different ethnic foods fit (breads and cereals, vegetables and fruits, meats and related protein foods, dairy, and fats and oils, and others, such as sweets and sauces).

Recent immigrants can find this new country a daunting place to find the familiar foods that formed their diets in their homeland. Labels are difficult or impossible for them to read if they have not yet learned the basics of English. The feeling of helplessness that shopping can create becomes easy to understand if you venture into an ethnic market and attempt to figure out what some of the foods are and how to prepare them. Fortunately, the large wave of immigrants in the last few years has created such demand for their basic food commodities in some communities that enterprising merchants are importing and stocking a wide assortment of the foods so important to immigrants (and to others who seek knowledge and experience in the foods of other cultures).

Most cities have some ethnic markets appropriate to the cultural diversity of the specific locale. Lingering visits at such markets provide an invaluable look at the most important ingredients needed to prepare the dishes of that specific cuisine. You will learn even more if you purchase some items and prepare them

Table 23.7 Selected African Foods Categorized by Food Groups

Breads and Cereals	Produce Vegetables	Fruits	Meats and Proteins	Dairy	Fats and Oils	Other
Corn	Amaranth leaves	Akee	Acacia seeds	Camel milk	Dendé oil	Cacao seeds
Fonio	Baobab pulp	Cape gooseberry	Agobono seeds		Palm oil	Coffee
Guinea Corn	Cassava	Cashew apple	Alligator			
Hungary rice	Chilies	Citrus	Antelope			
Kaffir corn	Fufu	Mango	Barracuda			
Millet	Gari	Melon	Bat			
Sorghum	Greens	Monkey bread pulp	Beef			
Tef	Iyan	Papaya	Bonito			
Wheat	Karkadeh flower pods and leaves	Roseapple	Bream			
	Manioc		Caterpillars			
	Peppers		Cod (dried, salted)			
	Plantain		Crickets			
	Potato		Crocodile			
	Sweet potato leaves		Dorado			
	Taro		Goat			
	Yam		Grasshoppers			
			Groundnuts			
			Grubs			
			Kaffir pea			
			Lamb			
			Legumes			
			Tilapia			

Table 23.8 Selected Asian Foods Categorized by Food Groups

Breads and Cereals	Produce Vegetables	Fruits	Meats and Proteins	Dairy	Fats and Oils	Other
Acorn noodles	Amaranth leaves	Durian	Azuki beans	Donkey milk	Pork fat	Barley tea
Bao	Bamboo shoots	Fuzzy melon	Barracuda	Yak milk	Sesame oil	Bird's nest
Buckwheat	Bok choy	Japanese plum	Bat			Boxthorn tea
Congee	Bottle gourd	Kumquat	Beans			Five spice powder
Millet	Bracken fern	Loquat	Blowfish			Ginseng tea
Mochi	Chinese cabbage	Lychee	Bonito			Rice vinegar
Rice noodles, sticky sweet flour	Chinese kale	Persimmon	Caterpillars			Rice wine
Soba	Chinese mustard greens		Chicken			Sake
Sorghum	Chinese spinach		Crab			Soy sauce
Udon	Cloud ears		Dog			
Wheat	Daikon		Dried beans			
Wonton	Eggplant		Duck			
	Garlic		Eel			
	Ginger root		Eggs (fermented, preserved, quail, turtle)			
	Gobo		Fugu			
	Hairy cucumber		Miso			
	Kelp		Mung beans, curd			
	Kimchee (cabbage, cucumber, radish)		Pigeon			
	Laver		Pork			
	Lotus root		Roe			
	Mushrooms		Sea cucumber			
	Nori		Sea urchin			
	Peppers		Shark fin			
	Purslane		Shrimp			
	Seaweeds		Silkworm pupa			
	Snow peas		Snail Snake			
	Taro		Soy products			
	Wasabi		Tofu			
	Water chestnut		Yellowtail			
	Winter melon					

Table 23.9   Selected Indian (Asian) Foods Categorized by Food Groups

Breads and Cereals	Produce — Vegetables	Fruits	Meats and Proteins	Dairy	Fats and Oils	Other
Barley	Agathi leaves	Bananas	Almonds	Buttermilk	Ghee	Chutney
Chapati	Amaranth leaves	Cape	Bengal gram dal	Milk	Peanut oil	Curry
Chickpea flour	Bottle gourd	gooseberries	Black gram dal	Yogurt	Rapeseed oil	Garam
Corn flour	Breadfruit	Cashew apple	Bombay duck		Sesame seed	masala
Millet	Lily root	Coconut	Bush beans		oil	Saffron
Oats	Okra	Durian	Cashew nuts			Sugarcane
Paratha	Onion	Jackfruit	Chana dal			
Puri	Plantain	Loquats	Chicken			
Rice	Purslane	Lychee	Chickpeas			
Roti	Spinach	Roseapple	Conger eel			
Wheat	Tampala		Crocodile			
			Fish			
			Goat			
			Green gram dal			
			Jujube			
			Kidney beans			
			Lentils			
			Mung beans, dal			
			Peanuts			
			Pigeon peas			
			Red gram dal			
			Squab			
			Turtle eggs			

yourself. Each cuisine around the world has the potential to broaden your eating excitement. If you have a chance to visit a range of ethnic markets, your experiences with food can be broadened still more.

Ethnic restaurants offer another way of experiencing food from other cultures. The variety available in many U.S. cities today is amazing. Try eating at an ethnic restaurant that features a cuisine you have never tried before. Read the entire menu and notice the items that are new to you. If you cannot read the menu, ask your server to explain each of the dishes so that you will know just what is available.

The server's specific recommendations may help you figure out what you want to order so that you get a good introduction to the cuisine. Look around to see what diners from the culture of the restaurant are eating. Their choices can give excellent clues to finding favorites of that cuisine. You may want to make some notes about the foods you eat at your first meal and jot down the names of dishes to order next time. Try other cultural restaurants too. Ask friends and acquaintances from other cultures where they like to eat and what they think are some of the best dishes to order.

World cuisines have developed in extremely varied settings over many centuries. However, foods sold in the United States are required to meet the legal standards established governing food safety in this country. In some instances, long-standing traditions of preparation of certain foreign foods may not meet legal requirements.

An illustration of such problems occurred in Los Angeles in the 1980s when the county's health department moved against a local producer of Peking duck because the steps in the production of this classical dish did not meet the temperature control standards for food handling in the city. Although no evidence was presented that Peking duck caused food-borne illnesses, action was initiated to

Table 23.10   Selected Caribbean Islander Foods Categorized by Food Groups

Breads and Cereals	Produce Vegetables	Fruits	Meats and Proteins	Dairy	Fats and Oils	Other
Barley	Amaranth leaves	Acerola	Bacaloa	Milk	Palm oil	Cocoa
Cornmeal	Beans	Akee	Barracuda	Yogurt	Pork fatback	Coffee
Rice	Breadfruit	Avocado	Beef			Rum
Rye	Calabaza (pumpkin)	Banana	Blood sausage			Sugarcane
Wheat	Callaloo	Barbados	Chicharrones			molasses
	Carrot	cherries	Chicken			
	Cassava	Caimito	Cod (dried, salted)			
	Celery root	Cashew apple	Dorado			
	Chayote squash	Citrus	Dried beans			
	Chichi	Coconut	Eggs (iguana, turtle)			
	Christophene	Cocoplum	Fish			
	Cocoyam	Mamey apple	Goat			
	Corn	Mango	Iguana			
	Dasheen	Naseberry	Lamb			
	Eddo	Pineapple	Mackerel			
	Malanaga	Roseapple	Marlin			
	Manioc	Sapodilla	Pigeon			
	Name	Soursop	Pigeon peas			
	Okra	Star apple	Pork			
	Onion		Turtle, green			
	Palm hearts					
	Peppers					
	Plantain					
	Potatoes					
	Pumpkin leaves					
	Squash					
	Swamp potato					
	Tanier					
	Taro					
	Tomato					
	West Indian pumpkin					
	White sweet potato					
	Yam					
	Yautia					
	Yuca					

halt its production. Finally, a truce was negotiated that included some modification of the original procedure.

In 2000, some Vietnamese and Korean rice specialties that were being marketed as ready-to-eat delicatessen items failed to meet required refrigerated storage conditions for selling them in California. Similar dishes sold in Vietnam and Korea are not refrigerated in those countries even during long, hot days. Clearly, such discrepancies cause hardships and misunderstandings for new immigrants, but cooperative efforts are now being made to help draft acceptable, safe methods and standards that will ensure safety without seriously altering palatability.

Shifting Food Patterns

No sudden transformation in food habits will occur the minute immigrants arrive in the United States, just as you probably are going to take a little time to accept some of the food specialties from their cuisines. However, changes in the habits

Table 23.11 Selected European Foods Categorized by Food Groups

Breads and Cereals	Produce Vegetables	Fruits	Meats and Proteins	Dairy	Fats and Oils	Other
Barley	Beans	Apples	Bacalhau	Cheeses	Butter	Coffee
Buckwheat and kasha	Beets	Cherries	Baccala	Clotted cream	Olive oil	Beers
	Bracken fern	Grapes	Bacon	Cornish cream		Brandies
Millet	Cabbage	Plums	Beef	Crème fraiche		Liquers
Oats	Cardoon	Olives	Black pudding	Devonshire cream		Sauerkraut
Pasta	Carrots	Lingonberries	Blood sausage	Ice cream		Tea
Rice	Chickweed leaf	Pears	Bush beans	Milk		Vinegars
Rye	Cucumber		Caribou	Sour cream		Wines
Wheat	Dock		Caviar			
	Laver		Chickpeas			
	Leeks		Cod (dried, salted)			
	Mushroom		Conger eel			
	Onion		Eggs			
	Peas		Fish			
	Potato		Goat			
	Sweet peppers		Ham			
	Tomato		Horse			
	Truffles		Lamb			
			Mutton			
			Pork			
			Reindeer			
			Sausage			
			Squab			
			Veal			

Table 23.12 Selected Mexican and Central American Foods Categorized by Food Groups

Breads and Cereals	Produce Vegetables	Fruits	Meats and Proteins	Dairy	Fats and Oils	Other
Amaranth grain	Amaranth leaves	Avocado	Bonito	Cheese	Lard	Atole
Cornmeal	Breadfruit	Banana	Chicharrones	Milk		Chocolate
Fideo	Calabacitas	Citrus	Chorizo			Coffee
Masa	(summer squash)	Guava	Cod (dried, salted)			Pulque
Pan dulce	Cassava	Nance	Dorado			Sugarcane
Polvillo	Chiles	Naranjilla	Frijoles			Tequila
Quinoa	Chilies	Papaya	Garbanzo beans			Vanilla
Rice	Jicama	Pineapple	Goat			
Sopaipilla	Nopales	Sapodilla	Legumes			
Thin spaghetti	Palm hearts	Sapote	Marlin			
Tortillas	Plantain	Soursop				
	Purslane	Starapple				
	Squash	Strawberry pear				
	Squash blossoms	Tree melon				
	Taro					
	Tomatillos					
	Tomato					

Table 23.13 Selected Middle Eastern and North African Foods Categorized by Food Groups

Breads and Cereals	Produce Vegetables	Fruits	Meats and Proteins	Dairy	Fats and Oils	Other
Bulgur	Amaranth leaves	Banana	Antelope	Camel milk	Olive oil	Coffee
Couscous	Cauliflower	Citrus	Bream	Donkey milk	Sesame oil	Grape leaves
Millet	Eggplant	Dates	Bush beans	Ewe milk		Mint tea
Pasta	Garlic	Figs	Camel	Feta cheese		Ouzo
Rice	Okra	Grapes	Caviar	Goat milk		Raki
Wheat	Onion	Loquat	Chicken	Yogurt		Retsina
	Parsley	Olive	Chickpeas			Tahini
	Potato	Papaya	Donkey			
	Spinach	Pomegranate	Lamb			
	Tomato		Legumes			
			Mutton			
			Nuts			

and food choices occur over time with repeated contact and immersion in aspects of new food choices. Among the factors influencing changes in eating patterns among immigrant populations are the generation (whether a first-generation new arrival, a second-, or third-generation immigrant), age of the individual, children in families, income level, occupation of workers, educational level (particularly of the food preparer), and living environment (rural or urban, isolated or in an ethnic community). These factors play roles of somewhat varying degrees of significance, depending on the individual and the unique cultural gap. For those with language differences, the transition has an added impediment. Children often pick up language skills rather quickly and can play a key role in helping parents learn about foods in the markets.

The first generation of immigrants (particularly if they are older when they arrive) is more resistant to giving up their original food patterns than is the

Table 23.14 Selected South American Foods Categorized by Food Groups

Breads and Cereals	Produce Vegetables	Fruits	Meats and Proteins	Dairy	Fats and Oils	Other
Cornmeal	Amaranth leaves	Avocado	Bacon	Cheese	Dendé oil	Coffee
Quinoa	Apio	Banana	Barracuda	Milk	Palm oil	Sugarcane
Rice	Arracacha	Cashew apple	Beef			
Wheat	Breadfruit	Citrus	Bonito			
	Cassava	Coconut	Chicken			
	Chayote squash	Cocoplum	Cod (dried, salted)			
	Chocho	Jaboticaba	Dorado			
	Chuno	Mamey apple	Egg			
	Garlic	Melonpear	Fish			
	Manioc	Nance	Goat			
	Onion	Naranjilla	Guinea pig			
	Palm hearts	Papaya	Horse			
	Peppers	Pepino	Iguana			
	Plantain	Sapodilla	Lamb			
	Potato	Soursop	Legumes			
	Pumpkin	Starapple	Mutton			
	Taro	Tree melon	Pork			
	Tomato		Sausage			
	Yuca					

Table 23.15 Selected Southeast Asian and Pacific Islander Foods Categorized by Food Groups

Breads and Cereals	Produce Vegetables	Fruits	Meats and Proteins	Dairy	Fats and Oils	Other
Mochiko (rice flour)	Amaranth leaves	Avocado	Aku	Carabao (water buffalo) milk	Palm oil	Bagoong (fermented fish)
Noodles	Bean sprouts	Banana	Bat	Milk	Sesame oil	Fish sauce
Rice	Breadfruit	Carambola	Bonito			Lemon grass
Wheat	Cassava	Cashew apple	Chicken			Sugarcane
Wonton	Chilies	Coconut	Dilir (fried fish)			
	Kelp	Durian	Dog			
	Laver	Fuzzy melon	Dolphin-fish			
	Manioc	Guava	Dried beans			
	Palm hearts	Jackfruit	Duck			
	Palmetto cabbage	Java plum	Egg			
	Plantain	Mango	Fish			
	Squash	Orange	Goat			
	Sweet potato	Papaya	Mahi-mahi			
	Taro	Pawpaw	Marlin			
	Tomato	Pineapple	Mung beans			
	Yam	Pomelo	Pork			
		Roseapple	Sea cucumber			
		Sapodilla	Seafood			
		Tamarind	Snake			
			Squab			
			Tempeh			
			Tofu			

second generation, according to Kalcik. Second-generation food preparers are likely to retain part of their original food preferences but often make adjustments in the techniques used to prepare them as a means of saving valuable time. This generation may even give up most of its food traditions, leaving revival of their heritage to the eager third generation. The meal that is most likely to retain many of the cultural foods is dinner, for this is a time when the family is most likely to be together and to have a bit more time available. Breakfast and lunch patterns from the country of origin may give way fairly quickly to U.S. patterns, particularly if these meals are eaten away from home.

The shift toward more U.S. dietary patterns certainly is not necessarily a shift toward improved nutrition, for clearly Americans as a group are rapidly becoming an overweight population with eating habits that are not noted for being healthful. The desirable transition obviously is for new immigrants to pick up new habits that improve their nutritional status rather than cause new health problems.

Romero-Gwynn et al. found that second-generation Mexican American immigrants reported some healthful dietary changes, including decreased consumption of lard, cream, and chorizo (Mexican pork sausage). Offsetting these improvements, however, were decreased consumption of such healthful foods as atole, fruit juices, and pasta dishes with vegetables.

Increased intakes of soda, mayonnaise, sour cream, white bread, and expensive ready-to-eat cereals are detrimental dietary changes. Increased consumption of flour tortillas rather than corn tortillas, although seemingly not a change, actually is a shift for many immigrants from southern areas of Mexico where corn tortillas are the norm. Unfortunately, flour tortillas contain as much as 4 grams of fat in comparison with the usual 0.5 gram in a corn tortilla. Substitution of lard with oil is a healthful change that many are making, although the amounts used may still be too high. Also, powdered, instant fruit drinks heavily sweetened with sugar are often an empty calorie replacement for the healthful fruit juices that were part of the diet in Mexico.

Satia et al. studied the dietary practices of 30 Chinese American women living in the Seattle area. They reported a shift to a U.S.-style breakfast but the retention of the Chinese-style lunch by the majority and the consumption of a Chinese dinner by all. Only some of the women still observed the importance of balancing yin and yang in food selections. Reasons cited for food selections included convenience of U.S. foods, better quality of U.S. beef, milk, and tofu (but poorer quality chicken and fish), and cost.

These examples illustrate possible shifts in dietary patterns that immigrants may make as they become assimilated into U.S. society. Individuals obviously will make their own adjustments to their personal needs and living situations. Dishes from the various cultures may be altered as they are integrated into the American scene. These changes may be due to the need to use somewhat different ingredients as substitutions when the original ones are not available. Restaurants and other food producers may alter some dishes a bit to attract Americans to their cultural dishes.

Interestingly, immigrants are not the only ones making changes in the food patterns of their heritage. Many Americans are learning more and more about foods from many points around the world. Even the fast-food industry reflects this development, as evidenced by the growth of Mexican American items on their menus. Food courts and restaurants abound in Chinese foods, Greek dishes, Thai menus, and Vietnamese items, for example. Obviously, U.S. tastes are changing and expanding.

Summary

Food patterns in the United States developed in different regions of the country because of the cultural background of the immigrants and the foods that were available in the new land. Indians in the Northeast added to the familiar foods of the English and other European settlers who came to that region. Early immigrants to this region were primarily European, particularly British, Irish, and German at first, followed by Scandinavians and later waves from Greece, Austria-Hungary, Italy, Poland, Russia, Portugal, and Spain.

In the South, African slaves significantly influenced the cuisine, bringing their traditional dishes and adding seasonings from home to the food they cooked in their new land. French, French Acadians, and Spanish brought their distinctive cuisines to southern Louisiana.

Immigrants from Germany and other northern European countries helped shape the food patterns in the Midwest. The Southwest was influenced very early not only by Native American Indians, but also Spanish and Mexican residents who had well-established food patterns very different from the other parts of the United States. Chinese came as workers in the western part of the country in the 19th century. Added to these earlier waves of immigrants today are political refugees from Vietnam and other countries, as well as people from Mexico, Central and South America, the Caribbean, the Middle East, and Asian countries seeking improved economic opportunities. The West developed a food pattern that today is best described as "fusion" because of the wide diversity of its immigrants.

These immigrants have brought along their cultural heritage, which includes their cuisines, religions, and holidays. This diversity has created many ethnic markets and restaurants as well as new food items available in regular grocery stores. Many Americans embrace the increasing dining choices that result from the growing diversity of cultures in this country. Immigrants also are adopting many of the foods and dietary practices of their new country. Sometimes these changes are nutritionally helpful, but others may be detrimental.

Selected Sites

http://www.infoplease.com/ipa/A0762156.html—Racial census data for the U.S. in 2003.

http://www.trinity.edu/~mkearl/race.html—Discussion and numerous references on the sociology of race and ethnicity.

http://food.oregonstate.edu/prodev/demos99.html—Discussion and related Web sites for studying demographic trends and food resources.

http://lilt.ilstu.edu/rtdirks/NOAMERIND.html—Bibliography on Indian food patterns.

http://www.keyingredients.org/—Information about food throughout the United States; on-line companion to Smithsonian's *Key Ingredients: America by Food.*

http://www.agmrc.org/agmrc/markets/Food/food+ethnic.htm—Bibliography of some ethnic food trends.

http://www.nal.usda.gov/fnic/pubs/bibs/gen/ethnic.html—Resource list of materials on food and ethnicity in the United States.

http://www.recipelink.com/rcpusa.html—Information on regional cooking.

http://lilt.ilstu.edu/rtdirks/SEASIA.html—Bibliography of Asian ethnic foods.

Study Questions

1. Describe traditional food patterns in these parts of the United States: (a) the Northeast, (b) South, (c) Midwest (d) Southwest, and (e) West.
2. What ethnic and cultural groups live in your area? For each group, describe the food markets, unique food ingredients, and special menu items in their restaurants.
3. Visit an ethnic market and read the labels on five items for ingredient and nutrition information. Describe any problems you have in reading and understanding the labels.
4. What are the racial demographics of your school? Does the campus food service include food items that reflect this population? If so, identify the foods and, if possible, their frequency of service.
5. During the past week, have you eaten any foods that are considered to be part of any cuisine different from your heritage? If so, indicate each item and the typical frequency with which you eat it, and briefly describe what you like about it.
6. Which meal of the day is likely to be the first one that an immigrant alters to the U.S. style? Which meal is the last to be changed? Why do you think these changes occur in the order you indicated?
7. Why are some prepared cultural foods encountering problems in relation to U.S. laws covering food in the marketplace?

Bibliography

Acevedo, M.C. 2000. Role of acculturation in explaining ethnic differences in pre-natal health-risk behaviors, mental health, and parenting beliefs of Mexican-American and European American at risk women. *Child Abuse and Neglect 24:* 111–127.

Adrogue, H.J. and D.E. Wesson. 1996. Role of dietary factors in hypertension of African Americans. *Seminar in Nephrology 16:* 94–101.

Algert, S.J., E. Brzezinski, and T.H. Ellison. 1998. Mexican American food practices, customs, and holidays. In *Ethnic and Regional Food Practices*. American Dietetic Association/American Diabetes Association. Chicago.

Altschiller, D. 1995. Turkish Americans. In R.J. Vecoli et al., eds. *Gale Encyclopedia of Multicultural America*. Gale Research. New York.

Bachman-Carter, K., R.M. Duncan and S. Pelican. 1998. *Navajo Food Practices, Customs, and Holidays*. American Dietetic Association/American Diabetes Association. Chicago.

Bouvier, L. F. 1977. International migration: Yesterday, today, and tomorrow. *Population Bull. 34*(1): 6.

Bradley, B. 2000. *Journey from Here*. Artisan. Victoria, Australia.

Brown, L.K. and K. Mussell, eds. 1984. *Ethnic and Regional Foodways in the United States*. University of Tennessee Press. Knoxville, TN.

Burke, C.B. and S.P. Raia. 1995. *Soul and Traditional Southern Food Practices, Customs, and Holidays*. American Dietetics Association/American Diabetes Association. Chicago.

Byars, D. 1996. Traditional African foods and African Americans. *Agriculture and Human Values 13*: 74–78.

Camarota, S.A. 2002. *Immigrants in the United States—2002: Snapshot of America's Foreign-Born Population*. Center for Immigration Studies. Washington, DC.

Claudio, V.S. 1994. *Filipino-American Food Practices, Customs, and Holidays*. American Dietetic Association. Chicago.

Dirige, O.V. 1995. Filipino-American diet and foods. *Asian American Business Journal 2/28/05:* 11–17.

Faneklli-Kuczmarski, M., R.J. Kuzmarski, and M. Naijar. 1995. Food usage among Mexican Americans, Cuban, and Puerto Rican adults. *Nutr. Today 30:* 30–37.

Gutierrez, C.P. 1992. *Cajun Foodways*. University of Mississippi Press. Oxford, MS.

Ikeda, J.P. 1999. *Hmong American Food Practices, Customs, and Holidays*. American Dietetic Association/American Diabetes Association. Chicago.

Kalčik, S. 1984. Ethnic foodways in America and the performance of identity. In L.K. Brown and K. Mussel, eds. *Ethnic and Regional Foodways in the United States*. University of Tennessee Press. Knoxville, TN.

Lee, H.G. 1992. *Taste of the States: A Food History of America*. Howell. Charlottesville, VA.

Lee, S.K., J. Sobal, and E.A. Frongillo. 1999. Acculturation and dietary practices among Korean Americans. *J. Am. Dietet. Assoc. 99(9):* 1084.

Leistner, C.G. 1996. *Cajun and Creole Food Practices, Customs, and Holidays*. American Dietetic Association/American Diabetes Association. Chicago.

Levenstein, H. 2003. *Paradox of Plenty: Social History of Eating in Modern America*. Rev. ed. University of California Press. Berkeley, CA.

Mandel, A. 1996. *Celebrating the Midwestern Table*. Doubleday. New York.

McIntosh, E.N. 1995. *American Food Habits in Historical Perspective*. Praeger. Westport, CT.

Norris, R.E., and L.L. Haring. 1980. *Political Geography*. Charles F. Merrill Publishing. Columbus, OH.

Pan, Y. L. et al. 1999. Asian students change their eating practices after living in the United States. *J. Am. Dietet. Assoc. 99(1):* 54.

Raj, S., P. Ganganna, and J. Bowering. 1999. Dietary habits of Asian Indians in relation to length of residence in the United States. *J. Am. Dietet. Assoc. 99*(9): 1106.

Rischin, M. 1989. Immigration. In *World Book Encyclopedia 10:* 82. World Book. Chicago.

Romero-Gwynn, E. et al. 1993. Dietary acculturation among Latinos of Mexican descent. *Nutr. Today 28*(4): 6.

Satia, J.A. et al. 2000. Use of qualitative methods to study diet, acculturation, and health in Chinese-American women. *J. Am. Dietet. Assoc. 100*(8): 885.

Shortridge, B.G. and J.R. Shortridge. 1998. *Taste of American Place*. Rowman and Littlefield. Lanham, MD.

Stoddard, R.H. et al. 1986. *Human Geography: People, Places, and Cultures*. Prentice-Hall. Englewood Cliffs, NJ.

Weaver, T., N. Kanelklos and C. Esteva-Fabregal, eds. 1993. *Handbook of Hispanic Culture in the United States: Anthropology*. Arte Publico Press. Houston.

Wilson, D.S. and A.K. Gillespie, ed. 1999. *Rooted in America: Food Lore of Popular Fruits and Vegetables*. University of Tennessee Press. Knoxville, TN.

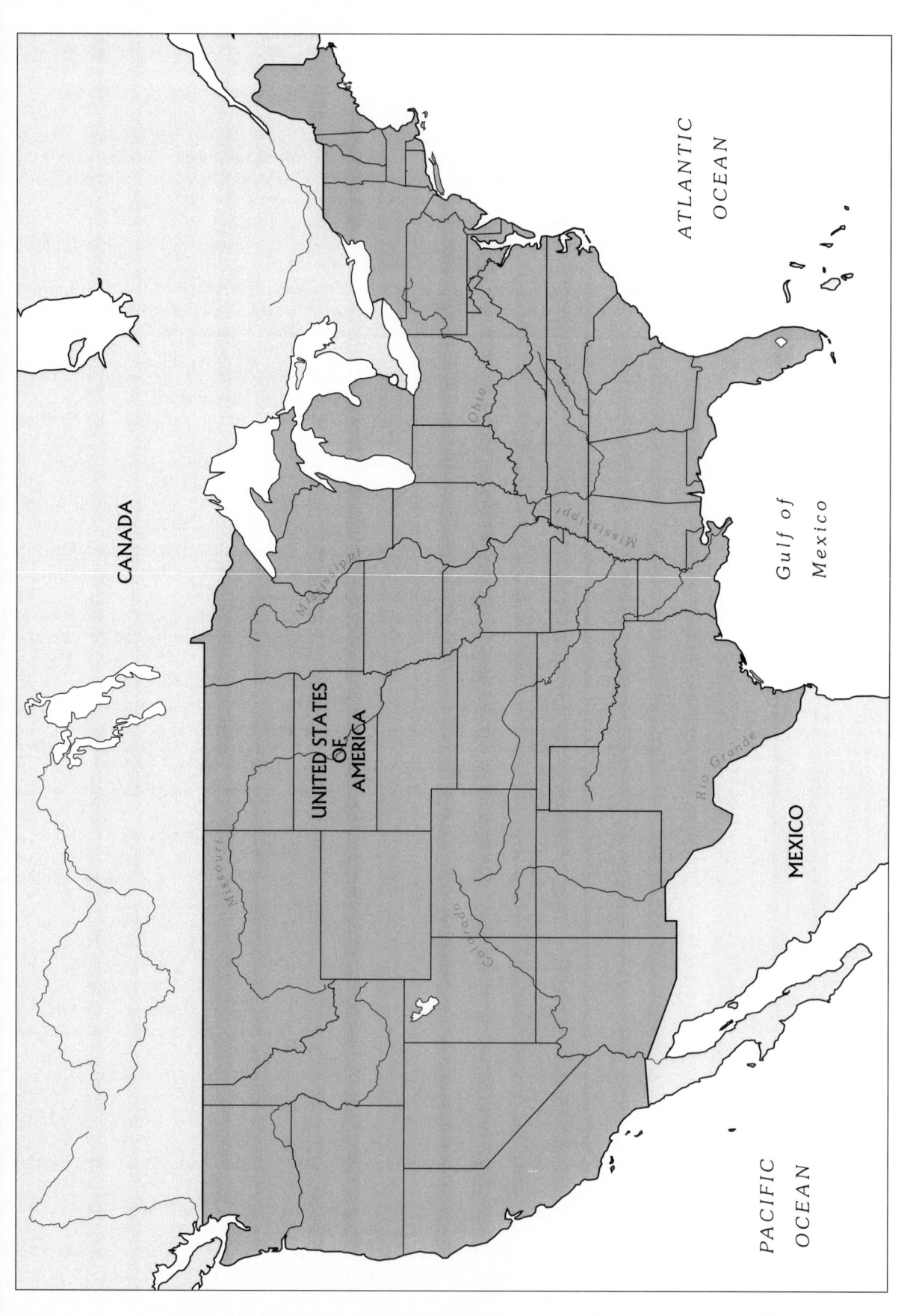

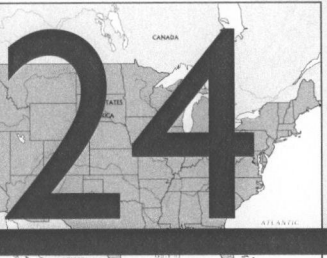

24 Diet Counseling in our Cultural Milieu

The rapidly expanding cultural milieu in the United States is presenting significant challenges to dietitians and others who are involved in communicating messages of good nutrition. For meaningful communication to take place between a client and a health professional, a mutual understanding needs to be developed. For this to happen, you, as the health professional, need to approach the counseling session with an understanding of the actual situation in which the client lives and a familiarity with the diet patterns that probably form the basis for the foods that will be accepted and consumed.

Familiarity with the culture and the foods associated with it is essential for people to accept suggestions about eating and diets. Obviously, there will be individual differences about the foods that immigrants from a particular country select as their favorites, but the general preferences within a country serve as a reasonable starting point for communication. This book gives you considerable information that will help you understand the culture and foods pertinent to individual clients. This chapter presents graphic nutritional guides that have been developed in some countries; these may be useful in counseling individuals or talking to groups.

The way in which you conduct each counseling session needs to be compatible with your client's culture, for one country's view of good manners often is significantly different from that of another country. Awareness of some of the possible pitfalls in communication is essential to effective counseling. This important topic is discussed in this chapter to provide a basic background in intercultural communication.

MyPyramid.gov
STEPS TO A HEALTHIER YOU

Figure 24.1 MyPyramid, the graphic developed by the U.S. Department of Agriculture, replaced the Food Guide Pyramid in 2005 as the tool for eating for good health in the United States.

Food Guide Pyramid and MyPyramid

Food Guide Pyramid— Educational tool used in the United States to guide people in making healthy food choices.

MyPyramid— Graphic guide to good nutrition introduced in 2005 to replace the Food Guide Pyramid as an instructional tool for nutrition education.

Graphics have been developed consistent with the food preferences of people living in some countries; these can be useful in presenting dietary suggestions to individuals or to groups. For example, the **Food Guide Pyramid** was used in the United States as a graphic to help transmit information on healthy eating to Americans for several years. It resulted in various proposals by professionals in other countries to adapt the concept to match the dietary preferences and available foods in their own countries or locales. In 2005, the Food Guide Pyramid was revised and replaced by the new U.S. graphic **MyPyramid** (Figure 24.1).

Other Food Guides

Some graphics developed for diet counseling in other countries are presented here.

The Filipino Pyramid Food Guide

Filipino Pyramid Food Guide— Food guide developed in the Philippines to guide people in making healthy food choices using the local foods.

The **Filipino Pyramid Food Guide** (Figure 24.2) was presented in the Philippines in 1996 as a visual means of teaching good dietary practices to help avoid overweight and obesity while eating for good health. This guide consists of five groups. The foods in the first group, rice, root crops, corn, noodles, breads, and cereals, are pictured and named as the base of the pyramid, with the advice to "eat most." The other groups are as follows:

FILIPINO PYRAMID FOOD GUIDE

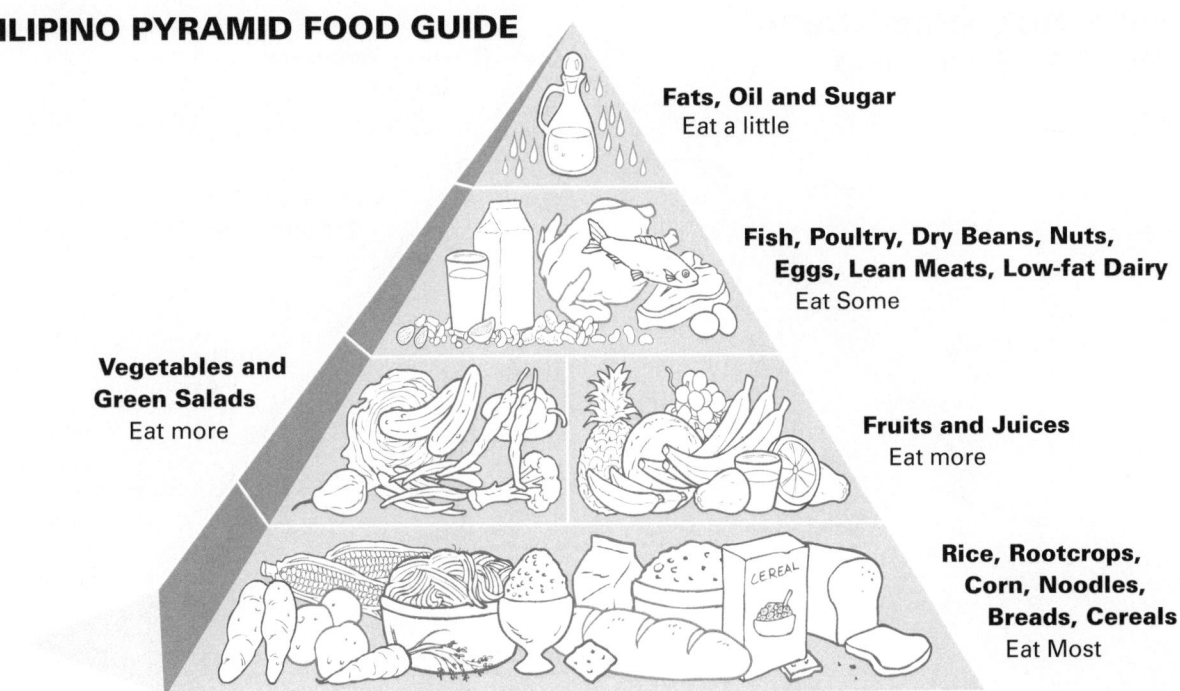

Figure 24.2 The Filipino Pyramid Food Guide. Developed by Sanirose S. Orbeta, M.S., R.D., and the Food and Nutrition Research Institute and endorsed by the Philippine Association for the Study of Overweight and Obesity. 1996.

- Two groups are included on the second level: Vegetables are pictured on the left half, fruits are on the right half, and captioned to "eat more."
- The third layer from the bottom is one group (fish, poultry, dry beans, nuts, eggs, lean meats, and low-fat dairy) and is captioned to "eat some."
- The apex of the pyramid includes fats, oils, and sugar, with the admonition to "eat a little."

An obvious departure in the Filipino guide from the pyramid developed by the United States is the elimination of the milk, yogurt, and cheese group, a move that was taken because of the paucity of dairy foods in the typical Filipino's diet. The lack of emphasis on dairy may result in a somewhat low intake of calcium. The other key difference is the use of action words rather than specific recommendations on numbers of servings and serving sizes. Proponents of this guide find this is a useful device for promoting interest in eating more of the lower two levels of the pyramid and less of the upper two levels.

Piramide Alimentaria para Puerto Rico

A Piramide Alimentaria para Puerto Rico (Macpherson-Sanchez, 1998) was developed in Puerto Rico (Figure 24.3) using the U.S. pyramid as its launching point, but adapting it to the unique requirements engendered by the tropical setting. To highlight the importance of adequate water intake to Puerto Ricans, a stylized triangle that looks like the pyramid's shadow appears at the base and reminds people to drink six to eight glasses of water daily. The foundation block of the pyramid is identified as cereales y viandas (7 to 12 portions) and includes pictures of some foods in this group. **Viandas** are defined as bland plant foods high

Viandas—Generic word used in the Piramide Alimentaria para Puerto Rico to include bland foods high in starch.

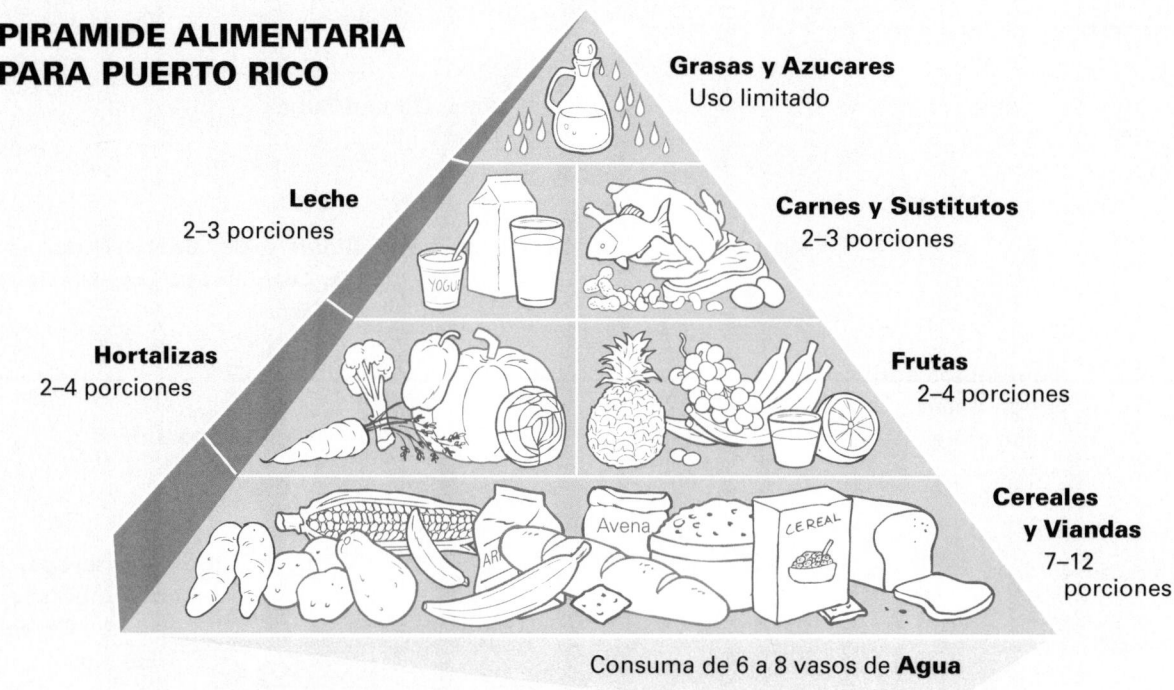

PIRAMIDE ALIMENTARIA PARA PUERTO RICO

Grasas y Azucares
Uso limitado

Leche
2–3 porciones

Carnes y Sustitutos
2–3 porciones

Hortalizas
2–4 porciones

Frutas
2–4 porciones

Cereales y Viandas
7–12 porciones

Consuma de 6 a 8 vasos de **Agua**

Figure 24.3 Piramide Alimentaria para Puertio Rico. Developed by the University of Puerto Rico with the U.S. Department of Agriculture. 2nd ed. 1995.

in starch, such as green bananas, yuca, breadfruit and its seeds, plantains, sweet potatoes, potatoes, white yams, yautia, and malanga. Cereals include rice, oats, wheat, barley, and corn (kernels as well as the dried, granular meal).

The second level is divided in half, with hortalizas (nonstarchy vegetables) on the left and frutas on the right (with the suggestion to eat two to four servings of each group). The next level also is divided in half: leche (milk and dairy) on the left and carnes y sustitutos (including legumes, nuts, and eggs in addition to meat and poultry with the suggestion for two to three servings for each group) on the right. The peak has grasas y azucares (fats and sugars, to be in limited use). Minor variations in recommended servings are the result of shifting starchy plant foods such as potatoes into the bottom category (cereales y viandas) rather than counting them as vegetables in this pyramid.

Chinese Food Guide Pagoda

Chinese Food Guide Pagoda—Educational tool developed in China to guide people in making healthy food selections.

The Chinese version of a guide for daily eating is a five-tiered pagoda (Figure 24.4). At the base of the **Chinese Food Guide Pagoda** are cereals (300 to 500 grams) such as rice, wheat and breads baked from wheat, noodles, and corn. The second tier has vegetables (400 to 500 grams) and fruits (100 to 200 grams). The third or middle tier specifies three different types of protein-rich foods daily: meat and poultry (50 to 100 grams), fish and shrimp (50 grams), and eggs (25 to 50 grams). The fourth tier has two categories: milk and milk products (100 grams), and beans and bean products (50 grams). The top tier is fats and oils (25 grams). No mention is made of sugars because they are not likely to be consumed in very large quantities in the typical Chinese diet. The pagoda reflects the limited intake of milk and dairy products that may be needed to accommodate those who are

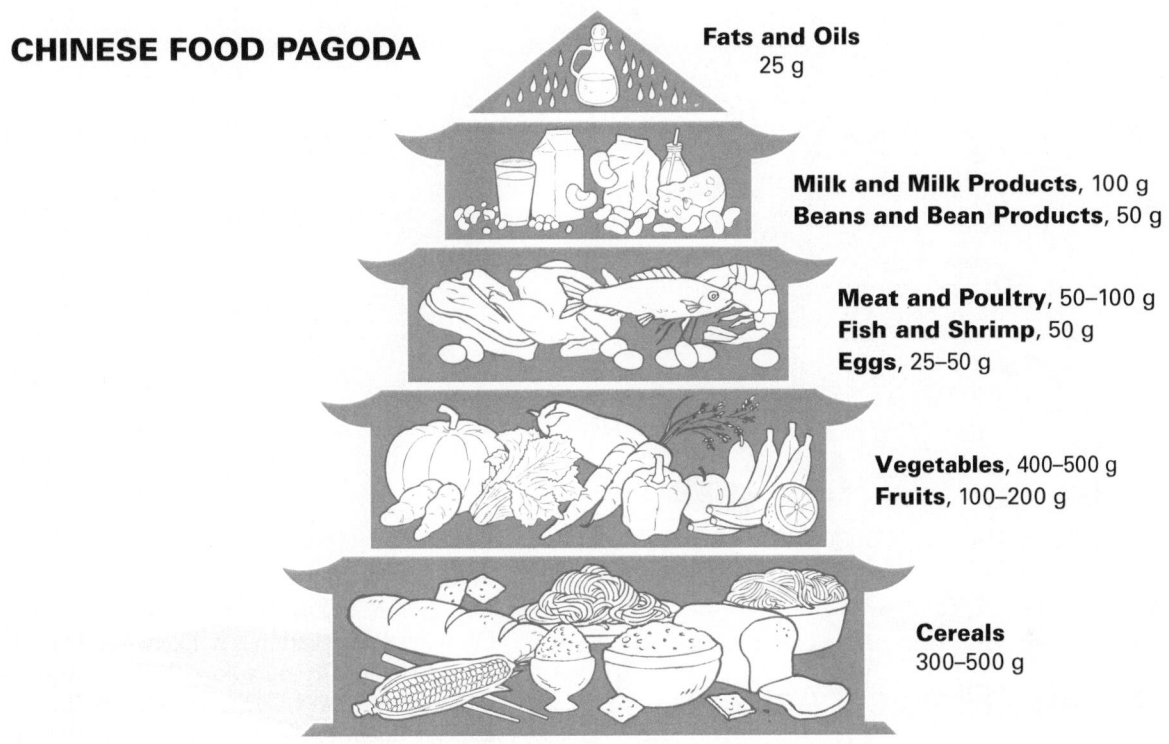

CHINESE FOOD PAGODA

Fats and Oils
25 g

Milk and Milk Products, 100 g
Beans and Bean Products, 50 g

Meat and Poultry, 50–100 g
Fish and Shrimp, 50 g
Eggs, 25–50 g

Vegetables, 400–500 g
Fruits, 100–200 g

Cereals
300–500 g

Figure 24.4 Food Guide Pagoda for Chinese Residents. Developed by the Chinese Nutrition Society. 1999.

lactose intolerant; inclusion of tofu or other bean products in the fourth tier encourages calcium intake from this supplemental source. Use of the pagoda for the graphic provides a clear message that this guide is specifically for Asians.

Mediterranean Diet Pyramid

Traditional Healthy Mediterranean Diet Pyramid—Food pyramid designed to incorporate the foods common to the Mediterranean in a pattern that has 11 categories.

The **Traditional Healthy Mediterranean Diet Pyramid** (Figure 24.5) presents the classic shape of a pyramid, but several modifications have created one that encompasses 11 categories and two additional suggestions that accompany this pyramid. Because of this detail, the pyramid must be read carefully. The base of the Mediterranean Diet Pyramid is composed of cereals (breads, pasta, rice, couscous, polenta, bulgur, other grains, and potatoes). As is basically true for the entire pyramid, the base does not indicate the number of servings, although foods from this foundation category are to be eaten daily. The next level, which is also to be eaten daily, places fruits on the left, covering about 40 percent of the space; beans and other legumes and nuts occupy about the middle 10 percent of this level; and vegetables compose the right half. Olive oil in variable amounts, but daily, is the thin block above the fruits and vegetables. Cheese and yogurt, to be eaten daily, represent the next thin layer. Fairly thin layers then rise above the dotted line. The proviso is given that these items (in ascending order on the pyramid) should be eaten a few times per week: fish, poultry, eggs (a very thin layer), and sweets. The tip of the pyramid is labeled red meat, with the recommendation that this should be eaten only a few times per month. To the left of the pyramid is the suggestion that individuals should have regular physical activity, and to the right is the suggestion to use wine in moderation. This guide reflects the basic diet from the Mediterranean region, but is somewhat challenging to remember.

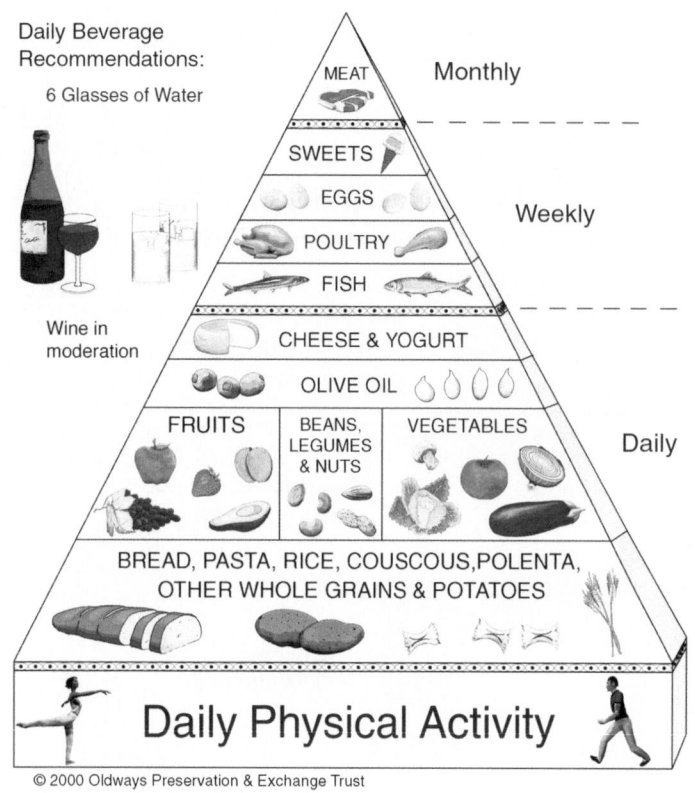

Figure 24.5 The Traditional Healthy Mediterranean Diet Pyramid. Codeveloped by Oldways Preservation and Exchange Trust, the World Health Organization (WHO) European Office, and the WHO/FAO Collaboration Center in Nutritional Epidemiology at Harvard School of Public Health. 1994.

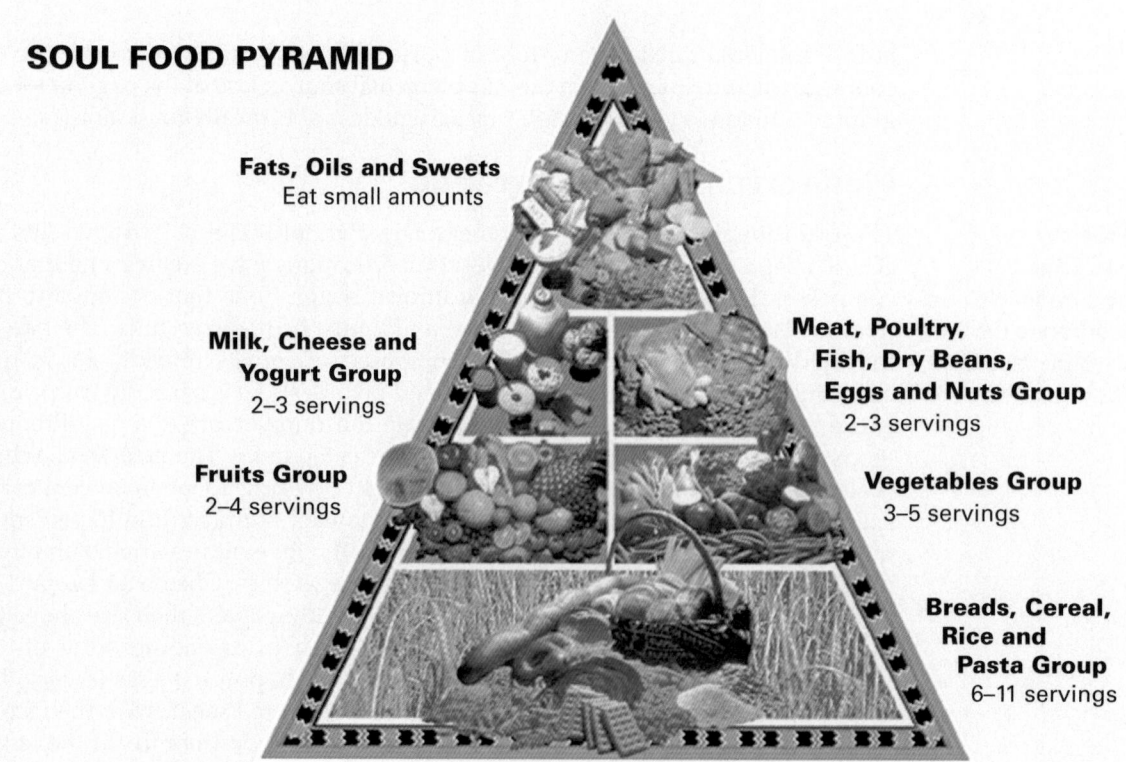

Figure 24.6 Soul Food Pyramid. Hebni Nutrition Consultants Inc., 4630 S. Kirkman Road, #201, Orlando, FL 32819. Web site: www.soulfoodpyramid.org.

Soul Food Pyramid

Soul Food Pyramid—Healthy food guide for persons who are lactose intolerant and need to limit fat intake to control weight.

Dietary suggestions for people wishing to follow a "soul food" diet are depicted in yet another pyramid, the **Soul Food Pyramid** (Figure 24.6). Lactose-reduced milk, yogurt (low fat or fat free), and reduced fat cheeses are excellent choices for reducing discomfort for those with lactose intolerance and keeping calories low if weight is a concern. To avoid high fat intake when selecting within the meat group, the pyramid suggests avoiding such high-fat items as chitterlings (chitlins), fatback, pig's feet, hog jowls, sausage, and pork neck bones. Keeping snack foods and sweets to a minimum also is emphasized.

Canada's Food Guide to Healthy Eating

Canada's Food Guide to Healthy Eating—Rainbow graphic used to teach good food patterns to Canadians.

Our neighbor to the north uses **Canada's Food Guide to Healthy Eating,** a rainbow graphic, to explain its dietary recommendations (Figure 24.7). The outer yellow band is grain products, the next green band is for vegetables and fruits, the blue band is for milk products, and the red innermost band is for meat and alternatives. The fact that the outer band encompasses the largest total space and each successive inner band is progressively smaller visually reinforces the quantities that are recommended for each category. The color designations subtly suggest the types of foods in the bands.

When counseling patients who are likely eating a diet that could be somewhat similar to one of these adaptions of the U.S. Food Guide Pyramid, you may

Figure 24.7 Canada's Food Guide to Healthy Eating.

find that the appropriate version is helpful in exploring food patterns and preferences. Then you might shape your suggestions to take advantage of this visual. The picture will help to convey the message even when your words may be a little difficult for your client to understand.

Intercultural Communication

Even when two people speak the same language but come from different countries, communication may be somewhat confused because of idioms, different definitions of the same word, or accents. When little or no knowledge of each other's language is added, communication can be very limited or nonexistent.

Unfortunately, the very different cultural backgrounds that the client and the health professional can have could magnify the problem because what the client may understand could be something other than what the health professional is saying even if an interpreter is helping with the session.

The challenges of effective communication with your clients are apparent. For success in helping your clients, you will need to be familiar with their general cultural traditions. Added to this knowledge is the need to establish the rapport with each client that will facilitate your understanding of the aspects of culture the client practices and considers important. Careful listening, including watching your client's body language, is a key to establishing good rapport and achieving effective counseling.

Body Language

Body language—Movements made that communicate attitude or feelings to another person.

Body language is an aspect of communication that needs to be considered. Body language is subtle, yet has a strong impact. The various movements you might make as a normal part of your style of interacting with another person happen automatically unless you make a conscious effort to control a behavior that may be misinterpreted in the culture of your client.

Possible problems related to body language include space you maintain between you and your client, whether any handshake or other physical contact is made, whether or not eye contact is acceptable or expected, and hand motion, particularly the manner of pointing. Even your feet could be conveying messages contrary to your client's culture.

Cultural Parameters

Customs—Traditions that are common to a cultural group, such as shaking hands or bowing.

Your recommendations to your clients need to be made in the context of the beliefs and **customs** of each individual. For example, you should be aware that some foods simply are not allowed by religious beliefs. Others may be totally outside the culture's typical diet. Special qualities could be attributed to some foods in a culture, thus giving them unique importance at special times, such as at childbirth.

Although each client presents a somewhat different communication challenge, consideration of the following points regarding cultural expectations will help you in establishing an appropriate context for your meeting.

- Language (English first or second, or none; other)
- Body language (personal space, greeting, eye contact, hands)
- Foods of the culture (kinds, beliefs, preparation, traditions)
- Religion (if it influences food choices)
- Values regarding time

An idea that you might find helpful in refining your counseling skills is to arrange for several friends to join you in videotaping a mock counseling session. One of the friends can be your client, and the other can videotape the session. You may be uncomfortable at first, but you probably will be able to relax enough to provide a good sample of your counseling techniques. You can review the tape privately if you prefer, or you can critique it with your friends to develop ideas that could be effective for you to use in actual counseling sessions. The chance to actually view yourself, as the client sees you, can be invaluable in improving counseling skills.

Obviously, the ability to speak in your client's language is extremely helpful, but often may not be possible. If your client has limited knowledge of English, you may need to speak slowly and in short sentences, using as simple a vocabulary as possible. Be sure to speak clearly, leaving a bit of space between words.

Watch the eyes (unless the client's culture does not permit) to help determine whether you are being understood. It could be necessary to say the same thing in more than one way to get your message across. If you and your client have no language in common, you will need to have an interpreter assist you in your meeting. Having appropriate visual materials and brochures written in the client's language also may be helpful.

If at all possible, counsel in a conversational format in which you provide a small amount of information and draw your client into the conversation, perhaps with a simple question that will help you know whether you have been understood before moving to the next point. This type of dialogue may take time to establish, but it is helpful in determining that your information is being understood correctly.

Avoid asking questions that can be answered with a simple yes or no. Many people of other cultures wish to avoid embarrassing you or themselves in giving an answer. For example, if you ask a client if he or she understands what has just been said, the answer will almost certainly be yes or a positive nod of the head, even if the client did not understand.

Food Attitudes and Traditions

Questioning your client regarding any special foods enjoyed by the family, particularly those served for holidays, can help strengthen the understanding between you and the client and aid you in creating dietary strategies that will be helpful to and used by the client. The insights you gain from such conversations may be of value in working with others from a similar background.

Also, exploring whether your clients avoid some foods will help you to create realistic dietary suggestions that accommodate religious dictates or health beliefs regarding foods. Because health beliefs regarding such implied attributes as hot and cold (yin and yang) foods and their balancing in the diet vary even among people of the same country, individual client input is essential if you are to proceed appropriately in diet counseling.

Try to create an ever-expanding knowledge base about the cultures and the food patterns of your clients. Your work will not only be more interesting, but also will become increasingly effective. In addition to using knowledge gained from interviews with clients, read books and articles about the their countries of origin, and eat at ethnic restaurants to expand your personal food experience and gain appreciation of the types of food that are familiar to them.

Cultural Differences

Many cultural differences—far more than can be included here—can be found around the world. However, the following discussion will help identify some of the distinctive ones that you may need to recognize. Although many people in a particular culture may fit the descriptions, keep in mind that you are working with individuals, and each one could have quite different beliefs and practices than those presented here. The key words to remember in your counseling are *listen, observe,* and *think about* your client as a unique individual, even though he or she is likely to follow certain cultural patterns.

Attitude toward Time Cultural attitudes toward time are highly variable and tend to linger long after immigrants have settled in the United States. The typical

U.S. system that requires one eye to be on the clock at all times simply refuses to mesh with the more leisurely attitudes of people from countries where personal interactions take priority over punctuality. To establish rapport with some of your clients, you may have to take a few deep breaths to shift gears into a more relaxed and friendly style. Your warm, welcoming smile will not only relax your client, but also be surprisingly helpful in easing your frustration regarding the wasted time. Try it.

Far East Cultural Insights

Space and Greeting   Customs and behaviors in the Far East vary a bit from country to country, but are generally somewhat restrained. The Japanese have a particular appreciation for private space. A bow serves as the greeting, with the depth of the bow reflecting the importance and/or age of the person being greeted. If there is a handshake, Japanese usually prefer a weak grip. Men from South Korea may bow slightly and shake hands, sometimes with both hands, but women do not ordinarily shake hands. Touching is uncommon among Chinese.

Business cards are very important when meeting people of Far Eastern background, who read them carefully to appreciate the title of the person on the card. Exchange of business cards is usually done in a formal manner that honors the donor of each card.

Body Language   Body language also is important in the Far East; for example, avoid any prolonged eye contact, do not expose the sole of your shoe, keep the palm of your hand downward when pointing or beckoning, and avoid showing your mouth open (Japanese and Koreans often cover their mouths when smiling or laughing).

Names and Family   Names may be confusing because the family name is often the first name in the sequence followed by the given name. Among key values is the importance of the family (superseding one's personal needs), respect for the elderly, and paternalistic and rigid hierarchy in family organization.

Other Values   The people of the Far East appreciate formality and rules as well as indirect and circuitous dialogues; they dislike confrontation and disagreements. Beliefs and superstitions (for example, these regarding hot and cold foods) are important. Personal questions may not be welcome. Beauty and style are particularly important to people from a Japanese background.

India and Southeast Asia

Greeting   In India and Southeast Asia, greetings vary a bit from those of the Far East, although there are certainly many similarities because of the numerous interactions over the centuries. Indonesians and Filipinos shake hands. Malaysians may extend their palms outward and touch fingers in greeting, while Thai, Balinese, Indian women, and some other Hindus greet people with their hands together in a prayerlike manner and sometimes with a slight bow. Indian men shake hands.

Middle Easterners

Family Values   The customs of the Middle East often reflect its religious heritage. For Muslims, women are important within their families and may be quite protected from the rest of the world, which is evidenced in their wearing of the chador (or similar enveloping outer garment). The family and its honor are at the center of values; males are clearly recognized as the leaders of their families, and male children are especially cherished.

Interactions   Men may embrace each other in greeting, may touch, and may stand quite close to others while talking. Punctuality is not a value in this part of the world, but warm hospitality is important. Expressing interest in the family's well-being precedes any business. Generosity often is so great that Middle Easterners may give you an item that you admired. Friday is the Islamic religious day, and no business is to be conducted.

Eating Traditions   Women and children may eat separately, after the men, but the foods served both sexes usually follow Muslim laws: no alcohol or pork, goat, dog, crabs, lobsters, or products containing them. Fasting is required during Ramadan.

Jewish Practices

Judaism is prominent in Israel, which means that the religious day is Saturday. The food laws differ from those of Muslims: pork and shellfish are prohibited; Orthodox Jews require that their food be kosher (see Chapter 3) and that dairy and meat products be kept separate.

Hispanic Values

In the western hemisphere, Hispanics are characterized as a family-oriented, paternalistic society, which places the family (and extended family) as its dominant value. Typically, women are expected to take care of the children and home while men make the important decisions.

When talking with others, sharing news of family takes priority over proceeding with the business at hand. Sociability is valued more than punctuality. Conversation and greetings often involve touching and standing close. However, South Americans often greet each other with a handshake rather than an embrace.

Summary

Health professionals today counsel many clients with cultural backgrounds quite different from their own heritage. Successful communication requires an understanding of the food patterns and cultural practices commonly followed in the client's culture. The Food Guide Pyramid has been adapted to some other parts of the world and can provide a basis for dietary counseling. In the United States, MyPyramid replaced the Food Guide Pyramid as the tool for nutrition education in 2005. The food guides presently available in various countries include the Filipino Pyramid Food Guide, the Piramide Alimentaria para Puerto Rico, the Chinese Food Guide Pagoda, the Mediterranean Diet Pyramid, the Soul Food Pyramid, and Canada's Food Guide to Healthy Eating.

When counseling clients from other cultural backgrounds, professionals should consider many dimensions in addition to actual dietary information if communication is to be effective. Among these dimensions are language, body language, food appropriate to the culture, religion, and values (particularly about time). Some of the basic considerations for counseling Asians, Middle Easterners, and Hispanics are mentioned in this chapter.

Selected Sites

http://www.nal.usda.gov/fnic/etext/000039.html—Information on nutritional guidelines for various nations.

http://www.mypyramid.gov/global_nav/media.html—Information on the revised pyramid.

www.**mypyramid**.gov/—Discussion of dietary recommendations for individual Americans.

http://www.hc-sc.gc.ca/fri-an/food-guide-aliment/index_e.html—Canada's Food Guide to Healthy Eating information.

http://www.cyborlink.com—Background information on culture and traditions in many different countries; designed for business and professional interactions.

Study Questions

1. What food and cultural practices need to be considered before beginning to counsel a recent immigrant from the Middle East?
2. What food and cultural practices need to be considered before beginning to counsel a recent immigrant from China?
3. What food and cultural practices need to be considered before beginning to counsel a recent immigrant from Mexico?
4. Are there habits in your style of talking with another person that might need to be altered when you are working with clients from different backgrounds? If so, what are they, and how do you plan to make these changes?

Bibliography

Axtell, R.E. 1990. *Do's and Taboos of Hosting International Visitors.* John Wiley and Sons. New York.

Baldridge, L. 1985. *Complete Guide to Executive Manners.* Rawson Assoc. New York.

Basaran, P. 1999. Traditional foods of the Middle East. *Food Technol.* 53(6): 60.

Chinese Nutrition Society. 2000. Dietary guidelines and the Food Guide Pyramid. *J. Am. Dietet. Assoc.* 99(2): 886.

Curry, K.R. 2000. Multicultural competence in dietetics and nutrition. *J. Am. Dietet. Assoc.* 100(10): 1142.

Devine, E. and N.L. Braganti. 1995. *Traveler's Guide to Customs and Manners.* St. Martin's Press. New York.

Dresser, N. 1996. *Multicultural Manners.* John Wiley and Sons. New York.

Elkort, M. 1991. *The Secret Life of Food.* St. Martin's Press. New York.

Ge, K. and K. McNutt. 1999. Publication of the Chinese Guidelines and Pagoda: How it happened. *Nutr. Today 34*(3): 104.

Gordon, B.H.J. et al. 2000. Dietary habits and health beliefs of Korean-Americans in the San Francisco Bay Area. *J. Am. Dietet. Assoc.* 100(10): 1198.

Hampden-Turner, C.M. and F. Trompenaars. 1997. *Riding the Waves of Culture: Understanding Diversity in Global Business.* McGraw-Hill. New York.

Hampden-Turner, C.M. et al. 2000. *Building Cross-Cultural Competence: How to Create Wealth from Conflicting Values.* Yale University Press. New Haven, CT.

Harris, P.R. and R.T. Moran. 1987. *Managing Cultural Differences.* 3rd ed. Gulf Publishing. Houston, TX.

Harris-Davis, E. and B. Haughton. 2000. Model for multicultural nutrition counseling competencies. *J. Am. Dietet. Assoc.* 100(10): 1178.

Kleiner, S.M. 1999. Water: Essential but overlooked nutrient. *J. Am. Dietet. Assoc.* 99(2): 200.

Lukins, S. 1994. *All Around the World.* Workman Publishing. New York.

Macpherson, A.E. 1998. Food Guide Pyramid for Puerto Rico. *Nutr. Today 33*(5): 198.

Orbeta, S. 1998. Filipino Pyramid Food Guide: Perfect match for the Philippines. *Nutr. Today 33*(5): 210.

Packard, D. and M. McWilliams. 1993. Cultural foods heritage of Middle Eastern immigrants. *Nutr. Today 28*(3): 6.

Painter, J., J. Rah, and Y. Lee. 2002. Comparison of international food guide pictorial representations. *J. Am. Dietet. Assoc. 102*(4): 483.

Peterson, B. 2004. *Cultural Intelligence: Guide to Working with People from Other Cultures.* Intercultural Press. Yarmouth, ME

Sonnenfeld, A. 1996. *Food: Culinary History from Antiquity to Present.* Columbia University Press. New York.

Storti, C. 2001. *Art of Crossing Cultures.* Nicholas Brealey Publishing. London, England.

Glossary

Achaemenid Empire: Empire that extended from the eastern end of the Mediterranean eastward to central Asia, and then southward to northern India and the Persian Gulf (also called the *Persian Empire*); conquered in 331 BCE by Alexander the Great (Ch. 1).

Adobo: Filipino stew using meats marinated in vinegar seasoned with bagoong before being fried with onions and garlic, and then stewed (Ch. 16).

Aebleskiver: Small Danish doughnuts prepared in a special pan (Ch. 5).

Afrikaans: Language spoken by Afrikaners (South African farmers of Dutch heritage); one of the official languages of South Africa (Ch. 14).

Agave: Century plant; source of the sap used to make tequila and pulque (Ch. 22).

Aji: Very hot Andean chili pepper; pronounced ah-hee (Ch. 20).

Aksum: Early, well-developed settlement in the highlands of Ethiopia of importance in the 4th and 5th centuries CE (Ch. 14).

Almuerzo: Typical late-morning light meal (usually tortilla-based dish and a beverage) in Mexico and Central America (Ch. 22).

Alsace-Lorraine: Eastern region of France bordering Germany (Ch. 9).

Angkor Wat: Very large temple complex built by the Khmers in northwest Cambodia (Ch. 2).

Antipasto: "Before the pasta" (hors d'oeuvre); wide variety of tidbits or appetizers, often olives, bread sticks, pickled vegetables, or other simple items (Ch. 8).

Apfel strudel: Austrian pastry made with extremely thin dough spread with melted butter and an apple filling, then rolled into a log, sliced into 3-inch lengths, and baked (Ch. 6).

Appelflappen: Fried, batter-dipped slices of apple sprinkled with confectioner's sugar (Ch. 6).

Aquavit (akvavit): Aged whiskey made in Scandinavian liquor distilled from potato mash and flavored with car-away; considered possibly to be the national Scandinavian drink (Ch. 5).

Arawaks: Peaceful Indians who greeted Columbus when he arrived on Hispaniola (Ch. 21).

Ardennes: Region north of Paris to the English Channel (Ch. 9).

Arepas: Corn flour–based small pancake that is baked or fried; eaten throughout the day in Colombia and Venezuela (Ch. 20).

Atole: Gruel-like, thick beverage with a cornmeal base (Ch. 22).

Avatar: Person who is so saintly that he is thought to be an incarnation of a deity (Ch. 3).

Aztec Empire: Empire extending to both coasts of central Mexico south to Guatemala that was controlled by Aztecs from 1345 to 1519 CE (Ch. 1).

Aztecs: Indians in power in Mexico City region from the 14th century until Cortés conquered them in 1521 (Ch. 22).

Bacalao: Dried, salted cod (Ch. 21).

Bachalhau: Salted, dried cod (Ch. 10).

Bagoong: Filipino fermented, salted shrimp paste (Ch. 16).

Baklava: Baked dessert made of multiple layers of phyllo brushed with butter and with honey or rosewater (or both) plus chopped nuts (Ch. 11).

Balsamic vinegar: Special herb-flavored vinegar made by aging a thick syrup boiled from sweet white wine grapes acidified with the addition of some aged balsamic vinegar; the best is made in the vicinity of Modena in northern Italy (Ch. 8).

Bannock: Pancake made with oat instead of wheat flour (Ch. 4).

Bantus: Very large group of Africans originally from west and central regions of Africa who spread east and south prior to colonial days (Ch. 14).

Barley: Cereal grain suitable for human and animal diets (Ch. 1).

Bar mitzvah: Celebration of maturity at which a boy reads from the Torah in the synogogue at age 13 (Ch. 3).

Bartolonneu Diaz: See Diaz, Bartolomew.

Bastilla: Flaky-crusted pigeon pie flavored with ginger, cumin, cayenne, saffron, and cinnamon and dusted with confectioner's sugar; Moroccan specialty (Ch. 12).

Basques: Group living in the Pyrenees Mountains near the Bay of Biscay in northeastern Spain; some are seeking independence from Spain (Ch. 10).

Bat mitzvah: Celebration of a girl reaching maturity (age 12) (Ch. 3).

Béarnaise sauce: Sauce similar to hollandaise but with vinegar, shallots, and seasoning used instead of lemon juice (Ch. 9).

Béchamel sauce: Basic white sauce made with cream or milk and thickened with flour (Ch. 9).

Belgian endive: Oblong, small head vegetable consisting of very pale leaves around a central core; grown in the dark to prevent greening and displayed in light only when being sold in the market (Ch. 6).

Belgian waffle: Oblong, crisp waffle with deep indentations (Ch. 6).

Berbers: Early inhabitants of much of Libya and the Maghreb; noted as fierce fighters (Ch. 12).

Berlin Conference of 1884–85: Meeting at which European colonial powers divided the African continent without including Africans in their decisions (Ch. 13).

Bet tai: Disc-shaped, yeast-leavened wheat flour Arab bread, usually about 14 inches in diameter (Ch. 12).

Betel nut: Nut from a climbing pepper that is chewed for its digestive qualities; it has a deep red juice (Ch. 15).

Bird's nest soup: Cornstarch-thickened soup made with the mucilaginous lining of the nests of the Asiatic swiftlet, chicken broth, minced chicken, and egg white (Ch. 17).

Biscuit: Flat cracker or cookie (Ch. 4).

Bitter melon: Vegetable resembling a cucumber with a wrinkled green skin and interior red seeds (Ch. 17).

Black beans: Cooked and fermented soybeans preserved with ginger and salt (Ch. 17).

Bliny: Small, thin Russian pancake (Ch. 7).

Blood (Black) Pudding: Sausages made of toasted oatmeal, blood, onions, and seasonings (Ch. 4).

Bocaloa al Pil-Pil: Basque dish made with salted cod served in a garlic sauce (Ch. 10).

Bodhisattva: Semidivine, mystical being incorporated in Mahayana form of Buddhism (Ch. 3).

Body language: Movements that communicate attitude or feelings to another person (Ch. 24).

Boer: South African of Dutch descent (Ch. 14).

Boeuf bourguignon: French beef stew with vegetables and red wine (Ch. 9).

Bok choy: Vegetable that grows as a bunch with thick, white stalks and a top of several large, coarse green leaves (Ch. 17).

Bolivar, Simon: Considered to be the liberator of South America from its European powers (Ch. 20).

Bolshoi Ballet: World renowned Russian ballet ensemble (Ch. 2).

Bombilla: Fancy silver straw and filter used to sip maté from a gourd (Ch. 20).

Bordeaux: Western region of France that is home to some outstanding wines, including cognac (Ch. 9).

Bordelaise: Dark sauce made with meat juices, bone marrow, tarragon, shallots, and red wine of Bordeaux (Ch. 9).

Borrel: Dutch gin (Ch. 6).

Borsch: Russian soup featuring beets and cabbage and topped with sour cream. (Ch. 7).

Bosporus: Narrow channel that separates Europe from Asia between the Sea of Marmara and the Black Sea (Ch. 11).

Bouillabaisse: Soup made with many types of sea food; created originally in Marsailles (Ch. 9).

Boulangerie: French bakery (Ch. 9).

Boxer Rebellion: Violent uprising of a secret sect that trapped foreigners and missionaries in Peking for two months in 1900 (Ch. 17).

Braaivleis: Barbecues in the southern countries of Africa (Ch. 14).

Brahma: Creator god in Hindu religion (Ch. 3).

Brahmans: Highest caste in Hinduism; priests and teachers (Ch. 3).

Brillat-Savarin: Author of *The Physiology of Taste* (Ch. 9).

Brioche: Rich, uniquely shaped bread that highlights the special butter of Normandy (Ch. 9).

Brittany: Peninsula jutting from the northwest corner of France (Ch. 9).

Bruschetta: Italian bread brushed with olive oil, garlic, and sometimes tomato, and then broiled (Ch. 8).

Bubble and squeak: Dish of leftover beef, potatoes, and vegetables that makes these noises while being fried together (Ch. 4).

Bulgogi: Grilled, marinated beef or other meat (Ch. 18).

Bulgur: Partially cooked and dried cracked wheat (Ch. 11).

Bunraku: Puppet shows featuring large, complicated puppets very skillfully presented, often in traditional stories (Ch. 19).

Burghul: Granular cereal product made by boiling and drying cracked wheat; also called *bulgar* (Ch. 12).

Burgundy: Region on the eastern side of France north of the Rhone Valley and southeast of Paris; wine is produced in the region (Ch. 9).

Burnoose: Dark, capelike, hooded garment worn by Arab men, particularly in Morocco (Ch. 12).

Burrito: Wheat flour tortilla wrapped around bean or meat filling (Ch. 22).

Byzantine Empire: Eastern part of the former Roman Empire; was powerful for almost a millennium (129 BCE to 1071 CE) (Ch. 11).

Byzantium: Early name for the city once called Constantinople but now called *Istanbul* (Ch. 11).

Cabral: Portuguese explorer who claimed Brazil for Portugal in 1500 (Ch. 20).

Café au lait: Coffee with milk, the most common breakfast beverage (Ch. 9).

Café con leche: Coffee with warm milk, the style preferred in South America (Ch. 20).

Caffe latte: Coffee with a generous amount of milk added (Ch. 8).

Cajun: Style of one-pot cooking developed in southern Louisiana based on combining fish or meat, local vegetables, and rice (Ch. 23).

Calabash: Dried hard shell of a gourd suitable for holding liquids and foods (Ch. 14).

Callaloo: Spicy, thick, green soup containing spinach or other green plus okra, salt pork, coconut, and crabmeat (Ch. 21).

Calvados: Apple brandy from Normandy (Ch. 9).

Camembert: Ripened dessert cheese originating from Camembert in Normandy (Ch. 9).

Canada's Food Guide to Healthy Living: Rainbow graphic used to teach good food patterns to Canadians (Ch. 24).

Cannelloni: Ridged tubes of pasta that are designed to be filled with various stuffings for entrées or desserts (Ch. 8).

Cape of Good Hope: Region at the southern tip of the African continent where the Atlantic Ocean meets the Indian Ocean (Ch. 14).

Capellini: Angel hair (very thin, spaghetti-like pasta) (Ch. 8).

Cappuccino: Espresso topped with frothy white milk (Ch. 8).

Carbonada: Argentinian beef stew with rice, corn, potatoes, squash, sweet potatoes, and apples (Ch. 20).

Caravels: Sturdy vessels with lateen sails (triangular sails extended on a spar and flying from a rather low mast) (Ch. 10).

Carcassonne: Walled city founded by Visigoths that served as a fortress in southwest France during the Middle Ages (Ch. 9).

Carib: Fierce Indian tribe originating in South America that subsequently conquered the tribes in the Caribbean (Ch. 21).

Carthage: Important trading city on the Mediterranean shore of Tunisia (Ch. 1).

Casbah: Walled part of Arab city in North Africa (Ch. 12).

Cassareep: Bittersweet flavoring used in pepper pot; made from the boiled juice of the cassava root (Ch. 21).

Cassava: Tropical plant that is harvested for the starch abundant in the roots (Ch. 23).

Cassava bread: Native, rather flat bread made with powdered roots of cassava (Ch. 21).

Cassoulet: Meat and bean casserole from Toulouse in Languedoc-Roussillon (Southwestern France) (Ch. 9).

Cawl: Welsh name for soup or one-dish meal, usually containing cabbage, leeks, and bacon, as well as other ingredients that may be available (Ch. 4).

Cena: Supper meal (light menu) served in Mexico and Central America in the evening (Ch. 22).

Ceviche: Raw fish marinated for 1 to 4 hours in lime juice and onion until flesh is opaque and the consistency of cooked fish; probably originated in Peru (Ch. 20).

Ch'a-shao-pao: Cantonese dish of steamed buns filled with roast pork (Ch. 17).

Chalupas: Fried tortillas topped with refried beans, slivered meat, chopped tomatoes and onions, and grated cheese (Ch. 22).

Champagne: Region east of Paris where sparkling wine is produced (Ch. 9).

Chapati: Pancake-like grilled whole wheat bread popular in India (Ch. 15).

Char siu bao: Steamed buns with a roast pork filling, a Cantonese specialty (Ch. 17).

Chicharrones: Fried snack of pork cracklings (Ch. 21, 22).

Chilaquiles: Shredded fried tortillas baked with chili sauce (Ch. 22).

Chima: Long, gathered skirt that is part of traditional dress for Korean women (Ch. 18).

Chinese cabbage: An elongated cabbage with crinkled green leaves extending from the long ribs; also called *napa cabbage* (Ch. 17).

Chinese Food Guide Pagoda: Educational tool developed in China to guide people in making healthy food selections (Ch. 24).

Chinese parsley: Cilantro or coriander (Ch. 17).

Chi pao yu: Shanghai specialty; bits of seasoned raw fish wrapped in wax paper and fried in deep fat, then unwrapped, and eaten (Ch. 17).

Chogori: Short jacket tied off-center and worn with chima to complete the traditional dress for Korean women (Ch. 18).

Chorizo: Sausage flavored with paprikas and chilies that may be seasoned to be picante (hot) or dulce (sweet) (Ch. 10).

Choucroute garnie: Casserole of sauerkraut, sausage, and pork that is popular in Alsace (Ch. 9).

Chorten: Tibetan religious (Buddhist) monument, often with some gold or silver gilding (Ch. 3).

Chow mein: Parboiled noodles fried briefly with other ingredients; a Cantonese stir-fry with noodles (Ch. 17).

Churro: Spiral-shaped fried quick bread similar to a doughnut but extruded into a fluted, thick stick before frying. (Ch. 10).

Chutney: Chunky and flavorful sauce often served as an accompaniment to curry (Ch. 15).

Cinco de Mayo: Celebration on May 5 honoring Mexican defeat of the French in 1862 at Puebla; celebrations in the United States also recognize the Mexican Americans living in this country (Ch. 22, 23).

Circumambulate: Process of prostrating and prayings repeatedly while encircling a Buddhist temple once or many times (Ch. 3).

Cloudberries: Orange-yellow, plump berries that are similar in shape to blackberries; primarily available briefly from the far north of Scandinavia in summer (Ch. 5).

Cocido: Spanish meal consisting of three traditional courses (soup, cooked vegetables, and boiled meats) with specific ingredients varying. (Ch. 10); hearty Filipino stew containing a variety of meats, Spanish sausage, chickpeas, saba (sweet cooking bananas), tomato sauce, and lard (Ch. 16); hearty Caribbean stew containing beef, sausage, vegetables, and sofrito (Ch. 21).

Cockaleekie soup: Hearty soup containing chicken, barley, and leeks (Ch. 4).

Coconut cream: Pureed and strained creamy liquid prepared from freshly grated white meat of mature pared coconut and hot water (Ch. 16).

Coconut milk: Coconut liquid similar to coconut cream but with more liquid (Ch. 16).

Coconut water: Liquid drained from fresh coconut by puncturing its eyes; used as beverage, but not as a cooking ingredient (Ch. 16).

Colcannon: Scottish recipe for boiled potatoes, cabbage, turnips, and onions that are sautéed in butter (Ch. 4).

Comal: Flat, cast iron griddle used to bake tortillas (Ch. 22).

Comida: Heaviest meal of the day, eaten in midafternoon, in Mexico and Central America; includes soup, main dish, beans, rice, tortillas, dessert, and a beverage (Ch. 22).

Congee: Rice gruel often served at breakfast in southeast Asia (Ch. 16); in China, flavoring, meat, or fish are sometimes added (Ch. 17).

Coo-coo: Cornmeal pudding with okra, which is served either hot or cold (Ch. 21).

Coq au Riesling: Chicken cooked in Riesling, a white wine (Ch. 9).

Coq au vin: Chicken cooked with red wine (Ch. 9).

Coquilles St. Jacques: Dish made by poaching scallops before serving in white wine sauce (Ch. 9).

Corned beef and cabbage: Cured (corned) beef simmered about 3 hours before cabbage wedges are added and cooked with the meat for about 20 minutes (Ch. 4).

Cornish pasties: Turnovers filled with meat and vegetables; pronounced pas tē (rhymes with nasty) (Ch. 4).

Cortés: Spanish explorer in Central America, particularly Mexico, in the 16th century (Ch. 10).

Coui sauce: Popular Caribbean hot sauce made with cassava juice and hot peppers (Ch. 21).

Couscous: Cereal product made by drizzling water on wheat flour and rolling it into small pellets, which are then steamed until fluffy (Ch. 12).

Crayfish: Freshwater crustacean; apparently introduced to Scandinavia via ships from Britain (Ch. 5).

Creole: Flavorful cuisine of New Orleans and southern Louisiana that integrates spices from the Caribbean with cuisines brought by French, Spanish, and African immigrants (Ch. 23).

Creoles: People born in the Caribbean of European ancestry, often mixed with Negro blood (Ch. 21).

Crêpe: Thin French pancake served with a variety of fillings and sauces (Ch. 9).

Crumpet: Similar to an English muffin, but somewhat thinner and more springy (Ch. 4).

Culture: Way of life of a group of people (what they create, do, and think) (Ch. 2).

Curry: Hearty and well-seasoned stewlike dish featuring meat or legumes and served with several accompaniments (Ch. 15).

Customs: Traditions that are common to a cultural group, such as shaking hands or bowing (Ch. 24).

Cuzco: Center of the Incan civilization in a very high (11,000 feet) Andean valley in Peru (Ch. 20).

Cyrillic alphabet: Alphabet developed by Cyril and Methodius, Byzantine monks who lived in the 9th century; used in Russia and many Slavic regions (Ch. 7).

Daeborum: Annual celebration of First Full Moon Day, which celebrates the first day of full moon in the first month of the Korean lunar calendar (Ch. 18).

da Gama, Vasco: Portuguese navigator who opened trade routes to India in 1498 and 1502 (Ch. 10).

Daikon: Large, long Asian radish that has a delicate flavor and slight pungency (Ch. 17, 23).

Dal: Puree of lentils or other legumes, usually rather blandly seasoned (Ch. 15).

Dashi: Clear soup stock made with dried fillet of bonito and kelp (Ch. 19).

Dendé: Yellow to reddish oil from a West African palm, which was introduced into Brazilian cooking by African slave women (Ch. 20).

Desayuno: Breakfast (usually coffee and pastry) eaten early in the morning in Mexico and Central America (Ch. 22).

Devi: Hindu goddess, the wife of Shiva (Ch. 3).

Diaspora: Settling of Jews outside Palestine (Ch. 3).

Diaz, Bartolomeu: Portuguese navigator who sailed around the Cape of Good Hope (southern tip of Africa) in 1488 (Ch. 10).

Dim sum: Small, steamed dumplings filled with any of a variety of meat or vegetable fillings and many other small servings of food ranging from appetizers to sweets. (Ch. 17).

Dolmas: Stuffed grape leaves usually containing rice and often other ingredients; may be served hot or cold (Ch. 11).

Dravidians: Early people of southern India (Ch. 15).

Dulceata: Romanian dish of simmered fruits in very heavy syrup (Ch. 7).

Durian: Large Asian fruit with bumpy skin and extremely strong smell (Ch. 23).

Dutch East India Company: Trading company that established Cape Town as a post to restock its ships plying between the East Indies and Holland (Ch. 14).

Eastern (Shanghai) school: Designation of cuisine of the eastern seaboard of China, notably of Shanghai; light broths, seafood, egg rolls, and paper-wrapped foods are characteristic (Ch. 17).

Einkhorn: A type of wheat grown in Syria around 9000 BCE (Ch. 1).

Eintopf: Hearty German stew of meat, vegetables, and a cereal or dumplings (Ch. 6).

El Cid: Spanish military hero who fought many battles for both the Moors and the Catholics, and freed Valencia from the Moors in 1094 (Ch. 10).

Emmer: An early form of wheat farmed in Palestine by 10,000 BCE (Ch. 1).

Empañadas: Fried or baked semicircular pastries filled with meat and raisins; prominent in Argentina, but also found in other South American countries (Ch. 20).

Empire of Ghana: Dominant power in West Africa from 5th to 11th centuries (Ch. 13).

Empire of Mali: Empire dominating trade from Senegal to Egypt from the 13th to the 15th centuries (Ch. 13).

Empire of Songhai: Dominant empire in West Africa (including Timbuktu) after splitting from Mali in the 14th century and into the 16th century (Ch. 13).

Enchiladas: Corn tortillas rolled around a filling and covered with a sauce before baking (Ch. 22).

Escabeche: Cooked fish marinated in vinegar and spices (Ch. 21).

Escargot: Snails, usually served with butter or other sauce in Burgundy (Ch. 9).

Escoffier: Chef considered to be the definitive writer about French cuisine (1846–1935) (Ch. 9).

Espresso: Very strong Italian coffee made by brewing dark-roast, finely ground coffee with steam (Ch. 8).

Ethnicity: Affiliation with a race, people, or social group (Ch. 2).

Etruscan: Group who settled in Tuscany and moved south, ultimately taking over Rome and contributing their alphabet, speech, and ability to wage war (Ch. 8).

Fado: Distinctive sad musical form of the blues sung to a guitar accompaniment (Ch. 10).

Falafel: Dish made by creating a paste of soaked chickpeas and seasonings, shaping into balls or other forms, and frying in deep fat (Ch. 11).

Fan: Grain foods considered to be important as a balance (yin) with the ts'ai (other foods in the meal) (Ch. 17).

Färikäl: Thick lamb stew with cabbage; popular in Norway (Ch. 5).

Feijoada completa: Celebrated Brazilian dish of several meats (including sausages and bacon), beans, rice, hot sauces, manioc meal, and sliced oranges (Ch. 20).

Feta: Soft cheese made from ewe's milk (Ch. 11).

Filipino Pyramid Food Guide: Food guide developed in the Philippines to guide people in making healthy food choices using the local foods (Ch. 24).

Finnan haddie: Smoked haddock poached in milk on a bed of onions (Ch. 4).

Fish and chips: Batter-dipped pieces of cod or other fish that are deep-fat fried; served with deep-fat fried thick strips of potato (Ch. 4).

Fiskebeller: Norwegian fishballs (Ch. 5).

Five Pillars of Islam: Requirements of Islam: Shahada (creed), Salat (prayers), Saum (fasting), Zukat (purifying tax), and Hajj (pilgrimage to Mecca) (Ch. 3).

Five-spice powder: Popular Chinese spice made by mixing star anise, Szechwan pepper, cinnamon, cloves, and fennel (Ch. 17).

Fjord: Narrow, steep-sided inlet from the sea (Ch. 5).

Flan: Baked custard dessert, usually containing caramel; served in Spain, Portugal, Central America, and Mexico (Ch. 10, 22).

Flautas: Tightly rolled corn tortillas containing a small amount of filling that are fried until crisp (Ch. 22).

Flying buttress: External architectural feature to support the relatively thin, windowed walls of Gothic cathedrals (Ch. 9).

Fondue: Swiss dish prepared by melting cheese with wine in a chafing dish and using long-handled forks to dip cubes of bread into the cheese mixture (Ch. 6).

Fontina: Cheese well suited for making fondue; originally from Valle d'Aosta in northern Italy near Great St. Bernard Pass (Ch. 8).

Food Guide Pyramid: Educational tool used in the United States to guide people in making healthy food choices (Ch. 24).

Foo-foo: Mashed plantains with okra (Ch. 21).

Fool: Sweetened fruit puree blended with custard or cream; served cold (Ch. 4).

Forbidden City: Walled area in Beijing built by Chinese emperors as the seat of government and power (Ch. 2).

Foul: Mixture of cooked chickpeas and black or broad beans that have been soaked together for at least two days before being cooked; served with topping of garlic, olive oil, lemon, tomato, and cilantro (Ch. 11).

Franco: Spanish dictator for about 40 years in the 20th century (Ch. 10).

Frijoles refritos: Cooked beans mashed and fried with lard to create a somewhat bumpy texture (Ch. 22).

Frikadeller: Danish meatballs (Ch. 5).

Fruit soup: Dessert soup popular in Scandinavia; often made with various dried fruits that are readily available through long winters (Ch. 5).

Fufu: Starchy paste produced by pounding and boiling manioc or other rich source of starch and then dipping each bite in a spicy sauce; popular in West Africa (Ch. 13); starchy paste or dough made of cassava; popular specifically in Kenya (Ch. 14).

Funchi: Cornmeal pudding prepared in the Caribbean (Ch. 21).

Fungi: Designation for mushrooms in some Chinese recipes; may include shiitake, enoki, oyster, button, or other types, usually dried (Ch. 17).

Fusilli: Wavy, spaghetti-like pasta (Ch. 8).

Garam masala: Basic mixture of spices usually prepared in quantity and used as desired to season many different dishes in India (Ch. 15).

Gari foto: Stew of hard-cooked eggs, onions, and tomatoes (Ch. 13).

Gazpacho: Chilled soup made with many chopped vegetables of Spain plus beef or chicken stock, red wine vinegar, and olive oil (Ch. 10).

Gelato: Italian ice cream (Ch. 8).

Ghandi, Mahatma: Famous pacifist in India who led a 200-mile march to the sea in 1930 to protest the salt tax (Ch. 2).

Ghee: Clarified butter made by boiling to evaporate the water and precipate the milk solids before filtering to clarify it; clarified butter that has been cooked down a little to add flavor; expensive, but preferred fat for cooking in India (Ch. 15).

Ghiveciu: Romanian casserole consisting of browned chunks of pork or veal and vegetables combined with tomato paste, red wine, and green grapes (Ch. 7).

Gibanica: Yugoslavian layered cheese pie (Ch. 7).

Ginger root: Gnarled root of ginger, which usually is peeled and grated; adds flavor as well as some heat to a recipe (Ch. 17).

Gnocchi: Yugoslavian small dumplings of wheat or cornmeal, or both (Ch. 7, 8).

Gorditas: Thick, small tortilla fried and slit to form a pocket that is stuffed with meats or seafood (or both), lettuce, and cheese served topped with salsa, shredded lettuce, chopped tomatoes and grated cheese (Ch. 22).

Goree: Island just off the coast of Dakar, Senegal, from which vast numbers of slaves were shipped to the Americas and Caribbean islands (Ch. 13).

Gorgonzola: Blue-veined cheese that originated in Gorgonzola near Milan in northern Italy and is now produced in the Po Valley (Ch. 8).

Gothic: Style of cathedral featuring pointed arches, high and thin walls containing stained glass, and strengthened by flying buttresses on the exterior (Ch. 9).

Gravet: Smoked salmon, a Norwegian delicacy (Ch. 5).

Great Rift Valley: Vast depression in the earth extending from Jordan south and west to Mozambique (Ch. 14).

Great Zimbabwe: Settlement in Zimbabwe featuring the Great Enclosure built of stone in the 14th century (Ch. 14).

Guacamole: Mashed avocado, chilies, tomatoes, cilantro, and lemon juice; served as an accompaniment or a garnish (Ch. 22).

Gulyás: Hungarian stew made with chunks of braised meat, seasoned with onion and paprika, and cooked with varying amounts of liquid (Ch. 7).

Haggis: Scottish traditional pudding of oatmeal, variety meats, suet, onions, and seasonings boiled in a sheep's stomach; often served at dinners honoring Robert Burns, Scotland's famous poet (Ch. 4).

Hajj: Pilgrimage to Mecca; one of Five Pillars (Ch. 3).

Hallacas: Colombian version of a tamale made by wrapping a layer of corn flour dough and a filling of meat or other ingredients in banana leaves and then steaming the packets (Ch. 20).

Han-gŭl: Phonetic Korean alphabet developed under the leadership of King Sejong in the 15th century (Ch. 18).

Hapsburg: Family that ruled Austria and its neighbors for about seven centuries until World War I (Ch. 6).

Harira: Hearty soup containing legumes, meat, and vegetables and seasoned with spices and lemon; important for suppers during Ramadan (Ch. 12).

Hellenistic Greece: Ancient Greek civilization that reached its peak of political dominance and cultural influence from about 323 BCE to 27 BCE (Ch. 1).

Hispaniola: Caribbean island where Columbus landed and that eventually became the countries of Haiti and the Dominican Republic (Ch. 21).

Hittites: Civilization occupying parts of Turkey to Syria and Mesopotamia for more than four centuries, ending in about 1200 BCE (Ch. 11).

Hmongs: People native to the northern hill regions of Laos (Ch. 16).

Hohenzollern: Family that ruled Prussia and neighboring regions for three centuries, ending with the end of World War I (Ch. 6).

Hoisin sauce: Thick, dark, garlic-flavored bean sauce (Ch. 17).

Hollandaise sauce: Sauce made of an emulsion of butter, egg yolks, lemon juice, and seasoning (Ch. 9).

Honshu: Largest of the islands of Japan; Tokyo is on Honshu (Ch. 19).

Hot cross buns: Easter yeast buns containing cinnamon, allspice, and raisins, and topped with a cross of candied orange peel or a strip of dough to represent the cross of Christ (Ch. 4).

Hummus: Dip made with pureed, cooked chickpeas, tahini, lemon juice, garlic, and olive oil (Ch. 11).

Hutspot: Hearty stewlike dish made in the Netherlands by simmering a large cut of meat with vegetables and then mashing the cooked vegetables before serving them with the sliced meat (Ch. 6).

Iberian Peninsula: Peninsula composed of Spain and Portugal forming the western part of Europe (Ch. 10).

Ibrik: Turkish coffee maker designed with a long handle and a narrow neck (Ch. 11).

Id al-Fitr: Three-day holiday celebrating the end of the Ramadan, the month of fasting (Ch. 3).

Idlis: Rice cakes (Ch. 15).

Ikebana: Japanese art of arranging cut flowers (Ch. 19).

Ile de France: Region within a 50-mile circle of Paris (Ch. 9).

Illyrians: Group of people settling the Balkans prior to the Romans (Ch. 7).

Imam: Person who leads Muslims in their daily prayers (Ch. 3).

Incan Empire: Region of Andes in Peru controlled by Incas from about 1300 CE until Pizarro conquered it after his arrival in 1533 CE (Ch. 1).

Inquisition: Period when Spain required non-Catholics to convert or leave the country; torture sometimes was part of the imprisonment process in Spain, Peru, and Portugal (Ch. 10).

Irish soda bread: Round loaf of bread leavened by carbon dioxide produced from buttermilk and soda, ingredients in the dough (Ch. 4).

Irish stew: Stew featuring lamb cubes or other meat, potatoes, onions, leeks, cabbage, and/or other vegetables; frequently served with red cabbage in Ireland (Ch. 4).

Jenné-Jeno: Very early town (before 500 CE) in Mali (Ch. 13).

Jicama: Brown root vegetable with crisp white interior, often served in raw slices with chili powder sprinkled on them (Ch. 22).

Jollof rice: Dish composed of layers of meat, tomatoes and other vegetables, and steamed rice (Ch. 13).

Jugged: Slow, moist-heat cooking of meat in a covered clay pot (Ch. 4).

Ka'ba: Black stone cube with a meteorite in its wall; shrine in the center of Mecca that pilgrions circumambulate as part of the Hajj (Ch. 3).

Kabob (kebab): Meat grilled, sometimes with other items, on a skewer (Ch. 11).

Kabuki: Traditional, highly stylized drama performed by men in elaborate costumes and makeup, often featuring dancing and some music (Ch. 19).

Kacca: Hindu term for level of food just below pakka, but made without ghee (Ch. 3)

Kama: Hindu god of love (Ch. 3).

Kami: The supernatural form of a deceased ancestor (Ch. 3).

Kaoliang: Sorghum (grain) crop grown in northern China (Ch. 17).

Kapi: Thai salty, dried shrimp paste (Ch. 16).

Karma: Force generated by actions in a Hindu's life that will determine what the next life will be Ch. 3).

Kasha: Buckwheat groats (or sometimes other cereals) boiled in liquid until light and fluffy; popular in Russia and its environs (Ch. 7).

Kashruth: Requirements outlining the preparation and types of food that Orthodox and other Jews may eat (Ch. 3).

Keshy yena: Edam cheese stuffed with grated cheese, meat mixtures, and seasonings and then baked; from Netherlands Antilles (Ch. 21).

Khatib: Person who reads the Friday sermon (Ch. 3).

Khmers: People native to Cambodia (Ch. 16).

Kibbeh: Deep-fat fried, egg-shaped shell of finely minced lamb and cracked wheat paste encasing a filling of another meat (Ch. 11).

Kielbasa: Polish sausage made of ground beef and pork, well seasoned with garlic (Ch. 7).

Kimchi: Fermented, pickled vegetables (particularly cabbage) (Ch. 18).

Kippers: Herring prepared in the traditional Scottish way of splitting them and then salting, drying, and smoking to preserve them (Ch. 4).

Kitchen god: Spirit of the hearth who determines wealth and longevity of people in the household; reports to Heaven annually regarding family's behavior (Ch. 17).

Knedliky: Flat, circular potato or bread dumplings popular in the Czech Republic and Slovakia (Ch. 7).

Kochujang: Red pepper and bean paste used as a condiment and as an ingredient in Korean recipes (Ch. 18).

Koldt bord: Literally, cold table; bread, butter, and cold dishes that are the beginning part of a smørgasbørd (Ch. 5).

Koran: Writings from Allah given to Muhammad by Angel Gabriel to define the spiritual life of Muslims (Ch. 3).

Koryŏ: Dynasty that ruled Korea from 918 to 1392 and subsequently was the source for the name Korea (Ch. 18).

Kringle: Nut-filled coffee cake from Denmark (Ch. 5).

Krishna: Hindu god celebrated as the eighth incarnation of Vishnu (Ch. 3).

Kshatriyas: Second caste in Hinduism; warriors and rulers (Ch. 3).

Ku lao jou: Dish containing starch-coated fried cubes of pork, stir-fried green peppers, various vegetables, and pineapple cubes in a thickened sweet-sour tomato sauce (Ch. 17).

Kulich: Russian traditional yeast-leavened Easter bread containing candied and dried fruits, nuts, and liqueur (Ch. 7).

Kutho: Kind or generous act that brings merit to help strive toward Nirvana (Ch. 3).

Kwanzaa: African-American holiday lasting a week at the end of the year to celebrate African-American heritage (Ch. 23).

Languedoc-Roussillon: Region in southern France that includes the marshy delta of the Rhone River (Ch. 9).

L'apéritif: Cocktail hour preceding dinner in France (Ch. 9).

Lapin: Rabbit, a popular meat in Belgium (Ch. 6).

Lapskaus: Chunky and thick meat and potato stew (Ch. 5).

Lasagne: Broad, ribbonlike pasta used in casserole dishes (Ch. 8).

Lascaux: Area in southern France where cave paintings from prehistoric people have been found (Ch. 9).

Laver: Edible seaweed popular in Korea (Ch. 18).

Laverbread: Jellylike mass resulting from boiling a special seaweed harvested along the coast of Wales (Ch. 4).

Lavosh: Armenian cracker bread; basically a very thin version of pita without a pocket (Ch. 11).

Lebkuchen: German gingerbread cookies baked in picture molds (Ch. 6).

Lebneh: Soft cheese made by draining whey from yogurt (Ch. 11).

Lefse: Norwegian flatbread (Ch. 5).

Le goûter: Afternoon snack (Ch. 9).

Lemon curd: Egg yolk-thickened sweet filling flavored with lemon juice and rind; often used as filling for tarts and pies (Ch. 4).

Le petit déjeuner: French breakfast (typically a croissant and coffee) (Ch. 9).

Levant: Land at the eastern end of the Mediterranean Sea (Ch. 11).

Lingonberries: Mountain cranberrylike fruit particularly popular in Sweden (Ch. 5).

Longyi: Long, saronglike cloth worn in Burma, tucked in at the waist; can be hiked up in the very hot weather (Ch. 16).

Lotus root: Crunchy root of lotus (water lily) cut crosswise to use in stir-fries and soups, where its porous appearance due to many lengthwise cavities in the root adds visual interest (Ch. 17).

Lumache: Large, conch shell–shaped pasta suitable for stuffing (Ch. 8).

Lutefisk: Cod soaked in lime until very soft (about 3 days) before being rinsed in running water for 2 days and subsequently poached or boiled (Ch. 5).

Mace: Reddish coating on nutmeg, which is removed and dried for use as a spice (Ch. 21).

Madeira wine: Sweet, fruity wine produced on Madeira, the Portuguese island in the North Atlantic Ocean (Ch. 10).

Magellan: Portuguese navigator who led the first circumnavigation of the world from 1519 to 1522 but died in the Philippines during the trip (Ch. 10).

Maghreb: Countries in the northwestern part of Africa: Morocco, Algeria, and Tunisia (Ch. 12).

Magyars: Ancestors of today's Hungarians (Ch. 7).

Mahayana: Mystical form of Buddhism practiced in Tibet, Mongolia, and the Himalayas (Ch. 3).

Malagueta: Extremely hot South American pepper, also called *aji* (Ch. 20).

Mamaliga: Romanian cornmeal mush similar to Italian polenta (Ch. 7).

Manicotti: Long, plain tube of pasta appropriate for stuffing (Ch. 8).

Manioc (cassava): Inclusive name for group of related tropical plants native to the western hemisphere that had fleshy roots rich in starch (Ch. 1); granular flour prepared by peeling and then grating bitter cassava roots and squeezing out absolutely all of the juice, which is poisonous until the juice is subsequently boiled. The dry grated material is broken to a powder by pounding (Ch. 20).

Mantra: Hindu incantation (Ch. 3).

Manu: Source of Hindu laws on living, and ancestor of Hindus, progenitor of human race and source of Vedas (Ch. 3).

Marmitako: Basque stew made with tuna and potatoes (Ch. 10).

Masa: Cornmeal dough made by mixing masa harina and water; main ingredient of tamales (Ch. 22).

Masa harina: Ground corn that has been soaked in lime (Ch. 22).

Mascarpone: Unripened Italian dessert cheese made from fresh cream; may be flavored with honey, liqueurs, or candied fruit (Ch. 8).

Maté: Beverage brewed in a gourd by pouring hot water over crushed leaves of yerba maté, producing a caffeine-containing beverage that is sipped through a bombilla; pronounced ma-tay (Ch. 20).

Mayan Empire: Region including the Yucatan Peninsula and Guatemala controlled by Mayans from 300 BCE to about 1200 CE (Ch. 1).

Mayans: Indians living in Guatemala, Belize, and southern Mexico from 600 BCE to 1200 BCE (Ch. 22).

Mealie meal: South African name for cornmeal (*mealie* means *corn*) (Ch. 14).

Medici: Powerful Florentine banking family; Cosimo, Lorenzo, and Caterina (who carried the excellence of Florentine cuisine to France when she married future King Henri II) are credited with influencing the artistic and culinary renaissance particularly in the 15th and 16th centuries, (Ch. 8).

Medina: Old native quarter of a North African city (Ch. 12).

Mediterranean Diet Pyramid: Food pyramid designed to incorporate the foods common to the Mediterranean in a pattern that has 11 categories (Ch. 24).

Menorah: Jewish candelabra designed to hold four candles in a row on each side of a central holder slightly higher than the eight holders; one additional candle is lighted each day of the eight days of Chunukah (Ch. 3).

Merienda: Late afternoon light refreshment eaten in Mexico and Central America (Ch. 22).

Meseta: High central plain in Spain (Ch. 10).

Mestizo: Person of mixed heritage of Spainards and native Indians (Ch. 20, 21).

Metate: Stone quern used for grinding nixtamal to masa harina (Ch. 22).

Mihrab: Niche in an interior wall of a mosque indicating the direction of Mecca for worshipers during Salat (Ch. 3).

Minaret: Tower of a mosque from which people are called to prayer (Ch. 3).

Minbar: Staircase topped with a pulpit in a mosque (Ch. 3).

Minoans: Mediterranean people who developed a prosperous, artistic civilization on Crete that was ended by a tidal wave in 1625 BCE (Ch. 1).

Mirin: Sweet rice wine (Ch. 19).

Miso: Fermented soybean paste (Ch. 19).

Mochi: Rice cake made by pounding cooked sweet glutinous rice; traditional for New Year's celebration (Ch. 19).

Mofongo: Puerto Rican specialty made with mashed plantains, pork cracklings, and garlic and either fried in balls or baked as a pancake (Ch. 21).

Mongol Empire: Barbaric, short-lived empire ranging southward from central Asia and westward to threaten even Vienna in Europe. (Ch. 1)

Mongolian fire pot: Mongolian-designed unique chafing dish with a spot to burn charcoal, a chimney going up the center, and a surrounding round vessel where broth is kept hot enough for diners to cook their individual bites of meats and vegetables (Ch. 17).

Mons: People native to Burma (Ch. 16).

Moors: Islamic inhabitants of northwestern Africa (mixture of Arabs and Berbers) from Morocco who invaded Spain in the 8th century (Ch. 10, 12).

Moo shu pork: Slivered pieces of seasoned pork and bean paste or other ingredients wrapped in small, thin pancakes (Ch. 17).

Moros y Cristianos: Cuban specialty containing black beans and rice cooked with garlic, onions, green peppers, tomatoes, and seasonings (Ch. 21).

Mosque: Place of worship for Muslims; contains a mihrab pointing to Mecca, a minbar atop a staircase for delivering the Friday sermon and daily prayers, and at least one minaret (Ch. 3).

Moussaka: Eggplant casserole usually containing lamb, onions, tomato sauce, and eggplant slices (Ch. 11).

Mozzarella: Cheese used on pizzas, originally made from buffalo milk, but now often made from cow's milk (Ch. 8).

Muesli: Breakfast cereal of toasted oats, nuts, and dried apples developed by a Swiss doctor (Ch. 6).

Muezzin: Person who calls Muslims to prayer five times a day (Ch. 3).

Muhammad: *See* Prophet Muhammad.

Mulligatawny: Curry-flavored rich soup made with a chicken or lamb base; reflecting British period in India (Ch. 4).

Myceneans: Civilization centered on the Greek Peloponnesus that controlled Crete and other Mediterranean islands (Ch. 1).

MyPyramid: Graphic guide to food nutrition introduced in 2005 to replace the Food Guide Pyramid as an instructional tool for nutrition education (Ch. 24).

Naan: Oval-shaped whole wheat bread baked by sticking it to the wall of a tandoor (Ch. 15).

Nam pla: Fermented fish sauce popular in Thailand (Ch. 16).

Niger River: One of the longest rivers of the world traverses much of West Africa, running north before turning east and south; has an interior delta and one at the coast (Ch. 13).

Nixtamal: Hull-less, lime-soaked corn (Ch. 22).

Nopales: Leaves of prickly pear cactus (Ch. 22).

Nori: Dried seaweed available in thin, greenish-black sheets; used for wrapping sushi and other foods or as a garnish (Ch. 19).

Normandy: Northern region of France just east of Brittany that lies along the coast of the English Channel (Ch. 9).

Northern (Peking) school: Designation of cuisine of the northern region of China that includes Mongolian fire pot, and Peking duck as well as moo shu pork and other recipes that use wheat and wheat flour products (Ch. 17).

Nuoc cham: Vietnamese condiment made with chili peppers, citrus juice, garlic, onions, and vinegar (Ch. 16).

Nuoc mam: Fermented, salted fish sauce popular in Vietnam (Ch. 16).

Olmecs: Dominant cultural group in Central America from 1200 to 150 BCE; settled predominantly on the coast of the

Gulf of Mexico along the Bay of Campeche west of the Yucatan Peninsula (Ch. 1).

Om: Sound chant repeated by Hindus for long periods to generate religious energy (Ch. 3).

Opium War: War in 1840 caused by British involvement in the opium trade in China; resulted in the long-term lease of Hong Kong to Britain (Ch. 17).

Osso buco: Braised veal shanks simmered with herbs and wine until very tender (Ch. 8).

Ottoman Empire: Large empire centered in Turkey that ruled for more than 600 years, ending after World War I. (Ch. 11).

Ouzo: Greece's distilled alcoholic drink from grape skins that are cooked with star anise and a variety of other herbs prior to distillation (Ch. 11).

Oyster sauce: Salty, dark Chinese sauce made with soy sauce and the taste of oysters and other flavoring agents (Ch. 17).

Paella: Traditional rice dish colored and flavored by saffron and topped with cooked vegetables and meats (Ch. 10).

Pagoda: Shrine of several stories where Buddhists worship (Ch. 3).

Pakka: Hindu word for food containing ghee; offered to gods and then high-ranking guests (Ch. 3).

Pannetone: Coarse, sweet yeast bread containing raisins and candied fruit (Ch. 8).

Paratha: Whole wheat bread circles about 7 inches in diameter, made with ghee in the dough and fried in ghee on the griddle (Ch. 15).

Parmesan: Hard cheese often aged for more than two years; frequently grated over Italian dishes (Ch. 8).

Parrillada: Grilled mixture of meats, typical of Argentina (Ch. 20).

Parthenon: Classical Greek structure dominating the Acropolis in Athens (Ch. 2).

Paskha: Pyramid-shaped Russian Easter cake (Ch. 7).

Pasteles: Puerto Rican specialty made by spreading mashed plantain or cornmeal on a plantain leaf, adding a savory filling, wrapping, and steaming (Ch. 21).

Pastelitos: Savory, small turnovers with meat filling made in the Dominican Republic (Ch. 21).

Patis: Fermented, salty fish sauce popular in the Philippines (Ch. 16).

Peking duck: Traditional dish of northern China, which involves special roasting of a duck until the skin is very crisp; skin, a bit of duck meat, and green onion are wrapped in a thin pancake liberally splashed with hoisin sauce. Plum sauce is also served (Ch. 17).

Peloponnesus: Peninsula extending off the southwestern region of Greece (Ch. 11).

Penne: Tubular pasta cut diagonally into pieces about an inch long (Ch. 8).

Pepper pot: Long-lived stew common throughout the Caribbean, flavored with cassareep, containing meats and vegetables that are replenished from time to time as needed and available (Ch. 21).

Perigord: Area north of the Pyrenees where truffles are found (Ch. 9).

Pesto: Flavorful thick sauce made by pulverizing fresh basil and adding such ingredients as piñon nuts, parmesan cheese, garlic, and olive oil (Ch. 8).

Phoenicians: People living in Lebanon who sailed extensively to trade with many other regions by 1000 BCE (Ch. 1).

Phyllo: Extremely thin dough that is formed into large sheets and serves as the main ingredient for desserts and some main dishes (Ch. 11).

Pierogi: Polish dish consisting of small pockets of dough containing a filling (vegetable or sweet) (Ch. 7).

Pikelet: Small pancake served at tea in Wales and Scotland (Ch. 4).

Pirozhki: Small Russian pastry filled with meat (Ch. 7).

Pita: Pocket bread that is common throughout the Middle East (Ch. 11).

Pizarro: Spanish explorer who conquered the Incas in Peru in the 16th century and established Spanish dominance there (Ch. 10, 20).

Plantain: Very starchy banana, which is cooked before serving (Ch. 23).

Plum sauce: Chutney made with plums, apricots, vinegar, chili, and sugar (Ch. 17).

Plum pudding: Dense, steamed pudding containing some suet and a generous amount of dried and candied fruits that is served warm, usually with hard sauce and often flamed with brandy (Ch. 4).

Poe (poi): Starchy paste of boiled and pounded peeled taro root popular in Polynesia (Ch. 16).

Polenta: Traditional northern Italian dish; cornmeal cooked in milk or other liquid with frequent stirring until it forms a mushy, soft paste, at which time butter and sometimes other ingredients are added (Ch. 8).

Pombe: Kenyan beer (Ch. 14).

Porchetta: Whole, suckling pig flavored with fennel, peppercorns, and garlic and roasted; popular entrée in Tuscany (Ch. 8).

Porrusalda: Basque soup that features potatoes and leeks. (Ch. 10).

Posados: Procession of Mary and Joseph's search for lodging reenacted from December 16 until Christmas Eve as part of Christmas festivities (Ch. 22).

Potala: Seat of Tibetan Buddhism and the former home of the Dalai Lama (Ch. 15).

Pot stickers: Assorted fillings of shredded meats and/or chopped vegetables wrapped in a thin pancake, fried, and then simmered in chicken stock (Ch. 17).

Prester John: Mythical Christian leader of a domain originally rumored to be in India and then reported to be deep in Africa (Ch. 14).

Prince Henry the Navigator: Portuguese leader who sponsored voyages of exploration aboard caravels to very distant places (Ch. 10).

Prophet Muhammad: Arab man who founded Islam in the 7th century (Ch. 3).

Prosciutto: Thinly sliced, well-cured Parma ham (Ch. 8).

Provence: Region in southern France adjacent to the French Riviera (Ch. 9).

Puja: Hindu worship ritual that begins with seating, cleansing, and dressing a deity. Food is offered to the god and then some is eaten by the worshiper (Ch. 3).

Pumpernickel: German dark, coarse bread made with unsifted rye flour (Ch. 6).

Punic Wars: Three wars fought between Carthage and Rome between 264 and 146 BCE (Ch. 1).

Puri: Deep-fat fried rounds of whole wheat bread that are puffed in the middle during frying (Ch. 15).

Quesada: Spanish conquistador credited with conquering Colombia (Ch. 20).

Quesadilla: Flour tortilla folded over a layer of grated cheese and heated (Ch. 22).

Quiche Lorraine: Tart featuring a bacon and custard filling originally made in Lorraine region of France (Ch. 9).

Quinoa: Grain grown in the high Andes by Indians and eaten as a rich source of protein and starch in Peru and Chile; pronounced keen-wah (Ch. 20).

Raclette: Swiss favorite consisting of melted cheese served with a sliced, boiled potato, sweet gherkin, and pickled pearl onions (Ch. 6).

Raki: Distilled Turkish alcoholic beverage made from grape residue and with anise for added flavor; turns milky if water is added. (Ch. 11).

Ramadan: One-month period of fasting from sunrise to sunset each year; one of the Pillars of Islam (Ch. 3).

Rastafarianism: Jamaican religion traced to teachings in the Old Testament; members may have dreadlocks; reggae music originated in this group (Ch. 21).

Ratatouille: Highly flavorful medley of vegetables and herbs from Provence (Ch. 9).

Ravioli: Rectangular pasta pouches stuffed with ground meat or cheese (Ch. 8).

Red cooking: Braising meat mixtures in a sauce containing some soy sauce (Ch. 17).

Retsina: Greek rosé or white wine flavored with pine resin (Ch. 11).

Rijsttafel: Rice table originating in Indonesia; brought to the Netherlands by the Dutch East Indies Company; consists of some highly spiced dishes and many other somewhat bland dishes, which are prepared at the table (usually in restaurants) (Ch. 6).

Risotto: Rice dish from northern Italy made by sautéing Arborio or other short-grain rice before slowly adding a bit of white wine and other liquid while cooking and stirring until grains are tender and the texture is creamy (Ch. 8).

Roma: Nomadic group originating from India but particularly numerous in Romania that has spread into most parts of Europe (Ch. 7).

Roman Empire: Vast empire based in Rome that gradually was formed to cover much of the areas along the Mediterranean coast into Turkey, France, and England. (Ch. 1)

Romano: Sharp, aged sheep's milk cheese; very hard cheese, ideal for grating (Ch. 8).

Rømmegrøt: Norwegian porridge of milk and sour cream thickened with flour and flavored with cinnamon and coarse sugar granules (Ch. 5).

Rösti: Swiss dish of parboiled, grated potatoes sautéed in sizzling butter to make a pancake-like disk that is browned well on both sides (Ch. 6).

Roti: Indian word for bread (Ch. 15).

Sachertorte: Austrian dessert; layered chocolate cake spread with apricot jam and topped with a chocolate glaze (Ch. 6).

Sacred cow: Wandering cow where Hindus live; protected from harm because of respect for life (Ch. 3).

Sadza: Zimbabwean name for a stiff cornmeal porridge (Ch. 14).

Saffron: Orange to yellow spice; the stigma of purple crocus; adds color and flavor to dishes (Ch. 10).

Safsari: Robes worn by women in North Africa to cover their bodies, including a headpiece with a veil to cover their face except the eyes. (Ch. 12).

Sahel: Broad band of land across West Africa between the Sahara and the lush vegetation along the southern coast (Ch. 13).

Sake: Strong rice wine, usually served warm (Ch. 19).

Salat: Muslim daily prayer according to the Five Pillars (Ch. 3).

Sally Lunn: Light yeast bread baked in a tubular pan, sliced in half, and then topped with whipped cream or melted butter; originated in Bath, England (Ch. 4).

Salsa: Sauce containing finely chopped vegetables and seasonings used to add flavor excitement to many Mexican and Central American dishes (Ch. 22).

Sambar: Spicy purée of lentils, which often is served with idlis (Ch. 15).

Samgye t'yang: Whole small chicken stuffed with rice, ginseng, and chestnuts, covered in broth, and baked until meat almost falls from bones (Ch. 18).

Sami: Nomadic reindeer herders (Lapplanders) living in the arctic reaches of Scandinavia; shorter stature and darker coloring than the Scandinavians from the lower parts of this region (Ch. 5).

Samosa: Fried pastry enclosing a filling (Ch. 15).

Samovar: Elaborate Russian device equipped with a chimney, a teapot for the essence of the tea, and a large area where the water is boiled for dispensing from the spigot (Ch. 7).

Sancocho: Stew popular in the Dominican Republic; contains plantain, chicken, cassava, vinegar, and pepper (Ch. 21).

Sang-chi-sam: Lettuce-wrapped meal containing many tidbits from numerous dishes selected by the diner (Ch. 18).

Sangria: Red wine blended with fruit juices (Ch. 10).

Sashimi: Very carefully cut and arranged slices of raw fish (Ch. 19).

Sauerbraten: German dish; roast marinated in vinegar and wine and simmered with seasonings until very tender, and then served with a gingersnap-containing gravy and red cabbage cooked with tart apples (Ch. 6).

Sauerkraut: Pickled shredded cabbage, a German specialty (Ch. 6).

Saum: Ritual of fasting (Ch. 3).

Schnitzel: German term for thin cutlet of veal or other meat that is dipped in a batter prior to cooking (Ch. 6).

Scone: Quick bread made from a dough that is rolled and cut into triangles or circles, and then baked in a very hot oven; popular for teatime (Ch. 4).

Scotch Broth: Thick soup made of vegetables and a meat broth (Ch. 4).

Seaweed: Various types of edible seaweeds and sea grass, as well as purple laver; usually used dried in soups (Ch. 17).

Sejong the Great: Dynamic 15th-century Korean leader who sponsored development of han-gŭl, written music, movable type, astronomy, and a medical book (Ch. 18).

Shahada: One of the Five Pillars; chanting of creed, "There is no god but God; Muhammad is the Messenger of God" (Ch. 3).

Shark's fin: Usually transparent, yellowish, dried cartilage from the fin of a shark; requires rehydration when used in soup (Ch. 17).

Shashlyk: Russian version of shish kebabs (Ch. 7).

Shawarma: Thinly sliced chicken as lamb layered tightly with fat and formed into a solid that is grilled vertically on a rotisserie and sliced off in very thin, long slices while still on the skewer (Ch. 11).

Shchi: Cabbage-containing soup made in Russia (Ch. 7).

Shepherd's pie: Deep-dish meat pie made with cooked meat and onions, and topped with a crust of mashed potatoes before baking (Ch. 4).

Shiite: Branch of Islam practiced by those who follow Ali, the prophet's son-in-law (Ch. 12).

Shin sul ro: Korean hot pot (Ch. 18).

Shinto: Early religion of Japan that focused on nature and considered the Emperor to be a descendant of the sun goddess (Ch. 19).

Shiva: Destructive Hindu god, also called *Siva* (Ch. 3).

Shofar: Hollowed out ram's horn blown in the synagogue during Rosh Hashanah to call man to be aware of his shortcomings and to emphasize that God is the divine king (Ch. 3).

Shogun: Term for military rulers in Japan prior to 1867 (Ch. 19).

Shortbread: Very rich, buttery cookie (biscuit) rolled into a circle and cut into wedges before baking (Ch. 4).

Sibelius: Composer from Finland who lived from 1865 to 1957; his most famous orchestral work is *Finlandia* (Ch. 2)

Simon Bolivar. *See* Bolivar, Simon.

Sinhalese: Descendants of Aryans living in Sri Lanka (Ch. 15).

Sinterklaas: Name for Saint Nicholas in the Netherlands (Ch. 6).

Sizzling rice soup: Rice that has formed a crust on the bottom of a wok before being deep-fat fried and then added to a hot broth, causing great sizzling sounds as it is stirred into the soup (Ch. 17).

Slatko: Sweet Serbian dish made of fruit simmered with blossoms in a thick sweet sugar syrup (Ch. 7).

Slivova: Bulgarian plum brandy (Ch. 7).

Slivovitz: Plum brandy liqueur drunk by Czechs and Slovaks (Ch. 7).

Smørgasbørd: Very elaborate Scandinavian buffet with ample arrays of cold foods and hot dishes, as well as dessert choices (Ch. 5).

Smørrebrød: Scandinavian open-faced sandwiches, usually with a base of rye bread and butter and artfully arranged toppings (Ch. 5).

Snow peas: Flat, green peas in tender, crisp, edible pods (Ch. 17).

Soba: Noodles made from buckwheat flour from northern Japan (Ch. 19).

Sofrito: Hot, spicy sauce featuring chilies, tomatoes, garlic, ham or bacon, and coriander (Ch. 21).

Sopa de ajo: Garlic soup popular in Spain (Ch. 10).

Sopa de pescado: Fish soup (Ch. 20).

Sopito: Fish chowder made with coconut milk in the Netherlands Antilles (Ch. 21).

Sosaties: Barbecued pieces of meat on a stick (Ch. 14).

Soufflé: Baked foam of egg whites combined with a yolk and chocolate (or cheese or other flavoring ingredient) sauce (Ch. 9).

Souk: Arab marketplace featuring specific types of shops that sell items such as spices and gold (Ch. 12).

Soul Food Pyramid: Healthy food guide for persons who are lactose intolerant and need to limit fat intake to control weight (Ch. 24).

Southern (Cantonese) school: Designation of cuisine of the southern Chinese that features stir-frying, such dishes as egg rolls, dumplings (dim sum), and pork specialties, as well as generous use of vegetables, rice, and fruits (Ch. 17).

Spanakopite: Main dish consisting of many layers of phyllo, spinach, and various other ingredients according to taste (Ch. 11).

Springerle: Anise-flavored German picture cookie popular at Christmas (Ch. 6).

Spritsar: Swedish ring-shaped cookie often made at Christmastime (Ch. 5).

St. Peter's Basilica: Very large cathedral in the Vatican in Rome (Ch. 8).

Stamp and go: Jamaican dish featuring salted, dried cod suspended in a heavy batter containing chilies, onions, and annatto and fried as a fritter (Ch. 21).

Steak-and-kidney pie: Hearty, savory pie containing pieces of beef steak and kidneys in the filling (Ch. 4).

Stoemp: Mashed potatoes made with plenty of butter, cream, and seasonings in Belgium (Ch. 6).

Stupa: Covered mound, often containing a relic of significance for Buddhists (Ch. 15).

Sudras: Lowest Hindu caste; menial workers (Ch. 3).

Suimono: Clear Japanese soups (Ch. 19).

Sukiyaki: Thinly sliced beef simmered with Japanese vegetables, soy sauce, mirin, and dashi in a pot at the table (Ch. 19).

Sunni: Branch of Islam practiced by those who follow the descendants of the fifth caliph (Ch. 12).

Sunomono: Vinegared salads (Ch. 19).

Sushi: Vinegared rice and small bits of other ingredients pressed into a mold or rolled tightly into a long log encased in a layer of nori and sliced vertically (Ch. 19).

Sukkot: Nine-day Festival of Tabernacles; celebrated five days after Yom Kippur (Ch. 3).

Tabouli: Salad containing soaked bulgur, minced parsley and mint, diced tomatoes, olive oil, and lemon juice (Ch. 11).

Taco: Crisply fried or soft tortilla folded in half over a filling of beans, meats, and other ingredients (Ch. 22).

Tagine: Stew prepared in a round pottery bowl topped with a conical lid (bowl and conical lid also called *tagine*), a unique product of Morocco (Ch. 12).

Tahini: Paste of finely ground sesame seeds, sesame oil, and lemon juice (Ch. 11).

Taj Mahal: Mausoleum built by Shah Jahan in Agra, India, to honor the memory of his favorite wife, Mumtaz (Ch. 2, 15).

Tajaditas: Fried banana chips (Ch. 22).

Tak paesuk: Whole small chicken stuffed with rice, covered in broth, and baked until meat almost falls from bones (Ch. 18).

Talik: The colored mark (often red) that many Hindus wear on the forehead between the eyebrows. (Ch. 3).

Talmud: Authoritative body of Jewish tradition (Ch. 3).

Tamale: Masa harina spread on cornhusk and wrapped around a filling of meat or other ingredients, and then steamed until done (Ch. 22).

Tamils: Descendants of early invaders of Sri Lanka (Ch. 15).

Tandoor: Thick-walled, deep jar-shaped clay oven used for roasting meats and baking naan (Ch. 15).

Tapa: Small plate of tidbits of food designed for nibbling while having a drink in the late afternoon or early evening (Ch. 10).

Taro: Starchy root vegetable that thrives in tropical climates (Ch. 1).

Tarte tatin: Apple tart made by arranging apples neatly in a tart pan and covering with a pastry; tart is inverted after baking (Ch. 9).

Tatars: Mongol invaders who originally gathered military might under Genghis Khan and who conquered Russia under his grandson's leadership (Ch. 7).

Tempura: Batter-coated, deep-fried shrimp and thinly sliced vegetables (Ch. 19).

Theravada: Buddhist sect practiced in Southeast Asia in which monks carry begging bowls in the mornings. (Ch. 3).

Thousand-year egg: Egg (usually duck) preserved by packing them in a lime-clay mixture and storing for between 6 weeks and 100 days, which transforms the white into a very dark, gelatinous material with a slightly fishy taste as the chemicals from the packing penetrate through the shell and throughout the egg (Ch. 17).

Toad-in-the hole: Sausages cooked in a quick-bread batter (Ch. 4).

Tofu (soybean curd): Precipitate formed by adding calcium sulfate to a cooked soybean solution made from water and strained, ground soybeans; may be pressed to form firmer curd (Ch. 17).

Torah: First five books of the Old Testament that are the foundation for Judaism (Ch. 3).

Torii gate: Distinctive gateway to a Shinto shrine (Ch. 19).

Tortiglioni: Spiral-shaped pasta (Ch. 8).

Tortilla: Dough of masa harina (or flour) and water, which is pressed into thin disks and baked (Ch. 22).

Tostada: Fried tortilla filled with beans, meat, chopped vegetables, guacamole, grated cheese, and sour cream; sometimes flour tortilla is fried in the shape of a bowl and filled with the same ingredients (Ch. 22).

Tostone: Twice-fried slice of plantain pounded to be thin before the second frying (Ch. 20).

Transylvania: Region in western Romania bounded by the Carpathian Mountains (Ch. 7).

Treacle: Very thick, sweet molasses (Ch. 4).

Trekboer: Boer who made the Great Trek to settle the interior of South Africa (Ch. 14).

Trifle: Elaborate dessert made in a pretty glass bowl, which has been lined with lady fingers or slices of pound cake and then filled with layers of stirred custard, whipped cream, slivered almonds, and raspberries and generously laced with sherry (Ch. 4).

Truffle: Dark, subterranean fruity body of a fungi; especially rare and flavorful ingredient prized in French recipes (Ch. 9).

Ts'ai: Term designating the various other dishes in a meal that balance the meal with the rice or fan (yin) in the meal; the yang part of the meal (Ch. 17).

Tsetse fly: Vector for sleeping sickness, a very serious disease in parts of West Africa (Ch. 13).

Tsukemono: Pickled vegetables (Ch. 19).

Tuk-kuk: Rice cake soup (Ch. 18).

U.S. Immigration and Naturalization Service: Federal agency responsible for enforcing immigration and naturalization regulations and laws (Ch. 23).

Udon: Noodles made with wheat flour, typical of southern Japan (Ch. 19).

Ugali: Kenyan name for stiff cornmeal porridge (Ch. 14).

Untouchables: Person unworthy of belonging to a caste (Ch. 3).

Vaisyas: Third level Hindu caste; farmers and businesspeople (Ch. 3).

Valdivia: Captain under Pizarro who led the Spanish expansion to Chile from Peru (Ch. 20).

Vasco da Gama: *See* da Gama, Vasco.

Vassilopita: Rich sweet bread containing a good-luck coin to celebrate the New Year (Ch. 11).

Vedas: Four volumes of the collective wisdom on how Hindus must live (Ch. 3).

Velouté: Basic flour-thickened sauce made with a fish or chicken stock (Ch. 9).

Viandas: Generic word used in the Piramide Alimentaria para Puerto Rico to include bland foods high in starch (Ch. 24).

Vishnu: Preserver god of Hindu religion (Ch. 3).

Voodoo: Type of worship found in Haiti based on spells, hexes, and animism traced to African roots (Ch. 21).

Voortrekker: Boer who used oxen and covered wagons to make the Great Trek between 1835 and 1839; also called *trekboer* (Ch. 14).

Wasabi: Finely grated, delicate green horseradish; also available as a powder (Ch. 19).

Wassail: Traditional spiced wine or ale drink served at Christmas in the United Kingdom (Ch. 4).

Water chestnut: Tuber that is sliced and used as a vegetable to add a crisp, distinctive texture; usually available canned (Ch. 17).

Waterzooi: Belgian fish stew (Ch. 6).

Welsh rarebit: Sauce usually made of cheddar cheese and beer that is served over toast or other bread as a main dish (Ch. 4).

Western (Szechwan) school: Designation of cuisine developed in western China, that is quite spicy and hot in character and uses considerable garlic, ginger, and oil (Ch. 17).

West Indies: Islands of the Caribbean, ranging from near Florida to the northeast coast of South America (Ch. 21).

Weiner schnitzel: Traditional Viennese dish consisting of thin veal cutlets dipped in flour, egg, and bread crumbs before being fried in butter (Ch. 6).

Winter melon: Green, oblong melon similar in outward appearance to a watermelon, but with a white, pulpy interior and a seed-filled center (Ch. 17).

Wok: Round-bottomed, two-handled metal pan used for stir-frying or as the container for boiling water to steam food in bamboo steamer trays stacked on the wok (Ch. 17).

Wonton: Small pouch of food wrapped in thin wheat dough (wonton wrapper) and cooked in a broth or deep-fat fried (Ch. 17).

Worcestershire sauce: Pungent sauce made of soy sauce, vinegar, and garlic and used quite universally at British tables; originated in Worcestershire, England pronounced wüs-ta-shir (Ch. 4).

Yang: Positive principle including male, sun, heaven, fire, brightness, good, wealth, and joy; complementary balance to yin (Ch. 17).

Yarmulke: Skullcap worn by Jewish men (Ch. 3).

Yassa: Dish made with lemon-marinated chicken or meat (Ch. 13).

Yin: Passive principle including female, moon, earth, water, darkness, evil, poverty, and sadness; complementary balance to yang (Ch. 17).

Yom Kippur: Day of Atonement; celebration 10 days after Rosh Hashanah (Ch. 3).

Yorkshire pudding: Puffy, crusty pudding baked on meat drippings in a very hot oven; batter is thin egg–milk–flour mixture similar to popover batter (Ch. 4).

Yuca: Sweet cassava; root used as a starch in the tropical regions (Ch. 20).

Zapotec: Indians who developed the city of Monte Alban near Oaxaca in Mexico around 500 BCE (Ch. 22).

Zeljanica: Yugoslavian cheese and spinach pie (Ch. 7).

Zukat: Purifying tax; one of the Five Pillars (Ch. 3).

The Essentials of Wine:
with Food Pairing Techniques

by John P. Laloganes

PREFACE

HOW THIS TEXTBOOK IS ORGANIZED

The Essentials of Wine with Food-Pairing Techniques is a straightforward approach to understanding wine and provides a framework for making intelligent food-pairing decisions. The units (and the chapters within the units) in this book have been arranged by a **building-block** approach that was developed through trial and error over a period of several years of classroom testing. The units and chapters build upon one another (particularly Units 1 and 2) until a certain point when the textbook allows for **flexibility** if the instructor desires, in order to adjust and adapt the order of units presented according to the skill level of the learners or the appropriateness of the curriculum. The units also allow teachers to utilize the text in a single course or multiple courses, either as a main textbook or as a supplement in conjunction with other wine, culinary, or pastry books. The book can work in single classes such as "Introduction to Wine," "Wine Appreciation," "Wine and Food Pairing," or "Food and Beverage Operations." It can also be used as a supplementary text in "Culinary 101," "Baking 101," "Guest Service," and "Hospitality Marketing and Retail Sales" courses.

Unit 1—**The Basics of Wine** introduces the learner to fundamental wine concepts, professional tasting, and the process of how grapes are grown and wine is made. *Unit 2*—**Wine and Food Compatibility** outlines the most significant and common grape varietals and then proceeds to the foundations and advanced information about wine- and food-pairing concepts. *Unit 3*—**Wines of the New World** introduces the learner to the major New World wine-producing countries and the most notable regions within them. *Unit 4*—**Wines of the Old World** introduces the learner to the major Old World wine-producing countries and the most notable regions within them. *Unit 5*—**Other Types of Wine** provides vital information that exposes the learner to sparkling, fortified, and dessert wines. Not all culinary, pastry, and hospitality management programs have the classes or allowance for advanced wine content in their programs. Unit 5 allows instructors to forego such content or to manipulate the order of the chapters to suit their situation. *Unit 6*—**Wine Management** provides some necessary techniques for managing wine successfully. Discussed here are the processes controlling the flow of wine, cost control, and the development of a wine menu. This material can be useful either in a wine course, cost control, or in a menu-planning course.

To get the maximum benefit and depth of information out of the book, follow the units and chapters in order while periodically flipping through the **Appendix, Wine Glossary: From A to Z.** This appendix acts to support the other chapters and should be used as a reference throughout the textbook. The six units into which the book is broken down are described in more detail as follows:

- *Unit 1*—**The Basics of Wine:** The student is exposed to the fundamentals of wine, beginning with what wine is, how grapes are grown, how wine is made, and the three main categories of wine. The differences between Old World and New World wine is analyzed, and bottle shapes and labelling are then discussed.
- *Unit 2*—**Wine and Food Compatibility:** The significant white and red wine grape varietals are discussed, with an eye toward gaining a strong analytical understanding of how to pair wine and food together. This unit is fairly "culinary heavy" as a means of providing a solid foundation or review of cookery. The culinary

information affords a bridge for the student by reinforcing techniques learned in order to truly understand the analytical approach to pairing wine with food.

- *Unit 3*—**Wines of the New World:** The student is introduced to the major wine-producing areas of the United States (California, New York, Washington, and Oregon) and Canada. Also explored are other New World wine-producing countries, such as Chile, Argentina, Australia, New Zealand, and South Africa.
- *Unit 4*—**Wines of the Old World:** The student is introduced to the major wine-producing areas of France, Italy, Germany, and Spain.
- *Unit 5*—**Other Types of Wines:** The student is introduced to the various production methods and different styles of sparkling wines, fortified wines, and dessert wines.
- *Unit 6*—**Wine Management:** This unit provides a solid foundation for the new or already working beverage manager.
- **The Appendix** is a comprehensive glossary complete with the pronunciations of difficult or foreign wine terms.

MAJOR COMPETENCIES

Upon completion of this textbook, the reader should be able to do all of the following:

- ☑ Classify wines according to type, and recognize their distinguishing styles and classification methods. (Chapter 1—Introduction to Wine)
- ☑ Apply wine-tasting assessment techniques for table, fortified, and sparkling wines. (Chapter 2—Wine Tasting)
- ☑ Identify the major elements within the grape-growing and winemaking processes. (Chapter 3—Viticulture and Enology)
- ☑ Distinguish between different grape varietals, their major locations of production, and their unique personalities. (Chapter 4—Performance Factors of Grape Varietals)
- ☑ Apply the analytical approach to wine and food pairing. (Chapter 5—Foundations to Wine and Food Pairing)
- ☑ Comprehend specific food types with their respective pairing strategies. (Chapter 6—Advanced Wine and Food Pairing)
- ☑ Discover the wine philosophies and major wine-producing areas of American and Canadian wines. (Chapter 7—Wines of the United States and Canada)
- ☑ Discover the wine philosophies and major wine-producing areas of Chile, Argentina, Australia, New Zealand, and South Africa. (Chapter 8—Other New World Wine Countries)
- ☑ Discover the wine philosophies and major wine-producing areas of France and the notable wines that are produced in those areas. (Chapter 9—Wines of France)
- ☑ Discover the wine philosophies and major wine-producing areas of Italy, Germany, and Spain. (Chapter 10—Other Old World Wine Countries)
- ☑ Distinguish between the different production methods and major styles of "other wines" (sparkling wines, fortified wines, and dessert wines). (Chapter 11—BUBBLES: Sparkling Wine, Chapter 12—BOLD: Fortified Wine, Chapter 13—NECTAR: Dessert Wines)
- ☑ Identify the elements within each control point throughout the flow of wine. (Chapter 14—The Flow of Wine)

☑ Demonstrate fundamental wine opening and serving techniques. (Chapter 14—The Flow of Wine)

☑ Comprehend different variables needed to arrange and compile an effective wine menu. (Chapter 15—Developing a Wine Menu)

☑ Acquire a comprehensive vocabulary of wine terminology. (Appendix, Wine Glossary: From A to Z)

ADDITIONAL TOOLS

Practice Quizzes—At the end of each chapter, there are "Check Your Knowledge" quizzes that include a combination of 20–30 multiple choice, true/false, matching, and short answer essay questions. Unit 2, "Wine and Food Compatibility," offers several worksheets at the end of each chapter to assist the learner with gaining a solid understanding and practice of pairing guidelines and principles.

Key Words—These terms have been set in italics throughout each chapter within the book. Most words can also be found in the Glossary for quick reference if a definition or pronunciation is needed.

Colorful maps—Maps of key grape/wine production areas help to illustrate terroir in a general sense. Certainly, it is helpful to have a sense of place, particularly an understanding of where regions or countries are in relation to one another. Each winemaking region has its own character and heritage, and its wines represent both the unique properties of the land and local winemaking practices. The climates and topographies within a country or even a wine region can vary dramatically, so knowing where the wine is made gives clues as to the grape varieties and flavors one can expect.

Pronunciation Guides and Glossary—Some wine terms can be challenging to articulate, because they are taken from French, Italian, German, or Spanish (or even, in some cases, from Portuguese or Hungarian). The first time a "foreign term" appears and is expanded upon within the text, a phonetic guide is included for English speakers. The guide provides an approximate pronunciation in English and does not necessarily reflect the nuances or specific dialects that may be apparent with the use of these terms in the country or wine region of origin. Certainly, a French word will sound best as said by a French-speaking person, but the guides provide a close approximation that would be acceptable to use throughout the world.

Vocabulary that is used throughout the book is summarized in a Glossary at the back of the book. The reader is encouraged to reference the Glossary throughout the text upon encountering a term whose meaning he or she does not know. Unit 4, "Wines of the Old World," presents easy-to-locate wine bottle labelling terminology at the beginning of each chapter.

INTRODUCTION BY THE AUTHOR

The GOAL of This Textbook

The Essentials of Wine with Food-Pairing Techniques is a resource that educates the reader through the presentation of a practical and straightforward approach to understanding wine and by providing a framework for making intelligent, well-informed wine- and food-pairing decisions.

The textbook provides both a foundational wine education and guidelines and principles for pairing wine and food. Of course, the book discusses the "typical" classic wine and food combinations that are in all wine books; yet it emphasizes the necessity of understanding the pairing strategies for "World Cuisine" that is prevalent around us today and for food found in everyday types of restaurants.

Throughout the book, broad-brush strokes will be used to present information in a user-friendly format. Sometimes, however, a fine brush will be applied to emphasize areas that are foundational concepts in the text. The writing style and format of the book have been designed in a way that allows simplicity to guide the student through the maze of wine information by keeping it on a level that learners can relate to.

This textbook strives to provide relevant, to-the-point information that saves the reader from personal or long-winded stories. There are other books for that. This book and all of its contents (study quizzes, tasting sheets, etc.) have been designed and tested in a classroom environment for a period of several years. While things aren't perfect, they hopefully will ensure greater success of the transition of the content from the book into a classroom or training environment.

The Current State of Wine Textbooks

Currently, many wine and wine-and-food-pairing textbooks fall short of effectively delivering information that will train and educate students in the essentials of both topics. Some of the books discuss only wine pairing and veer towards being more of a cookbook or "coffee-table" type of book, rather than a "cut to the chase" wine-and-food book. Other books are extensively researched treatises on wine and devote a meager page or two to the subject of wine pairing—and that only out of obligation.

Many of these books are written at two extremes of imparting information about wine. At one extreme, the books that are available are incredibly basic, often written in a first-person narrative and even comedic style and not very academic for an educational institution. At the other extreme are books written by wine experts for other wine experts, without regard to the level of comprehension or to whether they can give the reader a foundation of wine knowledge to build upon. These books, while certainly informative, are written at such a complex level that they require the novice wine reader to read and speak several foreign languages as he or she sifts through and pronounces foreign terms and relevant concepts. Also, such books sometimes require the reader to be an expert in geography and decipher maps detailing the most obscure wine-producing areas and vineyards in, for example, Burgundy, France. These books often leave the novice to intermediate wine reader confused or overwhelmed. The Essentials of Wine With Food Pairing Techniques doesn't contain all the information one needs to know about the topic of wine. There are many advanced books available for enhanced knowledge, but this text provides a solid foundation that will prepare the reader for those other books.

Whom This Book Is for . . .

The Essentials of Wine with Food-Pairing Techniques is ideal for anyone who desires a strong, solid foundation to understanding wine, as well as wine and food pairing. The book is targeted not only at students who are presently enrolled in culinary or hospitality management programs, but also for individuals working within the restaurant industry and salespeople in wine retail. The book will be useful to the novice cook, but also to the culinary student and the seasoned chef. The Essentials of Wine with Food-Pairing Techniques will be most valuable (though, not necessary) to those who have some initial foundation in a basic culinary training because of the pervasive theme of wine and food pairing throughout.

The book strives to demystify wine and food pairing. A difficulty of many wine textbooks is their inadequate coverage of information about food, while food textbooks don't cover enough about wine. This leaves a large gap in wine and food education, but also an opportunity to bridge that gap.

There appears to be a dichotomy of wine perspectives out there in the world. Certain people espouse the idea that wine shouldn't be a routine drink: In drinking wine, rituals and customs go with the wine experience. Other wine drinkers champion the notion that wine is simply another beverage for enjoyment, and barriers that limit access and consumption should be avoided as much as possible. As an avid wine drinker, I value both approaches and see no right or wrong with either as the motivation and meaning of wine is different for every individual who consumes it. If I could make one suggestion, it would be the following: Pour a glass of your favorite wine to sip as you read these pages. Allow this book to uncover all the intrigue, seduction, and complexity that wine has to offer. If it hasn't already, it is my hope that you permit wine to enrich your life as it has mine.

ABOUT THE AUTHOR

John Peter Laloganes

John has worked in the restaurant industry since the mid-1980s and works avidly with Chicago restaurants and related establishments in assisting them to become more successful.

He has taken extensive coursework in culinary arts, earned a bachelor's degree in hospitality and tourism management from the University of Wisconsin–Stout and a master's degree from the University of Minnesota. John was an associate professor at the Cooking and Hospitality Institute of Chicago–Le Cordon Bleu schools, he earned the "Educator of the Year" award in 2004 and the "Customer Service Award" from North American Le Cordon Bleu Schools in 2005. John also was awarded the distinctive Sommelier Diploma (level III) through the International Sommelier Guild (ISG) in 2007.

John is currently a sommelier/management instructor at the International Culinary School at the Illinois Institute of Art–Chicago and, in addition, teaches wine fundamentals, levels I and II, for the International Sommelier Guild.

John is a current member of the Society of Wine Educators (SWE), the American Culinary Federation (ACF), and the National Restaurant Association (NRA). Feel free to visit John's web-site at www.johnlaloganes.com or blog-site at www.laloganes.blogspot.com for additional informational resources and services.

ACKNOWLEDGMENTS

The construction of any textbook is the result of dozens, if not hundreds, of different people pulling together. This book is a collection of efforts from so many different individuals through the years, some of whom I have never met and some of whom I have had the pleasure of meeting at different points throughout my life. For those who have assisted me through this project, but whom I may have failed to mention, I thank you, too.

I would like to acknowledge the following individuals (not in any particular order) for their assistance:

Cheryl Kabb, for initially getting this project rolling and to Bill Lawrensen, for making it all happen. This book would never have been possible if not for your seeing the need for an accessible, user-friendly text about wine and food pairing.

Sharon Hughes, for your guidance and support throughout the review process. Your encouraging nature and helpful advice were always beneficial.

Julie Mason, for your assistance with image procurement. Thanks for adding a dimension to the textbook that would not have occurred without you.

Thomas Moore, for your excellent and speedy development of some fantastic maps.

Janel Syron, for providing me with the opportunity to have intelligent wine conversations on a regular basis.

Kerri Williams—a huge thanks—for your assistance with providing feedback on the dessert chapter and for the development of some support materials.

Tara Jobe, for your dedication in helping me complete the initial draft, oh so long ago!

Chef Mark Facklam, Chef Alisa Sattler, and Mr. Bert Lindstrom, for your support and encouragement that help me balance all the crazy stuff in life and allow me to do what I do best in the classroom.

Jamie Kluz, for your always inspiring approach to living life and your memorable quote, ". . .such a sexy, challenging and complex thing wine is!"

Peter D'Souza (from University of Wisconsin-Stout), Evan Saviolidis (from WineSavvy Consultants (www.winesavvy.ca), and Wayne Gotts (from International Sommelier Guild) for being inspiring and knowledgable wine educators.

Denise and Martin Cody, for providing me an additional opportunity to educate consumers about wine. You both continue to work to demystify wine for the public—and you do it with such tireless enthusiasm.

Thanks to the reviewers for all of their insightful comments. They are Marc DeMarchena, *Johnson & Wales University;* Brian Hay, *Austin Community College;* Dr. William Jaffe, *Purdue University;* Ken Jarvis, *Anne Arundel Community College;* Dr. Joe LaVilla, *Art Institute of Phoenix;* Greg Lemaire, *Manchester Community College;* Joe McCully, *Lane Community College;* Robert Pierson, *W. Delaware Valley College* and Sue Slater, *Cabrillo College.*

Edyta and Amelia, for your patience and support. I missed way too many trips to the park :)

Mrs. Cooney (my eighth-grade math teacher). Your prediction was obviously incorrect.

WEB RESOURCES

All Purpose

www.state.il.us/lcc/

The Alcohol and Tobacco Tax and Trade Bureau (TTB)

http://www.ttb.gov/appellation/index.shtml

Wine Institute of California

www.wineinstitute.org

Local wine events that can be searched internationally, by individual state or city.

http://www.localwineevents.com

Grape Radio

http://www.graperadio.com/

UNIT 1—The Basics of Wine

Riedel Stemware Company

http://www.riedel.com

UNIT 2—Wine and Food Compatibility

Food recipes from *Bon Appetit* and *Gourmet* magazines

http://www.epicurious.com/

UNIT 3—Wines of the New World

Wine Trade Group

http://www.wineinstitute.org/

American Wine Trade Group

http://www.wineamerica.org/

Wines of Napa Valley

http://www.napavintners.com/

Wine Appellation

http://wine.appellationamerica.com/wine-region-index.aspx

Wines of Monterey

http://www.montereywines.org

Wines of Sonoma

http://www.sonomawine.com

Wines of Washington State

http://www.washingtonwine.org/

Wines of New York State

http://www.newyorkwines.org/

Wines of Oregon State

http://www.oregonwine.org

Wines of Canada

http://www.canadianvintners.com/woc/index.html

Wines of British Columbia

http://www.winebc.com/

Wines of South Africa

http://www.wosa.co.za/

Wines of Chile

http://www.winesofchile.org/

http://www.chileinfo.com

Wines of Argentina

http://www.winesofargentina.org/

Wines of Australia

http://www.wineaustralia.com/australia/

Wines of New Zealand

http://www.nzwine.com/

UNIT 4—Wines of the Old World

Wines of France

http://www.frenchwinesfood.com/

Wines of Alsace

http://www.vinsalsace.com/en/index.html

Wines of Loire Valley

http://www.loirevalleywine.com/

Wines of Bordeaux

http://www.bordeaux.com/

Wines of Beaujolais

http://www.beaujolais.com/eng/page.htm

Wines of Rhône Valley

http://www.rhone-wines.com/pages/home-en.asp

Wines of Provence

http://www.provenceweb.fr/e/mag/terroir/vin/

Wines of Banyuls and Collioure

http://www.banyuls.com/banyuls/

Wines of Spain

http://www.winesfromspainusa.com

http://www.winesfromspain.com

Wines of Germany

http://www.germanwineusa.org/

Wines of Portugal

http://www.vinhoverde.pt/en/default.asp

Wines of Austria

http://www.winesfromaustria.com/eindex.php

UNIT 5—Other Types of Wine

The official website for Champagne

http://www.champagne.com/en_indx.html

Office of Champagne, USA

http://www.champagne.us/

The Port and Douro Institute (IVDP)

http://www.ivp.pt/index.asp?idioma=1&

http://www.infoportwine.com/

Consejo Regulador de las denominaciones de Origen

http://www.sherry.org/en/intro.cfm?CFID=144672&
CFTOKEN=71113649

http://www.enjoysherry.com/sherry/index.html

Chocolate

http://www.fieldmuseum.org/Chocolate/exhibits.html

http://www.scharffenberger.com/

Wine Publications

Decanter magazine

http://www.decanter.com/

Wine Spectator magazine

www.winespectator.com

Wine X magazine

www.winexmagazine.com/

Food and Wine magazine

www.foodandwine.com

Wine Enthusiast magazine

http://www.winemag.com/homepage/index.asp

Wine and Spirits magazine

www.wineandspiritsmagazine.com

Unit 1
THE BASICS OF WINE

"... from so simple a beginning endless forms most beautiful and most wonderful have been, and are being, evolved".
—Charles Darwin

1

Introduction to Wine

Whether a wine is modest or distinguished, it's intended for pleasure; yet somehow, it unfortunately has developed a mystique and pretentious image that many people find intimidating.

LEARNING OBJECTIVES

Upon completion of this chapter, the learner will be able to:

- Understand the basic composition of a grape and its contributions to a wine.
- Identify each of the three distinctive categories and several styles of wine.
- Comprehend the broad distinctions between the Old and New Worlds.
- Discern clues about a wine through various bottle shapes and colors.
- Identify common wine closures as well as advantages and disadvantages of each.
- Recognize the distinctions between glassware for the different categories and types of wine.
- Identify the four approaches for labelling table wine.
- Discover the five most significant components of information found on wine labels.

THEN AND NOW OF THE WINE INDUSTRY

There is evidence that, originally, wine was made as early as 6000 BC and is thought to have originated in the Middle East. It is believed that the Greeks were making wine around 4500 BC and that they eventually influenced the Romans. The Roman Empire is, in turn, largely responsible for influencing the spread of the grapevine throughout Europe and the Mediterranean.

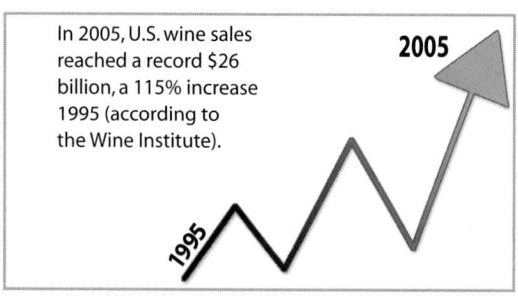

In 2005, U.S. wine sales reached a record $26 billion, a 115% increase 1995 (according to the Wine Institute).

FIGURE 1–1 Increase in U.S. wine sales
(Thomas Moore)

Some 8000 years later, the popularity and consumption of wine throughout the world and, in particular, the United States has reached new heights. This success is evident in the overall upward demand for wine in the United States and certain other countries throughout the world. In 2005, U.S. wine sales reached a record $26 billion, a 115% increase since 1995 (according to the Wine Institute). The American wine industry has maintained 14 years of consecutive sales growth, with over 304 million cases consumed in 2007 (according to Wine Impact Group) (see Figure 1–1).

The food wholesaler COSTCO, which operates a chain of international warehouses, is currently the nation's largest retailer of wine, with over $700 million in wine sales. This upward consumption of wine is becoming more evident, and current data indicate that America will overtake France as the world's largest consumer of wine by volume in 2015. In all likelihood, by that year France will still have the United States beat in per-capita wine consumption, as it does today: The average French person outdrinks the average American by nearly eight to one.

The United States is home to over 5,000 wineries spread through all 50 states. This state of affairs is dramatic, considering that the U.S. government implemented prohibition from 1920 to 1933, making it illegal to produce, distribute, or consume any alcohol (with a few exceptions) in the nation. The wine industry was near dead, with only a handful of wineries surviving to produce wine for sacramental purposes.

It wasn't until 1975 that the industry started to gain back some growth; that year, there were 579 wineries in the United States. With this slight revival of U.S. wine, France and Italy ruled the market, and the majority of American wine states and New World countries and regions were unknown. Then, in the course of 20 years, the wine industry experienced explosive growth and vast changes. As the eighties approached, wine consumption increased with the coming of age of the new wine consumer known as the *"Baby Boomer"*. The popularity carried throughout the nineties, but the dominant American wine consumed was low-quality jug wine named after classic European wine regions such as Burgundy or Chianti. Then wine consumption saw another explosion in 1991 after the CBS news program *60 Minutes* reported on the "French Paradox," an inconsistency of lifestyles and rates of heart disease among people in America and France. This report provided evidence of medical benefits derived from the moderate consumption of wine. These newly discovered advantages have led people to drink wine more now than ever before. As the new millennium approached and the industry matured, the majority of wine consumed became grape name or "varietally" labelled and newly evolved wine cultures from countries such as New Zealand, Australia, Chile, Argentina, and South Africa, together with the United States, had an impressive impact on the wine industry, setting new standards and styles for the wine-drinking public.

The New Wine Consumer

A 2006 Gallup poll study from several different age groups named "wine" as America's most preferred alcoholic beverage. The study identified 39% of respondents claiming wine as their alcoholic beverage of choice, compared with 36% for beer and 21% for spirits. Unfortunately, these results were short lived as the study has been repeated to only have beer regain its "number one" status. The study does illustrate the ground that wine has gained in reputation. Wine's popularity is partly propelled by a nontraditional wine consumer: individuals in their twenties and thirties known as the "*Millennials.*" These young adults are showing the same interest in wine as their baby boomer parents, who originally fueled a previous wine explosion in the early eighties. The Millennials have become a significant growth factor in the wine industry, as the popularity of wine has trickled down to this new generation of wine drinkers. The millenials acquire approximately 25% of total wine purchases and are more likely to spend an average of $20 and even more substantially on bottles of wine, particularly if they are living at home with parents (as many of them are), allowing them greater disposable income without sacrificing quality of life.

User-Friendly Approach

The popularity of wine is owed to numerous factors. To a large extent, it has been fueled by the accessibility of wine retail stores and restaurants that increasingly focus on hiring and training intelligent salespeople to help guide the consumer to an enjoyable wine selection and one that can enhance their dining experience. Some progressive restaurants and wine stores have designed wine menus in user-friendly formats, listing wines by "style" as opposed to "geographical origins". Some adventurous beverage managers have even coordinated the wine list with the food menu, offering useful recommendations after each description of food, to enhance the guest's experience.

New Styles of Wine

Other factors that contribute to increased acceptance and consumption of wine include the process of making wine in fruit-forward style. Many New World wines contain aromas and flavors that make them easy to drink, with or without food. Most of this wine is being produced to encourage a "drink it now" mentality. It's no longer necessary to bottle-age a wine and hold it for 5 or 10 years, as has been the tradition associated with old world wines.

Reasonably Priced, Yet Good Quality, Options

Many wine countries, such as Australia, Chile, New Zealand, and the United States, are making wines of good value that encourage consumption on a daily basis. This notion is illustrated by some of the successful brands, such as Charles Shaw (California) or Yellow Tail (Australia), which retail anywhere from $3 to $10 a bottle. Wine options at this price point dismiss the mentality that consumers should wait and drink wine only for special occasions; instead, they encourage buyers to consume as often as they desire.

A new breed of wine stores has exploded with popularity, offering value wine largely near or below the $25 price point. The international wine chain "WineStyles" has been designed to be user friendly in the staging of their wine. The customer is greeted with wines categorized according to eight styles that describe the basic personality and characteristics of the wine.

Packaging and Closures

Wine is being bottled with easy-to-read and eye-catching colorful labelling. Some producers have redesigned the bottle in an effort to make it easy to open, store, and transport. Screw-cap closures, single-serve bottles, and better quality bag-in-box allow consumers to drink wine in nontraditional situations and places, such as the beach, park, and sporting events, without the concerns of breaking a glass bottle or having to aquire a special tool to open

This photo represents wine having gained considerable popularity, allowing it to be viewed as more of an everyday beverage around the world instead of one only being reserved for the fine-dining restaurant.
(Lluís Real/AGE Fotostock America, Inc.)

the container. Screw–cap closures have gained considerable popularity, allowing wine to be viewed as more of an everyday beverage, but have also been criticized by some wine aficionados as an abomination to tradition.

Direct Shipping

Direct-shipping laws allow wineries to ship wines to consumers, though not in all states. This is important because many small wineries do not have the means to market or sell their wines in any other way. The Internet has provided greater accessibility and a venue for consumers to scout out small producers, who then legally can ship the product directly to customers at their front door.

Changing Eating Habits

Throughout thousands of years, wine has evolved with cuisine, and at one time in our modern world, classical French cuisine was the rage. The idea of matching wine with food had mostly been tied to a natural connection of evolution of regional cuisines. However, over the last decade, American eating patterns changed dramatically, with globalization exerting an ever-growing influence on contemporary cuisine. Americans have turned food into a hobby. With the success of restaurant and food television shows and the heightened status of *chef* as a profession, people have become more experienced in terms of restaurant usage, menu items, ingredients, seasonings, and spices. More Americans are growing up with ethnic flavors and are well traveled, which makes the world a much smaller place. In fact, salsa surpassed ketchup as the "number-one" condiment in America back in 1991. The culinary landscape has been rapidly expanding as new cuisines, flavors, and ingredients (such as North African, Peruvian, Indian, etc.) evolve and become more mainstream in the United States.

In 2008, "world cuisine" was available to most Americans on television without their ever having to leave home to experience it. In any medium-sized to large city, we are likely to walk down the street and find a Thai restaurant next door to an Italian restaurant, and a few doors down is a hot dog stand. The influx of immigrant food ingredients and cuisines, and Americans' diverse experiences, are contributing to more discerning tastes and to not only an understanding of food, but also a desire to drink wine and find wine that pairs well with the food. Diners are becoming more adventurous, and American palates more knowledgeable, than ever before. Food and wine pairing has become less about the classical combinations and more about matching a type and style of wine with what is being eaten at the moment.

World Wine Producers

As of 2006, the top five wine-producing countries—France, Italy, Spain, the United States, and Argentina—produced over 178,133 hectoliters, representing 62.8% of the world's wine production.

2006 COUNTRY RANK	HECTOLITERS	PERCENTAGE OF MARKET
1. ITALY	52,036	18.3
2. FRANCE	51,700	18.2
3. SPAIN	39,301	13.9
4. UNITED STATES	19,700	6.9
5. ARGENTINA	15,396	5.4
World Production	283,600	100.0

Source: International Organisation of Vine and Wine, *OIV State of the Vitiviniculture World Report*, March 2007.

♦ In Europe, Canada, and the South American countries, wine production figures are commonly expressed in hectoliters (hl), equal to 100 liters, or 26.418 U.S. gallons.

World Wine Consumers

As of 2006, the top five wine-consuming countries—France, Italy, the United States, Germany, and Spain—consumed over 119,500 hectoliters, representing 49.6% of the world's wine consumption. A study conducted by VINEXPO (the largest wine trade organization), in conjunction with IWSR (a leading London-based beverage research organization), forecasts that by 2015, the United States will overtake France and Italy as the world's largest wine consumer.

2006 COUNTRY RANK	HECTOLITERS	PERCENTAGE OF MARKET
1. FRANCE	32,800	13.6
2. ITALY	27,300	11.3
3. UNITED STATES	25,900	10.8
4. GERMANY	19,850	8.2
5. SPAIN	13,650	5.7
Forecasted World Consumption	240,800	100.0

Source: International Organisation of Vine and Wine, *OIV State of the Vitiviniculture World Report*, March 2007.

Summary

Many factors are contributing to the continued increased growth of wine, including the perception and acceptance of wine as a part of everyday life. Indeed, wine is becoming a part of mainstream society in America, something that for decades has been a part of everyday life in European wine countries such as France, Italy, and Spain.

THE NOVICE WINE CONSUMER

Whether a wine is modest or distinguished, it's intended for pleasure; yet somehow, it unfortunately has developed a mystique and pretentious image that many people find intimidating. The world of wine can be frightening for restaurant and retail customers, employees, and students of wine. The common belief is that one has to be an expert or connoisseur to appreciate wine. Ultimately, as with all matters of taste (music, food, or clothing, for example), wine is a matter of preference, but appreciating wine takes experience. To truly understand wine and, even more, to comprehend how it can integrate with food (this is the good news), one must continue to experiment and taste it. With enough patience and practice, it's possible for a wine drinker to develop a palate and truly identify and differentiate the subtle or significant nuances associated with wine. Presented next are some perspectives that may be useful for the novice and intermediate wine drinker to reference in beginning or continuing his or her exploration in understanding the somewhat complex world of wine.

Perspective 1: There Is No Bad Wine

Take comfort in knowing that there is no one ideal wine or style of wine for everyone. This truism is evident in the thousands of different wines produced around the world that individuals enjoy or appreciate. Culture can influence adult taste preferences, and Americans raised over the last 40 years have typically been raised on milk, juice, or soda drinks at mealtime and throughout the day. Therefore, it's likely and quite common for beginning wine drinkers to gravitate and appreciate wines with greater sweetness and little complexity associated with them. Even if there is a wine that one may find too simple or too sweet for personal tastes, know that someone, somewhere, is drinking it. Also, wine still has other applications other than drinking. Wine can be a very important culinary ingredient. Ultimately, people have a right to like what they like, whether or not it's a style that is preferred by the mass wine consumers and collectors around the world.

Perspective 2: There Is a Wine for Every Purpose

In some situations, a wine may not pair well with food items as presented on a menu, but it may still have some application in the kitchen or as a part of another beverage. For example, it's possible to use a wine as an ingredient in a food marinade, as part of a cooking liquid, or in a sauce to accompany a food item. For Friday evening a Chardonnay can be combined with cassis to create a wine cocktail called "Kir" or Sunday mornings, sparkling wine can be added to orange juice to create a Mimosa.

Perspective 3: The Wine Drinker's Palate Is the Only One That Matters

Wine ratings conducted by professional evaluators may be considered a useful tool; however, they should not necessarily be the defining influence. A wine rating may be the equivalent of a film critic rating a new movie release. The critic may declare, "Thumbs up"; however, the movie might not be enjoyed and held in the same opinion by the average moviegoer. Similarly, if a wine critic declared a particular wine "excellent" or "90+ points," this doesn't necessarily guarantee enjoyment by every wine consumer. Wine ratings have played a role in facilitating wine purchases for some people, but caution is advised when using them as the only source to make wine decisions.

In 2006, the results of a survey of 869 wine drinkers were published in *Nation's Restaurant News,* offering some interesting statistics about the views and preferences of these wine consumers (See Figure 1–2). An important objective of this textbook is to address many of the issues and to demystify wine in order to help the reader more effectively understand, comprehend, and communicate the story of wine to others. The communication can happen in multiple ways, depending on the situation. It could occur in a classroom with a teacher and a student, in a restaurant or store with a server or retail salesperson and a customer, at the workplace with a manager and an employee, or just about

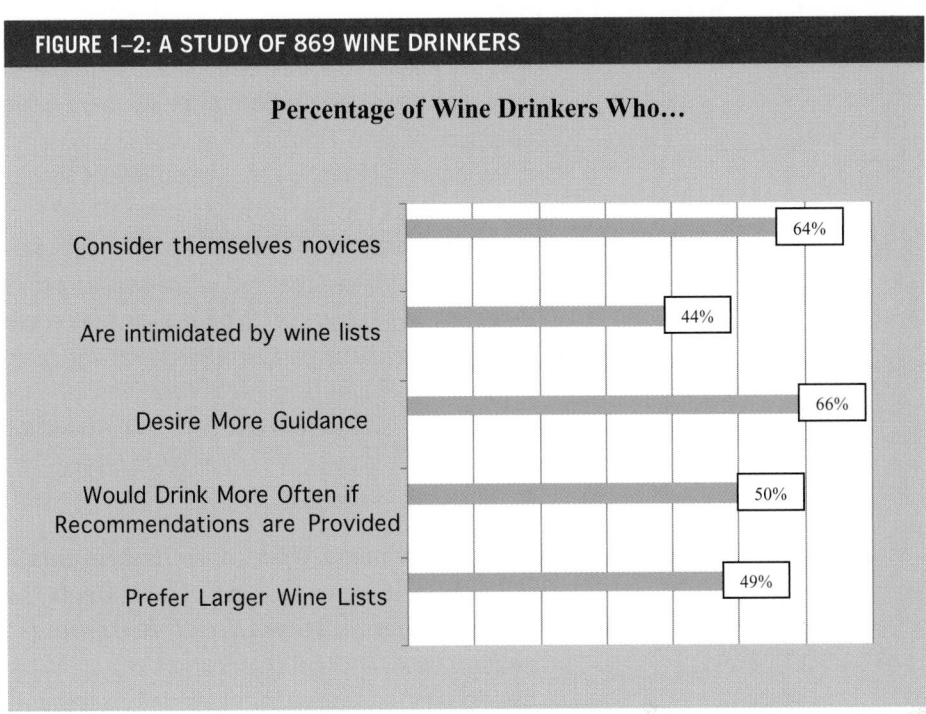

FIGURE 1–2: A STUDY OF 869 WINE DRINKERS

Percentage of Wine Drinkers Who...

Consider themselves novices — 64%

Are intimidated by wine lists — 44%

Desire More Guidance — 66%

Would Drink More Often if Recommendations are Provided — 50%

Prefer Larger Wine Lists — 49%

(Russel Research, New York)

anywhere between friends. Presented next is a bit of perspective on the results of this study that may provide insight into the state of wine being sold and consumed in restaurants and retail stores. Hopefully, it raises some cautionary flags to the saleperson who is directly assisting the consumer in making wine decisions and to the manager who is accountable for producing wine revenue.

"64% of 869 Wine Drinkers Classified Themselves as Novices When It Comes to Their Wine Knowledge"—This statistic should identify some of the challenges for the frontline service employees who suggest and/or sell wine to others. It points to the fact that many consumers desire guidance on some level when selecting wine. Here are some relevant questions that can be used by the salesperson making decisions about which wines to sell to customers:

- Are you looking for a wine to pair with dinner or to drink by itself? If with dinner, what will you be ordering for dinner? Do you have a certain price parameter in mind? What kind of wine do you usually enjoy?

Once a salesperson can discover the type and style of wine a consumer enjoys, it's possible to now suggest different producers, regions, or comparable grape varietals, just as it's possible to seek out new variations on a genre in art, film, or music. It's an effective way for a wine drinker to develop the palate and gain a sense of stylistic differences. For example, someone who enjoys the rock group the Rolling Stones may also appreciate the sounds of Pete Townsend and The Who.

Encouraging a salesperson to ask wine drinkers the appropriate set of questions allows the salesperson to determine an adequate and sometimes even a great wine selection. The goal of the saleperson is to identify a wine selection that can suit the personal taste preferences and meal selection of the customer.

"44% of These Wine Drinkers Indicated That They Often Feel Intimidated by Wine Lists at Restaurants"—It's amazing how the novice wine consumer can make any sort of intelligent wine decision based on the wine lists or, in some cases, wine catalogues offered in some restaurants. Most wine stores are filled with endless aisles of shelves that may be labelled merely by a country, offering little helpful information about the style or type of wine. How are consumers supposed to be able to comprehend a wine list and the entire geographical mystique, foreign languages, and unfamiliar words that are necessary in order to identify many of the wines? Some progressive restaurants and wine shops are beginning to address this concern with user-friendly wine lists that have been organized by either wine styles or food-pairing recommendations. But the vast majority seem to expect the wine consumer to have taken wine courses or to have a degree in geography, French, or Italian. The paradigm has been designed to confuse the novice wine drinker and discourage future purchases. Whether a customer is in a wine shop or a restaurant, the goal, of course, should be to sell wine to make money, but also to ensure that the customer is satisfied with his or her selection and, hopefully, with the least amount of pain in the attempt to select a wine.

"66% of Customers Wish More Restaurants Would Provide More Guidance in Choosing Wine to Go with Their Meals," and "50% of Respondents Said They Would Drink More Often if Restaurants Provided Recommendations"—Wine (or, indeed, any beverage) can be one of the biggest moneymakers for a restaurant. It has become imperative for chefs and managers—but most importantly, the frontline worker who is selling and making suggestions—to understand what wine is and how it can enhance a diner's experience. Unfortunately, in some restaurants and wine stores it's difficult for managers and chefs to provide guidance and training to their staff. Common reasons for this are that they don't understand wine or they lack the ability to effectively communicate and provide training to the people who sell wine.

There is a famous saying in the hospitality industry: "If you are not serving the customer, then serve the person who is." By learning more about wine, the manager is equipped to assist others with well-informed and satisfying wine-related decisions. Also, chefs and managers may be accountable for the revenue and cost control of wine or other beverages within the wine store or restaurant. These individuals may be responsible for creating wine lists, purchasing wine, storing and issuing wine, training staff on wine, pairing wine with the daily specials, conducting wine seminars, designing wine dinners, etc. For many restaurants, these are opportunities to attract new customers and stimulate sales through understanding and promoting wine.

"49% of Participants Said They Would Prefer Restaurants with Large Wine Selections"—This particular statistic is a bit baffling, considering that a large percentage of consumers (according to this study) are confused with the current state of wine programs. If one is confused, why desire to add more confusion by having a larger wine selection? Perhaps what wine drinkers are referencing (and this is purely speculative) is their preference that a restaurant or wine store offer ample options to more effectively suit their particular needs. It's unfortunate, but many wine stores stock shelves with wines that are enjoyed by the manager and only minimally alter or adapt to consumer trends or up-and-coming wine-producing regions or producers. And similarly, restaurants may develop wine lists that are never changed again. A stagnant wine selection that doesn't evolve or adapt can create a waning guest. Increasing options should include having a wine-by-the-glass program, offering half-bottle selections, providing a sample taste, and so on. A wine selection should keep up with the times and evolve with that of the customer base.

Final Comments on This Study—Perhaps the insight of this study speaks to us about current practices of how wine is marketed and sold across America. Possibly, the current approaches and practices should be rethought. Granted, U.S. wine sales are increasing, as are the number of wine stores and restaurants. But could wine sales and customer satisfaction be increased? By taking a new approach, wine sellers can educate and guide the consumer without embarrassment and intimidation, and that can demystify wine's sometimes pretentious image. Ultimately, this more "suitable" approach can provide the consumer with a more enjoyable experience, and in the process, the beverage operation can produce more revenue.

WHAT IS WINE?

Wine is, very simply, an agricultural product produced from the fermented juice of fruit. It's almost always the fermented juice of grapes (legally, unless otherwise specified), although apples, blackberries, rhubarb, and other fruits can be substituted. On the surface, grapes are no different from tomatoes or olives. Taking a step further, all fruits, including grapes, have several varieties or types that can yield a multitude of different personalities. A wine's personality is derived from several different stages throughout the production process, wherein thousands of different compounds influence aromas, flavors, body, and more. This is what makes each grape unique, with its own set of performance factors. Some of the personality-influencing compounds are inherent in the original grape and its juice; others are created during fermentation or through processing or aging methods.

Wine Defined

Wine grapes, in some ways, are just like people. Some individuals grow up in the suburbs, others in the city. Depending on where grapes grow up, they can be influenced and molded the same way a person can be, according to their surroundings. On the surface, people are all the same: human beings. However, as one learns more about them, it becomes obvious that individuals are different. The same holds true for wine grapes: On the surface they contain skins, pulp, seeds, and stems, and like people, they have been influenced partially by their environment. Grapes deliver their distinctiveness in many ways: their color (red, white, or rosé), body (lightness to fullness), aroma and flavor (fruit, to vegetables, to tobacco shop), and texture (acidity, sweetness, spiciness and bitterness). Wine can be made from a single grape varietal or a blend of different complementary grapes. The grape variety, or blend of grapes, will impart a specific style or personality into a wine. *Table grapes* are a basic agricultural product that yields about $1.50 per pound, but *wine grapes* can deliver a complexity that can yield anywhere from $3.00 to $16,000 a bottle, and sometimes even more.

Wine grapes are generally described as either white or red. White wine grapes are not actually white, but any shade between green and an amber-yellow. White wine can also be made from red grapes that have had the skins removed from the juice and pulp before fermentation begins.

Red wine grapes are generally not actually red, but instead can range from blue to deep purple-black. Red wine can also be made from a blend of red and white wine grapes. The red grape skins remain with the juice and pulp during fermentation and provide color.

Rosé wine is made either from a blend of red and white wine or from the more common process known as the French "Saignée" (san-YAY) method, allowing some of the color from red grape skins to bleed into the fermenting juice, creating a pinkish color.

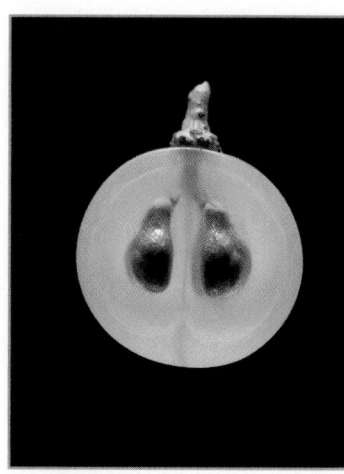

FIGURE 1–3 Pulp of a Chardonnay grape

(Collection CIVC. Photographer: CORNU Alain)

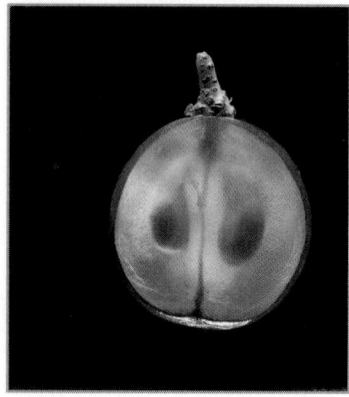

FIGURE 1–4 Pulp of a Pinot Noir grape

(Collection CIVC. Photographer: CORNU Alain)

The grape is made of three major components: pulp, skin, and seeds/stems. Figure 1–3 and 1–4 are sample cross sections of a white wine grape and red wine grape.

Pulp—(Pulp is found on the inside of the grape, where the juice, acid, sugar, and flavor can be found.) Pulp makes up approximately 75% of a grape by weight. It plays a major role in providing acid, which is present in the juice, and is pivotal to giving both red and white wine good structure. A wine without acid falls flat on the palate and has a difficult time standing up to food when they are paired together. When a wine has inadequate acid, it is frequently referred to as *flat* or *flabby*. A flabby wine is often lost when paired with an otherwise compatible food item.

Skin—(Skin is on the outside of the grape, where the tannin, flavor, and color can be found.) Skin makes up approximately 20% of the grape by weight. Skin plays a greater influence on the style and structure of a red wine, which are achieved when the skins are allowed to ferment with the juice. Anthocyanins (ann-thoa-SY-ann-inns) and other natural pigment chemicals found in the skins of red wine grapes are responsible for contributing the color to a wine.

Grape skins also contribute tannin to a red wine. The tannin is pivotal to providing a red wine with good structure and aging potential. Tannin is a compound that causes the same dry feeling on the tongue and around the gum line that one feels after drinking black, heavily steeped tea. Tannin content varies with grape variety and wine style. Like a wine with insufficient acid, a red wine without adequate tannin falls flat on the palate and is often referred to as *flat* or *flabby*. (Tannin is discussed in greater detail in Chapter 2, "Wine Tasting". The contribution of grape skins in the winemaking process is discussed in greater detail in Chapter 3, "Viticulture and Enology.")

Seeds and Stems—(Seeds are found on inside and stems are found on the outside of the grape and may contribute a bitter component if crushed or used in excess.) Stems and seeds contribute approximately 5% of the grape by weight. In most cases, they are a minor component of a wine, but can have a pronounced negative influence if handled poorly. Seeds and stems can yield an undesirable bitterness to the finished wine if the grapes have been handled too harshly in the harvesting and production process.

CATEGORIES OF WINE

Wine may be broadly divided into three groups (see Figure 1–5):

1. **Table Wine**—This category of wine gets its name because it's made to be drunk at the table with meals. The alcoholic content of table wine generally is between 8% and 15%. Table wines are white, pink, or red wines that can be dry, sweet, or somewhere in between.

2. **Sparkling Wine**—This category of wine consists of a table wine as the base, with the addition of large amounts of CO_2 for carbonation. Sparkling wine typically contains between 10% and 13% alcohol. The most prestigious of all sparkling wines is Champagne. However, many other sparkling wines of varying quality are produced throughout the world and can rival the excellence of Champagne.

    Sparkling wine can be made into white, pink, or red wine that can be dry, sweet, or somewhere in between. However, the majority of sparkling wines are white and made into a dry style. It's possible to find options of varying levels of sweetness, particularly from Italian and German sparkling wines.

3. **Fortified Wines**—This category of wine consists of table wine as the base, with additional alcohol (in the form of a distilled spirit—often an unaged brandy) added.

Fortified wine typically contains between 17% and 22% alcohol, and it's possible to have white or red options that can be made into dry, sweet, or somewhere in between.

Dry—Drier fortified wines are commonly consumed prior to a meal as an aperitif to help stimulate the appetite and cleanse the palate.

Sweet—Sweeter fortified wines are commonly consumed after a meal for satiety or fullness.

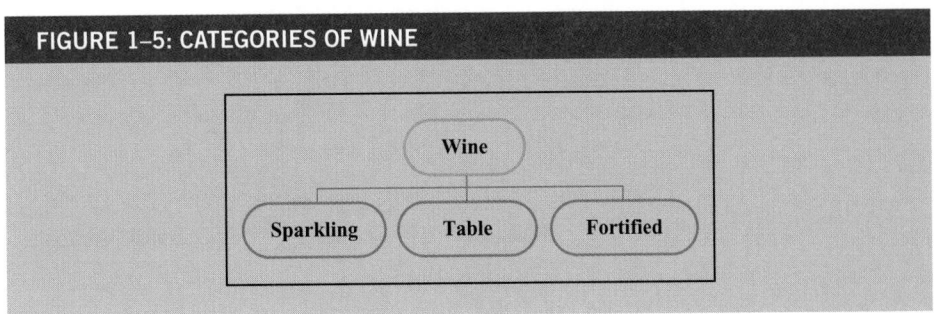

FIGURE 1–5: CATEGORIES OF WINE

All wine categories have specific production methods that will be discussed and expanded upon throughout this book.

WINES OF THE OLD WORLD VS. WINES OF THE NEW WORLD

The world of wine has expanded from its origins in Europe to new possibilities in the far west. For the grapes to truly flourish and ripen appropriately, they need warmth, sunshine, and water, but not too much of any one. These conditions are located primarily between the latitudes of 30° and 50° north, and 30° and 50° south, of the equator. In some cases, grapes are found in areas that don't normally grow a quality wine grape; however, these areas will have mitigating influences such as varying elevation levels, coastal waters, and rivers that all help moderate temperature extremes. Figure 1–6 highlights the significant wine-producing countries throughout the world.

There are two broad schools of thought and practice in the wine world, and they are identified by broad geographic concepts: Old World and New World. These designations separate the wines by geography, but also by a perspective that stylistically will affect the wines. What follows are generalizations between the two worlds; however, drawing similarities and differences between the two assists in the broad understanding of wine concepts.

Old World: Primarily Inside Europe

The Old World references the long-established tradition of winemaking within the European countries of France, Italy, Germany, and Spain. These countries have nurtured and developed many of the vines and winemaking techniques that form the foundation for modern practices of wine throughout the world. The Old World generally believes in the terroir (tehr-WHAR) concept. *Terroir* loosely translates to the connection to the land. Since grapes are the product of the earth (or soil), they will have characteristic aromas and flavors tying them to the land in which they are grown. In Europe, the region also often predetermines how the wine must be made.

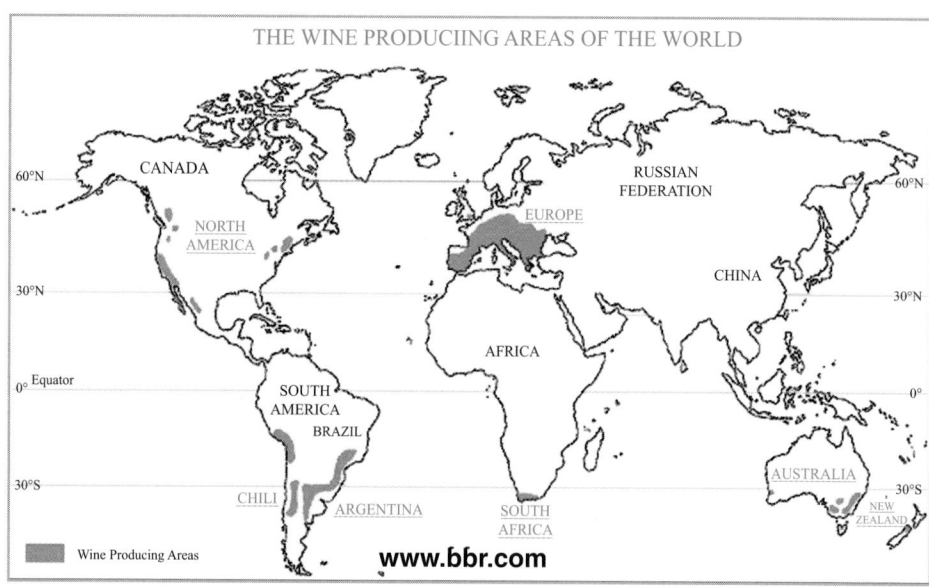

FIGURE 1–6 Wine producing areas of the world
(Berry Bros & Rudd)

New World: Primarily Outside Europe

The New World is a concept used primarily to reference the wine-producing countries of America, Canada, Australia, Argentina, Chile, South Africa, and New Zealand, which have a relatively brief history and culture associated with grape growing and wine production. These countries were settled within the last 500 years or so and are known as some of the most significant New World wine-producing countries. The grapevines and some techniques were transported into them by European settlers and through trade and wars. In the New World, producers aren't bound by tradition, instead they can utilize different techniques and can radically alter the style of wine from one vintage to the next or as they see fit.

Climate Influences

Climates within both the Old and New Worlds have a large influence on the development of grapes. (The topic of climate's influence on wine grapes is discussed in greater detail in Chapter 3, "Viticulture and Enology.") Aroma, flavor, and textural components (acid, tannin, sugar and, ultimately, after fermentation, alcohol) are dependent to some extent on the area where the grapes are grown, because vines are very sensitive to climate and soil.

COOL/WARM CLIMATES Cooler to warmer climates can suggest inconsistently ripened grapes that have not seen adequate warmth and/or sunshine throughout the growing season. The more slowly the grapes ripen, the richer is their aroma. Grapes grown farthest from the equator in both hemispheres are the most fragrant. Wines produced in this climate are often incredibly food friendly because of their substantial acidity and freshness.

In cool/warm climates, **GRAPES** are less pigmented, less consistently ripe, low in sugar, and high in acid, compared with identical grapes found in a warm/hot climates.

In cool/warm climates, **WINES** have the following characteristics compared with identical wines found in a warm/hot climates:

Sight. Pale to light in intensity, green tint to straw yellow in hue for white wines.
Smell/taste. Muted to highly aromatic; lighter, more subtle citrus; tree fruit, vegetables, herbs, and mineral aromas and flavors. These wines are often stainless steel aged or lightly oaked and are high in acidity and low in alcohol content.

WARM/HOT CLIMATES Warmer and hotter climates can suggest a ripe grape that has seen ample sunshine and/or heat during the growing season. Wines produced in this climate are often *easy drinking wines* and work well with or without the consumption of food.

In warm/hot climates, **GRAPES** are more pigmented, very ripe, higher in sugar, and lower in acid, compared with identical grapes found in cool/warm climates.

In warm/hot climates, **WINES** have the following characteristics compared with identical wines found in a cool/warm climate:

Sight. Medium in intensity, high straw to golden yellow in hue for white wines.
Smell/taste. Flavors that predominate with riper fruit and that suggest cooked or dried fruit rather than fresh-off-the-vine fruit. These wines are often oak aged and are lower in acidity with high alcohol content.

The following table summarizes the broad distinctions between Old World and New World wines:

CHARACTERISTICS	OLD WORLD	NEW WORLD
MAJOR COUNTRIES	France, Italy, Germany, and Spain	United States, Australia, New Zealand, Argentina, Chile, and South Africa
CLASSIC EXAMPLE	France	United States
VITICULTURE PERSPECTIVE	Strict laws define acceptable viticultural practices, depending on level of classification. Grape growing areas can be small and relatively fixed.	Limited laws regarding viticultural practices. Grape growing areas can be large and relatively flexible.
TERM FOR GEOGRAPHIC LOCATIONS	Appellations	American Viticultural Areas
WINEMAKING HISTORY	Thousands of years	Hundreds of years
WINEMAKING PHILOSOPHY	Traditional wines are made to reflect the local style. Intervene as little as possible.	Experimental wines are made to reflect an international style. Control the winemaking process in order to produce the best wine possible, given the raw material.
GRAPE DESIGNATIONS	Legally defined on the basis of appellations	Not legally defined
GENERAL STYLE	Subtle; more about finesse and complexity. Lower to medium alcohol levels. Expression of the individual terroir through the fruit.	Bolder, rich, and oaky, with great expression of fruit. Often made with medium to higher levels of alcohol—around 13% or more.
LABELLING PRACTICES	Primarily labels according to place of origin (or appellation)	Primarily labels according to the dominant grape found within the bottle
PRIMARY AROMAS / FLAVORS	Earth, barnyard, vegetable, mineral	Fruit

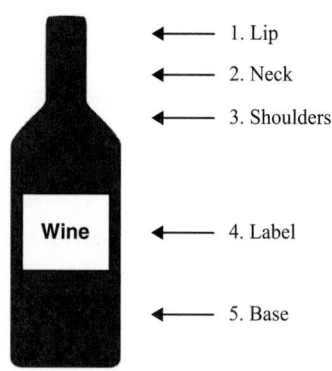

1. Lip
2. Neck
3. Shoulders
4. Label
5. Base

FIGURE 1–7 The anatomy of a wine bottle

WINE BOTTLE SHAPES

During the Greek and Roman periods, wine was originally transported in a two-handled vessel called an *amphorae* (ahm-FOR-uh). Possible evidence suggests that this was not only a crude form of a wine bottle, but also part of an early appellation system. The shape of the container could indicate the city or region, winemaker, and vintage of the wine. During the 1700s and 1800s, the glass bottle was invented. Once it became more durable, it was evident that wine could be aged in glass bottles to mature in flavor. Eventually, various bottles shapes were developed to hold different types of wine. The shapes of the bottles made it easy to identify the type or style of wine that was within each bottle. This became particularly useful if it wasn't possible to read the label. Today, the wine bottle can assist in the same way. Recognizing the bottle shape can quite possibly lead a wine drinker in the general direction of understanding the grapes or particular style of wine that might be found within.

Even before reading a wine label, it's possible to learn a large amount of information about a wine by examining the color and shape of a wine bottle that the wine is stored in. The shape and color of the bottle can provide some basic information about the region or country of origin and grape varietal within the bottle. Many wine regions have their traditional bottle shapes, and winemakers throughout the world typically respect the traditions of those wine regions and the grapes that are produced in them. Winemakers can choose any bottle shapes, but for recognition purposes, when winemakers anywhere in the world produce a wine from a grape from a particular traditional place, the bottle that the wine is sold in is usually consistent with the wine region.

Wine bottles have been used for centuries and appear in a variety of shapes and sizes, but have been standardized to generally contain 25.4 oz (750 ml) of liquid. The half-bottle (contains 12.7 oz/375 ml) has become popular over the last decade as an alternative to provide a source of high-quality wine for single diners. Figure 1–7 is an example of the anatomy of the bottle.

Bordeaux Wine Bottle

The Bordeaux bottle, shown in Figure 1–8, has straight sides with steep, tall, shoulders. It's an excellent shape for wines that tend to exude sediment (typically, old red wines and Bordeaux reds are known to age well) because the steep shoulders can serve to hold back the sediment as the wine is poured. This can be particularly useful if a decanter is not available.

FIGURE 1–8 Bordeaux wine bottle
(Thomas Moore)

RED WINE: The Bordeaux shape is the most common shape used for red wine around the world and is often found in dark green or black glass. Red wine grapes commonly found in this style of bottle include *Cabernet Sauvignon* (KAB-er-nay SOH-vin-NYOHN), *Merlot* (mehr-LOH), and *Zinfandel* (ZIN-fun-del).

WHITE WINE (Dry or Sweet): The Bordeaux shape can also be used for white wine in a light green or clear glass bottle. White wine grapes commonly found in this style of bottle include *Sauvignon Blanc* (SOH-vihn-YOHN BLAHNK), particularly if the wine is from Bordeaux or California, *Semillon* (seh-mee-YOHN) and Pinot Grigio (PEE-noh GREE-joh) when it comes from Italy.

Burgundy Wine Bottle

The Burgundy bottle, shown in Figure 1–9, typically is sturdy and heavy, with shallow, gentle sloping shoulders.

FIGURE 1–9 Burgundy wine bottle
(Thomas Moore)

RED WINE: The Burgundy shape can be used for red wine in a light green or black glass. Wine grapes found in this bottle include *Pinot Noir* (PEE-noh-NWAHR), *Gamay* (gah-MAY), and *Syrah* (SEAR-ah) and *Syrah blends*.

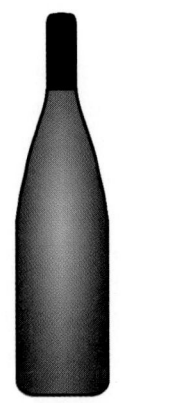

FIGURE 1–10 German wine bottle
(Thomas Moore)

FIGURE 1–11 Sparkling wine bottle
(Thomas Moore)

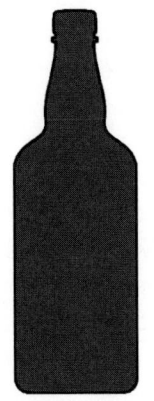

FIGURE 1–12 Fortified wine bottle
(Thomas Moore)

WHITE WINE: The Burgundy shape can also be used for white wine in a light green or clear glass bottle. Wines commonly found in this bottle include *Chardonnay* (SHAR-duh-nay) and *Sauvignon Blanc* (SOH-vihn-YOHN BLAHNK) when the bottle comes from New Zealand or Loire Valley France.

German Wine Bottle

This narrow, thin, tall bottle, shown in Figure 1–10, has a very gently sloping shoulder and is typically light green or brown in color. Some have brown glass for wine produced from the Rhine (RINE) region in Germany, and green glass for wine from the Mosel-Saar-Ruwer (MOH-zel sahr ROO-vayr) region in Germany.

WHITE WINE (Dry or Sweet): Wine grapes commonly found in this bottle include *Riesling* (REEZ-ling), *Gewurztraminer* (guh-VERTZ-trah-mean-er), and *Pinot Gris* (PEE-noh GREE) when it comes from Alsace, France.

Sparkling Wine Bottle

This bottle, shown in Figure 1–11, is made from a very thick glass, with gently sloping shoulders and a long neck. The sparkling wine bottle also contains a rather large *punt,* or indentation in the bottom of the bottle, to assist in durability. The punt is needed to help reduce the pressure felt along the bottom of the bottle.

Classic Champagne uses a blend of three grapes, including Chardonnay, Pinot Noir, and Pinot Meunier (muh-NYAY). Other sparkling wines from around the world may use the same or similar grapes.

Champagne bottles are designed with thick glass because of the need to withstand the high pressures exerted by the carbonation development after bottling. Pressures can yield 80–120 lbs per square inch (psi), approximately two to three times the pressure of a car tire.

Fortified Wine Bottle

Fortified wines such as Port, Madeira, and Sherry typically use sturdy bottles, as shown in Figure 1–12. Vintage Port may often have tall shoulders and a larger bulge in the neck to help capture the sediment when it is decanted. Often, these are wines that need many years to properly age and tend to contain some sediment.

With the exception of vintage or late-bottled vintage port, these bottles usually have a cork stopper rather than the traditional larger corks typically used for other wines. The cork stoppers allow easy opening and closing of a bottle after each serving.

WINE CLOSURES

There are various types of closures or stoppers available for a winemaker to seal a bottle of wine. There are advantages and disadvantages for all, but each one must perform the essential function of preserving the wine and, if necessary, promote conditions conducive to appropriate development.

Most wines are produced for early consumption shortly after purchase. Only a small percentage of wines are created to benefit from and to be enhanced by bottle development through long-term aging. Bottle development occurs when a wine closure allows the optimal amount of oxygen (too much air can lead to oxidation) to positively affect the wine. The type of wine closure can affect the outcome of the finished wine by determining the personality and overall quality of the finished wine. Ultimately, a winemaker's vision of the finished product will determine the appropriate wine closure.

Cork

Cork has been used since the 18th century to seal bottles and has been the primary closure ever since. Wine corks come from the bark of the cork oak, a tree found in Portugal, Spain, North Africa, and other Mediterranean countries. After the tree reaches maturity (16 to 25 years), it is harvested by hand every 9 years in a labor-intensive process that strips the bark, only for it to regenerate throughout the coming centuries.

Corks are flexible, lightweight, and natural, and when the cork is wet, it swells to form a tight seal within the neck of the bottle. Therefore, wine bottles closed with corks must be stored either upside down or on their sides in order to keep the cork wet and the bottle tightly sealed. If a wine bottle closed with a cork is stored upright for too long, then the cork can dry out and contract over time, allowing air to enter the bottle, causing a darkening of the wine and a loss of aroma and flavor.

Besides proper storage, another concern is the development of an off-flavor from tainted corks. During the corks' preparation for use as wine closures, they are bleached, and if a certain mold is present in the cork, a highly aromatic compound called *2,4,6-Trichloroanisole* (try-clore-AN-iss-all), or TCA, is formed. This TCA has a disagreeable smell that is detectable in very low concentrations and will destroy a bottle of wine by imparting a "wet cardboard" character to wine. Winemakers refer to a wine having detectable levels of TCA as being *corked*. It has been estimated that between 3% and 5% of the corks are tainted with TCA, and unfortunately, there is no efficient way to determine whether a cork is tainted until a bottle of wine is opened.

Screw Caps or Twist Offs

New World (largely in New Zealand) winemakers are leading a campaign to replace the traditional wine cork with a high-tech aluminum screw cap, named the *Stelvin* after the company that created it. Screw caps first appeared in the 1970s; however, the connotation that they were "cheap" didn't help their success. More recently, there has been a renewed push for screw caps for short-term aging of wines because they are inexpensive, easy to open (not requiring a special tool—the corkscrew), and easily resealable and because they limit the passage of oxygen.

Philosophically, it seems natural to use the screw cap, particularly if the wine has been stored only in stainless steel prior to bottling and is destined to be consumed early. This carries on the intended style of the winemaker of pure essentials of fruit and preservation of acid and youthfulness of the wine that oak aging and a cork would otherwise alter.

Wine traditionalists find it difficult to accept the screw cap because the lost romance surrounding the opening of a corked bottle is now replaced by twisting the cap off of the bottle. Because of the tradition and mystique that are pervasive in the wine industry, wine drinkers still tend to associate a screw cap with inexpensive wines of low quality. Nonetheless, the more adventurous winemakers in Australia and California, and even some Old World producers, have begun to bottle some of their prestigious wines with a high-quality screw top. Ultimately, the biggest test will be the acceptance by the consumer.

Synthetic

The popularity of artificial or plastic corks for early-drinking wines has been on the upswing in response to the problem of cork taint in natural corks. But synthetic corks are not without problems of their own and have not been widely embraced by the industry. For long-term storage, the biggest problem has been the quick passage of oxygen, which, after a period of time, can result in oxidized wines that exhibit symptoms of aging sooner than if sealed with other closures. Others are hesitant to put their wines in contact with the elastic polymers that make up a synthetic cork for fear that some undesirable compounds may be extracted from the corks.

Technicals, or Composites

Technicals, or composites, are formed with pieces of natural cork and bonding materials and usually incorporate disks of natural cork at each end.

Glass Stopper

The glass stopper is a recent creation that can be made out of either glass or Plexiglas.

WINE GLASS SELECTION

Wine glasses are often referred to as *stemware* or *glassware*. They are generally composed of three parts: (1) bowl, (2) stem, and (3) foot. It's generally believed that the construction and shape of a glass can significantly improve the aromas and flavors of a wine. Some companies go as far as to create particular shapes suited for specific grape varietals, in addition to making several different price points based on what the glass is made out of. Stemware can be made out of glass or crystal. Glass provides a more durable and inexpensive alternative to crystal stemware, which is delicate and expensive, but viewed as better quality. In handling stemware, it's important to hold the glass by the stem to avoid smearing the glass with fingerprints and to avoid warming the wine.

Two of the most common types of glassware are a white and red wine glass used for table wine. In addition, two more glasses are used: the sparkling (flute) and fortified wine glasses.

White Wine

FIGURE 1–13 White wine glass

(Thomas Moore)

Table Wine Glassware

Many restaurants utilize an all-purpose wine glass that can be used for both white and red wine. For those restaurants that choose a more extensive wine list or have the budget to allow for better glassware, they can opt for the minimum white wine and red wine glasses.

Some high-end restaurants with extensive wine budgets carry several different styles of stemware for individual grapes or types of table wine. Not only is there a variety of various shaped glassware, but consisting of various quality levels as well. *Crystal stemware* is often (but not always) made with lead to provide a higher index of refraction than normal glass affords. It gives the wine a greater "sparkle" at a more expensive price.

Red Wine

FIGURE 1–14 Red wine glass

(Thomas Moore)

An effective size for wine glassware should be large enough (about 10–12 ounces) to allow for the standard portion size of wine (about 4–5 ounces) to be swirled in the glass without being spilled.

White wine glasses are tulip shaped, with a small bowl, generally narrow, and with a slightly inverted lip, which allows the concentration of the wine's aromas to the nose after being swirled. The narrow surface area also allows the wine to retain its chilled temperature by reducing surface area. Figure 1–13 shows a sample white wine glass.

Red wine glasses usually are larger in size, with a bigger bowl and wider surface area, which allows the wine to have greater air contact to cause the softening of tannin and integration of aromas. Figure 1–14 shows a sample red wine glass.

Stemless

FIGURE 1–15 Stemless wine glass

(Thomas Moore)

The Austrian glass company Riedel (ree-DEL) created a "*stemless*" line of glassware for the more casual and trendy wine drinker. The stemless glassware comes in a variety of shapes and sizes. Figure 1–15 shows a sample stemless wine glass.

Flute

FIGURE 1–16 Flute

(Thomas Moore)

Saucer

FIGURE 1–17 Saucer

(Thomas Moore)

Fortified
Wine

**FIGURE 1–18 Fortified wine
glass**

(Thomas Moore)

Sparkling Wine Glassware

Sparkling wine glassware should be designed to maximize the idea of what a sparkling wine is about: bubbles. The *flutes* are the most suitable stemware for all types of sparkling wine, as they are tall, thin, and designed to bring the delicate aromas toward the nose. The length of the flute allows the preservation of carbonation as it slowly rises to the surface. Figure 1–16 shows a sample flute glass.

The *saucer glass* (sometimes called *coups*) is an inferior option (and still sometimes used) because it causes the dissipation of effervescence at a fast rate. In addition, it has a large surface area that makes it difficult to drink from without spilling the wine. Figure 1–17 shows a saucer glass.

Fortified Wine Glassware

Fortified wine is enhanced with additional alcohol. Therefore, the portion size (about 2 ounces) is much smaller than other types of wine. Since the portion size is more reserved, the glassware size corresponds to the amount of wine—generally small and capable of holding about 2 ounces. Figure 1–18 shows a sample fortified wine glass.

TABLE WINE CLASSIFICATION

Varietal Labelled Wine

Varietal based wine is a concept applied to most non-European wine labels, including those from Australia, New Zealand, South Africa, South America, Canada, and the United States. The names of wines in this category are derived from their predominant grape variety. A grape variety is like an ice cream. At a basic level, ice cream is ice cream no matter how it's made, and you may say the same thing about wine. On the other hand, chocolate ice cream tastes quite different from vanilla, and likewise, Cabernet Sauvignon tastes very different from Chardonnay. The greatest distinction from one variety to the next is in the aroma, taste, and texture of the resulting wine. If wine is made from predominantly one grape variety, it can be called a *varietal* wine.

Serious wine-producing countries and states regulate the amount of a particular grape that must be present as an ingredient before the wine can be identified by that grape's name. Throughout the United States, any wine with a designated grape varietal must contain at least 75% of that grape within the bottle. Each state within the United States can choose to be stricter with this rule. For example, most varietals in Oregon must contain a minimum of 90% (for most varietals) of the grape identified on the label.

Geographically Labelled Wine

Geographically based wine is a concept applied to most European (Old World) wine labels, where the wines are named after the place they come from. Europe's wines are intimately linked to their terroir concept rather than to the name of the grape variety. Geographically based wines refer to wines that are labelled and produced from strictly regulated areas of the wine-growing country. For example, the bottle may read "Burgundy" (a French region that specializes in Pinot Noir) rather than identifying the name of the grape. Over the past 200 years, the Europeans have used trial and error to understand which varieties will make the best wines possible in each region. *Terroir* is a sense of place with special characteristics that can't be duplicated elsewhere. It's a sort of thumbprint that contributes to a particular "personality" for a given wine.

The following table lists some renowned wine-producing areas and the wines named after them:

THE MOST RENOWNED WINE-PRODUCING PLACES AND THE WINES NAMED AFTER THEM	
PLACES/NAME OF WINE	COUNTRY
Barbaresco	ITALY
Barolo	ITALY
Beaujolais	FRANCE
Bordeaux ⟶	FRANCE
Burgundy	FRANCE
Chablis	FRANCE
Champagne	FRANCE
Chianti	ITALY
Port	PORTUGAL
Rioja	SPAIN
Sauternes	FRANCE

All European wine-producing countries have their own regulations controlling labelling. To further complicate the labeling, regions are divided into districts (subregions), subdistricts (sub-subregions), villages (communes or neighborhoods), and localities as specific as a vineyard (someone's house). For example, Burgundy has five significant districts, several subdistricts, dozens of villages, and hundreds of vineyards. A general rule that can assist with reading and understanding a label is to identify how much specificity is given on that label. A broader place on the label generally indicates less quality; the more specific label indicates better quality. (View the Place chart at the end of this section.)

Currently, winemakers around the new world are showing more interest in this kind of regional and local specialization. As non-European countries establish reputations for the wines of certain regions, they often add the region's name to the varietal name. Examples are Napa Valley Cabernet Sauvignon and Russian River Pinot Noir.

The following table shows some labelling conventions:

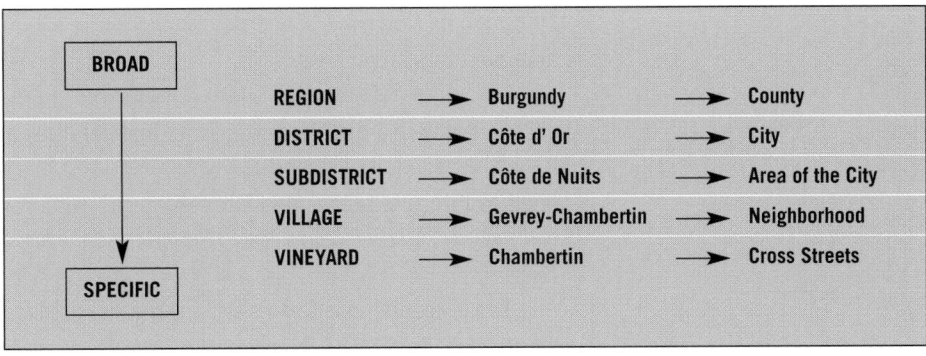

BROAD ↓ SPECIFIC			
REGION	⟶ Burgundy	⟶ County
DISTRICT	⟶ Côte d' Or	⟶ City
SUBDISTRICT	⟶ Côte de Nuits	⟶ Area of the City
VILLAGE	⟶ Gevrey-Chambertin	⟶ Neighborhood
VINEYARD	⟶ Chambertin	⟶ Cross Streets

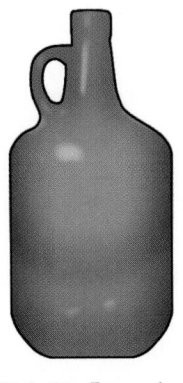

FIGURE 1–19 Jug wine
(Thomas Moore)

Generic Labelled Wine

Generic wines were widely popular in the early 1900s and up until the 1980s, but are still available today. Throughout the United States, these wines have been commonly referred to as jug or generic wine because they were often purchased in a jug or box, shown in Figure 1–19.

Generic wines generally consist of a blend of different grapes that often are of lower quality than grapes that compose varietal labelled wines. The grapes used are often high-yielding varieties that can be grown and produced at low cost. In many cases, the grape is not even known to the consumer, because these wines may be labelled so vaguely.

Up until the 1990s, it was quite common for California winemakers to freely borrow the names of European wines and regions to label their jug or generic wines, rather than give them grape varietal names, as is the common current practice in the rest of the United States. The common practice in America was to use names such as "Burgundy," "Chablis," or "Champagne" (names based on famous wine-growing regions where the grapes were produced), even though the wines were not from those areas. This sort of imitation irritated the wine growers of Europe, who argued that these names had very specific meanings in terms of local origin, grape types, vineyards, and cellar practices. The American winemakers, however, felt that if a red wine tasted similar to the red wine of Burgundy, France, it seemed perfectly reasonable to call it as such. The names of American wines in this category are unrelated to the geographic or varietal origin associated with European wines using the same designation.

Proprietary Blends/Trademark Labelled Wines

The types and kinds of proprietary blends are endless. Many wineries have opted to create opportunities by blending various complementary grape varietals to distinguish their wines from the traditional varietal-based wines that are most prominent in the New World.

Many (but not all) of the proprietary-based wines are respectable high-quality American versions of the classic red or white Bordeaux (bohr-DOH) style. These wines (as in Bordeaux) are a blend of several complementary grape varietals.

Back in 1988, a few Napa Valley winemakers started their own association and devised an official name for this style of wines: Meritage (rhymes with the word "heritage"). The name *Meritage* is a combination of two words, "merit" and "heritage," to symbolize the quality and history associated with the origination of these wines made in a Bordeaux style. These wines tend to be the best a particular winery produces.

According to the Meritage Association, the wine must contain at least two of the approved grapes (classic to Bordeaux), with no single variety containing more than 90% of the blend. The approved varietals for red Meritage are Cabernet Sauvignon, Merlot, Cabernet Franc, Petit Verdot, and Malbec. The combination and proportions of these grapes are completely determined by the individual producer. However, most often, the wines tend to be dominated by either Cabernet Sauvignon or Merlot, with smaller amounts of the other approved varietals.

Throughout California, other winemakers produce red Bordeaux-styled wines, but choose not to use the Meritage name. Instead, they have chosen to create and market alternative names that sound fancy or unique to the particular winery without being confined to the rules associated with Meritage. Some producers have identified their wines variously as *Affinity, Opus One, Rubicon,* and *Insignia;* or they call them simply *Reserve Bottlings.*

These blends in many cases are a winery's flagship option, and prices often start at around $50 to $100 a bottle. In addition to possessing fancy names, they have stylish labels and tall-shouldered heavy glass bottles. Craig Williams, winemaker at Joseph Phelps Vineyard, was the first winemaker in California to produce a proprietary red—Insignia—in 1974.

Many winemakers have also opted for other blends. The popularity of white and red Rhône-style wines has increased dramatically. These wines tend to be dominated with Syrah and other varietals.

READING A TYPICAL WINE LABEL

What does a wine label tell us? In addition to a bottle informing us about the shape and color, a wine label can provide a great deal of information as to the contents within the bottle. Law mandates most of the information offered on a label, but additional information is sometimes provided to assist the consumer with making a well-informed decision. Every wine-producing country has its own set of government wine laws that regulate grape growing, winemaking, and labelling. The following are five categories of wine label information:

1. **WHO:**—The producer (winery or estate or negociant)
2. **WHAT:**—The grape variety (not always listed, particularly in Europe)
3. **WHERE:**—The geographic location (where the grapes are grown)
4. **WHEN:**—The vintage year (the year the grapes were picked and the wine was made)
5. **HOW:**—The level of quality or some other classification. Whereas these are not always listed or known, there may be clues that imply (but do not necessarily guarantee) quality, such as the specific geographical location of the vineyard(s), whether the wine came from a single vineyard, and, in the case of many French vineyards, the rating or quality classification of a particular vineyard.

Typical New World Wine Label

A sample of a common United States wine label is pictured in Figure 1–20. The most prominent items on a U.S. wine label are the following:

1. The name of the winery or vintner that produced the wine. The producer's name usually is the largest text on the label and the easiest element to identify. In the example, the producer is St. Supéry.
2. The identification of the wine grape(s). A wine predominantly from a single grape varietal identified on the label means that at least 75% of that varietal is used in the wine. When the wine is blended from several varieties or regions, it will not be labelled as a varietal wine. In the example, the grape is predominately Cabernet Sauvignon.
3. The geographical location where the grapes were grown. In the United States, these are legally defined as American Viticultural Areas (AVAs). Some are as broad as "California," whereas others are narrowly defined as a section of a river valley. In the United States, vineyards can be named if a minimum of 95% of the grapes came from that vineyard. If a region is identified on the label, 85% or more of the grapes must come from that specific locality. In the example, the location is predominately Napa Valley.
4. The vintage is the "year" in which the grapes were harvested and the wine was made. If a vintage year is displayed, it means that at least 95% or more of the wine was produced from grapes grown in the stated year. In the example, the vintage date is 2003.

Wine labels can be particularly confusing, because they are loaded with foreign terms. The remainder of this book attempts to illuminate some of this mystery. Key label terms for France, Italy, Germany, and Spain are discussed within their individual chapters, "Wines of France," in Chapter 9, and "Other Old World Wine Countries," in Chapter 10.

FIGURE 1–20 Wine label
(St Supery Winery)

INTRODUCTION TO WINE

NAME: _____ Score out of 20 points_____.

Use these questions to test your knowledge and understanding of the concepts presented in the chapter.

I. MULTIPLE CHOICE: Select the best possible answer from the options available.

1. A disadvantage of using screw caps as closures is

   a. the ability to easily reseal the cap.

   b. the cost is high, compared with that of corks.

   c. the perception of low quality.

   d. the ease of opening the caps.

2. The number one country producing the most table wine is

   a. the United States.

   b. Australia.

   c. Italy.

   d. France.

3. The number one country consuming the most table wine is

   a. the United States.

   b. Australia.

   c. Italy.

   d. France.

4. Which of the following are among the disadvantages of using corks as closures?

   a. the perception of low-quality and cheap wines

   b. having to store wines on their side for extended storage periods

   c. TCA/cork taint

   d. All of the above

   e. Answers b and c

5. A broader geographic label on a wine label usually indicates that the grapes are

   a. of less quality.

   b. of better quality.

   c. of undetermined quality.

   d. Not enough information is given to answer the question.

6. Jug and generic wines take their names (such as Chablis) from

   a. the grapes.

   b. famous Old World regions.

   c. where the wine was produced.

   d. where the grapes were grown.

II. TRUE / FALSE: Circle the best possible answer.

7. Old World wines tend to be made in a fruit-forward style. **True / False**

8. Grape skins contribute to the color in a wine. **True / False**

9. The three categories of wine are table wine, sparkling wine, and dessert wine. **True / False**

10. A purpose of a wider bowl for red wine glassware is to assist in aeration of the wine. **True / False**

11. Fortified wine glassware generally is smaller in size in order to accommodate a smaller portion size. **True / False**

12. The amount of sugar present in the grape juice can have an influence on the amount of alcohol that is produced. **True / False**

13. If fermentation is stopped before the yeast has had a chance to ferment all the sugar, the wine will have some sweetness. **True / False**

14. In Europe, the wines often are named after the place the grapes come from. **True / False**

15. Proprietary blends are styled after either red or white Bordeaux wines. **True / False**

16. The "Old World" refers to the long-established tradition of winemaking within the European countries of France, Italy, Germany, and Spain.
True / False

17. Wine bottles have been used for centuries and appear in a variety of shapes and sizes, but have been standardized to generally contain 33.8 oz.
True / False

III. IDENTIFY:

18. Given a typical wine label as shown, draw an arrow to the most prominent items that may be found on them.

- Name of winery
- Varietal
- Location
- Vintage date

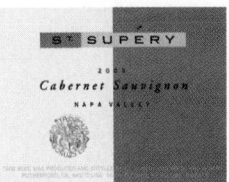

19. For each bottle, identify the name of the bottle and the common grapes found in them.

a. _____

_____

b. _____

_____

c. _____

_____

IV. SHORT-ANSWER ESSAY / DISCUSSION QUESTION: Use a separate sheet of paper if necessary.

20. List at least two reasons for increased popularity and consumption of wine in America. Explain.

2

Wine Tasting

Tasting wine (as opposed to just drinking it) adds an extra dimension to the basic routines of eating and drinking; it turns obligation into pleasure.

LEARNING OBJECTIVES

Upon completion of this chapter, the learner will be able to:

- Exercise the professional four-step tasting technique used to assess and evaluate wine.
- Understand and communicate using key wine-tasting terminology.

THE TASTING RITUAL

Drinking wine is easy, but tasting wine can be more of a challenge, as it involves a concentrated sensory approach. Wine tasting is a technique used to determine the *performance factors* of wine by the senses of sight, smell, and taste. It is an attempt to capture a sensory experience in order to understand the unique personality of a given wine and, possibly, communicate it in simple terms to others.

Tasting wine (as opposed to just drinking it) adds an extra dimension to the basic routines of eating and drinking; it turns obligation into pleasure. Tasting wine can be as simple as "I like it" or "I don't like it" or as complicated as "Is it good or poor quality?" There are four essential steps in tasting: (1) looking at the wine (sight), (2) smelling the wine (smell), (3) tasting the wine (taste), and (4) spitting or swallowing the wine.

The ability to isolate and identify specific aromas and smells can be challenging, but will develop through experience. "Practice" is the most important advice for any wine drinker, as it can improve the ability to identify a wine's obvious and subtle clues through the tasting process.

FIGURE 2–1 Wine tasting
(Getty Images-Stockbyte, Royalty Free)

Wine tasting is a sensory evaluation of a particular wine or grouping of wines in a formal or informal arrangement. A wine tasting can be conducted blind (without seeing the labels) or in full view (seeing the labels). Blind tasting ensures zero influence by a wine's reputation and allows the taster to establish both an uncontaminated objective assessment and a subjective opinion about the wine. A wine's color, smell, and taste all offer insight into its origin of production and distinctive personality. Figure 2–1 shows an arrangement of wines prepared for a blind tasting.

Beyond producing enjoyment of the senses, the object of a wine tasting is to deduce the characteristics (or performance factors) of the wine, such as the type of grape, the region of origin, grape growing and winemaking methods, and maybe even the vintage date. In a competitive tasting where a wine may be compared with another wine, such as Cabernet Sauvignon from California against Cabernet Sauvignon from Bordeaux, the tasting is done blind to ensure a fair outcome so that, for example, the more established reputation of the Bordeaux region doesn't yield more clout than it may deserve.

1. Looking at the Wine

The appearance of a wine can create initial expectations, as the personality can be assessed partly by sight. The first impression can provide clues to a wine's grape variety, climate it was grown in, age of the wine, the winemaking methods, and potential faults. The visual aspects can also provide valuable clues to what the wine may smell and taste like just as the color of an avocado or a banana may suggest its level of ripeness, taste, and texture.

In the majority of grapes (except for a handful of obscure ones), we know that only the grape skins contain pigment responsible for a wine's color. Therefore, smaller grape berries contain a higher ratio of skin to juice, yielding a deeper, more concentrated color pigment. In contrast, a larger grape has a lower proportion of skin in relation to juice, yielding a wine with a lower color pigment. For example, a pale or lighter white wine with a greenish-to-straw yellow appearance may suggest a youthful wine grape (possibly larger berries) that was grown in a cooler area and possibly aged in stainless steel to preserve color (as opposed to oak aging, which may contribute color). If any of the clues are accurate, the wine will have a fresh, youthful smell and contain low to moderate alcohol to yield a light- to medium-bodied wine with ample acidity.

Unlike a white wine with medium intensity, wine with a golden yellow hue may be older and more evolved—a wine that was made from grapes (possibly smaller berries) grown in a warmer to hotter area and perhaps picked later in the season, suggesting that they had reached ample ripeness and sugar content and were aged in oak. If any of the clues are accurate, the wine will have an evolved smell containing several secondary aromas and flavor characteristics indicating moderate to high alcohol that yields a medium- to full-bodied wine with moderate to low acidity and slight to heavy residual sugar.

Process of Sight—Ensure that there is only a small amount of wine in the glass (about 1–2 ounces). This allows for better assessment of color and, later on, helps to detect aroma. Hold the stem of the glass between the thumb on one side and the index finger and middle finger on the other side. Tilt the wine glass and hold it over an opaque white background (such as a placemat or tablecloth) in a well-lit area. This is the best way to observe and assess the *clarity* (freedom from particles), *depth* or *intensity* (its level of concentration), and *hue* (shade of color). It is more accurate to judge hue by viewing the wine as the glass is tilted. View the wine from its deepest color for *intensity* (located in the core, or center of the glass) to its very thinnest and lightest color for *hue* (located at the rim, or edge of the glass), which is the first place to show signs of either youth or age.

> **WHITE WINES COLOR SCALE:** White wine can range in color from a greenish tint, to pale straw yellow (both are a possible sign of cool climate, youth, bone dryness, and stainless steel aging), to deep golden yellow (probably indicating a warmer climate, well-aged wine, exposure to oak barrels, or, possibly, some level of residual sugar). brown-amber (showing signs of possible death or spoilage).
>
> **RED WINES COLOR SCALE:** Red wine may appear any color from purple to ruby red (both of which may indicate a youthful wine) to red and brick red (indicating an evolved, more mellow wine), showing signs of age then finally to brown (showing signs of death or spoilage).

Swirl the wine in the glass, and notice how quickly or slowly the wine filters down after it has stopped moving. The patterns and viscosity of the wine remaining on the glass are together referred to as *legs* or *tears*, which provide a visual measurement of the wine's body. Slower moving and more viscous legs indicate a higher alcohol content, extract, or a high volume of sugar, all of which are characteristic of a wine with a fuller body. Quickly moving legs may indicate a wine low in alcohol or low in sugar, signifying a wine with a lighter body.

2. Smelling the Wine

Smell is probably the most important and certainly the most evocative sense we have. This is our key sensory tool for wine tasting because the nose can detect and distinguish an estimated 10,000 different odors, depending on the training of the individual. Even those lacking the ability to smell and detect specific odors can often be prompted to learn them by repeated exposure. The focus of initial training for wine tasters is the repetition of the common grape varietals for the purpose of building both a memory base for subsequent recognition of a wine and a solid foundation of common odor associations.

When smelling wine, it's possible to detect some of the same smells that might be associated with other food ingredients, the farm, or even a forest. The smells associated with a particular variety of grape have been influenced by that grape's cultivation under certain environmental conditions throughout the growing season. The actual scents associated with the grape (and all its environmental effects) are known as the *primary aromas*. These smells are combined with additional, more complex ones (known as *secondary* or *tertiary* aromas) that emerge from chemical changes of fermentation, from barrel and bottle aging, and through various winemaking techniques, to culminate in what is known as the wine's *bouquet*. Whether they are primary or secondary, the most common and detectable aromas associated with wine are broken down into *common wine aroma/flavor categories*. (See charts of the wine flavor categories in Chapter 4, "Performance Factors of Grape Varietals.")

Winemaking and maturation or aging techniques create and impart aromas often associated with bakery, cigar shop, and coffee shop smells and flavors. For example, the smell of butter or cloves may suggest that the wine has been adulterated with butter or cloves when it hasn't. Many of the aroma compounds we find in other places and food items that are actually derived from the same aroma compounds found in wine. The aroma in butter is actually derived from a chemical compound called *diacetyl* (die-ASS-ih-tahl), which is a by-product of malolactic fermentation. (This technique is discussed in Chapter 3, "Viticulture and Enology.") The smell of cloves is really caused by the chemical compound *eugenol* (u-jen-ahl), extracted in wine through aging in oak barrels.

The tasting experienced can be enhanced by learning aroma and flavor terms (see Chapter 4, "Performance Factors of Grape Varietals") in order to communicate better with others and, most importantly, to develop a memory of their likes and dislikes.

Perception of Aroma and Taste—We perceive the aroma of a wine in two ways and in two areas: by actively smelling the odors on the outside through the nose, and by holding the wine in the mouth to taste its flavor on the inside, through the *retronasal passage*. We differentiate the two kinds of odors by referring to the external odor as *smell* or *aroma*, and the internal odor as *flavor* or *taste*. These terms are commonly confused and used interchangeably, but are actually two different elements in wine tasting. Often, we taste more flavors than we smell aromas, because once the wine is in the mouth, it warms up as well as react with saliva to release more odor components.

When smelling a wine, we can also determine its level of *intensity*. The level of intensity provides an impression whether a wine has a somewhat diluted aroma or a concentrated one, which can be an association of its quality of production but of course, also the typicity of a particular grape varietal.

Process of Smell—To get a strong sense of the wine's smell, use the proper glass in order to concentrate the aroma molecules in the wine. Fill the glass only about one-third full or less to allow space for the wine's vapors to be released.

Next, swirl the wine to release and intensify the aroma of the wine. Then immediately bring the glass up to the nose and take several small whiffs. As the wine clings to the inside of the glass, the alcohol evaporates and carries with it the aromas of the wine.

The first impression of aroma is important, as the nose is at its freshest point and maintains the ability to identify subtle nuances. Concentrate on the smell in order to form an initial description of the wine's aroma personality. The longer a particular wine is smelled, the more the nose fatigues and loses its keen sense of discerning subtle aromas.

One of the most effective methods employed to develop the palate is to keep notes or tasting sheets of the wines tasted. This allows us to record connections between different styles and kinds of wines. Write down impressions and associations to help establish an aroma memory. Different wine tasters will have different sets of associations with which to identify a wine's aroma personality; however, there are some common smells associated with each particular grape variety that should be universal. In describing the aromas and flavors, the terms should be objective, not subjective. For example, *floral* is a more specific descriptive term and more useful to record than "It tastes good," which is a subjective opinion.

Fatigue and Adaptation—Smell is the most easily stimulated sense, but it is also the most fragile. The nose will *fatigue* after a short period of smelling (primary olfaction) something and will become temporarily unable to detect additional aromas. Simultaneously, *adaptation* sets in, which is the self-adjustment to a constant level of stimulus in an environment. For example, most of us, from time to time, have applied a noticeable amount of cologne or perfume to our bodies. After a short time, however, the odors may no longer be noticeable to us. This experience of fatigue and adaptation is no different when one is sniffing wine and will certainly influence the tasting process. A solution is to use quick sniffs, make an assessment, and move on, rather than sniffing a single wine for an extended period.

3. Tasting the Wine

When we taste a wine, our palates can break down different characteristics within the wine. The tastes that the tongue senses in wine are four *taste components*: (1) sweet, (2) sour, (3) bitter, and (4) salty. The palate can also detect texture (a combination of weight, tannin, and alcohol) associated with a wine.

When wine drinkers order and describe wine, they often refer to the flavor components they desire in their wine, whether they are aware that they are doing so or not. In many cases, it will be necessary to interpret their preference for components, because the thresholds of perceptible levels of sweetness, alcohol, tannin, and acidity can vary significantly among individuals. It's important to understand that perceived sweetness can be affected by levels of alcohol and acidity in a wine as well as perceived tannin can be affected by the level of fruit concentration.

Taste Components

Body can be light, medium, or full and can be comparable to skim milk, 2% milk, or whole milk.
- Light Body ⟶ Skim Milk
- Medium Body ⟶ 2% Milk
- Full Body ⟶ Whole Milk

Tasting a wine also involves detecting a wine's body. *Body* can be thought of as the boldness, thickness, or viscosity of a wine. The body of a wine can be felt as light, medium, or full-bodied, which is merely the impression of the weight and size of the wine in the mouth. The description *full bodied* is frequently applied to wines that are high in alcohol, sugar, extract, or tannin.

These elements (alcohol, sugar, extract, or tannin) are distinguishable, with each simultaneously influencing the other. If one element is dominant, a proficient taster will still be able to identify the other elements and possibly predict the effects of further aging. For example, a young red wine might be overly tannic, but have definite fruitiness and acidity, suggesting that in a few years the tannin will have softened, while the fruit will have become more complex.

The Process of Tasting—Place approximately one-half ounce of the wine in your mouth, suck in some oxygen (in order to aerate and open the wine's aromas and flavors), and swish the wine around in your mouth to ensure sure that as large an area of the tongue as possible has a chance to judge the wine's components (acid, sweetness, tannin, and salt). While doing this, simultaneously sense the body, flavors, and effects of other components.

The Purpose of Sucking Oxygen—Sucking oxygen volatilizes the wine and sends it to the back of the nasal cavity, then up into an interior nasal passage in the back of the mouth called the retronasal passage. The smell and flavor are now intensified. This could be referred to as *smelling the wine on the inside,* which we often associate with the term *flavors.*

The Four Taste Zones on the Tongue—Tastes are sensed by nerve receptors called buds, and there are about 9,000 of them on the average tongue. Combinations of

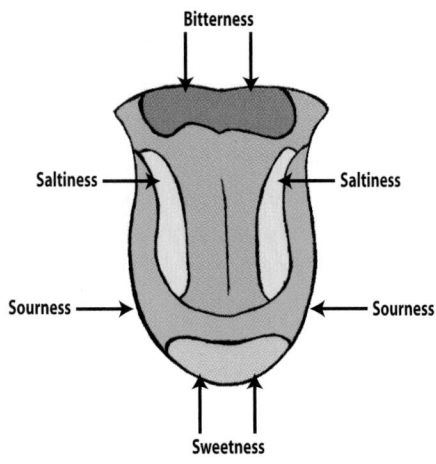

FIGURE 2–2 Tasting zones
(Thomas Moore)

tastes, along with the accompanying combined aromas (smelling from the inside), account for different flavors. Sensitivity to specific tastes varies considerably among individuals. Figure 2–2 is a visual representation of the taste zones on the tongue.

While there may be a vast array of aromas, historically only four taste components have been considered: sweet, sour, bitter, and salty. These four building blocks differentiate and describe common taste sensations.

Sugar—(Perceived as Fruit) Sugar is derived from the grape pulp and juice that contain equal amounts of both glucose and fructose. Sugar is the needed catalyst for yeast to produce alcohol and create wine. The amount of sugar fermented determines the wine's alcohol level. If yeast consumes most or all of the sugar present in the grape juice, the wine will be dry. If yeast consumes some but not most of the sugar, the remaining sugar after fermentation, is known as *residual sugar* or *RS*, the wine may have some detectible level of sweetness.

Sugar is sensed throughout the palate, but it is concentrated at the tip of the tongue. Most wine (particularly, red wine with some exceptions) is intended to be dry. Often, wine drinkers associate a fruit-concentrated wine with sweetness. Fruit is a smell and flavor through the nasal passage, and sweetness is a taste component. The effects of sweetness may be perceived more or less on the basis of varying amounts of other components such as acidity, fruit, and alcohol. For example, a wine with ample acidity may convey less sugar onto the palate.

If a wine is described as dry, there is no perceptible sugar. An off-dry wine may be described as having a hint of residual sugar, and a sweet wine has noticeable amounts of residual sugar.

Terms used to describe sweetness: *Sweet, ripe, luscious.*

Acid—(Perceived as Sourness) Acid derives primarily from the grape pulp and juice, but may also come from skins. Acid is best perceived as sourness and is a vital and fundamental structural component of both white and red wines. Without an adequate level of acid, a white wine is considered *flabby*, or falls *flat*, when paired with a food. Acid is sensed throughout the palate, but it is concentrated on the sides of the tongue and causes salivation. Sourness derives from various kinds of acids that are all found in wine in varying degrees such as tartaric (one of the main acids in wine), citric (also prevalent in lemon and grapefruit), malic (also found in apples and pears), lactic (also prevalent in dairy products), and acetic (also prevalent in vinegar). Collectively, these acids also acts as preservatives, but unlike tannin, they add a fresh, crisp sensation to the wine.

Terms used to describe acids: *Bright, lively, crisp, firm, zesty, fresh, and sharp.*

Tannin—(Perceived as Bitterness) Tannin originates primarily from grape skins, seeds, and stems (through the fermentation process) and also in part by the amount of contact with oak aging. Large oak casks impart less oak flavor and less tannin than smaller oak barrels do. Tannin is a vital structural component of a red wine and is, for the most part, undetectable in white wines. Fundamental to a red wine are its acid and tannin. Without an adequate level of either tannin or acid, a red wine becomes *flabby*, or *flat* and will fall flat when paired with food. Tannin is sensed throughout the palate, but it is concentrated toward the back of the tongue and around the gum line of the mouth. It causes a drying sensation that creates a "puckery" feeling and acts to cancel out the salivation caused by acid. In young red wine, tannin is most apparent and perceived as astringent and rough.

Tannins vary in type, strength, and character, depending on grape type and aging methods. The longer the maceration (juice and skin contact) period, the more tannin will be extracted. Tannin, therefore, helps wine age by acting as a natural preservative and suppressing oxidation throughout the aging process. Over time, tannin (in combination with color pigment) will *polymerize* (Puh-LYM-err-ize) (separate or fall out of the liquid solution) and form sediment in the wine bottle.

While there are several sources of tannin, not all tannin is created equal. The tannin present in skins, and particularly that found in seeds and stems, is known as *condensed tannin* (or unripe tannin). This type of tannin tends to taste slightly harsh on the palate, particularly if the grapes were harvested too soon before they had an adequate chance to ripen. Wines with condensed tannin are less likely to benefit and soften from aeration associated with aging and decanting. The type of tannin extracted through oak barrels is a *hydrolyzable tannin* (or ripe tannin). Hydrolyzable tannin benefits the wine by softening it from aeration during the aging process.

Tannin can significantly effect the texture and body of a wine. Low tannin usually is associated with light-bodied red wines, medium tannin with medium- to full-bodied red wines, and high tannin with full-bodied red wines.

Terms used to describe tannin: *Chewy, rough, gritty, dry, firm, rich, and puckery.*

Salty—(Perceived as Tangy) It is commonly believed that salt is not detected or sensed when tasting wine (with the exception of Manzanilla Sherry). Salt is more often associated with food items such as smoked meats or fish, baked goods, and canned or processed foods. Salt becomes integral to our understanding of wine when wine is paired with a food item that has a noticeable salt content. (This topic will be discussed in greater detail in Chapter 5, "Foundations to Wine and Food Pairing.")

Other Factors That Influence Taste, Flavor, and Texture—Texture in reference to wine is the feel of the wine on the palate. It is driven by a combination of factors, such as *tannin* (level of smoothness or roughness), *alcohol level* (feel of burn or lack of burn in the back of the mouth and down the throat), *extract* (number of particles of fruit suspended in the finished wine), amount of *residual sugar* (which creates a more weighty feel and viscous consistency), and impact of *temperature*.

Terms used to describe body: *Weight, richness, fullness, and intensity.*

Alcohol—(Perceived as a burning or spicy sensation) Alcohol is produced through the fermentation process of yeast consuming sugar. Alcohol plays a large role in the style, body, structure, and taste of wine. The level of alcohol in the finished wine is most often related directly to how much sugar the grapes contained at the harvest.

Alcohol is perceived as fullness or body in a wine. It frequently can be detected through a warming sensation that is largely noticed by a slight burn or spiciness toward the back of the mouth and throat. Alcohol can act somewhat similarly to the way acid is sensed, by assisting with cleansing the palate and having the ability to cut through rich types of foods and sauces. When the proportion of alcohol is too high for the other flavor elements, alcohol may give a burning sensation in the nose as well as a hot feeling in the back of the throat or the roof of the mouth. Sometimes, alcohol can be perceived as sweetness.

Fruitiness—(Perceived as sweetness) *Fruitiness* means the aroma and taste of the character of fruits (such as strawberry, blueberry, pineapple, etc.); it does not mean sweet. Although some fruity wines may be sweet, fruity wines more often are dry. Keep in mind that fruitiness and sweetness are two different things and that real sweetness is detected on the tongue, not in the nose.

Temperature—(Influences the perceptions of the other components) The temperature of a wine can affect the other components of wine (acid, tannin, sugar, fruit, and alcohol) by either emphasizing or de-emphasizing their sensations. A white wine served very cold gives a taste impression that is less fruity and more acidic than the same wine at a warmer temperature. A red wine served too warm yields more perception of alcohol than the same wine served cooler. (The topic of proper serving temperatures is discussed in greater detail in Chapter 14, "The Flow of Wine.")

The Theory of Umami—In the early 1900s, a Japanese scientist identified a fifth basic taste on the human tongue: *Umami*, which describes a savory sensation of foods high in glutamate. Such foods include meat, milk, mushrooms, and walnuts. The sensation creates a fullness or completeness of flavor upon tasting.

4. Spit or Swallow the Wine

After spitting or swallowing, notice which flavors and sensations are left and how long they linger in order to determine the *finish* or *persistence* (how long the aftertaste lasts in your mouth after you spit or swallow) of the wine. Many associate a longer finish with a better quality wine. However, this is not always the case. Some wines are not meant to have a longer finish, as they were created to be simple and perhaps one dimensional. The best measure is to understand that if a wine (such as Cabernet Sauvignon) typically has a long, lingering finish, and, during a tasting, it has been observed a glass of that wine has a short finish, then the quality of that particular wine should be called into question. The following chart approximates how to judge the persistence of a wine:

11 or more seconds	Long Finish
6–10 Seconds	Medium Finish
0–5 Seconds	Short Finish

Wine Flaws and Faults

A wine flaw is a minor error that still allows the wine to be drinkable, whereas a wine fault is a major error rendering the wine undrinkable. Both wine flaws and wine faults are defects and are generally considered undesirable and unpleasant characteristics of a wine, often caused by poor winemaking practices or storage conditions that lead to wine spoilage. Flawed and faulty wines are inevitable, and many of the flaws are undetectable until the bottle is opened and the tasting process begins.

Many of the compounds that cause flaws and faults are naturally found at insignificant levels in wine. Depending upon the perception of the drinker, the concentrations of the compounds may impart positive characteristics to a wine. However, when these compounds are at significant, noticeably perceptible levels, they adversely influence the wine by overpowering desirable aromas, flavors, and other pleasing components.

In 2006, the London-based International Wine Challenge (IWC), the largest wine competition in the world, revealed that some 13,000-plus wines (7% of all wines) tasted were identified as faulty. If a wine fault is detected, most credible suppliers, restaurants, or wine stores will allow the tainted product to be exchanged.

Six Common Flaws in Wine

1. **VOLATILE ACIDITY**—This encompasses both compounds of *acetic* acid and *ethyl* acetate. Acetic acid often is referred to as *vinegar taint,* and ethyl acetate in large doses contributes to the smell of fingernail-polish remover in a wine.
2. **CORK TAINT**—Often referred to as a wine being *corked,* a wine with *cork taint* is not to be confused with a wine being enclosed by a cork. Cork taint is caused by the compound *2,4,6-trichloranisole* (try-clore-AN-iss-all), or TCA, which originates from

mold present on cork or barrels when they are treated with chlorine for preparation. This is one of the more common wine flaws, and evidence suggests that it occurs in 2% to 4% of wines. Wine that displays this fault is characterized by an aroma reminiscent of wet cardboard or wet dog.

3. **HEAT DAMAGE**—Often referred to as *maderized*, heat-damaged wine contains a cooked aroma, flavor, and color. Visually, the cork may be pushed partially out of the bottle, the wine will look brick colored or brownish around the edges of the glass (whether red or white), and it may have an aroma and a flavor of caramel.

4. **SULFUR**—Sulfur is a naturally produced compound derived from the winemaking process. It is also a common additive used as an antioxidant (to stop oxidation) and as a preservative (to prevent undesirable microorganisms). If an excessive amount of sulfur is used, the perception is reminiscent of rotten eggs or burnt matches. The perception of sulfur may also cause a prickly sensation in the nose of the drinker smelling the wine. A closely related compound called *mercaptans* (mer-KAP-tuhns) is associated with a strong cabbage or onion-skin smell.

   U.S. federal regulations require any alcoholic beverage that contains more than 10 parts per million (ppm) of sulfites to print the phrase, "contains sulfites" on the label. The absence of the term on a label does not mean that the product is sulfite free, however; rather, it means that it has from 0 to 10 ppm of sulfites.

5. **ACETALDEHYDE (ass-ah-TAHL-duh-hide)**—This is a compound that causes a wine to have oxidized qualities, caused by the unintentional and undesirable effect of oxygen. Visually, an oxidized wine has a darkening or browning appearance, similar to an apple that turns color when cut open and not eaten right away. In table wines, acetaldehyde is generally considered a fault. However, an exception is made in the case of certain styles of fortified wines, in which such an aroma is desired.

6. **BRETTANOMYCES (breht-tan-uh-MY-sees)**—Often referred to as *brett*, this is a spoilage yeast that can grow on grapes and be present in wineries to affect a wine during processing. Brett can add a horse-saddle aroma and flavor to a wine.

DETAILED TASTING SHEET

WINE

Producer, varietals, location, vintage, etc.
_____

SIGHT

CLARITY → Clear—sediment   **INTENSITY →** Watery — pale — medium — deep — opaque

COLOR

     White Wine ⟶ Greenish — straw yellow — golden yellow — Brown amber

     Red Wine ⟶ Purple — ruby red — red — brick red — brown

SMELL

HEALTHY → Yes – No   **INTENSITY →** Muted — lightly aromatic — fairly aromatic — highly aromatic

WHITE WINE AROMA CHARACTERISTICS

1. FRUIT

TREE → Apricot, peach, pear, apple, cherry   DRIED → Raisins, figs, apricots

CITRUS → Lemon, lime, grapefruit, orange, tangerine   BERRY → Strawberry, blueberry, raspberry, blackberry

TROPICAL → Melon, banana, lychee, coconut, pineapple, passion fruit, fruit salad, mango

2. BAKESHOP

NUTS → Toasted hazelnut, walnuts, almond, nutmeg   BREAD → Yeast, toast, biscuit, dough

SAUCES → Caramel, vanilla, butterscotch, honey, cream, butter, custard

SPICES → Cinnamon, cloves, orange peel, anise, ginger

3. MINERAL/CHEMICAL → Chalk, flint, petrol, ammonia, rubber, steel

4. BARNYARD/HERBACEOUS → Grass, hay, straw, tomato vine, dill, fresh chives, Earl Grey

5. FLORAL → Rosé, peonies, orange blossom, honeysuckle, violets

6. VEGETABLES → Olive, asparagus, bell pepper, cucumber

RED WINE AROMA CHARACTERISTICS

1. FRUIT

FRESH FRUIT → Cherry, black cherry, raspberry, blackberry, blueberry, plum, cranberry, strawberry, banana

BAKED/DRIED FRUIT → Prune, raisin, jam, baked/dried cherry, baked/dried raspberry, baked/dried blackberry, currants, fig

2. COFFEE SHOP → Cinnamon, cloves, black pepper, orange peel, chocolate, vanilla, coffee, tea, black tea, licorice/anise, bubblegum, toffee

3. GARDEN → Green pepper, green olive, black olive, mushroom, eucalyptus, mint

4. FLORAL → Rosé, rosehips, violet, geranium, orange blossom

5. EARTH → Forest, mud, dirt, chalk, manure, dust

6. TOBACCO SHOP → Pine, cigar, cigarettes, leather, cedar, tar

TASTE

DRYNESS/SWEETNESS → Dry — off dry — sweet   ACID → Low — medium — high

TANNIN LEVEL → Low — medium — high   BODY → Light — medium — full

ALCOHOL LEVEL → Low (11% or below) medium (11%–13.5%) high (13.5%–15%)

Did the palate confirm the nose? YES or NO. If no, then identify _____
_____

FINISH → Short — medium — long

CONCLUSION

PRICE CATEGORY → Budget friendly ($15 or less) — moderate ($16–$30) — expensive ($30+) PRICE $_____

QUALITY → Poor — acceptable — good – outstanding

READINESS → Drink now (within the year) — could age (a couple of years) — definitely needs aging — tired

COMMENTS: _____
_____
_____

WINE TASTING

NAME: _____ Score out of 20 points_____.

Use these questions to test your knowledge and understanding of the concepts presented in the chapter.

I. MULTIPLE CHOICE: Select the best possible answer from the options available.

1. What term would apply when a white wine is lacking in adequate acidity or a red wine is lacking in acid and/or tannin?

   a. flat
   b. dry
   c. sweet
   d. tart

2. The first step of the tasting process begins with

   a. smell.
   b. taste.
   c. sight.
   d. spit or swallow.

3. The second step of the tasting process begins with

   a. smell.
   b. taste.
   c. sight.
   d. spit or swallow.

4. The third step of the tasting process is

   a. smell.
   b. taste.
   c. sight.
   d. spit or swallow.

5. The fourth step of the tasting process is

   a. smell.
   b. taste.
   c. sight.
   d. spit or swallow.

6. A white wine with a green-to-straw-yellow color may mean that the wine is

   a. youthful.
   b. aged in stainless steel.

   c. made from grapes grown in a cool climate.
   d. all of the above.

7. When looking at the wine, the best place to view youth or age is in the wine's

   a. core.
   b. rim.
   c. center.
   d. all of the above.

8. A wine's acidity causes

   a. salivation.
   b. dryness.
   c. spiciness.
   d. none of the above.

9. A wine's tannin causes

   a. salivation.
   b. dryness.
   c. spiciness.
   d. none of the above.

10. The purpose of decanting a wine is

   a. to aerate a young red wine in order to soften tannin and integrate aromas and flavors.
   b. to remove liquid from the sediment in an older red wine.
   c. to soften acid in a white wine.
   d. none of the above.
   e. all of the above.
   f. only answers a and b.

II. TRUE / FALSE: Circle the best possible answer.

11. White wine color ranges from green yellow, to straw yellow, to golden yellow, to amber, to brown. **True / False**

12. Red wine color ranges from purple, to ruby red, to brick red, to red, and then to brown. **True / False**

13. The best way to remember a wine's personality is to make an association of the aromas and flavors. **True / False**

14. The purpose of sucking oxygen into the mouth when tasting is to open up the wine's aromas and flavors. **True / False**

15. Smelling wine through the nose (on the outside) is done to perceive what is known as flavor. **True / False**

16. Smelling the wine in the mouth (on the inside) is done to perceive what is known as flavor. **True / False**

17. If a wine's alcohol content is relatively high, it generally can be sensed from a slight burn in the back of the throat. **True / False**

18. We have the ability to detect thousands of smells. **True / False**

III. SHORT-ANSWER ESSAY / DISCUSSION QUESTIONS: Use a separate sheet of paper if necessary.

19. Explain the difference between drinking wine and tasting wine.

20. Explain the four-step tasting process.

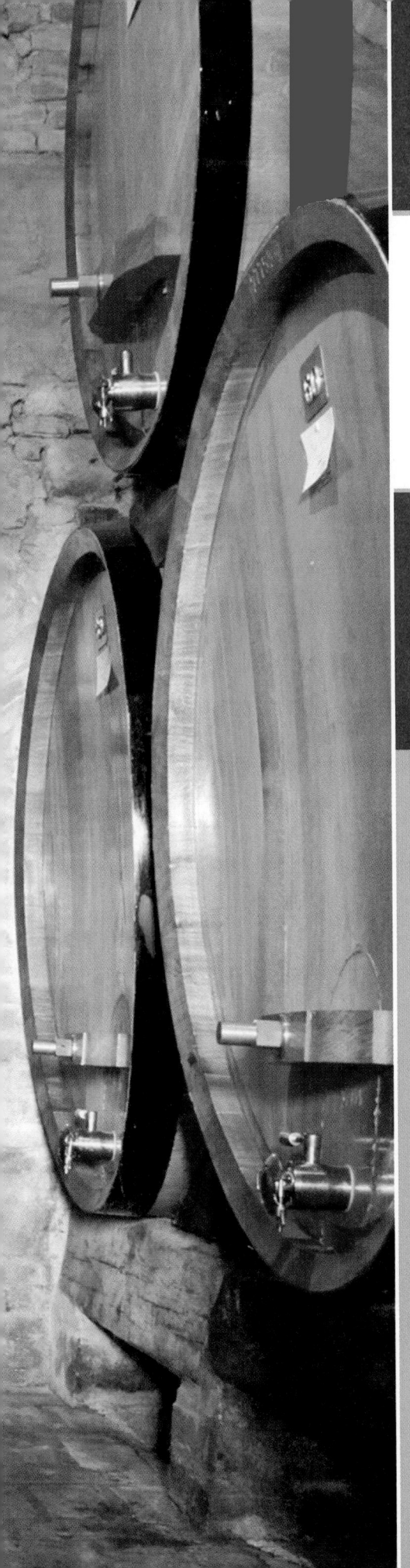

3

Viticulture and Enology

The wine in a glass is a product of nature, guided by the human hand from its initial conception in the vineyard, to its adolescence in the winery and, finally, to its maturity in the bottle.

LEARNING OBJECTIVES

Upon completion of this chapter, the learner will be able to:

- Learn how grape growing and winemaking can influence a type and style of wine.
- Discover how terroir can influence a wine's style.
- Understand the impact of key viticultural decisions and techniques on the flavors and style of a wine.
- Understand the impact of key enological decisions and techniques on the flavors and style of a wine.

FROM GRAPES TO GLASS

The wine in a glass is a product of nature, guided by the human hand from its initial conception in the vineyard, to its adolescence in the winery and, finally, to its maturity in the bottle. To produce a first-rate wine, the process must begin with the nurturing development of quality grapes, as the overall excellence initially comes from the combination of vine, grape, climate, and soil found within the vineyard. Figure 3–1 shows the two significant elements needed to create a wine.

The common phrase "Great wine is made in the vineyard" illustrates how a grape's personality is influenced much in the same way that a child is raised and nurtured. The upbringing in the vineyard can determine how the grapes behave later in life as they are transformed into wine. Once in the winery, the grapes are influenced by the numerous decisions made by the winemaker. The multiple factors in the winemaking process work collectively to alter grapes into a beverage that is desirable to drink from a glass (or for some, directly out of the bottle).

Producing wine involves two major steps typically done by two different individuals (or two different teams of individuals). The first person, responsible for growing the grapes, is called the *viticulturist* or simply, *farmer*. The second person, the specialist in creating the wine, is called the *enologist* or *winemaker*.

VITICULTURE

The science and practice of growing grapes in the vineyard

Viticulture (from the Latin word for *vine*) refers to the cultivation of grapes. When the grapes are used for winemaking, the practice is known as *viniculture*. Viticulture is the science, production, and study of grapes and deals with the series of events that occur in the vineyard.

A *vineyard* is a grape-growing area characterized by its *terroir*, a French term loosely translated as "a sense of place" and used widely throughout the wine world to distinguish one grape-growing area over another. All the nonhuman factors present in a vineyard area, such as soil, altitude, terrain, and microclimate (rain, wind, temperature, humidity, and so on), can identify the charecteristics of a vineyard and an appropriate grape to be planted. Each vineyard around the world is distinct and unique in its own way, whether it is geographically or geologically based. Every varying element of a vineyard can impart its characteristics into the grape varietal. Even though the differences may be indetectable at times, no two vineyards in the world have the exact same terroir.

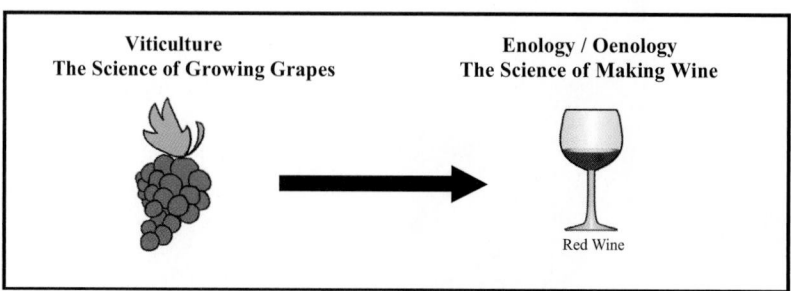

FIGURE 3–1 Viticulture and enology
(Thomas Moore)

Factors That Influence the Grape

In the vineyard, the personality of a wine is initially affected by the age of the grapevines, how they have been raised, and the soil composition (types of soil the vines are grown in). Later, the grape is influenced all the way through the growing season by exposure to sunlight, rainfall, temperature, pruning methods, and time of harvest.

The Viticulturalist

The vineyard manager commonly is responsible for monitoring and controlling pests and diseases, for fertilization and irrigation, for monitoring fruit development, for vine pruning throughout the season, and, finally, for determining when to harvest the grapes.

The most influential factor in determining the taste of wine is the grape. Therefore, viticulturalists often are intimately involved with the vision of the winemaker, because vineyard management and the resulting characteristics of the grape provide the basis from which winemaking can begin.

The Life Span of the Grapes

The grapevine is a deciduous plant that loses its leaves in the fall, becomes *dormant* (below a temperature of 50°F) in the winter, and follows the basic process of *bud break, flowering, fruit set, summer pruning, and véraison* throughout the spring and summer. Grapevines follow a growing season based on the combination of sunlight and weather. In the Northern Hemisphere, grapes usually are harvested in the late summer or early fall (September or October). In the Southern Hemisphere, harvest time (six months behind that of the Northern Hemisphere) occurs in the late winter to early spring (February or March).

FIGURE 3–2 Dormancy
(Photo by Jason Tomczak. Knudsen Vineyard, Dundee Hills AVA, Argyle Winery.com)

Dormancy—The dried vines are cut back during winter pruning to assist in conserving their energy throughout the season. Winter pruning will also train the vine for the approaching growing season. Figure 3–2 shows grape vines in dormancy.

Budbreak—In spring, the vines emerge from dormancy as sap begins to rise. As daytime temperatures warm, the emergence of green buds, or *budbreak*, occurs, where shoots begin to swell and open. At this point, growers watch the weather with concern, as the buds are extremely sensitive to frost and can easily be killed, significantly reducing or even destroying an entire crop. Figure 3–3 shows a vine at budbreak.

FIGURE 3–3 Budbreak
(Photo by Jason Tomczak. Knudsen Vineyard, Dundee Hills AVA, Argyle Winery.com)

FIGURE 3–4 Flowering
(Photo by Jason Tomczak. Knudsen Vineyard, Dundee Hills AVA, Argyle Winery.com)

FIGURE 3–5 Fruit set
(Photo by Jason Tomczak. Knudsen Vineyard, Dundee Hills AVA, Argyle Winery.com)

Flowering—When temperatures begin to reach into the mid-60s (May in the Northern Hemisphere and November in the Southern Hemisphere), the buds bloom and *flowering* occurs. It is during this phase that self-pollination and fertilization of the grapevine take place. At this point, excessive rain or hail can prevent flowering, and a significant amount of potential crop may be lost. Figure 3–4 shows a bud flowering.

The flowering stage can be of concern if the spring climate is unusually cool, rainy, or windy. Either of those conditions can cause *coulure* (coo-LYUR). Coulure occurs when the flowers have been improperly pollinated, resulting in insufficient fruit set and causing berries to abort or fall off the clusters. Another vineyard concern is *millerandage* (mill-lehr-AHN-dahj), in which grape bunches contain berries of varying sizes and maturity levels.

Fruit Set—*Fruit set* will occur during summer as the flowers form into green, hard berries. The berries continue to gain sugar and ripen throughout the summer. Figure 3–5 identifies fruit set.

Summer Pruning—Pruning is the process of removing excessive grapes and foliage from the grapevine for the purpose of influencing yield, which affects flavor development in the grapes. Pruning forces a vine to exert more energy into its fruit rather than its foiliage.

Véraison—Near the middle to end of summer, *véraison* (vehr-ray-ZOHN) occurs, where the green berries begin to change color and become recognizable as grapes. Toward the end of the summer to early fall (depending on grape varietal and climate), the grapes are at the optimal level of ripeness (level of sugar and acid) and flavor content to begin the harvest. Figure 3–6 identifies some grapes going through véraison.

FIGURE 3–6 Véraison
(del Amo,Tomas/Photolibrary.com)

1. THE GRAPEVINE

Grapevines are fairly adaptable, growing in a wide range of soils and temperature range. The most successful wine grapes are grown in temperate climate bands in the range from 30° to 50° north of the equator and from 30° to 50° south of the equator. The areas located in the temperate climate bands generally provide the right combination of sun, rain, and temperature.

As the grapes grow throughout the growing season, they gradually lose acid, and sugar levels increase through photosynthesis. The grapes also gain color and take on flavor as they begin to ripen. The grape grower's challenge is to ensure that there is enough acid in the juice to balance the sugar content, while simultaneously making certain that the grapes are neither underripe, nor overripe with sugar and flavor.

The first step in producing a quality wine is to select a grape variety best suited to the particular growing environment. Some varieties can tolerate more winter cold than others; some, more summer rain. Some varieties ripen earlier than others, making them desirable for areas with short growing seasons, whereas some mature later and are ideal for a location with a long growing season. Once the grower has decided which grape varieties to plant, a process begins that will take several years to bear fruit.

The types of grapes used to make a wine probably are the single most important factor in the taste and style of wine. Indeed, at the dinner table, the grapes and the style of wine are the dominant consideration in deciding which food items eventually are paired with a wine.

There are about 20 different species of grapevines, but only one of them, *Vitis vinifera,* the European species, produces all the grapes used in high-quality wine.

The native North American *Vitis labrusca* is another grape-growing species used by some winemakers, mainly in challenging climates. The labrusca is a hardier vine able to withstand extreme cold temperatures, but its musky off flavors tend to rule it out as a serious wine producer. Labrusca possibly is most famous for its Concord grape used in the production of jams, jellies, and grape juice.

Within the *vinifera* species, there is estimated to be as many as 10,000 strains, clones, and hybrids of different variations of grapes. Most of the wine world depends on perhaps 30 to 40 grapes, of which an even smaller number are considered *classics*, or Noble grape varietals.

Clones are grapes that are produced through the replication of an original vine that may arise over time through natural evolution or manipulated intentionally through grafting vines (referred to as, scions) onto rootstocks. Either method may allow the clone to become modified due to climatic effects. Cloned grapes may develop characteristics that differ from the parent as the grapevines evolve and mutate with changes in their surroundings. The differences in the flavor profile can range from being very pronounced to being extremely difficult to discriminate on the palate. For example, the Sangiovese grape that is prevalent throughout central Italy varies significantly enough with its location that it is commonly identified by different names to point out the various distinctions.

Cross-pollination occurs between two different grapes of the same vine species, either naturally through evolution or intentionally within a vine nursery. For example, current evidence suggests that the Cabernet Sauvignon grape varietal is derived from the natural crossing of the Cabernet Franc and Sauvignon Blanc varietals.

Hybrid grapes are created from cross-pollinating two different vine species, such as American vine (to obtain hardiness) and European vine (to obtain complexity) varieties. Some notable hybrids are Seyval (say-VEL) Blanc and Vidal (vee-DAHL) Blanc, which are both prevalent in New York State and Canada.

This textbook will concentrate on *the Big Six grapes produced from the* vinifera *vine species*—Riesling, Sauvignon Blanc, Chardonnay, Pinot Noir, Merlot, and Cabernet Sauvignon—but will also discuss other important grapes grown throughout the world. The list easily could include so many more magnificent grape varieties, but the Big Six grapes are selected because of their adaptability in multiple locations to produce quality wines throughout the world.

The Vineyard

Vineyards can vary in size and in spacing between individual vines. Varying quantities of grapes can be grown, depending on the age of the vine, the variety of grape, the amount of rainfall, and various viticulture practices. In addition, different grape varieties have the ability to yield larger or smaller amounts of juice per pound. Figure 3–7 depicts the orderly arrangment of a vineyard.

As a rough guideline, one vineyard acre can contain 900 to 1300 vines, which collectively can yield from 2 to 12 tons of grapes, equal to about 300-plus cases of wine bottles. A single vine can produce between 15 and 45 clusters of grapes, which collectively can produce somewhere between 40 and 75 grapes. A single vine can produce about four to six bottles of wine annually. In Europe, Canada, and South America, vineyard size is commonly measured in hectares (ha), as opposed to acres in the United States. (For reference, 1 hectare is equivalent to 2.47 acres.)

FIGURE 3–7 Vineyard rows

♦ Exact figures vary greatly from vineyard to vineyard, according to the variety of grape, desired yields, the planting formation, the age of the vines, and so on.

(Ron Redfern © Dorling Kindersley)

2. CLIMATE

Weather and location

The geographical location and related climate significantly dictate the type of grapes a vineyard is able to successfully grow. A producer selects varieties specifically for their style and their suitability to a particular site—varieties that will perform best under the climatic conditions within the producer's specific vineyards. Through hundreds of years of trial and error, the French invented and perfected this system of matching varietal to location.

Today's winemakers have many methods for manipulating wine; however, the basic climatic influence will always be one of the most significant factors affecting the personality of a given wine. Grapevines do not tolerate extended periods below freezing, nor can they take tropical heat. Therefore, wine grapes grow best in temperate climates associated with both the Northern and Southern Hemispheres. The length of the growing season, daily temperatures, and amount of sun and rain all influence the sugar–acid balance and flavor development.

Climate factors are important considerations in wine and often may influence the appropriateness of a food pairing. Climate can affect a wine's fruit ripeness, acidity level, alcohol level, tannin, and aromas and flavors. White wines from cool climates have aromas and flavors associated with cool-climate tree fruits such as apples and pears. Warm climates give aromas and flavors associated with warm-climate trees and tropical fruit such as mango, banana, and pineapple. Cool-climate red wines promote fresh fruits such as cranberries and red cherries, whereas warm climates encourage dried and stewed fruits such as figs, plums, and dried cherries. These examples highlight aroma and flavor differences between grapes grown in different climates, but certainly also will influence other variables such as acidity and alcohol content. The aroma and flavor difference (as well as other factors) can be used as a basis for establishing and justifying a particular wine and food pairing (discussed in greater detail in Chapters 4, 5, and 6).

In warm climates such as in California, grapes maintain high sugar levels because of their magnified exposure to sun and excessive heat throughout the growing season. In addition, as the grapes sugar content rises, the acid level drops. This can result in a wine with low acid and high alcohol. In a warm climate, sugar development is automatic, but if the climate is too hot, the grapes will not ripen fast enough. In some warm wine-growing areas, winemakers are allowed to add acid (a method known as acidification) during the winemaking process to balance the drop in acid due to the increased sugar content.

In cool climates such as in Germany, grapes maintain higher acid levels because the cooling influence limits the production of sugar and maintains the grapes' natural crispness. This climate produces grapes with lower natural sugar levels because the grapes have not been exposed to the sun and warmth consistently for a long enough period. The result may be a wine with low alcohol content and, possibly, slightly underripe flavors.

In some wine-growing regions such as Germany, as well as Champagne, Burgundy, and Alsace, in France, winemakers may be allowed to manipulate the ripening process to make up for the limitations imposed by the climate. Depending on the classification level, some winemakers may add sugar in the process known as *chaptalization* (shap-tuh-luh-ZAY-shuhn) or reserve grape juice during the winemaking process to make up for the lack of sugar that was not naturally produced in the grapes. This sugar is necessary in some cases in order to eventually ferment the grapes and turn the juice into alcohol.

Climates can be broadly classified for the purpose of understanding grapes that may grow and prosper. Four major types of climates (often referred to as *macroclimates*) are found throughout the major wine-producing areas:

1. **Maritime Climates** have large bodies of water that moderate the temperatures throughout the year by keeping summers cool and winters mild and, overall, the environment moist. Examples are New Zealand and Bordeaux.
2. **Continental Climates** have four distinct seasons with short, hot summers and cold winters. Examples are Champagne and Burgundy.
3. **Mediterranean Climates** have long warm-to-hot growing seasons with mild winters, low moisture, and low rainfall. Examples are Rhone, Provence, and Southern Spain.
4. **Alpine Climates** have influences of altitude from vineyards being perched upon mountainous areas. Examples are parts of Northern Spain, Argentina, and Southeastern France.

Within the macroclimate, there are smaller growing areas that may have different weather or climate patterns. Growing areas can be influenced by such local factors as lakes or rivers, or even hillsides with greater or lesser sun exposure. This type of smaller climate pattern, known as a *microclimate,* has the ability to alter the personality of a given grape or even influence the growth of a grape variety completely different from those that might be found in the larger, broader climate area.

3. SOIL

Soil is the medium necessary for a grapevine to grow, as it supports the root structure and controls drainage levels and amounts of minerals and nutrients that the vine is exposed to. Grapes have the ability to extract flavors and attributes from the geological conditions that they are partnered with.

These conditions include soil and all of the other non-human factors (or terroir) that contribute to the personality of a wine. Terroir is a guiding principle behind most of European winemaking, apparent from the practice of labelling the wines according to their location of origin. The Europeans, and certainly the French, believe that the place influences the personality and distinction of the grapes in its own unique way that cannot be duplicated elsewhere, similar to the unique and distinguishing mark of a fingerprint.

Influence of the Soil

Soil is a mixture of minerals, organic matter, and particles that are of different sizes and textures. Grapevines grow in a combination of *topsoil* and *subsoil* with varying particles. The sizes of the particles determine the texture of the soil, which influences a grapevine's root structure, water drainage, temperature, and absorbtion levels of minerals and nutrients. Essentially, the best soils for grape growing are lightly textured soils because they allow for good drainage, have a good capacity to hold nutrients, and are relatively infertile. Ideally, well-drained infertile soils force the vine to struggle for its nutrients, which results in a good concentration of flavor characteristics in the grapes.

Different types of soil are available in different geographic wine-growing areas. High importance is placed on matching the correct or suitable soil type with the appropriate type of grapes. However, soil is highly variable even in individual vineyards. Soils can affect vines in several ways:

1. Soils can influence the temperature of the vineyard. Darker soils retain heat well, whereas light-colored soils reflect sunlight either toward or away from the vines.
2. Soils can influence water management. Free-draining soils force roots to grow downward to reach nutrients and water.
3. Soils can affect flavor development. In cooler climates such as Champagne, where grapes ripen slowly, the strong mineral content of the soil influences the flavor profile of the wine.

Figure 3–8 shows the chalky soil that is highly prevalent in the Champagne region of France.

Topsoil and subsoils are extremely important to vine development and consequently influence the personality of the grapes. In rich topsoil, the vine does not need to dig hard because its nutrients are found close to the surface. Thus, yields are likely to be high and quality may be low. However, if the vines are given poor, low-nutrient soil, the roots are forced to dip deep, and this results in better grapes, according to the *struggling vine philosophy*. This philosophy theorizes that the farther the vine's roots must dig to find nutrients, the fewer, but better-quality, grapes will be produced, with thicker skins and more concentrated flavor. In order for the vine and the grapes to retrieve their nutritional requirements, the vines grow slowly and thus produce fewer grapes, but with greater flavor development. Ultimately, a better wine may be produced because of a better-quality ingredient. The chart shown in Figure 3–9 lists some general characteristics associated with how various types of soil may function.

Classic Soil Types

In some famous wine regions, the soils produce certain varieties of grape that are considered almost legendary in the manner that they are expressed. This is not to say that the same grapes can't be grown in alternative soil types and still produce high quality. But in the wine world, the degree of distinction associated with something such as soil that can't be duplicated by humans carries a certain romance and desirability. The following table lists some legendary kinds of grapes grown in their respective soil types and regions:

FIGURE 3–8 Chalk cliff in the Champagne vineyard
(Collection CIVC.
CIV Photographer: SPAANS ERIK)

FAMOUS SOIL TYPES				
GRAPE		**SOIL**		**REGION**
Chardonnay	→	Chalk	→	Champagne, France
Cabernet Sauvignon	→	Gravel	→	Bordeaux, France
Pinot Noir	→	Limestone	→	Burgundy, France
Riesling	→	Slate	→	Mosel, Germany

Appellations

The French term *appellation* refers to a viticulture region distinguished by geographical features that produce wines with shared characteristics. In simple terms, an appellation is a place where the grapes are grown. Though the term has a specific meaning to European grape growers, most wine-producing countries use it loosely. The idea of appellation is that the soil, climate, sun, and water quality of a region combine to produce a style of wine that cannot be duplicated elsewhere. The size of an appellation can range from very small plots of land to huge areas that cover hundreds of miles.

In 1935, France founded the Institut National des Appellations d' Origine (an-stee-TYOO nah-syaw-NAHL dayz ah-pehl-lah-SYOHN daw-ree-ZHEEN), or INAO, becoming the first nation to set up a countrywide system based on geography for controlling the origin and quality of wine. The *Appellation Controlee* system, or AC, is a French term meaning "controlled appellation of origin" and is applied to standards of production for various kinds and types of products such as wine, cheese, butter, and so on. The designation is given and controlled by the French government, and it guarantees that the products have been held to a set of rigorous production standards.

This plan originated during the Great Depression as a preventative measure to protect French winemakers and consumers from fraudulent and inferior wine-blending methods practiced by some unethical French wine brokers.

INFLUENCE OF COMMON SOIL				
Stones >	**Gravel** >	**Sand** >	**Silt** >	**Clay**
Larger Particles				Smaller Particles
Poor Nutrients				Rich Nutrients
High Drainage				Low Drainage
Warmer Soils				Colder Soils
Retains Heat				Reflects Heat
Heat of Minerals				Retains Minerals
Early Ripening				Late Ripening

FIGURE 3–9 **The influence of common soil types in Southern Rhone Valley**
(Vineyards Domaine de la Mordoreé)

The system is based on several levels, with the highest and most stringent tier called the *Appellation d' Origin Controlee* (AOC). This top category is reserved for wines meeting quality criteria in seven areas: (1) land, (2) grape varieties used, (3) viticulture practices, (4) permissible yield, (5) alcohol content, (6) winemaking practices, and (7) official tasting.

The system is the model in the wine industry and parallels other systems throughout the world, such as the Denominazione Di Origine Controllata Garantita (DOCG) in Italy and the Denominacion De Origen Calificada (DOCa) in Spain. Outside of France, the systems may or may not be as strict or as comprehensive.

The European Union (EU)

The European Union (EU) has registered place names called appellations of origin. Each EU country defines the specifics of its appellations of origin in terms of standards for type of grapes grown, processes for grape growing, and wine-making methods. Each appellation serves as a definition of the wine, as well as the wine's name. The EU regulates the wine appellations. The chart on the left identifies the quality levels of top classifications for France, Italy, Spain and Germany.

In the United States, appellations are known as *American viticulture areas*, or AVAs. In simple terms, a viticulture area is a place where the grapes are grown. However, the American viticulture areas carry a different connotation than the French appellations of origin. American labels may identify a wine's AVA or location when a minimum of 85% of the grapes used for the wine come from the AVA specified on the label. The French AOC regulations have stricter guidelines, which include standards regulating vineyard location, grape varietal, growing technique, crop yield, grape ripeness, ensuing alcohol content, and winemaking practices.

Generally, the French rely more on topography and the effect of nature upon grapes than do Americans. It is the basis on which the entire French wine classification and terroir concept are built. However, American winemakers do recognize what important elements regional flavors and style characteristics are to wine identification and classification. To illustrate, a wine labelled simply "California Chardonnay" could originate from anywhere in California, rather than only from the Sonoma-Napa County wine region or even the more specific, "Carneros" AVA that is within Napa and Sonoma.

Sustainable Agriculture and Biodynamics

The sustainable, or "green," concept is gaining momemtum as the world becomes more aware of and concerned not only about its food supply and other resources, but also about the environment in general. Sustainable viticulture is known to be ecologically sound. With today's more educated customers, the wine world has started to implement a bit of green philosophy. This trend not only benefits the earth's natural resources, but, many believe, results in better-tasting grapes and, thus, more flavorful wine that can reflect the distinctiveness of the land.

Biodynamics is a view of the land as a living system and of the vineyards as an ecological self-sustaining whole. Biodynamics takes organic farming to a new level. The concept was developed by Austrian philosopher Rudolph Steiner in 1924 as a way to express the authenticity of the vineyard in which the produce (grapes, in this case) has been grown. It bans pesticides and artificial additives and strives for a self-contained sustainable farming system in which water and organic materials are recycled to regenerate the land.

As of 2007, there are over 20 certified biodynamic wineries in the United States and 200 more throughout the world; however, this number is growing each day.

4. GRAPEVINE MAINTENANCE

Grapevine maintenance is a lot like nurturing a child going through adolescence. We attempt to raise children with values and principles and to help them create futures filled with an excellent quality of life. As parents, we attempt to keep children away from predators and other elements that may do them harm and stifle their development. With grapes, the goals are similar as the grape grower attempts to guide them, provide nourishment, nurture them to develop excellent qualities, and keep them protected from predators.

Pruning

Crop control involves the adjustment of grapevines by *pruning*—an important factor in determining the quality of the grapes and, ultimately, of the wine. Pruning is the process of removing excessive grapes and foliage from the vine for the purpose of affecting yield, which influences flavor development in the grapes. It forces a vine to exert more energy into its fruit rather than its foiliage.

If pruning is limited, the results will be a high yield of grapes per vine with less intense flavors and reduced concentration. Alternatively, if high pruning is conducted, the result will be lower quantity, but higher-quality, concentrated grapes. Theoretically, the fewer grapes there are on a vine, the more concentrated is the juice of the grape.

Pruning requires a delicate balance. The answer is neither to always prune excessively nor not to prune at all. In both situations, the grapes can be prone to viticultural and financial hazards. Too much pruning can cause the grape crop to be uneconomical, as it creates an expensive wine, whereas too little pruning can cause diluted grapes, creating a low-quality wine.

Typically, high-quality vineyards produce around two tons of grapes per acre or less, whereas vineyards of lower quality levels may produce in excess of 12 to 14 tons of grapes per acre.

In many vineyards, the method of *dropping crop* is practiced, according to which some of the grape bunches are picked and dropped on the soil next to the vines. This practice has two benefits:

1. The flavors are more strongly concentrated in the remaining grapes left on the vine.
2. The dropped crop gets absorbed back into the topsoil, adding nutrients to the grapevine.

Canopy Management

Canopy management is the practice of adjusting or positioning the vine's leaves, shoots, and fruit as the vine grows, in order to gain such beneficial advantages as increased sunlight exposure and air movement. Canopy management improves varietal character and decreases problems with fungal rot and insects.

COMMON HAZARDS IN THE VINEYARDS

There are numerous microorganisms, pests, and disease that can attack and kill grapes and vines. Both temporary and permanent solutions have been developed to combat these viticultural challenges.

Microorganisms

Fungal Disease—Managing fungal diseases such as odium, mildew, grey rot, and so on is a constant concern in the vineyard. Fungal disease is often associated with vineyard locations with excessive rain or with constantly moist climates without adequate sunshine. In some cases, wind can assist in drying the vines and helping to prevent some fungal disease.

Widespread control methods to lessen fungal disease have included chemical sprays such as *bouillie bordelaise* (Bwee-YEE Bor-duh-LEZZ) (a solution of copper sulfate, lime, and water) and better knowledge of canopy management.

Glassy Winged Sharpshooter—These pests are named after the glassy or transparent appearance of their wings. The sharpshooters have caused widespread disease by passing on the bacterial infection known as *Pierce's disease*. Insecticides have been used to deter the ailment, but have not worked as a complete solution. Currently, experimentation with biological control by natural enemies is underway.

Animals/Pests

Phylloxera (fil-LOX-er-uh)—This aphid feeds on the roots of grapevines (especially on the highly vulnerable Vinifera roostock species), causing the vine to starve and thus preventing fruit development.

In the 1800s, phylloxera was unknowingly transported from hardy Native American vine species (which are resistant to phylloxera) in the United States to the Vinifera species in Europe. Over the next 100 years, the vineyards of France, Spain, and other countries were nearly devastated. It took Bordeaux over three generations to recover.

The solution was to graft Vinifera vines to the American rootstock. *Grafting* in the vineyard is the technique of securing a vine to a rootstock. In most Vinifera vineyards (except for those in Chile and vinyards in some parts of Australia), cuttings of the desired varieties are grafted onto rootstocks of Native American varieties that are resistant to phylloxera.

Birds—Birds eat grapes as a source of nourishment. Large nets are often placed across the vineyards in order to deter birds. Other animals such as deer and raccoons have been known to consume fruit and cause vineyard damage.

Weather

Wind—Wind may prevent pollination of the flowers during the early part of the season. Later in the season, the winds can knock fruit off the vine and heavier winds can knock vines over. Some of the heaviest winds occur in Southern France (the Mistral) where they have been known to rip vines right out of the ground.

Frost—Frost is a serious danger in many vineyards, especially those located on the valley floors where the coldest air settles on frosty nights. Sprayers, burners, and wind machines can all be used collectively or separately where frost is a constant danger to the buds, flowers, or berries. Wind machines are used to distribute heat from a central heat source, such as a fire or chaufferettes (gas heaters), that warms the grapes (or vines) to keep them free of frost. (See Figure 3–10, which depicts "Chaufferettes" in a Champagne vineyard protecting the vines against the frost.)

FIGURE 3–10 "Chaufferettes," protection against the frosts

(Collection CIVC.
Photographer: DIVERS)

FIGURE 3–11 Sprinklers

(Collection CIVC.
Photographer: HODDER JOHN)

FIGURE 3–12 Against the frosts: a bud wrapped by ice to protect it from the frosts

(Collection CIVC.
Photographer: HODDER JOHN)

Many grape growers located in cold climates (particularly with early budding grapes) may also use *aspersion*, which involves sprayers that release water into the air. The water that lands on the grapes (or buds) forms an outer ice shell, but a warm, protected state is maintained on the inside. Figures 3–11 and 3–12 show water spraying on grapevines to form a protective coating around a bud to protect it from damage due to frost.

Rain—Heavy rains are a concern both in early spring and at harvest time. Too much rain can prevent pollination of flowers in the spring. If it rains near harvest time, the fruit may be over-saturated and the flavors, sugars, and acid that have been developing throughout the growing season may be diluted.

In locations such as Argentina and Australia, where lack of rain is a consistent problem, select vineyard areas may be allowed to use irrigation systems created to feed off nearby rivers or lakes.

5. HARVESTING

Picking the grapes

All grapes start out as unripe, hard, green berries. Finally, after the grapes have been exposed to enough sun and heat, the white wine grapes change to yellow and the red wine grapes to purple in a process known as *véraison* (vehr-ray-ZOHN). This is part of the ripening process, when grapes change color, acid decreases, and sugar content, or *brix,* increases. Véraison is an indicator that the grapes are evolving along their path, eventually to be harvested.

In the Northern Hemisphere, grapes ripen in late summer or early fall, depending on both the varietal and the climate. As the growing season progresses, the winemakers ultimately decide when the grapes will be ready for harvest on the basis of sugar ripeness and flavor development. The winemakers' concern is to pick grapes at the correct level of ripeness and near the harvest; grapes are often measured multiple times throughout the day. There is a small window of time when the grapes (depending upon the climate and the type of grape) should be picked, because if picked too early, the grapes will be underripe, and if picked too late, they will be overripe.

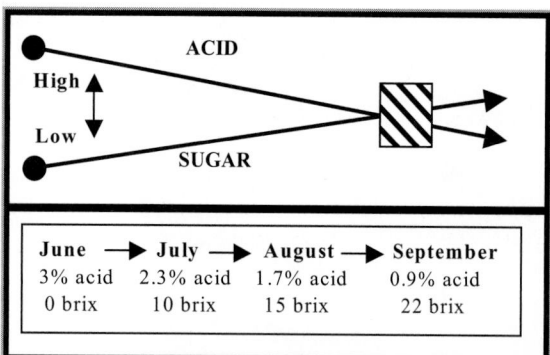

FIGURE 3–13 Acid/sugar ratio

(John Laloganes)

The ability to evaluate grape ripeness is vital for determining the suitable time of harvest. The evaluation should involve both an objective approach, by measuring grape sugars (through the use of a refractometer), and a subjective one, by measuring flavor through the use of taste. Flavor ripeness (otherwise known as phenolic ripeness) is represented by a group of compounds that contribute color, aroma, flavor, and tannin to a grape. This kind of ripeness allows the tannins to become softer as the growing season progresses. Phenolic ripeness often trails sugar ripeness, but is important for allowing the maximum flavor of the grape to be obtained. Grape ripeness can be compared with teenagers in this regard; Often, their bodies (a grape's sugar content) mature faster than their minds (a grape's flavor development), leading the teens to believe that they are older and more mature than they really may be.

A recent 10- to 15-year trend has been to extend the "hang time" (the delay of harvest) of the grapes, with the expectation of increasing flavor development. This practice produces very ripe fruit that yields a "jammy" quality in the finished wine. In some cases, certain producers have been criticized for too much hang time, allowing the grapes to become overripe with a surplus of sugars to yield a wine that is higher in alcohol and can be excessively out of balance.

There has to be sufficient sugar in the juice of wine grapes for yeast to feed on and convert into alcohol. When there is too much sugar, the wine becomes cloyingly sweet, or flabby; when there is too little sugar, the wine becomes thin and unsatisfying. Figure 3–13 offers a perspective on sugar and acid balance throughout the growing season.

In warm-to-hot climates, sugar/acid ripeness is almost automatic, but it presents a problem. Phenolic ripeness and sugar ripeness don't happen simultaneously, and the concern is when sugars develop too quickly before phenolic ripeness has caught up. In this environment, the grower is forced to harvest grapes earlier than desired or risk losing the grapes' acid. Unfortunately, at this time, the flavor of the wine may not have developed as fast as the sugar, leaving somewhat of an underripe flavor in the wine.

In cool climates, both types of ripeness are a concern because each will inhibit the ability of a vine to produce sugar and develop flavor. Most often, grapes are planted at various angles on hillsides for the maximum exposure to sunlight, to assist in the development of sugars and flavors. In these environments, the vines develop at a slower rate, and the greater concern tends to be frost striking in early fall, damaging the grapes before they are ready to be picked.

ENOLOGY

The science of making wine in the winery

Methods of production can vary greatly from country to country, region to region, and even grower to grower. Among the influential factors that shape the quality and style of a wine are the grower's philosophy and whether it is based on tradition or innovation. Figure 3–14 shows the common steps in white and red wine production.

Making Wine

In the winery, personality of the wine is influenced by how the grapes are handled and fermented, the types of yeast used, and whether the wine is aged in wood or stainless steel.

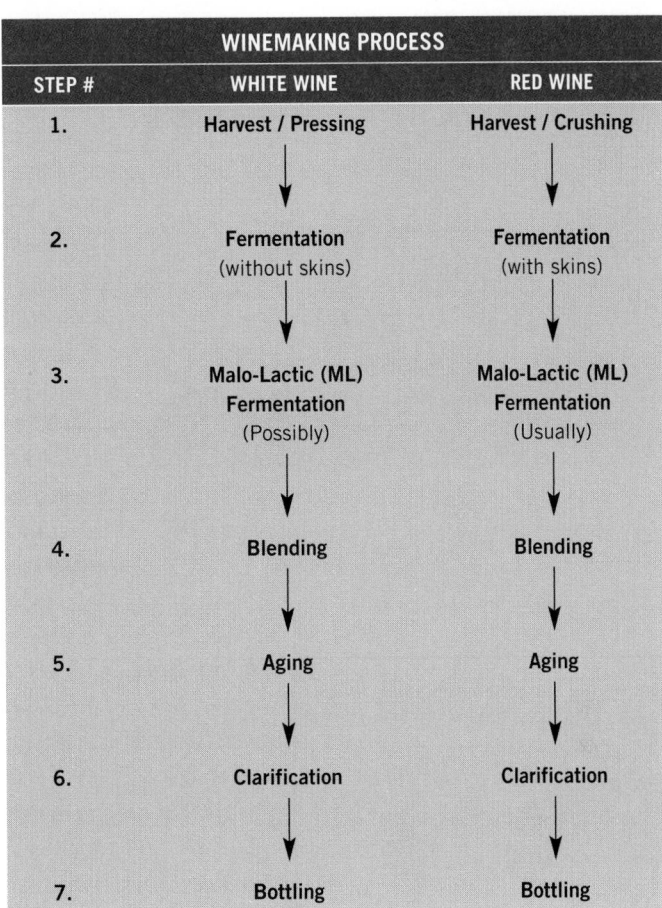

WINEMAKING PROCESS		
STEP #	WHITE WINE	RED WINE
1.	Harvest / Pressing	Harvest / Crushing
2.	Fermentation (without skins)	Fermentation (with skins)
3.	Malo-Lactic (ML) Fermentation (Possibly)	Malo-Lactic (ML) Fermentation (Usually)
4.	Blending	Blending
5.	Aging	Aging
6.	Clarification	Clarification
7.	Bottling	Bottling

FIGURE 3–14 The winemaking process
(John Laloganes)

♦ It is important to note that some of the winemaking process steps outlined here may occur in practice in a slightly different order, and/or some steps may occur multiple times throughout the winemaking process.

FIGURE 3–15 The harvest time in Champagne
(Collection CIVC.
Photographer: HODDER JOHN)

Therefore, the same grape varietals can be grown in France, Italy, Australia, and California, but various factors will result in wines with differing flavors and aromas.

The winemaker is similar to the chef, as they both create something out of raw ingredients according to a preliminary vision. Both require specialized skills and have been taught the best manner to bring out the maximum potential from the ingredients they are using to create their finished product. Initially, the winemaker has to envision the type and style of wine he or she wishes to create. A winemaker's goal is to make the best-tasting wine possible from the raw product available. Ultimately, however, as the philosophy goes, great wine is made in the vineyard.

1. HARVESTING AND PRESSING/CRUSHING—Great care is taken to ensure that grapes are picked at the right time and in the correct manner. At harvest time, the quality of the grapes represents the greatest potential of any wine that can be created. Just as a chef takes painstaking efforts to select the best-quality ingredients to produce a dish, winemakers search for the most excellent grapes to make the greatest wine possible. Pictured in Figure 3–15 are Champagne vineyards ready for harvesting.

The harvest and crush typically will take two to three weeks before all desirable grapes are obtained. Freshly picked bunches of grapes are put into mechanical crushing

FIGURE 3–16 Crushing grapes
(Alice Grulich-Jones/Omni-Photo Communications, Inc.)

and destemming machines. The higher-quality wines are made from the first pressing of grape juice, known as *free run*, while lower-quality wines are made from progressive pressings called *press wine*. With olive oil, the first pressing of the olives yields what is known as extra virgin oil because of its purity. It is the same with wine grapes: Secondary pressings release additional juice, harsh and not as pure as the free run. Figure 3–16 illustrates the destemming process that is necessary prior to crushing red wine grapes.

The remains of the grapes after the juice has been pressed out are known as *pomace* (PUHM-ess) which is a dry mass of pulp, skins, and grape seeds. The pomace can be used to fertilize the vineyard or sold to spirit producers to distill and make into brandy. As the grapes are being pressed or crushed, until fermentation is complete the grape juice is known as *must*.

Yeast consumes sugar and releases by-products of:
1) Alcohol 2) Carbon Dioxide 3) Heat

Alcohol
CO2
Heat

Yeast   **Grapes**

FIGURE 3–17 Fermentation process
(Thomas Moore)

2. FERMENTATION—The *bloom*, or white powdery film on the grape skin that gives the grapes their dusty look, contains millions of *wild yeast* cells. The problem with wild yeasts is that the effects of their fermentation are difficult to understand and predict. In most cases, winemakers use *sulfur dioxide* to destroy the wild yeasts (and, in the process, also kill bacteria and mold) so that the wild yeasts cannot interfere with the *cultured yeasts* which are universally chosen because they are more predictable and understood.

Some winemaking purists produce wine with wild yeasts because they believe that wild yeasts are indigenous to the origin of the grape's vineyard and winery. They believe that natural yeasts are an essential aspect to the terroir, as they provide a wine with personality derived from a specific place.

The diagram in Figure 3–17 illustrates the fermentation process.

Yeast is eventually added to the grape must, where it gradually breaks down the sugar into carbon dioxide, alcohol, and heat. The alcohol will be in the flavor or personality of the grape used. As the grape juice (or must) is fermenting and converting into wine, the carbon dioxide is allowed to escape (except in the case of sparkling wine) and the release of heat is controlled through refrigeration.

The level of alcohol produced during fermentation depends primarily on the sugar content of the grapes and the point at which the winemaker decides to stop fermentation. In most situations, the winemaker allows the yeast to consume all or most of the grape sugar (particularly for red wine), yielding a dry wine with higher alcohol. If the winemaker halts fermentation prior to the yeast consuming all or most of the sugar, then unfermented sugar known as *residual sugar* or RS will remain and leave a sweet wine with lower alcohol.

The amount of alcohol produced from fermentation depends largely on the amount of sugar that is available for yeast consumption. Of course, there are ways to manipulate this equation, but it is not always legal or advantageous to participate in them.

Fermentation takes place in large containers called *vats*. For red wines, the skins are present; white wines are fermented without the skins; and for rosés, the skins are left on for a portion of the time. This is referred to as *maceration* or juice and skin contact time.

SACCHAROMYCES CEREVISIAE

(sack-row-MY-ceese)

This is the common and famous yeast used in the production of various wines and beers, with more than 700 catalogued strains. Wild yeast was beginning to be understood in the 1850s through the work of Louis Pasteur. Currently, winemakers can purchase specific strains of cultured yeasts that are suited for particular tasks. Some strains can ferment high amounts of grape sugar, while others can highlight specific flavor profiles.

Climate's Effects on Winemaking Methods   In warm-to-hot climates, winemakers are sometimes allowed to add acid in a process known as *acidification* to make up for what was lost throughout the long growing season.

In cool climates, winemakers are sometimes allowed to add sugar in a process known as *chaptalization* to make up for the lack of sugar developed throughout the short growing season.

White Wine Fermentation   As the grapes are pressed, the clear juice is fermented on its own without skins. This is not only because the skins are not needed for color, but also because any potential tannin extracted from skins may detract from the subtle flavor nuances associated with a white wine.

Because of the heat produced during fermentation, most delicate white wines are fermented in stainless steel or temperature-controlled vats to preserve the delicate fruit aromatics. Control of temperature during fermentation is critical: Too high of a temperature will burn out any fruit aromas and flavors. If the wine is fermented at too low of a temperature, not enough alcohol will be created.

White wine is usually fermented and maintained within a range of 45 to 70°F. Because of the low temperature, the fermentation time for white wine often takes several weeks. During this process or after it has been completed, the wine is often held in stainless steel vats or wood barrels for a few months.

Red Wine Fermentation   When the grapes are crushed, the juice is allowed to remain in contact, or macerate, with the skins and seeds for a period during red or rosé wine fermentation. The longer the maceration period, the more certain it is that components such as tannin, color, and aromas/flavors will be extracted from the skins. To ferment red wine, the temperature of the must is brought between 70 to 90°F. The fermentation time for red wines is somewhere between several days to a few weeks. For most fuller-bodied red wines, this process takes about four weeks for extended maceration in order to extract more color, flavor, and tannin.

The Relation of Skins to Juice and Tannin

Some grape varietals such as Cabernet Sauvignon have small berries with a larger proportion of skin and seeds compared with pulp. The thicker skins not only minimize the evaporation of water from inside the grape during hot weather, but also give the wine its characteristic deep color. The skin and seeds (possibly along with the stems) contribute to tannin that acts as a natural preservative, but also adds a desired dryness to wine. In comparison, grapes such as Pinot Noir have thin skins and tend to produce lighter-colored wine.

The amount of tannin varies significantly within wine. Tannin levels depend on many factors: grape variety, growing season, winemaking methods, and so on. Tannins can add a desirable, tactile, dry complexity to the wine. It is important that winemakers not add too much (by longer extraction time or by too many stems or seeds), because excess tannin (in addition to being underripe phenolics) will give an undesirable astringent quality to the finished wine.

The thin skins also allow more evaporation from within the grapes, which makes Pinot Noir more difficult to grow successfully in hot climates. Wines made from thin-skinned grapes also tend to have less color pigment, low tannin, and less structure compared with those made from thicker-skinned varieties.

Other Fermentation Techniques

Carbonic Fermentation   *Carbonic fermentation,* also called "whole-berry fermentation," is a popular technique for producing light, fruity, red wines. The purpose is to make a red wine that accentuates its youthful fruitiness and avoids excessive, unwanted tannin.

Since the red wine grape juice is allowed to ferment with the grape skins, carbon dioxide produced during fermentation pushes a thick layer of the purple skins, stems, and seeds to the surface of the fermenting vessel, forming a *cap*. It is necessary to sub-merge the cap within the must; otherwise, it will be exposed to oxygen and subject to bacterial growth. As the cap is pushed back into the must, greater color and flavor extraction occur.

1. **Punching Down**—The gentle process of pushing the cap down into the wine as it is fer-menting is common in Bur-gundy, France. This method is used to minimize air contact and allow for minimal extract of excessive tannins.

2. **Pumping Over**—The aggres-sive process of pumping and circulating the juice (with a giant hose) over the cap dur-ing fermentation is commonly used in Bordeaux in order to extract maximum color, juice, and tannin from skins.

3. **Rotary Fermenters** — A large mechanical device periodi-cally rotates the juice and skin in order to maintain contact between them. The process is similar to that of a cement mixer.

REASONS FOR BLENDING

✓ Adjust or fine-tune the aromas/flavors.
✓ Adjust the components of acid, tannin, alcohol, or fruit.
✓ Adjust the color.
✓ Adjust the price.
✓ Add greater dimension or complexity.

Carbonic maceration is a quick process that takes about one to two weeks and produces a simple, one-dimensional type of wine. This fermentation technique is indigenous to the Beaujolais subregion of Burgundy, France.

Barrel Fermentation *Barrel fermentation* means that the unfermented grape juice was converted to wine in wood barrels. The term typically applies only to white wine.

Micro-Oxygenation *Micro-oxygenation* is a winemaking technique that introduces small amounts of controlled oxygen into the barrels of a red wine as it ages. This method produces a young red wine that tastes older than it is, by softening tannins and speeding the aging process.

3. MALOLACTIC FERMENTATION

Also called "secondary fermentation" Winemakers sometimes use a secondary technique based on a biochemical reaction. Malolactic fermentation (ML) transforms crisp, sharp *malic acid* into softer, creamier *lactic acid*. The result is a reduction of tartness and added buttery aromas and flavors, along with added texture. The release of the butter-like flavor derives from a natural chemical known as *diacetyl* (die-ASS-ih-tahl).

This effect of ML is similar to the difference between the taste of a tart Granny Smith apple, which contains malic acid, and the taste of creamy milk, which contains lactic acid. The winemaker may perform malolactic fermentation on all of the wine or on only a portion, depending on how much acid is desired to be converted.

Malolactic fermentation is applied to most red wines and a select few white wines. For white wine, the winemaker typically uses this process for Chardonnay, particularly from California and Australia, and generally, in smaller doses throughout the rest of the world.

4. BLENDING—Blending can take place during various stages of the winemaking process. In some cases, it can take place immediately after fermentation or just before clarification. It truly depends on the training and vision of the winemaker.

Some of the most famous wines in the world consist of a blend of complementary grape varietals. For example, Champagne contains a combination of Pinot Noir, Chardonnay, and Pinot Meunier. Bordeaux is another classic blended wine that consists of varying quantities of Cabernet Sauvignon, Merlot, Cabernet Franc, and others. A wine blended from several grapes may often be more complex than one which is not. For example, a blend of Caber-net Sauvignon and Merlot is often more complex than a wine that is solely 100% Cabernet Sauvignon. This is not to say that a predominant single varietal wine is inferior to a blended wine, some grape varieties have the ability to provide enough dimension (such as Pinot Noir or Riesling) on their own without the assistance of other grapes. Ultimately, blending is a matter of the style of wine that is desired and the grapes that typically make that style.

There are different methods and reasons for blending wine, depending on the wine-maker's vision of the finished product.

To achieve these objectives, it is possible to blend several complementary grapes from the same or different appellations or to blend the same grape from different appellations. For example, a winemaker may blend 75% of a Cabernet Sauvignon grape with 25% of a Merlot grape. This approach can adjust or fine-tune components and add complexity or di-mension to the wine.

Some wines are blended for the purpose of maintaining a certain cost parameter, by incorporating into the blend a small percentage of either an inexpensive grape or the same grape that has been harvested from a less desirable appellation. An example is blending 85% of the Chardonnay grape from Russian River with 15% of the Chardonnay from the larger Sonoma County. This approach allows the winemaker to incorporate grapes from locations where the cost of land (ultimately, the cost of the grape) is less expensive.

Other wines may skip the blending process; it depends on the style chosen by the winemaker. In some cases, laws or tradition prohibit the blending of different grapes or grapes from different locations.

Natural Grape Partnerships Some grapes are considered natural or compatible partners. The grapes of origin of wines are not always obvious when grapes are blended together, particularly if a wine is dominant with one varietal and has a tiny percentage of others.

Within each box in the following is a list of grape varietals that are commonly blended together in various parts of the world:

COMMON BLENDING PARTNERS	
Cabernet Sauvignon and Merlot	Syrah and Grenache
Sauvignon Blanc and Semillon	Shiraz and Cabernet Sauvignon
Chardonnay and Pinot Blanc	Sangiovese and Merlot or Cabernet Sauvignon

5. AGING—The aging process significantly influences the style and body of the wine. Think of the aging process as if the wine is going to etiquette school to lose its rough edges. The winemaker's vision of the finished wine is the determining factor as to whether and, if so, how it will be aged.

The aging process can be conducted in one of two ways: "*oxidative* or *reductive*". If the wine is aged by an oxidative technique, then it is wood aged. If the wine is aged by a reductive approach, then the wine is aged (or, more accurately, preserved) in stainless steel.

Stainless Steel *Stainless steel tanks* are used primarily for white aromatic wines whose primary flavors and crisp acidity need to be preserved. Stainless steel doesn't truly age the wine; rather, it preserves the wine and prevents the passage of oxygen that would otherwise alter the wine's personality. The preserving process allows the wine's flavors to integrate fully before the wine is bottled. Most tanks are double-jacketed, circulating cold water between the inner and outer walls in order to adjust and maintain the temperature throughout fermentation and the aging process.

Wood Barrels *Wood barrels,* a centuries-old tradition, are vessels used to store and age most red wines and many full-bodied white wines. The industy standard is to use French or American oak as the preferred wood. Oak from other places, such as Slovenian oak, is sometimes still used. In the past, different wine regions have used different kinds of wood, such as mahogany, chestnut, and pine. For the most part, use of these wood barrels have been disregarded over time due to their distinguishable flavors overpowering the aromas and flavors of the wine. Figure 3–18 shows some wood barrels used to age wine.

A *cooper* is someone who constructs the barrels—an age-old profession. The barrels are made from various types and sizes of wood and various levels of *toast* (the effect of exposure of the wood to varying degrees of fire and varying lengths of time during which the fire burned). *Barrel aging* is the process of holding the wine in wood barrels for a maturation period of months to years, whereby various components present in the wine slowly combine to create complexity and finesse.

The Barrel's Influence on Wine Personality A wood (typically oak) barrel's porous nature allows for the slow passage of oxygen and a small amount of evaporation, which is a beneficial interaction between the wine and the air. Wood barrels contribute their own flavor of complex chemical compounds, each of which lends its own flavor to wine.

FIGURE 3–18 Wood barrels called "pièces" in Champagne
(Collection CIVC.
Photographer: CORNU Alain)

Typical flavor characters are in the category of *bakeshop/coffee shop* (coffee, chocolate, caramel, vanilla, almond, and toasted nut), *cigar shop* (tea and tobacco), and *bakeshop spice* (nutmeg, cinnamon, and allspice).

The Barrel's Influence on a Wine's Personality   Wood can soften a wine's texture, alter the wine's color (from more golden-yellow, depending on the length of aging), and assist in creating a more complex beverage.

Factors that affect the ability of barrels to impart flavor and that influence the extent of the aging process include (1) type of wood (2) the size of the barrel, (3) age of the barrel, (4) the level of toast, and (5) the aging time.

Type of Wood   Winemakers select wood for their wine barrels from different forests, for the effect on the finished wine. American and French oak are the standards. Barrels made from American oak typically cost less than half the price of French oak barrels. The most prestigious and expensive barrels derive from white oak trees that come from several French forests and that are hundreds of years old, such as *Limousin* (lee-moo-ZAHN) and others whose wood has distinctive characteristics.

The type of wood can have a dramatic influence on the wine through the aging process. American oak has bigger grains that allow greater passage of oxygen and so contributes stronger, more significant aromas and flavors. French oak has smaller grains to permit less flow of oxygen and thus maintains more subtle aromas and flavors than American oak.

Typical Barrel Size   The size of the barrel influences the flavor of the wine as well. A smaller barrel contributes stronger and faster flavor because more wine is in contact with greater surface area. The typical wine barrel holds 225 liters (almost 60 U.S. gallons) and is commonly called a *barrique* (ba-REEK) or the *piece* (pee-YESS). One wine barrel can yield roughly 20 cases of wine. Between wine regions, barrel names and capacities will vary. Other barrel sizes include the *butt,* which is an English term for Spanish cooperage that consists of 151 U.S. gallons.

Age of the Barrel   The flavor distinction and prominence of wood tannin is most pronounced in new, unused barrels and becomes less significant with older barrels that have been previously used. By the time a barrel is about five years old, it is virtually neutral as far as its influence on the taste of the wine. Every time that a barrel is reused (for each yearly vintage), it contributes less flavor and fewer components and becomes more of a holding vessel rather than a contributor to the quality of the wine. A barrel can be thought of as a tea bag. The first use of a tea bag yields the most flavor and components. It is possible to reuse the tea bag and still extract benefits, but the effects are less intense and become somewhat diluted.

Level of Toast   The amount or degree of toast (or seasoning, as it's sometimes called) in the barrel has an affect on the flavor profile of the aging wine. Barrels can be ordered with varying levels of toast: Light toast contributes subtle aromas and flavors to the wine, and medium toast and heavy toast both contribute greater intensity of aromas and flavors to the wine. The toast decision will be made on the basis of the variety of grape to be used and the style of wine to be produced.

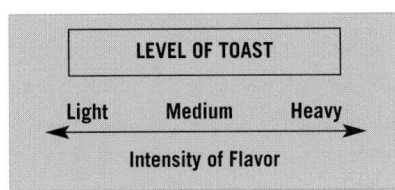

Length of Aging   Wines are aged anywhere from a few months, to several years in cases where small amounts of evaporation occur through the aging process. Lengthy aging assists to soften harsh tannins and allow desirable flavors to develop. As red wine ages, its tannins and color compounds *polymerize* (PUH-lym-err-ize), forming a larger molecule until they eventually fall out of the suspended wine solution, becoming sediment in the bottom of the barrel.

Shortcuts have been created to gain the benefits of oak flavor without actually going through the time or expense of traditional oak barrel aging. Such methods include using oak chips or oak shavings in a large "tea bag" placed inside stainless steel tanks or flavorless barriques. Using barrels in winemaking (though not appropriate for all grapes) can be compared with a chef's use of salt and pepper to enhance and bring out the natural flavors of a food. Without the seasonings, the dish may be bland, but the correct amount adds a certain something to the food. With the appropriate use and application of barrel aging, a wine can be enhanced to better showcase itself.

Sur Lie Aging   The French term *sur lie* (soor-LEE) *aging* refers to the process of aging the wine *on the lees*. Lees are the yeast deposits that add a toasty quality, making the wine rich, smooth, and complex.

Examples of Typical Unoaked and/or Lightly Oak Aged and Oaked Wines

COMMON UNOAKED LIGHTLY OAKED AND OAKED WINES		
	WHITE WINE	RED WINE
Stainless Steel and/or Lightly Oak Aged	Riesling, Chardonnay (from Chablis, New Zealand), Sauvignon Blanc, Pinot Grigio, Gewürztraminer, Grüner Veltliner, Pinot Blanc	Gamay, Dolcetto, Rioja (Joven or Crianza), Barbera, Pinot Noir, Cabernet Franc
Oak Aged	Pinot Gris (Oregon or California), Chardonnay, Fume Blanc, Viognier	Shiraz, Syrah, Syrah blends, Merlot, Cabernet Sauvignon, Nebbiolo, Rioja (Reserva and Gran Reserva)

6. CLARIFICATION—Clarification is the process of removing undesirable particles and making a wine more stable. The methods are similar for both red and white wine; however, the particles may be more obvious in a white wine because of its lack of color pigment as associated with a red wine. After fermentation is complete, new wines appear cloudy, so the wines are allowed to rest. Over time, residues settle out and the wines will become more stable. All methods of clarification remove undesirable particles from wine and assist with stabilization (preventing the chance for refermentation) until the bottle is purchased and opened by the consumer.

Clarification is a major concern because of the potential risk of stripping the wine of desirable aromas, flavors, body, color, and other components. Therefore, most quality-oriented winemakers opt for the softest, gentlest method and least amount of clarification. At some point during this stage—and truly, all throughout the winemaking process—sulfites are added to stop oxidation (browning) of the wine in order to preserve the wine during the aging process and during distribution.

The clarification process can be carried out by several different methods and, possibly, in combination with one another, depending on the grapes or the traditions associated with a particular winemaking region. The five common methods are *racking, cold stabilization, centrifuge, fining,* and *filtering.*

1. Racking   The racking method is considered one of the gentlest methods for limiting the loss of desirable components in the wine. Racking involves periodically draining the sediment, or dead yeast cells, called *lees,* by transferring the wine from one container to another, leaving sediment behind in the original container. Racking is a natural method because it relies on gravity to pull the unwanted particles to the bottom of the original container. Racking can be conducted once or several times before bottling, for greater clarification.

2. Cold Stabilization   This clarification process removes excess tartaric acid that would otherwise later form potassium *bitartrate crystals,* or *tartrates.* Tartrates have the appearance of shards of glass, but are completely safe and edible. Although a common practice is to remove this type of sediment, not all producers do so, and it seems more common in producers who believe in a "hands-off" type winemaking philosophy. Cold stabilization is accomplished through chilling a wine down to 40°F, causing the tartaric acid to crystallize, which allows the wine to then be racked, leaving the crystals behind.

3. Centrifuge   The wine is spun at very high speeds to pull out the impurities by centrifugal force.

4. Fining   This is a clarification method that incorporates a *fining agent* which forms a chemical bond with the undesirable particles, causing them to precipitate out to the bottom of the vessel. Then the wine is racked, leaving the particles behind in the original container. Some fining agents can include egg whites, blood, bentonite clay, bull's blood, gelatin, and isinglass (an extract from fish bladders). In addition to clarification, this process can soften harsh astringent tannins and allow desirable flavors to develop.

5. Filtering   This method passes the wine through a fine mesh filter with small holes that are smaller than the particles to be removed. Thus, the particles are collected and disposed of.

6. Bottling   Small quantities of sulfur dioxide (SO_2) are added to the bottle in order to limit oxidation and inhibit any further yeast activity. Ascorbic acid and antioxidants may be added as well.

Freshly bottled wines are usually held in stock for a few weeks to recover from *bottle shock,* a condition that causes a temporary loss of delicate aromatics due to the excessive agitation during the bottling process. The bottle will be sealed with either a cork or screw cap to prevent any oxygen from entering and destroying the wine.

If desired, the wine will be bottle-aged in order to integrate the wine components and add extra complexity. The fruit characteristics in white table wine tend to slowly develop into more complex characteristics (often described as "toasty" or "kerosene–like") with time in the bottle. These changes may take between six months and five years to become noticeable. In addition to influencing flavor changes, bottle aging has a softening and mellowing effect on the wine and integrates the oak and fruit flavors if the wine has been matured in barrels. A quality red wine will almost certainly be aged in the bottle before being released for sale.

Sulfur Dioxide   Sulfur is a compound found within most bottles of wine. It is created naturally in small quantities during the fermentation process, and the winemaker may also add it throughout the winemaking process.

Sulfur's antimicrobial and antioxidant properties assist in preventing a wine from refermenting within a bottle and prohibit oxygen exposure throughout the winemaking and bottling processes.

Producers are required to write "Contains Sulfites" (meaning sulfur dioxide) on the label of every bottle of wine in the United States if it contains 10 parts per million or more. Almost every bottle will contain this amount, whether the winemaker has added sulfur or not, because 10–20 parts per million may occur naturally. Levels of sulfur can range from 100 to 150 parts per million, but the U.S. allowable maximum is 350 within a single bottle of wine.

VITICULTURE AND ENOLOGY

NAME: _____ Score out of 20 points_____.

Use these questions to test your knowledge and understanding of the concepts presented in the chapter.

I. MULTIPLE CHOICE: Select the best possible answer from the options available.

1. Enology is the science of
   a. making wine.
   b. growing grapes.
   c. growing wine.
   d. making oak barrels.

2. The personality of a wine is *initially* affected by
   a. the type of grape.
   b. the winemaking techniques.
   c. whether the wine had malolactic fermentation or not.
   d. the amount of oak aging.

3. The major grapevine species that produces world-class quality wine grapes is
   a. Vitis labrusca.
   b. Vitis rotunda.
   c. Vitis vinisca.
   d. Vitis vinifera.

4. Chaptalization is the process of adding
   a. sugar to the finished wine.
   b. sugar to the grape juice prior to and/or during fermentation.
   c. acid to the finished wine.
   d. acid to the grape juice.

5. Pruning grapevines can produce
   a. higher quality grapes with higher yield.
   b. higher quality grapes with lower yield.
   c. lower quality grapes with higher yield.
   d. lower quality grapes with higher yield.

6. Grapes are harvested
   a. when the sugar has reached the desirable level.
   b. always in September.
   c. when the grape flavors are present.
   d. when a combination of sugar content and flavor development has reached the desirable level.

7. Large bodies of water (oceans, lakes and rivers) have the ability to moderate climate by
   a. regulating temperature extremes.
   b. regulating rainfall.
   c. regulating soil drainage.
   d. b and c

8. Grapevines grow best between the latitudes of
   a. 20–40 degrees.
   b. 30–60 degrees.
   c. 45–65 degrees.
   d. 30–50 degrees.

9. Terroir refers to
   a. the soil.
   b. the winemaker's influence.
   c. all environmental effects on the vine.
   d. the weather.

10. Viticulture is the science of
    a. making wine.
    b. growing grapes.
    c. growing wine.
    d. making oak barrels.

11. The most commonly used yeast for wine production is

    a. cultured yeast.

    b. wild yeast.

    c. a combination of both.

    d. none of the above.

12. Red wines are fermented with their skins in order to extract

    a. flavor.

    b. color.

    c. tannin.

    d. all of the above.

13. Racking refers to a method of clarification in which the wine is

    a. transferred into a series of new containers, leaving the dead yeast behind.

    b. incorporated with a protein such as egg whites.

    c. put through a centrifuge.

    d. passed through a fine mesh filter.

II. TRUE / FALSE: Circle the best possible answer.

14. A grape's sugar levels are the only factors that determine when the grapes should be harvested. **True / False**

15. Stainless steel aging is conducted in order to impart additional flavors into the wine. **True / False**

16. A winemaker may blend different grapes together for the purpose of reducing cost and increasing complexity. **True / False**

17. Malolactic fermentation is performed on most white wines when crisp fruit acids want to be preserved. **True / False**

18. The amount of sugar present in the grape juice can have an influence on the amount of alcohol that is produced. **True / False**

19. If fermentation is stopped before the yeast has had a chance to ferment all the sugar, the wine will have some sweetness. **True / False**

III. SHORT-ANSWER ESSAY / DISCUSSION QUESTION: Use a separate sheet of paper if necessary.

20. What are two types of aging? What does each do to the finished wine?

Unit 2
WINE AND FOOD COMPATIBILITY

*"Beauty of whatever kind, in its supreme development, invariably excites
the sensitive soul to tears."*
—*Edgar Allan Poe*

4

Performance Factors of Grape Varietals

"Performance factors" identify the distinguishable defining elements of color, aroma, flavor, body, style, and common locations associated with particular grape types produced around the world by varying viticulture and winemaking techniques.

LEARNING OBJECTIVES

Upon completion of this chapter, the learner will be able to:

- Understand the effects of how viticulture and enology and age can influence color, aroma, flavor, style, and body of a wine.
- Explore the performance factors (aromas, flavors, styles, and body) of the Big Six grape varietals and other common wine grapes.
- Realize the significant growing locations of the Big Six grape varietals and other common wine grapes.
- Discover wine pairing strategies and potential food partners of the Big Six grape varietals and other common wine grapes.
- Recognize wine styles and identify potential food pairings on the basis of classification.

PERFORMANCE FACTORS OF GRAPE VARIETALS

This chapter explores the more popular and significant grape varietals and the related *performance factors* associated with each one. Performance factors are a combination of aspects (color, aroma, flavor, acid, alcohol, tannin, body level, and so on) that cumulatively create the distinctive personality of a particular grape varietal. They can be used to identify the distinguishable defining elements linked with a particular grape as it has been produced around the world by varying viticulture and winemaking techniques. Once the performance factors are understood, it is then possible to seek out different producers, vintages, and regions, just as it is possible to seek out a new genre in art, film, or music. Understanding the performance factors of each grape and the variations they can produce can be an effective means of developing the palate and gaining a sense of the distinctive styles between the grape varietals as they are produced in different places around the world.

The Big Six grapes are arguably the most noble, as they are adaptable and produced around the world. Riesling, Sauvignon Blanc, Chardonnay, Pinot Noir, Merlot, and Cabernet Sauvignon are examined in detail here. Other notable grapes are discussed in lesser detail, not because they are any less important, but because they are outside the scope of this textbook. Figure 4–1 shows the famed Pinot Noir grape varietal.

Understanding the performance factors of each grape makes it easier to understand suitable pairings with food, as identified by the detailed pairing strategies offered here for each of the Big Six grapes. In this chapter, there are terms and concepts that may be foreign to some readers. The reader is strongly encouraged to reference the glossary in the back of the book A until he or she reaches those chapters in which the concepts are expanded upon.

FIGURE 4–1 Close-up of Pinot Noir grapes
(Collection CIVC. Photographer: CORNU Alain)

WHITE WINE GRAPE VARIETALS

White wine is made primarily from green and amber-yellow grapes, but can also be made from red, purple, and black grapes.

There are 50 major white-wine grapes grown in the world today, but the three most significant for producing high-quality wine are Riesling, Sauvignon Blanc, and Chardonnay. Other distinguishable white-wine grapes renowned for producing great wine in select locations include Albariño, Chenin Blanc, Gewürztraminer, Grüner Veltliner, Muscat, Pinot Blanc, Pinot Gris/Grigio, Sémillon, and Viognier.

The Colors Progression of White Wine

As white wines age, many factors affect their color progression. They can range from a slight green tint, straw yellow, golden yellow, and brown amber. This progression of a wine's color is very similar to a banana ripening from green to brown as sugars are converted.

Some factors that influence color are (1) the type of grape—some grapes contribute greater color just because smaller berries have greater skin-to-juice ratios, yielding greater color pigment; (2) oak aging, which can heighten the color; (3) residual sugar, which also may provide heightened color; (4) the age of the wine, which can enhance the color; and

(5) improper storage conditions (such as exposure to direct light for an excessive period), which, too, may heighten the color).

As whites wines mature, they gain color. However, as identified in the last paragraph there are numerous other variables that can also influence color:

- **GREEN TINT**—In young fruity wines about six months to one year from harvest, green tint is possible evidence of a cool climate and stainless steel aging.
- **STRAW YELLOW**—In the majority of white wines one to three years from harvest, this color is possible evidence of a cool climate and stainless steel aging or the subtle use of oak aging.
- **GOLDEN YELLOW**—In mature white wine two to five years from harvest, the golden yellow color is possible evidence of a warm climate, oak aging, or considerable residual sugar.
- **BROWN AMBER**—This color may indicate that the wine is past its useful life and likely to be oxidized.

Once a white wine has progressed to a brown amber color, the wine is generally considered undrinkable. Some white wines might progress to this color somewhat rapidly (within a few years); others may take as long as 20 years. The goal in consuming wine is to drink it when it is at its peak; for most wines, that means within months to a few years of its vintage date.

Aromas and Flavors of White Wine

Aroma and flavor categories are a means to create an association with a wine's smells and tastes and link it to memory. Associations can be used as memory "anchors" the same way that a ship or boat uses an anchor in the ocean to provide stability and foundation. Anchors help individuals remember the personality of a wine. There are six broad white-wine aroma/flavor categories and several smaller defined aromas/flavors. Once the general smell has been identified (which is often the easier aroma to identify), the specific, more defined aromas (which tend to be more difficult to identify) can be pinpointed. In some cases, it is possible to make an association between an aroma and flavor of a wine and an everyday type of item. For example, some Sauvignon Blancs have aromas and flavors that may be associated with hay, grass, herbs, or even cat urine (actually an ammonium smell associated with underripe grapes that have been shielded from the sun).

Climatic Influence

Hotter/Warmer Climates—In warm-to-hot climates, grapes are often more ripe and contain greater sugar, yielding a wine with a more pronounced deep-yellow color, rich overripe tropical fruit aromas, and flavors with lower acid. Because of the high sugar content, these wines provide more food for the yeast consumption and create greater levels of alcohol content. The increased alcohol may detract from the enjoyment of some wine consumers, but it replaces a somewhat desirable dimension that was lost with the acidity.

Cooler/Warmer Climates—In cool-to-warm climates, grapes are often less consistently ripe and contain less sugar, yielding a grape with less color pigment and therefore a wine with a lighter-yellow color. The wines also maintain lighter, more subtle aromas and flavors of citrus, tree fruit, vegetables, herbs, and minerals. Because of the lower sugar content, these wines provide less food for yeast consumption, resulting in a lower alcohol content. The cooler climate acts to preserve acidity and youthfulness; therefore, the wines are typically left un-oaked by aging in stainless steel for only a short period.

WHITE WINE AROMA/FLAVOR CATEGORIES

Common Aroma/Flavor Families Associated with White Wine

WHITE WINE AROMA/FLAVOR FAMILIES		
GENERAL AROMAS/FLAVORS	**SPECIFIC AROMAS/FLAVORS**	**VERY SPECIFIC AROMAS/FLAVORS**
1. FRUIT	Citrus	Lemon, lime, grapefruit, orange, tangerine
	Tree	Apple, pear, peach, apricot, cherry
→ Berry	Berry	Strawberry, blueberry, raspberry, blackberry
	Tropical	Melon, banana, coconut, pineapple, passion fruit, lychee
	Dried	Raisin, figs, apricots
2. BAKESHOP	Nuts	Toasted or untoasted (hazelnuts, walnuts, almonds)
	Sauces	Caramel, vanilla, butterscotch, honey, cream, butter, custard
→	Spices	Cinnamon, cloves, nutmeg, anise/fennel, ginger, orange peel
	Bread	Yeast, dough, toast, biscuit
3. MINERAL/ CHEMICAL	Mineral	Chalk, flint
→	Chemical	Petroleum, ammonia, steel
4. Barnyard/ Herbaceous	Barnyard	Grass, hay, straw
→	Herb Garden	Tomato vine, dill, basil, chives, Earl Grey tea
5. FLORAL	Floral	Rosé, peonies, orange blossom, honeysuckle, violets
6. VEGETABLES	Vegetables	Asparagus, cucumber, bell pepper, olives

THE BODY OF A WHITE WINE

A wine's *body* refers to how the wine feels in terms of weight or viscosity inside the mouth. White wine can range from light to medium to full bodied. Certainly, there are levels in between that a taster may describe by saying, "I give this wine a light body (but on the high side)" or "I give this wine a medium body (but on the low side)." However, describing a wine's body more precisely than low, medium, or full may only confuse the novice wine consumer.

An effective analogy is to think of the body of wine in terms of the weight or mouth feel of milk. For example, skim milk can be compared to a light-bodied wine, 2% milk to a medium-bodied wine, and whole milk to a full-bodied wine.

Some factors that can influence a white wine's body are as follows: (1) The size of the berries can alter the impact of acid, tannin, and overall extract. Large berries have more juice and less skin; smaller berries have less juice and more skin. (2) The level of alcohol affects body in that higher alcohol content can provide more body, while lower alcohol content can provide a lighter body. (3) Residual sugar yields a fuller mouth feel, while a wine that has been fermented dry can yield a lighter body. (4) *Extract* is a term used to indicate the level of concentration of several components (such as acid, alcohol, and fruit concentration) working together to create an impression of greater concentration. (5) Oak aging can influence body partly through the amount of evaporation of water content of the wine during the barrel aging process. Also, the addition of flavors associated with wood aging may add to the intensity of the wine.

Contributors to a White Wine's Body

CONTRIBUTORS TO A WHITE WINE'S BODY		
VARIABLES	**LIGHTER BODY**	**FULLER BODY**
Size of Berries	Larger berries with less skin-to-juice ratio	Smaller berries with greater skin-to-juice ratio
Level of Alcohol	11% or less	13% or more; sometimes as high as 14%
Dryness/Sweetness	Fermented dry	Fermented with allowing some varying amount of residual sugar.
Extract (concentration of fruit and other components suspended within the wine)	Lower	Higher
Oak Aging	None to light	Medium to heavy

♦ Generally, a fuller bodied wine is 13% alcohol or above, and a lighter bodied wine is low in alcohol, at 11% or below.

♦ Tannin is present in all wines, but is thought to be perceptible only in red wine.

Although there are many exceptions, understanding the relative weights and bodies of some common wines provides a good foundational beginning. On occasion, some wines can overlap in weight and body, depending on country or region of origin, or stylistic differences of producers. For example, Chardonnay can often be described as a light- to medium-bodied wine when it is produced in Chablis. In some cases, because of increased alcohol content, malolactic fermentation, sur lie, and oak aging (as with most California versions), Chardonnays become more medium to full bodied.

**RIESLING
(REEZ-ling)**

Riesling is native to Germany, where it is the most significant white wine grape and has been cultivated for hundreds (possibly thousands) of years. Though often consumed young, Riesling's substantial acidity, aromatic aromas, and concentration of flavors are suitable for extended aging, particularly of wines that have a high sugar content. It prefers to be a "stand-alone" varietal, as it is very rarely blended with other grapes. Riesling produces a range of wines from dry to sweet and from light- to full-body, largely dependent on the amount of residual sugar and tradition associated with area of production. Figure 4–2 shows the Riesling grape varietal.

Over the years, Riesling has become unfashionable because of the often oversweet versions with inadequate levels of acid created by some non-quality-oriented winemakers.

FIGURE 4–2 Close-up of Riesling grapes

(Ian O'Leary © Dorling Kindersley)

This has led many serious wine drinkers to consider that Riesling is reserved for the novice wine drinker. Riesling may be experiencing a bit of a renaissance, as producers are providing drier or sweeter options that balance the components that Riesling has to offer.

Aromas/Flavors

Riesling is a highly aromatic grape variety with concentrated aromas and flavors. Listed are some frequent (though not exclusive) aromas and flavors associated with Riesling:

- **Fruit**—tree fruit (peach, apricot), tropical fruit (pineapple), dried fruit (raisin)
- **Citrus**—grapefruit, lemon, lime, orange
- **Bakeshop Sauces**—honey
- **Mineral**—petroleum, flint, steel

The petroleum (or rubber band) aroma/flavor is associated less often with youthful wines and becomes more predominant with aged ones.

Body/Style

Rieslings can range from dry, to sweet and light, to full bodied, largely depending on the level of residual sugar left over in the wine after fermentation. Well-made Rieslings are high in tartaric and malic acids, which are necessary (although sometimes going unnoticed) to balance the wine's varying levels of sugar content and intense fruit aromatics. The acid also acts as a preservative for long aging capabilities. Rieslings are often left un-oaked (or at minimum, stored in old oaked barrels) in order to maintain the concentrated aromatic fruit and high acidity levels.

Riesling can often be seen in two differing styles. Winemakers either will ferment the wine dry, achieving higher alcohol levels, as in Alsace, France, or will leave considerable residual sugar (RS) through partial fermentation, leaving the wine with varying levels of sweetness, as in many German styles. The density and body increase with greater levels of sweetness, providing an effective pairing with more robust, fatty food items. Low-alcohol sweeter versions hover near 11% alcohol or less, and high-alcohol drier versions can be found at 12% or higher.

Riesling is also known for producing some of the world's most celebrated dessert wines. These wines can be made in a combination of methods. Three of the most well known dessert wines are *Late Harvest* (the grapes remain on the vine and gain additional sugar content), *Rot wine* (the grapes are attacked by a friendly fungus that concentrates the aromas, flavors, and sugar and causes evaporation), and *Ice wine* (where the grapes are frozen on the vine in order to extract water content). ♦ Riesling is discussed in greater detail in Chapter 10, "Other Old World Wine Countries," and in Chapter 13, "Nectar: Dessert Wines."

Significant Locations

Riesling is a late-ripening varietal which tends to prefer cooler climates that allow longer ripening periods.

Rieslings are capable of performing well in various types of soil, but some of the best examples of quality Riesling grapes derive from slate- or clay-based soils.

- **OLD WORLD**—Riesling wines come from Germany (Mosel and Rhingau), France (Alsace), Austria (Wachau), and Italy (Alto Adige, Friuli).
- **NEW WORLD**—Riesling wines also come from Washington (Columbia Valley), California (Central Coast), Australia (Clare and Eden Valleys), New Zealand (Marlborough, Martinborough, Nelson, Wairarapa), New York (Finger Lakes), and Canada (Niagara).

STYLE #1: German Style—German-style Rieslings have good concentration of fruit aromas and flavors, with some level of residual sugar. The sweetness creates a somewhat weighty palate and, coupled with lower alcohol (11% or less), allows the wine to be fairly food friendly.

Pairing Strategies

1. Riesling can pair well with salty, spicy, fatty, smoky, and sweet food items.
2. Riesling's varying level of residual sugar allows it to work well with cuisines that have some spicy or salty components, such as Asian food, including Chinese, Thai, and Japanese food.
3. Riesling's intense concentration of aromas and flavors increase the density of the wine, which allows it to work with fatty poultry (duck, goose), pork (pork loin, barbecued ribs), and game birds (quail).
4. Rieslings can couple with several dessert options such as fruit-based dishes (fruit tart, cobbler, pie, crisps, fruit mousse cake), chocolate-based desserts (white chocolate and varying types of nuts), pastry-based desserts (blueberry muffins, cranberry orange muffins, pineapple upside-down cake).
5. Rieslings that have considerable sweetness and density (such as German Auslese) work well with blue-vein cheese (Bleu, Gorgonzola, Stilton).

STYLE #2: Alsatian Style—These Rieslings also have a good concentration of fruit aromas and flavors and from having been fermented more fully, the resulting wine is drier and leaner with higher levels of alcohol (12% or higher). Thus, they work well with more delicate, lighter, and simpler dishes.

Pairing Strategies

1. Riesling can work well with lighter seafood preparations such as sushi and steamed, poached, or sautéed lean and fatty fish.
2. Riesling can pair with leaner poultry and pork that have been prepared by light to medium cooking methods.
3. This style of Riesling has substantial and detectable acidity that works well with food items (as mentioned previously) that are served with béchamel, hollandaise, and cream-based sauces.
4. Riesling pairs well with fresh/soft cheeses (goat, feta, and Neufchatel cheese).

FIGURE 4–3 Close-up of Sauvignon Blanc grapes
(Wines of Argentina)

**SAUVIGNON BLANC
(SOH-vihn-YOHN BLAHNK)**

Sauvignon Blanc is native to France and is found widely throughout the wine world. Sauvignon Blanc is one of the most versatile grapes and is known for producing food-friendly wines. This grape expresses its personality most effectively when aged in stainless steel or when a subtle use of oak has been used for aging. Sauvignon Blanc goes by various other names when found around the world. It is referred to as *Blanc Fumé* (few-MAY) in some areas of the Loire Valley, or it may be named after one of its two famous appellations within the Loire Valley: *Sancerre* (sahn-SEHR) and *Pouilly Fumé* (poo-YEE few-MAY). Figure 4–3 shows the Sauvignon Blanc grape varietal.

Oak aging can also be applied successfully to add an alternative dimension, such as in Bordeaux and California. Back in the 1980s, Robert Mondavi called his Sauvignon Blanc *Fumé Blanc* ("Fumé" is French for smoked) because he aged it in wood that would yield a smoky aroma to the wine. In the Loire Valley, the wines have a smokiness that comes from the minerality in the soil. In California, the wine may be called Fumé Blanc (particularly if it has been aged in oak); it is also known as white Bordeaux in Bordeaux, France.

Aromas/Flavors

Depending on the climate and growing methods, Sauvignon Blanc can range from grassy to tropical. When grapes lack sun exposure or are harvested underripe, aromas and flavors veer toward citrus, herbal and vegetable. If Sauvignon Blanc experiences lower yields and warmer, longer sun exposure, the grape expresses greater ripe fruit and tropical fruit elements.

- **Fruit**—tree fruit (peach, apricot), tropical fruit (gooseberry, pineapple), dried fruit (raisin)
- **Citrus**—grapefruit, lemon, lime
- **Herbs**—dill, cilantro, basil, thyme, fresh-cut grass, tomato vine
- **Vegetables**—bell pepper, jalapeno pepper, asparagus

Body/Style

Sauvignon Blanc is made in a variety of styles and can range from light- to medium-bodied and from dry to sweet. Either way, Sauvignon Blanc is always a crisp, highly acidic wine typically left un-oaked and drunk young to capture its youthful zesty acidity.

In Bordeaux's left bank, in and near the appellation of Sauternes (soh-TERN), the Sauvignon Blanc and Semillon grapes are allowed to obtain the desirable rot, or *Botrytis Cinerea*, producing some of the best sweet wines in the world.

Significant Locations

- **OLD WORLD**—France (Loire Valley and Bordeaux) and Italy (Northeastern) are notable.
- **NEW WORLD**—New Zealand (Marlborough, Martinborough), California (North Coast), Chile (Casablanca Valley), Australia, and South Africa are significant.

STYLE #1: The Loire Style—This style has become very popular as showcased in the Loire Valley and New Zealand, which arguably are now the world's leading producers of excellent Sauvignon Blanc. The Loire style creates a subtle to no oak influence in an effort to capture the pure essence of the grape varietals. These styles tend to be highly acidic and veer toward light- to medium-body. The high levels of acids maintained in this style allow the wine to work with other high-acid foods. Sauvignon Blanc's high acidity acts like a spark plug to the food and amplifies the food's flavors. Within this style, Sauvignon Blanc from Loire Valley and Sauvignon Blanc from New Zealand are actually quite different. Loire Sauvignon Blanc tends to emphasize herbal and vegetal qualities, whereas New Zealand Sauvignon Blancs tend to offer greater ripeness, with red grapefruit and gooseberry aromas and flavors.

Pairing Strategies

1. The dryness and acidity help to accentuate appetizers (artichoke dip, shrimp cocktail, oysters), salads (Caesar, seafood salad, Greek salad, Antipasto), and soups.
2. The light- to medium-body pairs well with similar body levels of protein, such as lean poultry (with or without skin) and seafood (lean to fatty fin fish, seviche, sushi, seafood brochettes).
3. Vegetarian friendly, it can work well with pasta and grains with or without any combination of seafood or poultry, with oil- or cream-based sauces.
4. This style pairs well with fresh/soft cheese (herbed or pepper-crusted goat cheese, feta cheese) and pasta filata cheese (Buffalo Mozzarella and provolone).

STYLE #2: The Bordeaux Style—This Sauvignon Blanc style is often blended with the compatible Semillon grape that adds richness and weight while calming some of the natural acidity. This dry (or even sweet) style has often seen a liberal use of oak aging. The Bordeaux style (often referred to as a white Bordeaux) derives from Bordeaux France, but has been also produced in California and may go by the name *Fumé Blanc*.

Pairing Strategies

1. The added weight of this Bordeaux allows it to work more effectively with cream- or milk-based sauces such as Alfredo or Béchamel sauce.
2. The grapes that produce this style are susceptible to botrytis and can create a sweet, luscious full-bodied dessert wine.
3. Pairs well with soft or rind cheese (Brie and Camembert) and semi-soft cheese (Edam, Gouda).

**CHARDONNAY
(SHAR-dun-nay)**

FIGURE 4–4 Close-up of Chardonnay grapes
(Collection CIVC.
Photographer: CORNU Alain)

Chardonnay is one of the most popular and widely planted grapes in the world. It is extremely adaptable to different climates and winemaking techniques. It has been said that virtually anywhere that there are vineyards, Chardonnay can be found.

Chardonnay is believed to have originated in the *Mâconnaise* (mah-kawn-NEH) region of Burgundy, France, where *Pouillly-Fuisse* (poo-YEE fwee-SAY) is currently produced. Chardonnay is vitally important in Champagne, France, where it is blended with Pinot Noir and Pinot Meunier to make the Champagne quartet. Some Champagne styles are even labelled *Blanc de Blanc* (white from white), where Chardonnay is made as a stand-alone varietal. Figure 4–4 shows the Chardonnay grape varietal.

A California Chardonnay wine was responsible for bringing great fame to California (and overall the new world) when a "Chateau Montelena Chardonnay" won the top place over French counterparts in the famous 1976 Paris wine tasting (discussed in greater detail in Chapter 7, "Wines of the United States and Canada").

Aromas/Flavors

Chardonnay is a fairly neutral grape that is quite adaptable both to its surroundings and to winemaking techniques. It is sometimes thought of as a painter's "blank canvas," as the grape is quite moldable and has the ability to be influenced greatly by the winemaker. The primary flavors include tree and citrus fruit, and in cool climates, mineral. Secondary flavors derived from winemaking techniques are commonly associated with bakeshop-type elements.

- **Fruit**—tree fruit (apple, pear, figs), tropical fruit (pineapple, banana, mango), citrus (lemon)
- **Mineral**—chalky
- **Bakeshop Spice/Sauces**—butter, toast, toasted nuts, caramel, vanilla, butterscotch, and honey

Body/Style

Chardonnay is medium bodied when aged in stainless steel or old oak barrels and full bodied when aged in new oak. Chardonnay grows well in many different regions and can be produced with various winemaking techniques.

Significant Locations

- **OLD WORLD**—Chardonnay is grown and made into wine in France (Burgundy, Champagne, and the un-oaked versions are found primarily in Chablis) or Italy (Alto Adige, Friuli).
- **NEW WORLD**—Chardonnay is also produced in California (Carneros, Russian River, Sonoma Coast, Monterey), Australia, New Zealand, and Chile (Casablanca Valley and Maipó).

STYLE 1: *The Chablis Style* — The Chablis style is a lighter Chardonnay that has gained renewed interest in the wine world. A classic "Chablis" is a Chardonnay produced in France's Burgundy region within the subregion of Chablis. Countries such as New Zealand and Australia have begun to model some of their Chardonnays in this style. The Chablis style is often left un-oaked or lightly oaked to showcase not only the subtle aromas and flavors of the grape, but also the expression of the type of soil and the high levels of acidity that are present.

Pairing Strategies

1. This version can work well with appetizers, soups, and salads.
2. Lean poultry, seafood (fin fish or shellfish), and pasta dishes prepared with either oil- or cream-based sauces are a good match.
3. The style works well as a vegetarian-friendly wine because of its leanness and ability to pair well with grains, pasta, and vegetables.
4. It pairs well with fresh/soft cheese (goat, feta, and Neufchatel).

STYLE 2: *The Burgundian Style* — In Burgundy, France oak is used as a seasoning to enhance the Chardonnay grape. California Chardonnay (and, to some degree, Australian versions) is Burgundian style, but with more overt and dominant oak influence. California versions can be tricky to pair because the riper fruit, high alcohol (from the warmer climate) and oak tend to be overpowering elements in the wine. Caution is advised when pairing with spicy foods, as spices can intensify the perception of alcohol.

Pairing Strategies

1. Burgundian style Chardonnays pair well with richer meats such as veal and pork and fatty poultry such as pheasant, hen, duck, and goose.
2. This style works well with richer fish and shellfish such as crustaceans (shrimp, scallops, crab, and lobster) and with fatty and meaty finfish (halibut, sea bass, monkfish, snapper, swordfish, salmon, shark, and tuna).
3. Chardonnay also works with leaner poultry (chicken and turkey), seafood, or pasta that use more robust cooking methods and/or incorporate butter or cream-based sauces.
4. Cream-based soups and chowders as well as dairy-based salad dressings go well with this style.
5. This wine pairs well with richer soft ripened or rind cheese (Brie, Camembert), fresh/soft cheese (feta or cream cheese), and semi-soft cheese (Edam, Gouda).

Other White Wine Grapes

**Albariño
(ahl-bah-REE-nyoh)**

Considered by many to be Spain's premier quality white wine, Albariño is labelled according to the grape varietal. Albariño is also known as Portugal's leading white wine in the Vinho Verde region known as Alvarinho (ahl-vah-REE-nyoh), where it is often labelled after the location.

- **AROMAS/FLAVORS** — Typically, wines made from Albariño are very aromatic, (because of its thick skins) often described as having the intense aroma of nuts (almonds), tree fruit (apricots, peaches, apples), and citrus.
- **BODY/STYLES** — The wine produced is unusually light to medium bodied, with high acidity and often with a slight "spritz" in Portugal.
- **SIGNIFICANT LOCATIONS** — Spain in the Rias Baixes (REE-ahs BY-shehs) region and sections of the Galicia (gah-LEE-thee-ah) region of Northwestern Spain produce this wine. The Portuguese region of Vinho Verde is also a producer.

**Chenin Blanc
(SHEN-ihn BLAHNK)**

Chenin Blanc is arguably the most versatile of all grape varieties. It can successfully produce dry table wines, sparkling wines, and off-dry and sweet dessert wines.

- **AROMAS/FLAVORS**—Honey, tropical fruit (melon), tree fruit (pear, peaches), exotic scents (Bergamot, Earl Grey tea), and mineral (wet stone).
- **BODY/STYLE**—Chenin Blanc can be made in a full range of styles, from dry and crisp to semi-sweet and fruity, and from sparkling wine to full-blown late-harvest dessert wines. Any style contains certain floral, honeyed aromas and flavors with zesty acidity, which are the trademarks of a Chenin Blanc. This grape can stand up to modest oak aging and is occasionally blended with Chardonnay and other varietals to add fruitiness and acidity.
- **SIGNIFICANT LOCATIONS**—The Loire Valley (several areas that will be discussed in greater detail in Chapter 9, "French Wine"), California (Central Coast), and South Africa.

Gewürztraminer (guh-VERTZ-trah-mean-er)

Gewürztraminer is a German word for "spicy grape." Sometimes the grape is referred to as *Gewürz* or *Traminer*. It is known for its spicy characteristics and high aromatics, often with some slight spritz on the tongue.

- **AROMAS/FLAVORS**—A distinctive wine, it can have citrus fruit (grapefruit), bakeshop spice (spicy cinnamon), tropical fruit (lychee), and flowers (rosé).
- **BODY/STYLES**—Gewürztraminer can be made light, dry, and crisp (Alsatian selections) to slightly full, sweet, and slightly flabby (California selections). It can also make luscious, honeyed sweet dessert wines.
- **SIGNIFICANT LOCATIONS**—This grape performs best in cooler climates such as France (Alsace), Germany, New York, Canada, California, Italy (Trentino and Friuli), and Washington State (Columbia Valley).

Grüner Veltliner (GROO-ner FELT-lih-ner)

Grüner Veltliner is indigenous to Austria, where it accounts for the most dominant grape varietal throughout every Austrian wine-growing region.

- **AROMAS/FLAVORS**—This style carries intense concentrated aromatics of citrus fruit (lime, grapefruit), tropical fruit, and bakeshop spice (white pepper).
- **BODY/STYLES**—Grüner typically produces a highly acidic wine that is medium in body.
- **SIGNIFICANT LOCATIONS**—Austria (Wachau) is a significant producer.

Muscat (MOO-scott)

Muscat goes by several different names and styles. In Italy's Veneto area, this grape is known as *Moscato*, where it makes the sparkling wine *Spumante* and a lightly carbonated version called *Moscato d'Asti*. In white France, Muscat makes sweet wine in Alsace and is considered most famous for the white Vin doux Naturals (VDN) sweet fortified wines produced in Southern France.

- **AROMAS/FLAVORS**—Musky, tropical fruit, tree fruit (peach and apricot), and citrus fruit (orange peel).
- **BODY/STYLES**—Muscat can range from dry wine (with occasional spritz) to sparkling wine and sweet wines.
- **SIGNIFICANT LOCATIONS**—Italy (Piedmont), France (Alsace and Provence), California, and Australia are significant producers.

Pinot Blanc (PEE-noh-BLAHNK)

This grape is grown primarily in northernmost wine regions throughout the world. It is called *Pinot Bianco* in Northern Italy (where it is produced in the Trentino-Alto-Adige, Veneto and Friuli areas) and *Weissburgunder* (VICE-buhr-gun-dehr) in Germany and Austria.

- **AROMAS/FLAVORS**—Subtle aromas and flavors of bakeshop (nuts, spice, yeast) and tree fruit (apple).

- **BODY/STYLES**—Pinot Blanc is part of the Pinot family (Noir, Gris, Grigio). It produces dry, light-to-medium-bodied wines with high acidity.
- **SIGNIFICANT LOCATIONS**—France (Alsace), Italy (Trentino-Alto-Adige, Friuli, Veneto) California, Germany, and Austria are significant winemaking locations for Pinot Blanc.

Pinot Grigio/Pinot Gris (PEE-noh GREE-joh)/PEE-noh GREE)

Pinot Gris is a darkly colored white wine grape that evolved from the Pinot Noir. *Gris* means grey, the color that comes from the grape skins' unique pinkish-gray hue.

Pinot Gris goes by different names, depending upon where it is produced. It is called *Pinot Gris* in France and the United States and is referred to as *Pinot Grigio* in Italy.

- **AROMAS/FLAVORS**—Has subtle aromas and flavors: citrus fruit (lemon), tree fruit (pear, apricot), bakeshop sauces and spice (almonds and honey), and mineral.
- **BODY/STYLES**—Pinot Grigio is often made in a crisp medium-to-high acid that is light to medium body. These wines are commonly aged in either stainless steel or old oak barrels, although some winemakers practice suble new oak aging to provide a touch of richness and increase complexity.
- **SIGNIFICANT LOCATIONS**—This grape thrives in cooler regions—France (Alsace), Italy (Trentino-Alto-Adige, Veneto, Friuli), and Oregon (Willamette Valley)—which assist in preserving its high acidity. In the New World, Pinot Gris receives greater sun and heat exposure, allowing more ripeness and concentration to be expressed, compared with many old world versions.

Sémillon (seh-mee-YOHN)

A well-known grape variety grown in Bordeaux, France, Sémillon is often blended in varying quantities with Sauvignon Blanc to produce a range of dry to sweet wines. It is often used to produce famous dessert wines from the Bordeaux appellation of Sauternes.

- **AROMAS/FLAVORS**—Dried fruit (figs), tree fruit (ripe apricots), citrus fruit (lemon), vegetables (grass), and bakeshop (honey).
- **BODY/STYLE**—Sémillon can be made in a dry or sweet style, producing a medium to full body. Sémillon is often a brilliant gold-colored wine with a soft, full, and sometimes even oily texture and low acidity. Sometimes this grape is used to fill out the leaner and highly acidic Sauvignon Blanc.
- **SIGNIFICANT LOCATIONS**—France (Bordeaux) and Australia (Hunter Valley, Margaret River) are significant producers.

Viognier (VEE-oh-NYAY)

Viognier has become one of the more "fashionable" white wine grape varietals throughout the wine world. Viognier is a highly intense aromatic grape varietal, often producing a distinctive deep golden-yellow wine with a rich full body.

Although often a stand-alone varietal, Viognier is unknowingly blended in small amounts in the red wines of France's Northern Rhône Valley and to create a white *Côtes du Rhône* in Southern Rhône.

- **AROMAS/FLAVORS**—Viognier has an aromatic, rich, and intense smell.
  If fermented in stainless steel tanks, it can produce an aromatic wine that shows off the fruit tree (peach), tropical (tangerine, pineapple, mango, and apricot), bakeshop sauce (honey), and floral.
  If Viognier is oak aged, the wood barrels add further complexity by contributing elements of bakeshop spice (anise, vanilla).

- **BODY/STYLES**—This grape is fairly low in acidity and is medium bodied when un-oaked and full bodied when aged in oak. Viognier is usually high in alcohol, which can compensate for the occasional limited acidity.
- **SIGNIFICANT LOCATIONS**—France (Rhône Valley, Languedoc-Roussillon), California (Central Coast), and Australia (Eden Valley, Adelaide Hills) are significant locations for making this wine.

ROSÉ/BLUSH WINE

Rosé (roh-ZAY) is French for "pink" and is named after its color that can range in shade from light pink to orange. The pink color identifies the fact that the wine was made from some type of black-to-purple grape varietals that bleed a small amount of red color into the juice when the grapes are pressed. Rosé combines the fruitiness of a red wine with the crispness and lightness of a white wine that are generally an appropriate warm-to-hot-weather drinking option and work very well with spicy or full-flavored foods.

Many rosés are created from a blend of grapes (Syrah, Grenache, Mourvèdre, and others), while others are made from a single grape varietal (Zinfandel, Merlot, or Cabernet Sauvignon).

Rosés are packed with berry fruit and occasional floral aromas and flavors, while pro-ducing a light- to medium-bodied wine (but it can be fuller if there is significant residual sugar) with low to medium in alcohol content. Most rosés are not oak aged, and if they are, it is only for a short period. Most rosés are released less than a year after they are made, as they are meant to be consumed to showcase their youth and fruity personality.

Some of the best-known rosés are made in Provence (praw-VAHNSS) and Tavel (ta-VEHL) in the Rhône region of Southern France. These wines are rarely complex and never aged in oak. Rosés are typically dry—at most, barely sweet, tart, and fruity. They gain their charm from their freshness, and most are served chilled. The United States and South Africa generally make their Rosé sweet in style, although there are increasingly dryer options to be found.

White Zinfandel was introduced in the United States in the late 1970s and filled a niche in the early 1980s as the desire and interest in white wine started gaining momentum. White Zinfandel is an American twist on rosé that is engineered to be sweet (with various amounts of residual sugar). White Zinfandels are made from Zinfandel red wine grapes and, during fermentation, have minimal skin contact, so they pick up a touch of the red color from the grape skins. Sutter Home Winery (located in Napa Valley) was one of the first wineries to promote White Zinfandels. Some consumers and wine experts frown upon sweet wines, particularly the White Zinfandel, not because it is sweet, but because it has an amount of acidity and alcohol that is inadequate to balance the sweetness in order to provide some element of structure to the wine.

Although Rosés are not complex, they do have a place for matching with some more difficult food items. They can work well with spicy Asian, Latin American, or Cajun foods and lemon sorbet, and they are enjoyed for sipping on the beach or with a splash of soda water.

Pink Wine Styles

1. **FRUITY AND DRY**—Typically called rosé wine, this style is produced primarily in Southern France or throughout Spain, although it is increasingly being produced around the world.
2. **FRUITY AND SWEET**—Typically, these pink wines are made in California. Their names sometimes begin with the term *white*, such as *White Zinfandel* or *White Merlot.*

RED WINE GRAPE VARIETALS

Made from red, purple, or black grapes that typically make red wine, but can also make pink or even white wine.

There are about 40 primary red wine grape varietals grown in the world today, but the 3 most significant for producing high-quality wine throughout the world are *Pinot Noir, Merlot,* and *Cabernet Sauvignon*. These primary varietals are listed and are ranked from typical light- to full-bodied, low to high in tannin level, lighter to deeper in color density (which generally corresponds to the perceived tannin level), and younger to older in ageability. There are many exceptions to the typical body of these wines. It is possible to find Pinot Noirs that are light or medium bodied, as well as some Cabernet Sauvignon based wines that range fom medium to full bodied. A lot of the determining factors are involved that influence variations of grape varietals such as climate, grape growing, and winemaking differences.

There are other red wine grapes famously known for producing great quality wine in select locations such as Barbera, Cabernet Franc, Carménère, Dolcetto, Gamay, Grenache, Malbec, Mourvèdre, Nebbiolo, Nero d' Avola, Pinotage, Sangiovese, Syrah/Shiraz, Tempranillo, Touriga Nacional, and Zinfandel.

The Color Progression of a Red Wine

As red wines age, many factors affect their color progression. They can range from a youthful purple to ruby red, red, brick red and, ultimately, a brown amber. Some factors that influence color are as follows: (1) Type of grape—some grapes contribute deeper color because smaller berries have a greater skin-to-juice ratio, yielding greater color pigment. (2) Oak aging can de-emphasize the color because of oxidation. (3) The age of the wine can also decrease the color because of loss of color pigment when pigmented particles fall out as sediment. (4) Improper storage conditions—exposure to direct light for an excessive period may cause the wine to lose color. (5) The degree of extraction (suspended particles in the wine) of color from the skins through the maceration period also affects the color.

- **PURPLE**—Young, fruity wines are ready about six months to one year from harvest. This is a possible indication of a cool to warm climate, minimal to no oak aging, or the application of carbonic maceration.
- **RUBY**—Slightly aged, these wines are ready about one to three years from harvest. This is a possible indication of a cool to warm climate, minimal to no oak aging, or the application of carbonic maceration.
- **RED**—These wines are ready only after several years of barrel aging, about three to five years from harvest.
- **BRICK RED**—These mature wines are ready about 5 to 10 years from harvest and often indicate extensive aging.
- **BROWN AMBER**—Definite signs of age, likely to be oxidized.

Over time, red wines lose their bright, youthful color shading because the color pigment particles (anthocyanins), in conjunction with tannin, fall out of the wine solution and form a sediment on the bottom of the bottle.

Once a red wine has progressed to a brown amber color, the wine is generally considered undrinkable. Some red wines might progress to this color rather rapidly (within a few years), and others may take as long as 20 or more years to reach brown amber. Factors that influence this color change are mostly the type and quality of the grapes. The goal in consuming wine is to drink it when it is at its peak or, of course, to satisfy the wine consumer.

Aromas and Flavors of a Red Wine

Aroma and flavor categories are a means of associating the way a wine smells and tastes with one's memory. We can use these associations as a sort of anchor to remember the personality of a wine. There are six broad general red wine aroma/flavor categories, with several smaller defined aromas/flavors. Once the general smell (which is often the easier aroma to recognize) has been identified, we proceed to identify smaller, more defined aromas (which tend to be more difficult to recognize). In some cases, it is possible to make an association between an aroma flavor of a wine and some everyday item, such as Beaujolais Noveau having an aroma/flavor of pear, cherry, and bubblegum.

Climatic Influence

Hotter/Warmer Climates—Hotter/warmer-climate grapes ripen with high sugar content and lower acid. They produce aromas and flavors of baked and dried jammy fruits. They can produce greater concentration of color with the possibility of high alcohol content and fuller body and texture that will provide a greater mouth-feel, with a slight or significant burn in the back of the throat.

Cooler/Warmer Climates—Cooler-climate grapes tend to preserve their natural acidity. Their color intensity tends to be lighter, and the grapes do not produce an abundance of sugar. Therefore, they tend to produce wines that are lower to moderate in alcohol levels. Aromas and flavors may be more pronounced—of fresh fruit berries or of mineral and vegetation associated with limited heat or sun exposure throughout the growing season.

RED WINE AROMA/FLAVOR CATEGORIES

Common Aroma/Flavor Families Associated with Red Wine

RED WINE AROMA/FLAVOR FAMILIES		
GENERAL AROMAS/FLAVORS	**SPECIFIC AROMAS/FLAVORS**	**VERY SPECIFIC AROMAS/FLAVORS**
1. FRUIT	Fresh fruit	Cherry, black cherry, raspberry, blackberry, blueberry, plum, cranberry, strawberry, banana
→	Baked/Dried Fruit	Prune, raisin, jam, cherry, raspberry, black cherry, currant, fig
2. COFFEE SHOP →		Cinnamon, cloves, black pepper, orange peel, chocolate, vanilla, coffee, tea, black tea, licorice, anise, bubblegum, toffee, caramel
3. GARDEN →	Vegetables	Green pepper, green olive, mushroom, black olive
	Herbs	Eucalyptus, mint
4. FLORAL		Rosé, violets, geranium, orange blossom, lanolin
5. EARTH		Forest, mud, pine, dirt, chalk, manure, dust
6. TOBACCO SHOP		Cigar, cigarettes, pipe, leather, cedar, tar

The Body of a Red Wine

A wine's *body* is the way it feels in terms of weight or viscosity inside the mouth. Red wine can range from light, medium, or full bodied. Certainly, there are levels in between that one arguably can say, "I give this wine a light, but on the high side or a medium, but on the low side." However, being so precise when describing a wine can sometimes contribute to more confusion for the novice wine consumer.

An effective analogy in describing wine is to think of the body of wine in terms of the weight or mouth feel of milk. For example, skim milk can be compared to a light-bodied wine, 2% milk to medium bodied, and whole milk to a full-bodied wine.

Some factors that can influence a red wine's body are as follows: (1) The size of the berries can alter the impact of acid, tannin, and overall extract because large berries have more juice and less skin (and vice versa). (2) The level of alcohol can be a factor because higher alcohol can provide a bigger body while lower alcohol content can provide a lighter body. (3) The level of tannin can influence the wine's body because higher tannin can provide a bigger mouth feel with substantial texture while lower tannin can yield a lower body. (4) Residual sugar can affect the body in that higher residual sugar yields a fuller mouth feel, while a wine that has been fermented dry can yield a lighter body. (5) *Extract* is a term used to indicate the level of concentration of several components (such as acid, alcohol, and fruit concentration) working together to create an impression of greater concentration. (6) Oak aging can influence body partly through the amount of evaporation of water content of the wine during the barrel aging process.

Contributors to a Red Wine's Body

CONTRIBUTORS TO A RED WINE'S BODY		
VARIABLES	**LIGHTER BODY**	**FULLER BODY**
Size of Berries	Larger berries with less skin-to-juice ratio	Smaller berries with greater skin-to-juice ratio
Level of Alcohol	11% or less	13% or more; sometimes as high as 14%
Level of Tannin	Lower	Higher
Dryness/Sweetness	Fermented dry	Fermented with allowing some varying amount of residual sugar.
Extract (concentration of fruit and other components)	Lower	Higher
Oak Aging	None to light	Medium to heavy

♦ Generally, a fuller bodied wine is usually 13% alcohol or above and a lighter bodied wine is low in alcohol, at 11% or below.

♦ Tannin is present in all wines, but is perceptible only in red wine.

**PINOT NOIR
(PEE-noh-NWAHR)**

FIGURE 4–5 Close-up of Pinot Noir grapes

(Collection CIVC.
Photographer: CORNU Alain)

The cultivation of Pinot Noir (or *Pinot*, as it is often coined) dates back over 2000 years and arguably produces some of the finest wines in the world. The grape is largely associated with the Burgundy and Champagne regions of France, where it originally gained its fame. Pinot Noir thrives in France's Burgundy region, particularly in the subregion of Côte d'OR (koht-d-OR). Figure 4–5 shows the Pinot Noir grape varietal.

Pinot is a difficult variety to cultivate and generally produces fairly low yields, which ultimately affects the selling price. With such limited production, good Pinots, when found, tend to be fairly expensive.

The name *Pinot* is used in the names of many different grapes because Pinot Noir is very prone to mutation. The widely used varieties Pinot Gris, Pinot Blanc, and Pinot Menieur are relatives of the Pinot Noir varietal.

Aromas/Flavors

- **Fruit**—tree fruit (cherry, cranberry, black cherry, raspberry, candied fruit)
- **Earth**—mushrooms, dust, dirt, wet leaves
- **Coffee Shop**—espresso, butterscotch, vanilla, cinnamon, clove, nutmeg, anise

Body/Style

Pinot Noir tends to be of light to medium body, with low tannin and medium to high acidity. The wine's color is often light and transparent in intensity because Pinot Noir is a thin-skinned grape that ends up contributing less color concentration (through anthocyanins) than other red wine grapes.

Significant Locations

Some of the best quality Pinot Noir is grown in cooler climates that allow the grapes to mature slowly.

- **OLD WORLD**—France grows, arguably, the best Pinot Noir in the world, especially in Burgundy and specifically in the areas of Côte d' Nuits (koht duh NWEE) and Côte'd Beaune (koht duh BOHN), and in Chamagne.
- **NEW WORLD**—California (Sonoma, Sonoma Coast, Carneros, and Central Coast), Oregon (Willamette Valley), and New Zealand (Central Otago, Marlborough, Martinborough, and Waipara) are significant producers.

STYLE #1: The Burgundian Style—Burgundy has always produced the classic Pinot Noir style that has been so widely imitated around the world. These wines typically offer medium body, with medium to high acid and medium tannin. The Burgundian style offers a wine that is harmonious and elegant. The alcohol content is typically found hovering around 13.5%. Oregon is another significant Pinot Noir producer that has traditionally been compared to Burgundian style.

STYLE #2: The California Style—In trying to mimic the Burgundian style, California and New Zealand have instead created something different. The Pinot from California generally offers a greater richness of fruit, with a bit more spice sensation coming from the often higher alcohol content hovering around 14% or higher. The high alcohol content can affect the type of food that is successfully paired with the wine, compared with Burgundian Pinots, which have a traditionally lower alcohol content.

Pairing Strategies

1. Pinot Noir is one of the most adaptable red wines and can pair well with roasted and braised preparations of lamb, pheasant, and duck. It works with meats such as poultry with skin; stewed or braised chicken such as Coq au Vin (chicken cooked in red wine); and other game birds such as quail and turkey; veal; and pork.
2. Pinot Noir pairs excellently with fatty fish prepared by robust cooking methods, such as tuna, salmon, shark, and swordfish. It is important that these fish be wild, as they contain greater flavor and fat content than farm-raised versions.
3. Pinot works excellently with coagulated beef such as Boeuf Bourguignon (beef stew), roast beef sandwiches, beef stroganoff, or any beef that is cooked medium well or greater. Because California style Pinot Noirs are often higher in alcohol, they have the ability to work with some steaks (Filet Mignon) that have been uncoagulated (that are rare to medium in level of doneness).
4. Pinot Noir can pair with some vegetarian dishes that have heightened flavors, such as mushroom risotto enriched with a touch of cream or butter.
5. Some Pinots that offer an intense concentration of fruit (common in the Sonoma Coast Pinots) can pair well with chocolate-based and nut-based desserts that offer some elements of caramel or toffee.

MERLOT
(mehr-LOH)

Merlot is the leading varietal consumed by Americans. It can be made as a stand-alone grape-varietal-based wine from California's Napa Valley or from Washington State. In Bordeaux, France, Merlot has been quite famous, blended in varying quantities with its natural

FIGURE 4–6 Close-up of Merlot grapes
(Chad Ehlers/Stock Connection)

companion, Cabernet Sauvignon, along with other varietals. This grape varietal is a great complement to Cabernet Sauvignon because it can assist in lightening the tannins and contributing greater fruit qualities, therefore making the wine a bit more approachable and adding a dimension of complexity at the same time. Figure 4–6 shows the Merlot grape varietal.

Aromas/Flavors

- **Fruit**—tree fruit (cherry, plum), tropical fruit (pineapple, banana, mango), citrus (lemon).
- **Vegetables**—green olives, bell pepper
- **Coffee Shop**—chocolate or cocoa, coffee
- **Tobacco Shop**—cigar or pipe

Body/Style

Merlot is medium bodied and deep in color intensity and can be fairly high in alcohol, with medium tannin (from thinner-skinned grapes) and medium acid.

Significant Locations

- **OLD WORLD**—France (Bordeaux), specifically in the areas of Pomerol (POAM-ehr-all) and Saint-Émilion (sahn-eh-meel-YOHN), and the northern regions of Italy are significant producers.
- **NEW WORLD**—Washington State (Columbia Valley), California (Napa Valley), and Chile also produce significant amounts of Merlot.

Pairing Strategies

1. Since Merlot often has less tannin than Cabernet Sauvignon, the wine can be paired with skin-on grilled and roasted poultry and game birds (including duck).
2. Roasted or grilled meats such as pork tenderloin, venison, veal, and lamb go well with Merlot. Grilled steaks with less texture and flavor such as beef tenderloin and steaks with minimal degrees of marbling such as skirt steak are also excellent partners.
3. Fruit-forward new world Merlots can pair well with pizza and burgers. Also, suitable Latin and Tex-Mex dishes such as chicken or steak fajitas and beef quesadillas are delicious with Merlot.
4. Some Merlots that offer an intense concentration of fruit (common in Washington) pair well with dark-chocolate-based desserts.

Often called just *Cab* or *Cab Sauv*, this is one of the most widely planted grapes throughout the world. It is frequently referred to as the king of red wine grapes and is often viewed as a winery's benchmark wine. Cabernet is a stand-alone varietal (though seldom 100%) but more often blended in a *Bordeaux style* (where it is a dominant grape, but blended with numerous others) as a *Super Tuscan* (blended with Sangiovese), where it has been the backbone of some of the world's most renowned wines.

**CABERNET SAUVIGNON
(KAB-er-nay SOH-vin-NYOHN)**

A California Cabernet Sauvignon wine was responsible for bringing great fame to California (and overall the new world) when a "Stag's Leap, Napa Valley, Cabernet Sauvignon" won the top place over French counterparts in the famous 1976 Paris wine tasting (discussed in greater detail in Chapter 7, "Wines of the United States and Canada"). Figure 4–7 shows the Cabernet Sauvignon grape varietal.

Aromas/Flavors

Intense aromas and flavors of

- **Fruit**—tree fruit (cherry, plum) dried fruit (black currents)
- **Garden**—black olives, bell pepper, eucalyptis
- **Coffee Shop**—chocolate or cocoa, coffee, black tea
- **Tobacco Shop**—cedar, clove, cigar or pipe

Body/Style

This deeply colored grape can produce medium-bodied wine (particularly when yields are high), but is often fuller bodied due to its thick skin. It is highly concentrated, rather high in tannin (smaller berry with thicker skin) and alcohol with medium acidity.

Cabernet Sauvignon is often blended with "fleshy" yielding grapes such as Merlot or Shiraz in order to lower tannin and balance flavors (by contributing a bit more fruit qualities). Cabernets are almost always aged in oak for at least 1–2 years from harvest, and are more likely bottle aged for years to decades to soften its tannin and to allow flavors and other components to integrate. World Class examples of Cabernet Sauvignon can often improve and be aged for decades.

Significant Locations

- **OLD WORLD**—France (Bordeaux), specifically in the areas of the Médoc (may-DAWK), Pessac-Léognan (peh-SAK leh-oh-NYAHN) and Graves (GRAHV) and Italy (Tuscany) are significant producers of Cabernet Sauvignon.
- **NEW WORLD**—California (Napa Valley), Australia (Barossa and Coonawarra), Chile, and Washington State (Columbia Valley) are significant producers.

Pairing Strategies

1. The firm tannins that are often present in Cabernet can be tempered in food pairing with robust cooking methods and uncoagulated meat protein found in beef, particularly steaks.
2. Cabernet Sauvignon can partner well with other meats such as lamb or veal shank.
3. As a Cabernet Sauvignon ages, it becomes less intense as the tannins soften and flavors come together. An aged Cab can alter a pairing and require meat that is less fatty as a successful partner.
4. Cabernet can pair with dark chocolate that has a high cocoa content.
5. Cabernet Sauvignon can pair with blue-vein-type cheese.

Other Popular Red Wine Grapes

Barbera (bar-BEHR-ah)

Barbera is one of the grapes most commonly planted throughout Italy. It is generally regarded as producing simple and inexpensive wine though there are some excellent high quality examples. Because of Barbera's high acid and lower tannin, it tends to be highly versatile with food. ◆ For a more extensive discussion of Barbera, refer to Chapter 10, "Other Old World Wine Countries."

- **AROMAS/FLAVORS**—Fruit (bright to sour cherry and berries) and light tobacco shop.
- **BODY/STYLE**—Barbera is a deep-ruby-colored, light- to medium-bodied wine with low to medium levels of tannin and high levels of acidity.
- **SIGNIFICANT LOCATIONS**—Italy (Piedmont) is a significant producer, and the wine is most recognizable in the areas of Asti and Alba, where they are known as Barbera d' Asti and Barbera d' Alba.

Cabernet Franc (ka-behr-NAY FRAHNK)

Cabernet Franc is widely used as a blending grape in the famous *Bordeaux Blend*. But Cabernet Franc is also famous as a stand-alone varietal in Loire Valley, France. ◆ For a more in-depth discussion of Cabernet Franc, see Chapter 9, "Wines of France."

- **AROMAS/FLAVORS**—Fruit (strawberry or berry fruit), garden (vegetables and herbs), cigar shop (slightly cedar and tobacco).
- **BODY/STYLE**—Cabernet Franc has low to medium tannin and tends to be light- to medium-bodied with high acidity.
- **SIGNIFICANT LOCATIONS**—France (Bordeaux, Loire Valley) is the significant producer in the Old World; California, Canada (Niagara Peninsula, and Okanagan Valley), and New York (Finger Lakes) in the New World.

FIGURE 4–7 Close-up of Cabernet Sauvignon grapes
(Michele/Tom Grimm/Creative Eye/MIRA.com)

Carménère **(car-men-YHER)**	In Chile, Carménère was originally thought to be Merlot, but its identity has been clarified as a separate, distinctive varietal. Carménère has since been rediscovered in Chile as a leading red grape capable of stand-alone single varietals wines. ♦ For a more thorough discussion of Carménère, refer to Chapter 8, "Other New World Wine Countries."

- **AROMAS/FLAVORS**—Fruit (fresh berries), bakeshop spice (cardamom, clove, nutmeg), vegetables (green pepper).
- **BODY/STYLE**—Medium bodied with low to medium tannin and medium acid.
- **SIGNIFICANT LOCATIONS**—Chile (Rapel Valley and Maipó).

Dolcetto **(dohl-CHET-toe)**	Dolcetto means "little sweet one," in reference to its early ripening, which allows the wine to be drunk sooner than other varietals. ♦ For further discussion of Dolcetto, see Chapter 10, "Other Old World Wine Countries."

- **AROMAS/FLAVORS**—Bakeshop (licorice), nuts (almonds), fruit (plums, blackberries).
- **BODY/STYLE**—Dolcetto produces a medium-bodied wine with low-acid and medium tannin.
- **SIGNIFICANT LOCATIONS**—Italy (Piedmont) is a significant producer, and the wine is most recognizable in the area of Alba, where it's known as Dolcetto d' Alba.

Gamay **(gah-MAY)**	Gamay is a French varietal most recognizable and dominant in Southern Burgundy in the area of Beaujolais, France. It produces the popular, simple, and highly fruity Beaujolais Nouveau and the more serious, complex, and well-structured *Crus* of Beaujolais. ♦ For a deeper discussion of Gamay, refer to Chapter 9, "Wines of France."

- **AROMAS/FLAVORS**—Gamay produces a highly aromatic wine with fruit (berries such as raspberry and cherry), tropical bakeshop (chocolate) in older vintages.
- **BODY/STYLE**—Most Beaujolais (Beaujolais and Beaujolais Village levels) are light bodied, low in tannin, and medium to high in acid. Many of the Crus of Beaujolais are heartier, with deeper, more intense fruit, and offer greater structure that can benefit from a short period of aging.
- **SIGNIFICANT LOCATIONS**—France (Beaujolais and Loire Valley).

Grenache **(Gren-AHSH)**	Grenache is a vigorously growing grape that has the ability to produce simple fruity rosés or powerful age-worthy reds. It is almost always blended (often with Syrah and Mourvèdre) and may even be a dominant grape in many of the blends. The Spanish call this grape *Garnacha* (gahrr-NAH-chah), or it is known as *Cannonau* (cahn-AH-now) in Sardinia, Italy. This varietal produces the famous French red based fortified wines called *Vin doux naturel* (VDN) in Southern France, specifically in the areas of Banyuls and Maury. ♦ For further discussion of Grenache, see Chapter 9, "Wines of France."

- **AROMAS/FLAVORS**—Fruit (fresh strawberries), bakeshop (chocolate), spice, earth (wet leaves) and tobacco shop
- **BODY/STYLE**—This grape produces a medium-bodied to full-bodied wine with medium acid and tannin.
- **SIGNIFICANT LOCATIONS**—France (Rhône Valley, Provence, Languedoc-Roussillon), Spain (Priorat and Rioja) is also a significant producer.

Malbec **(mahl-BEHK)**	Malbec has traditionally been a blending grape in red Bordeaux, but over the last decade, it has become the leading red wine grape as a stand-alone varietal in South America. Malbec goes by many synonyms, depending on the growing area. It is known as *Auxerrois* in Cahors (Southwestern France) or *Cot* in the Loire Valley. ♦ For a more in-depth discussion of Malbec, refer to Chapter 8, "Wines of the New World" or Chapter 9, "Wines of France."

- **AROMAS/FLAVORS**—Floral (violets, rosé), fruit (loganberries, black cherry, blackcurrant, plums), bakeshop (toffee, cinnamon, chocolate, coffee, anise), tobacco shop.
- **BODY/STYLE**—This deeply colored grape can range from medium to full bodied, with medium tannin and medium to high acid.
- **SIGNIFICANT LOCATIONS**—Argentina (Mendoza), France (Bordeaux, where it is blended in varying amounts in the famous *Bordeaux blend*; Loire Valley; and Southwest France) and California (North Coast, where it is blended in the *Bordeaux blend,* often called a *Meritage*) are the significant producers.

Mourvèdre (moor-VEH-druh)

Mourvèdre is traditionally used as a blending grape in the famous Côtes du Rhône and Châteauneuf-du-Pape. But it is becoming extremely popular as a stand-alone varietal, as it is primarily this grape that produces a *Bandol* in Southern France's Provence. Mourvèdre is said to have originated in Spain, where it still remains very popular and is known as Monastrel (mahn-ah-STRELL). ♦ For further discussion of Mourvèdre, see Chapter 9, "Wines of France."

- **AROMAS/FLAVORS**—Tree fruit (cherries), berry fruit (blackberries), spicy, cigar shop (animal, leather).
- **BODY/STYLE**—Medium bodied, with medium to high acid and tannin.
- **SIGNIFICANT LOCATIONS**—France (Rhône Valley, Provence, Languedoc-Roussillon), Spain (Jumilla) and California are the major producers.

Nebbiolo (neh-b'YOH-loh)

The name derives from the word *nebbia*, Italian for "fog," which is known to encase the Nebbiolo vineyards in Piedmont during the harvest time. Nebbiolo produces one of the most ageable and long-lived wines available. ♦ For more on Nebbiolo, refer to Chapter 10, "Other Old World Wine Countries."

- **AROMAS/FLAVORS**—Dried fruit raspberries and cherries, plums, prunes), earth (soil, mushrooms, tar), floral (rosés, violets), cigar shop (tobacco, licorice, leather), bakeshop (bitter chocolate).
- **BODY/STYLE**—Nebbiolo is generally full bodied, with high tannins and acids. It often needs several years of bottle aging before it is ready to drink.
- **SIGNIFICANT LOCATIONS**—Nebbiolo's main producer is Italy (Piedmont), where it is most famous in the appellations of Barolo, Barbaresco, and Gattinara.

Nero d'Avola (neh-ROH dah-voe-lah)

This grape, indigenous to Southern Italy, is known for producing a simple, rustic style wine that has similarities to wines made from the Zinfandel and Syrah varietals. ♦ For further discussion of Nero d'Avola, refer to Chapter 10, "Other Old World Wine Countries."

- **AROMAS/FLAVORS**—Fruit, dried fruit (berries, cherries), earth (soil), tobacco shop.
- **BODY/STYLE**—Nero d'Avola produces a medium-bodied wine with high acidity and medium tannin.
- **SIGNIFICANT LOCATIONS**—Italy (Sicily and Puglia) is the dominant producer.

Pinotage (pee-noh-TAHJ)

Pinotage is a grape unique to South Africa, where it was created in 1925 as a cross between Pinot Noir and Cinsault (SAHN-so) varietals. ♦ For further discussion of Pinotage, see Chapter 8, "Other New World Wine Countries."

- **AROMAS/FLAVORS**—Dried fruit, earth, animal (leather), tobacco shop (smoke), chemical (acetone).
- **BODY/STYLE**—Medium bodied with low to medium tannin and acid.
- **SIGNIFICANT LOCATIONS**—South Africa is this wine's major producer.

Sangiovese (san-joh-VAY-zeh)

Sangiovese is a famous and significant grape found throughout central Italy, primarily within Tuscany where the famous Chianti region is located. This grape varietal goes by various names, depending on the type of clone, such as *Sangioveto* in Chianti, *Brunello* in Montalcino and *Prugnolo* in Vino Nobile di Montepulciano.

Sangiovese is often a stand-alone varietal, as in Brunello di Montalcino, but is more often blended with small amounts of indigenous Italian grapes in Chianti or Vino Nobile di Montepulciano. It has also been blended with greater amounts of international varietals such as Cabernet Sauvignon and Merlot to create the Super-Tuscan wines of Tuscany. ♦ For further discussion of Sangiovese, refer to Chapter 10, "Wines of the Old World."

- **AROMAS/FLAVORS**—Fruit (cherry, black cherry), bakeshop (spice, nuts), cigar shop (tobacco, tea leaves, leather), floral (violet, rosé).
- **BODY/STYLE**—Sangiovese-based wines can range from medium to full bodied, with medium to high acid and tannin.

    Lighter versions may be labelled Chianti, Rosso di Montalcino; while medium versions may be labelled Chianti Classico and full-bodied versions Chianti Classico Riserva, Brunello di Montalcino, and Vino Nobile di Montepulciano.
- **SIGNIFICANT LOCATIONS**—Italy (Tuscany), and more specifically the area of and surrounding Chianti, boasts being the predominant producer of this wine.

Shiraz/Syrah (shih-RAHZZ)/(SEAR-ah)

The grape is called *Syrah* in France and California. In Australia, it is referred to as *Shiraz*. This grape is possibly the most significant of the emerging varietals throughout the entire wine world. It is beginning to play an important role in many wine areas and in some cases is being showcased as a particular country's calling card.

There appear to be two distinct styles of this grape. Syrah (and Syrah blends) tends more toward a spicy, rustic, or earthy style that can be medium to full bodied. Shiraz, on the other hand, is created in a bolder style that is intensely fruit forward.

Syrah or Shiraz is often created as a stand-alone varietal, but is also adaptable to blend with other grapes such as Grenache, Mourvedre, Cabernet Sauvignon, and Viognier. ♦ For further discussion of Shiraz/Syrah, refer to Chapter 8, "Wines of the New World," and Chapter 9, "Wines of France."

- **AROMAS/FLAVORS**—bakeshop spice (pepper), dried/baked fruit (jam and blackberry), animal (leather, wild game, tar).
- **BODY/STYLE**—A dense, dark red wine with a rich, full body, medium tannin and acid, with high alcohol content.

    Syrah blends tend to be a bit softer and with less tannin than Syrah, and with less alcohol than Shiraz.
- **SIGNIFICANT LOCATIONS**—In France (Rhône Valley), such as Cote Rotie or Crozes-Hermitage in Northern Rhône. California (Central Coast), Washington (Columbia Valley), Australia (Barossa Valley, Coonawarra), Chile (Colchagua and Maipó), and South Africa (Cape) are the main producers.

Tempranillo (tem-prah-NEE-yoh)

Tempranillo is often described as Spain's *Noble* grape. It can be produced as a stand-alone varietal, but shows more complexity when blended with grapes such as Garnacha (Grenache), Cabernet Sauvignon, and Merlot. Tempranillo is capable of producing deeply colored and concentrated fruity wines for early consumption, or richly flavored and age-worthy wine for later consumption. ♦ For further discussion of Tempranillo, see Chapter 10, "Wines of the Old World," and Chapter 12, "BOLD: Fortified Wines."

- **AROMAS/FLAVORS**—Fruit (dark cherry, strawberry), earth, bakeshop (spice), tobacco, floral.
- **BODY/STYLE**—Richly colored, Tempranillo is fairly low in acid and alcohol levels and medium to high in tannin levels (from thick-skinned grapes).

- **SIGNIFICANT LOCATIONS**—Spain (Rioja, Ribera del Duero, and parts of Penendes), Portugal, and Argentina are this wine's most significant producers.

Classically, Touriga Nacional has served as one of the most significant grapes used to produce the fortified wine, Port. Currently, this grape has gained renewed interest and popularity as a stand-alone varietal in an unfortified wine style.

- **AROMAS/FLAVORS**—This grape maintains the deep, concentrated flavor and aroma of the exotic spices of baked/dried fruit (blackberry, black cherry), floral (violets), bakeshop spice (black pepper, all spice, cinnamon), and cigar shop (smoke).
- **BODY/STYLE**—Touriga Nacional creates a wine with substantial concentrated color, with medium to high tannin (from thick-skinned grapes), medium acid levels, and medium-to-full body.
- **SIGNIFICANT LOCATIONS**—Portugal (Duoro and Dão Valleys) is the main producer.

The Zinfandel grape is native to Croatia and for centuries has made wine in Italy's Puglia region (where the grape is known as *Primitivo*).

In the United States, the Zinfandel grape has made resurgence after suffering from an image problem in the 1980s when people associated it mostly with its white counterpart, White Zinfandel.

- **AROMAS/FLAVORS**—Maintains a deep, concentrated flavor and aroma of exotic spices of fresh/dried fruit (jam, berry, currants, cherry, blackberry), bakeshop spice (black pepper, cinnamon), cigar shop (smoke), and vegetables (herbs, bell pepper).
- **BODY/STYLE**—Ranges from medium to full bodied and intense. Offering medium acid and tannin, with high alcohol.
- **SIGNIFICANT LOCATIONS**—California (Sonoma and Central Coast) and Italy (Puglia) are significant producers of this wine.

FRUIT WINES

A *fruit wine* is generally any wine fermented from a fruit other than grapes. There are many different types of fruit wines, but some of the most popular include red raspberry, blackberry, and cherry. These wines are big in flavor and intense in their fruit character, as it typically takes over 10 pounds of fruit to produce 1 gallon of premium fruit wine.

Fermentation techniques vary with the specific winemaker, but often the fermentation takes place under cold conditions to maximize the retention of fruit character. Well-made fruit wines are a delicate balance between the fruit's natural acidity and residual sugar. If the finished wine is too sweet, it tends to be cloying on the palate. If it is too dry, it tends to be sharp and astringent.

Well-made fruit wines come from the finest growing regions for that particular fruit. These include Willamette red raspberries and Marion blackberries from the Pacific Northwest and Montmorency cherries from Michigan. As in grape wine, optimal fruit quality translates into spectacular fruit wines.

Fruit wines have a multitude of uses. They are often consumed slightly chilled (55° F) with a dessert course. For example, blackberry and red raspberry wines are a delightful accompaniment to dense chocolate desserts, as the wine cleanses the palate of the sweet chocolate. Blueberry and cherry have a similar effect on cheesecake. Fruit wines can also be used in the sauté pan to make reductions or on roasts to create a glaze.

PERFORMANCE FACTORS OF GRAPE VARIETALS

NAME: _____ Score out of 20 points_____.

Use these quesetions to test your knowledge and understanding of the concepts presented in the chapter.

I. MULTIPLE CHOICE: Select the best possible answer from the options available.

1. Which is *not* a prominent location for high-quality Pinot Noir?

   a. Bordeaux, France

   b. Central Otago, New Zealand

   c. Willamette Valley, Oregon

   d. Burgundy, France

2. Which is *not* a prominent location for high-quality Cabernet Sauvignon?

   a. Napa Valley, California

   b. Chile

   c. Bordeaux, France

   d. Germany

3. Which is *not* a prominent location for Sauvignon Blanc?

   a. Germany

   b. Loire Valley, France

   c. Bordeaux, France

   d. New Zealand

4. Which is *not* a prominent location for Riesling?

   a. Germany

   b. Alsace, France

   c. Washington State

   d. Chile

5. Where is the *Gamay* grape grown?

   a. Bordeaux, France

   b. Beaujolais

   c. Napa Valley, California

   d. New Zealand

6. Which one of the following colors in white wine is a sign that the wine has been exposed to too much oxygen or has been bottled too long?

   a. very pale yellow with a hint of green

   b. straw yellow

   c. golden yellow

   d. brown

7. Which one of the following colors in white wine is a sign that the wine has been aged in oak?

   a. very pale yellow with a hint of green

   b. straw yellow

   c. golden yellow

   d. brown

8. Which one of the following colors in a red wine is associated with a wine that has been aged for a considerable period?

   a. purple

   b. ruby red

   c. red

   d. brick red

II. MATCHING: Match the correct grape varietal with its common aromas and flavors.

9. ____ Honey, raisin, petroleum, peach

10. ____ Earth (mushrooms, soil), bakeshop spice (anise, clove, cinnamon), fruit (berries)

11. ____ Black tea, tobacco, plum, cedar, black olive

12. ____ Bakeshop (cocoa, coffee), berries (cherries), green olive

13. ____ Bakeshop (vanilla, butter, toasted nuts), apple, pear

14. ____Citrus (grapefruit), barnyard (hay, fresh cut grass)

   a. Riesling
   b. Sauvignon Blanc
   c. Chardonnay

   d. Pinot Noir
   e. Merlot
   f. Cabernet Sauvignon

III. TRUE / FALSE: Circle the best possible answer.

15. Chardonnay is often known as a "moldable" grape varietal. **True / False**

16. Pinot Noir often produces a light- to medium-bodied red wine that is easy to grow, as seen in numerous growing locations around the world. **True / False**

17. Cabernet Sauvignon and Merlot are often blended together in varying amounts. **True / False**

18. Fumé Blanc is a white wine grape varietal. **True / False**

IV. SHORT-ANSWER ESSAY / DISCUSSION QUESTIONS: Use a separate sheet of paper if necessary.

19. List and briefly explain four factors that can influence the body of a wine.

20. List and briefly describe four factors that can influence the color in a red wine.

5

Foundations to Wine and Food Pairing

A large part of our daily food and beverage rituals involve our seeking some sort of balance, whether consciously or subconsciously, that we perceive as ideal for our palate, given the time of day, occasion, or mood. Pairing a glass of wine (whether extravagant or humble) with a food can elevate a meal and the dining experience from mundane to special occasion.

LEARNING OBJECTIVES

Upon completion of this chapter, the learner will be able to:

- Provide a framework for wine and food pairing choices by developing analytical and decision-making skills.
- Examine how various taste components can influence successful wine and food pairings.
- Discover the concept of bridge flavors and recognize how to reinforce a successful wine and food pairing.
- Describe the effects that moist- and dry-heat cooking techniques have on food and wine pairing.
- Discover how to select a wine on the basis of an analytical approach to pairing.
- Explore the effects that various cooking techniques have on the subsequent success of a wine and food match.

CUISINES AND HOW THEY AFFECT WINE PAIRING

Classical, or French, cooking is the foundation to most other cuisines. French cuisine became known as *haute cuisine* (OHT-kwih-ZEEN), which translates to "high cuisine" and identifies food prepared in an elegant or elaborate manner. Haute cuisine has maintained great influence because for many years France was one of the most important political forces in the world. Currently, European cooking methods and ingredients are still the foundation for modern-day cuisines the world over.

> As European influence spread through travels and trade, the Europeans left their thumbprint of food and beverage knowledge, as well as ingredients and techniques, throughout most modern-day cultures. Over time, changing eating and dining habits redefined cooking and *nouvelle cuisine* (NOO-vehl) eventually became the new healthy cooking philosophy. Popularized in the 1970s, nouvelle cuisine rose up in reaction to the rich and supposedly unhealthy nature of classic French cookery.

Creation of a Cuisine

A cuisine's foundation is a specific set of cooking traditions, techniques, and ingredients associated with a specific culture within a geographical area. Throughout the world, the diversity of cuisines is a reflection of the cultural dynamics derived from various factors that are particular to that specific area: geography, immigration, economics, trade, politics, religion and ethnicity. These factors act collectively to affect ingredients, traditions, and styles, which in turn affect our eating habits, flavor preferences, recipes, and dining etiquette. They are the primary drivers that sustain the distinction of a particular cuisine.

Throughout thousands of years, wine has evolved with cuisine. Traditionally, there has been a *classical* perspective on wine and food pairing that matches the regional cuisine to the local wine. This approach is still evident, and many wine drinkers live by it.

Currently, cookery has been modernized to create what is known as a *world cuisine*. Quite different from classical cuisine, it does not have defined geographic boundaries, but instead is rooted in the creation of food that incorporates aspects, ingredients, and techniques from around the world. Hence, a new approach to wine and food pairing has been established. The *contemporary* perspective is more appropriate for this new cuisine than the alternative, classical approach to wine and food pairing.

Classical Cuisine and the Classical Approach to Wine and Food Pairing

Classical cuisine is rooted in and produced according to tradition. Each culture around the world has its own unique culinary identity. The specifics of climate, politics, history, and geography all collectively influence the types of food that are readily available and that have evolved together.

With classical pairings, the idea of wine and food matching is tied to a natural connection of regional cuisines. These types of pairings are associated with Old World countries such as France, Italy, Spain, and Germany, where there is a strong sense of regionality that has taken hundreds and thousands of years for a cuisine to evolve. This is a somewhat romantic notion, to partake in a ritual of eating food and drinking wine that has a sense of time and place.

Sample of Classical Wine and Food Pairings

- Aged Tawny Port → Stilton Cheese
- Red Burgundy → Coq au Vin
- Chianti Classico → Bistecca Fiorentina

World Cuisine and the Contemporary Approach to Wine and Food Pairing

World cuisine in the broadest sense is food that has been created in the present day and that may incorporate a combination of modern or classical practices, ingredients, and techniques. Globalization has dramatically influenced contemporary cuisine, bringing to people the possibility to obtain almost any kind of wine and food ingredient at any time of the year. In addition, the fusion cuisine movement blends two or more cuisines collectively to create a new one. The World Cuisine movement began in the late 1980s and has now become pivotal in the United States, as a result of immigration, greater accessibility to foreign travel, and the renewed popularity of cooking. Professional and home cooks have been exposed to different cultures and the practice of combining different ingredients and techniques. As Americans' eating patterns have changed, so has the way wine is paired with food. Globally, cooking has been liberated and has led wine drinkers to rethink how wine is paired with food.

With contemporary matching, the idea of wine and food pairing is more about freedom—freedom from the evolution of food and beverage combinations that have been traditionally tied together because of culture. Instead, the contemporary approach is about finding a wine that is compatible no matter the origin of the food or cuisine. This notion may seem less romantic than a classical pairing; however, the world has become such a small place that it is not uncommon to find two or three different cuisines integrated together on a single plate.

Samples of Contemporary Wine and Food Pairings

- German Riesling → Roasted Honey and Ginger Glazed Pork Tenderloin Stuffed with Dried Fruits
- California Chardonnay → Corn Fritters with Dungeness Crab and Crème Fraiche
- Oregon Pinot Noir → Grilled Copper River King Salmon with Garlic Mashed Potatoes

FOUNDATIONS TO WINE AND FOOD MATCHING

"Wine is both a garnish and a condiment for food, changing and enhancing the way the diner tastes the finished product."
—*Danny Meyer, Restaurant Owner*

The Integration of Wine and Food

People pair wine and food out of tradition, for personal enjoyment, and for hedonistic reasons, by achieving a union between the two. When attempting to pair a wine with a food, it may help to think of wine as a condiment or just another ingredient to season the food. Wine can act much the same way that relish enhances the flavor of a hot dog, cream provides richness in coffee, and salsa adds dimension to tortilla chips. All these combinations are meant to enhance or alter the food item that is being consumed. Pairing a wine with food can be somewhat subjective because of personal tastes. While some individuals enjoy coffee straight-up black, others find balance in adding cream and or sugar, and yet more adventurous coffee drinkers add a flavoring such as vanilla or hazelnut syrup. Wine brings the same ability to the table by contributing such elements as acid, fruit, sweetness, tannin, aromas, flavors, and spiciness, the same way that condiments or ingredients do to food.

When choosing a food to go with a wine, a relationship is created, just as when two people come together. As with most relationships, these can be happy and can work for different reasons. Sometimes, opposites attract; other times, people are attracted to one another because of similarities. Either way, the couple has found some complementary qualities that work, just as with a wine and food pairing.

Wine pairing can be considered within the same context. Matching wine and food to enhance the quality of a meal can be fairly simple if a few basic principles and a moderate degree of gastronomic experimentation are applied. It is important to note that pairings are highly subjective and there is no perfect match that is right for everyone, just as romantic relationships are made on the basis of personal factors. Some romantic relationships are blah, some are good, and some are great! Do not be frustrated because of the occasional lack of a great wine and food pairing; sometimes, it is just like finding that romantic partner—it takes time and practice at applying the basic pairing techniques. With all the intricacies of wine and food, it's understandable how it can be easy to become overwhelmed by the concept, because every dish is dynamic and can comprise thousands of food ingredients and infinite combinations, which contribute to difficult and somewhat subjective pairings. However, it is possible to generalize and reasonably predict what might work for most people.

What Is an Effective Wine and Food Pairing?

Applying and practicing the pairing principles presented in this chapter make it possible to greatly improve the overall consistent satisfaction found in wine and food pairings. At the very least, wine and food should be able to intermingle with one another. In an effective pairing, neither overpowers the other and yet each one contributes something to the table to enhance the other. Generally, a successful wine and food pairing is one in which the interaction of the wine and food does not diminish the pleasure of either partner, but instead enhances each one, to contribute to a more fulfilling whole.

The Quick-Fix Approach

The common phrases "Drink what you like" and "Serve white wine with chicken and fish, and red wine with meat" are fine basic rules that have been preached over the last 20 or so years. However, these *quick-fix* approaches are limiting, as well as gross simplifications of the nature of wine and food pairing. Of course, one may drink and eat whatever he or she likes, but for one who loves and appreciates food, the ultimate goal is to create the best gastronomic experience by finding a suitable wine to enhance the food.

The quick-fix approach is similar to the old adage, "Give a person a fish, and he will be fed for a day," as opposed to the more analytical long-term approach, which we advocate in wine pairing, "Teach a person how to fish, and he will eat for a lifetime." People get stuck in the belief that there is only one wine or one perfect match to pair with a food item. In reality, there are often several different options that can be paired for similar, or in some cases very different, reasons. The old rules don't take into account the complexity of today's multi-ethnic World Cuisine and menus or the wide range of wines available from around the world.

The Analytical Approach

Rather than relying on the quick-fix approach, we can create successful pairings that work in most situations. Making intelligent wine and food pairing decisions involves a bit of analytical thought beforehand, relying on the approach of "Teach a person how to fish, and he will be fed for a lifetime." By broadening the quick-fix perspective and approaching wine and food matching with some basic principles, we can make pairing less intimidating, less stressful, and less limiting. The methodical three-step analytical approach will lead to greater satiety at the dining table. A good match can bring nuances to, and enhance flavors and characteristics in, both the food and the wine.

The three steps in the *analytical approach* are as follows:

1. Mirror the body and weight (or overall intensity) of the wine and the food to ensure neither one overwhelms the other.
2. Connect bridge ingredients in the food with flavors in the wine.
3. Compare or contrast taste components between the wine and food on the basis of the desired emphasis of the match.

The analytical process can be applied to both complex and even the simplest of dishes. By applying the analytical approach, it is possible to show a connection between the wine and a food and point out possible wine pairings. Throughout the analytical process, there are many techniques for building flavor or bridging elements in the wine and food to ensure and solidify a more effective pairing.

THE ANALYTICAL APPROACH:

Principle #1

Mirror the body and weight (or overall intensity) of the wine and the food to ensure that neither overwhelms the other.

Principle #1 is the most significant step to forming the foundation of a successful wine and food pairing. It involves mirroring the body, weight, or overall intensity of a given food item with a wine at a similar level. Principle #1 is focused on creating an equal balance, or "mirroring effect," of the body of both the wine and food so neither will overwhelm the other. The like characteristics allow the wine and food to remain compatible, and they work to keep the meal grounded. For example, a light- to medium-bodied white wine such as Sauvignon Blanc would be overwhelmed by a heavy dish such as a grilled porterhouse steak with melted bleu cheese. Likewise, a full-bodied wine such as a bold, powerful Cabernet Sauvignon may overshadow a delicate dish of poached scallops.

The first principle to the analytical approach involves breaking down the plate of food and determining the primary food type(s) to match with a particular wine. Every food type has a certain body and weight (or overall intensity) that need to be assessed to determine a possible wine pairing.

Intensity can be described as a certain richness or concentration of aromas and flavors. The *intensity* of a wine's aromas and flavors can sometimes compensate for the wine's not having as much weight or body. For example, fatty, rich foods like roasted duck or goose can be partnered in some cases with lighter- to medium-bodied (yet intense) wines such as German Riesling (Spätlese or Auslese).

After considering the main food type and its relative body level, we should consider two additional factors used to judge the influence of the body and weight (or overall intensity)

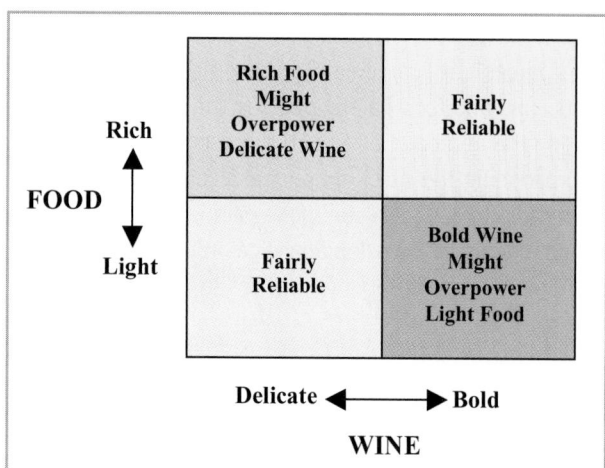

FIGURE 5–1 Comparison of food and wine types
(John Laloganes)

of a food: method of cooking and type of sauce. These elements can collectively alter the body or weight of a food item and subsequently determine a wine pairing.

Figure 5–1 depicts food types and their relative level of body compared with wines and their level of body and weight (or overall intensity). In pairing wine, the goal is to seek fairly reliable matches between the wine and the food and to prevent one from overwhelming the other.

Type of Food

In each dish, there tends to be a core food type, or core ingredient, on display. Often, this is referred to as the *food type* or *center of the plate* item. This main item, on stage within the dish, is the determining factor in choosing an appropriate wine. The food type that is the main item in a dish is often a protein; however, it can certainly be a pasta (or other grain), vegetables, or some other item, depending on the course of the meal or, simply, the preference of the diner. The core ingredient will not necessarily point to one specific grape varietal, but it should help narrow the options to a small, workable list of potential ones. It will provide a direction to suitable wines and help rule out others.

Every food item can be loosely categorized into levels of body on the basis of its individual chemical makeup. Some food items, such as vegetables and pasta, do not have the fat or proteins that meat contains. Therefore, vegetables and pasta tend to be thought of as a lighter food type than meat, which is a full-bodied food type. Presented next are some generalizations of several common food types and their possible levels of weight or body.

Keep in mind that other factors, such as cooking methods and sauces, can significantly alter the body and weight of these food items. For the purpose of simplicity at this point, think of the food items in their unadulterated, somewhat uncooked forms.

☐ **Light-Bodied Food Items**—Vegetables, grains, pasta, chicken, turkey, mollusks, lean finfish

☐ **Medium-Bodied Food Items**—Veal, pork, crustacean, fatty finfish, duck, goose, game birds

☐ **Full-Bodied Food Items**—Certain sausages, game, lamb, beef

Some other factors to consider that will influence the weight and body (overall intensity), of a food type include age of the animal, skin on or off, bone in or out, dark meat or light meat, quality grade, method of aging, wild or farm raised. These factors are not always known to the wine drinker; however, they are questions that can and should be asked prior to continuing with principles #1 and #2 and committing to a particular wine.

Cooking Methods

The more familiar with the food type and cooking techniques the diner is, the more successful wine selection he or she can make. It is possible to understand flavors and textures and how these are modified to pair most effectively with wine. The way a food item is cooked will have a significant effect on how it tastes and what wine pairings will be suitable. Cooking methods can adjust and influence a food's weight and body (overall intensity), but also texture, aroma, and flavor. A food type can be neutral and light in texture and body (such as chicken), but powerfully flavored (because it has been grilled).

Cooking methods can be used to enhance and adjust the body of a food type. A certain method can manipulate a food type to work with an alternative type and style of wine

FIGURE 5–2 Poached salmon dish
(Edward Allwright © Dorling Kindersley)

FIGURE 5–3 Grilled salmon dish

(Ian O'Leary © Dorling Kindersley)

Moist-Heat Cooking Methods

that may have not been previously possible. Understanding basic cooking techniques can help improve the possibility of a good wine and food match.

Hearty, more robust cooking methods and food items demand fuller-flavored and fuller-bodied wines, whereas subtle, more delicate cooking methods and food items necessitate low-flavored, less intense, and light-bodied wines. Choosing a light cooking method such as steaming or poaching can preserve simple and delicate flavors in food. However, more intense cooking methods such as grilling and smoking create rich, robust flavors in food and assist in amplifying the natural flavors. The more aggressive the cooking style, the more body a food type will have. For example, poached salmon tastes dramatically different from grilled salmon. This in turn greatly influences the wine pairing.

Figures 5–2 and 5–3, illustrating salmon being cooked in two different ways, can inform the appropriateness of the wine pairing. Figure 5–2 shows salmon cooked through the poaching method. This method preserves flavor and provides a lighter body to the fish, therefore demanding a lighter styled wine. Figure 5–3 shows the salmon cooked by the grilling method, which incorporates additional flavor to make the salmon more robust. Salmon cooked by this method demands a more substantial wine.

This method uses moist heat to cook food in water, steam, or the vapors of other liquids. Moist heat is used for tenderizing older or tougher cuts of meat by dissolving connective tissue, yielding a tender product. The goal of moist-heat cooking is to achieve the desired degree of doneness through cooking on low heat for a long period until doneness is indicated by tenderness (not by temperature, as is indicated in dry-heat cooking). In this cooking method, meat is cooked well done and beyond, but is still tender due to the breakdown of connective tissue.

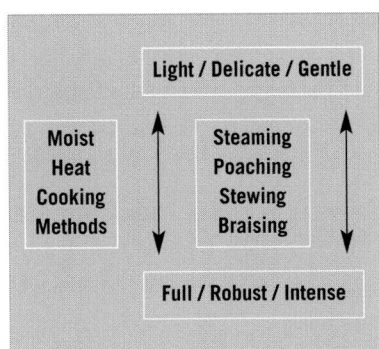

Steaming—Steaming involves lightly cooking small portions of food through the hot vapors of water or flavored liquid. A gentle, delicate process used mainly for delicate foods with fragile textures, steaming preserves a food item's natural flavors. Steaming is typically used for vegetables, dumplings, poultry, and seafood.

Poaching—This method involves submerging food in a simmering hot liquid. It is a slow, delicate cooking method for preserving delicate, tender foods (lean fish and poultry) or breaking down connective tissue in dense, tough meat (brisket). The poaching liquid can be as light and neutral as water or as distinguished as oil, butter, wine, or stock. Poaching is typically used for poultry and seafood.

♦ **En Papillote** (ohn-pop-ee-YOAT)—This is a unique moist-heat method that cooks food inside an individual enclosed pouch. It combines both the steaming and poaching processes, as the item is cooked both in a small amount of liquid in the pouch and through the release of vapors inside the pouch.

Braising and Stewing—These cooking methods produce foods with great dimension and layers of flavor. These methods are used for cooking tougher cuts of meat, older birds, and firm-fleshed fish. Braising involves browning larger pieces such as shoulders or shanks, and stewing involves browning smaller, bite-sized pieces on all sides in a small amount of oil and then simmering in a flavorful liquid until the meat is tender. The longer and slower the cooking process, the more tender the meat will become. The cooking liquid is critical and contributes significant flavor to the dish. The meats are often served with the sauce or gravy that they were simmered in. Braised and stewed food items include pot roast and coq au vin.

Wine Strategies for Moist-Heat Cooking

1. Poaching and steaming are the gentlest cooking methods used for delicate foods to preserve subtle flavors. These foods need an accompanying light- to medium-bodied white wine.

2. Sauces that accompany food items that have been poached or steamed often are emulsified or butter-based sauces that provide a touch of richness to the food item. But in some cases, the poaching liquid will replace these other sauces, thereby allowing a wine with a bit fuller body than what might normally be expected to be paired with the food item. Also, the sauce may play an interesting bridge, or compare–contrast element, with the wine. (See analytic principles #2 and 3, later.)

3. Braising and stewing are moist-heat cooking methods that incorporate significant body and weight to a dish. The cooking liquids usually coat the browned food to create a denser, more concentrated flavor. Food cooked in this manner calls for a medium- to full-bodied red wine, depending on the food type, which can range from seafood to poultry, sausage, or meat.

Dry-Heat Cooking

Dry-heat cooking comprises relatively quick cooking methods that use hot air, hot metal, or hot fat. This style of cooking is used for younger animals with less-exercised muscles that are naturally tender. The goal of dry-heat cooking is to achieve the desired degree of doneness (level of protein coagulation) while preserving the natural tenderness and juiciness. If a food item is uncooked or lightly cooked (from rare, to medium rare, to medium), it will be considered uncoagulated, with sufficient juiciness and internal fat content. In contrast, a food item that is overcooked (medium well or well done) will be drier, with less internal fat, because the item is considered coagulated. The level of protein coagulation is an extremely important consideration when pairing particular wines with food items. The less coagulation, the more fat, juice, and flavor are present in the meat. Generally, a bolder, more full-bodied wine that contains greater tannin would be an appropriate match with uncoagulated foods. When an uncoagulated piece of meat is paired with a tannic full-bodied wine, the fat in the meat can deactivate and soften the tannin to allow the flavors of both to meld together.

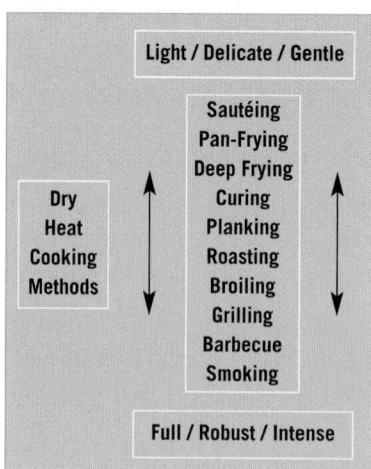

Light / Delicate / Gentle

Dry Heat Cooking Methods

Sautéing
Pan-Frying
Deep Frying
Curing
Planking
Roasting
Broiling
Grilling
Barbecue
Smoking

Full / Robust / Intense

Sautéing—Sautéing (saw-TAY-ing) is a quick-cooking method that uses high heat and a small amount of fat. It is usually reserved for cooking small pieces of food. Options for sautéing include shrimp, scallops, pasta, chicken breast, veal scallop or cutlets, and pork tenderloin. When cooked in this manner, the meat lends itself to a variety of flavors, depending on the pan sauces, which can be made from the addition of different types of wine or stock. The liquid can either be reduced down to make a syrupy glaze or finished with butter or cream for enrichment.

Pan-Frying—This method uses moderate heat with a moderate amount of fat and is used for more delicate items because there is less fat and the container is more shallow. The meat used in this cooking method is often tender and pounded (scaloppini) and may also be breaded or dredged in flour. The fat is needed to achieve a textured flavorful exterior while maintaining a juicy center.

Deep Frying—This method involves quick cooking small pieces of tender food product through immersion in a large amount of hot fat. The larger volume of fat is needed to crisp up the breading and allow the finished product to maintain a nice, crispy, flavorful exterior and a moist interior.

Curing and Planking—These are two of the more pronounced cooking methods used for seafood (mostly for finfish). The most common method of curing is a wet cure, otherwise known as picking. A wet cure consists of a brine solution of salted water possibly with the addition of sugar and spices. In some methods of brining, such as that used with the Latin American dish *seviche* (seh-VEE-cheh), a citrus acid solution is used to coagulate the proteins in the same manner that a pickling solution would.

Dry curing involves rubbing salt and perhaps other spices directly onto the fish, allowing the proteins to coagulate and the fish to lose some moisture content. The curing process can take place over a period of hours to weeks, depending on the desired predominance of flavor.

Planking is the technique of cooking meat, poultry, or seafood on a piece of seasoned wood in a dry-heat environment. The food absorbs the aromas and flavors of the wood throughout the cooking process.

Roasting—The roasting method involves cooking a food item on a suspended rack with the use of hot, dry heat within an oven. As the heat cooks and browns the outside of the roast, the flavors are concentrated by the creation of a slightly crusty, rich surface. (The chemical process by which this surface is created is called the maillard reaction.) The juices on the inside of the food item are intensified by the evaporation of moisture. Throughout the cooking process, the juices are released and collected into the roasting pan to become the foundation of a sauce.

Broiling and Grilling—These methods use very high heat to cook meat quickly. If properly done, broiling and grilling will create a brown, flavorful, crusty surface on the exterior of the meat and maintain a juicy center. Grilling can be used successfully with steaks, chops, burgers, poultry with skin on, and fatty finfish such as tuna, salmon, and shark, that are meaty, full flavored, and oily, either with or without skin to assist in holding the fish together. This method works well for chops and steaks that are about 1 to 1½ inches thick. If the meat is much thinner, it will cook inside before there is enough time for a proper crust on the exterior to form. If the meat is much thicker, it will take too long to cook the meat through to reach a desired degree of doneness, risking burning and drying out the exterior in the process. Figure 5–4 illustrates the grilling process.

FIGURE 5–4 Grilling method of cooking

(Dennis Lane/Photolibrary.com)

Barbecued/Smoking—True barbecuing is a long cooking process over a low, smoky heat to develop colorful, flavorful, and tender meat. It is often done outdoors, but can be done indoors, and is referred to as *smoking*. This cooking technique is used for tougher pieces of meat that can benefit from the long, dry-heat cooking process. Barbecuing is the process of cooking, preserving, and flavoring by exposing the food to burning or smoldering material such as wood. Smoking can be conducted by either the hot or cold method. The hot method is conducted over hot smoke (for several hours), often from burning hardwoods such as maple or oak (even from old whiskey or wine barrels), mesquite, and even tea leaves. Cold smoking is conducted at lower temperatures for an extended period, from days to weeks.

Wine Pairing Strategies for Dry-Heat Cooking

1. Most foods cooked by dry heat cooking methods (except for those which are deep fried) generally go well with oak-aged white and red wines because of the creation of caramelization on the food from sautéing, grilling, broiling, and roasting that mimics the flavor of the toasted oak barrel.

2. Sautéed and pan-fried foods (poultry and seafood) go well with medium- to full-bodied white wines that have been lightly or heavily oak aged.

3. Deep-fried foods contain an exterior coating that contains fat and some level of saltiness. Therefore, medium-bodied white wines or sparkling wines that have ample acidity are excellent at cutting through the fat content and providing a respite on the palate.

4. Because barbecued and smoked foods generally contain large amounts of fat and an intense smoke smell and flavor, they pair well with a medium- to full-bodied red wine that either is rich in fruit qualities or contains a qualities of earthiness and/or tobacco shop.

5. Broiling and grilling are robust methods (used commonly for steaks and chops) that can pair excellent with medium to full-bodied red wine that is medium to high in tannin.

Sauces

A sauce is a flavorful liquid that has been lightly thickened and is used to enhance foods such as meat, poultry, seafood, and vegetables by adding flavor, richness, and moisture. Most sauces act to provide a counterpoint of textural, visual, and flavorful dimensions to a dish. They can add a complementary or a contrasting flavor or structural component. Choosing a sauce with a base flavor similar to that of the main item tends to complement and intensify the flavor of the main item; a contrasting sauce, such as a red wine reduction, adds a contrasting acidity component to a rich fatty steak. Figure 5–5 illustrates sauce.

FIGURE 5–5 Sauce
(Richard Embery/Pearson Education/
PH College)

Sauces are an important consideration when attempting to construct an effective wine and food pairing. Understanding the nature of a sauce, such as its texture and flavors, can dictate a particular type or style of wine.

Classic Sauces

Having an understanding of classic base sauces can assist with a more effective understanding of derivative sauces and subsequent wine pairings. These sauces stem from classical French cookery and are still widely used today. The base sauces, sometimes referred to as *mother sauces*, include the following:

1. **Espanole** (ehs-pah-NYOHL)—Brown sauces derived from concentrated beef or veal stock.

2. **Béchamel** (bay-shah-MEHL)—White sauces derived from roux (a common thickening agent of equal parts fat and flour) thickened milk.

3. **Velouté** (veh-loo-TAY)—White sauces derived from roux thickened stock.

4. **Tomato**—Tomato sauces derived from cooking tomatoes.

5. **Hollandaise** (HOL-uhn-dayz)—These sauces are derived from an emulsion of clarified butter and egg yolks.

The base sauces are created from a base liquid with the addition of some sort of thickening agent. Then, additional flavorings may be added to create other variations of sauces known as *secondary sauces*. All classic base sauces have two major components:

Liquid + Thickening Agent = Base Sauce

Liquid (or the body of the sauce)—The classical base sauces (also known as mother sauces) use either clarified butter; chicken, fish, vegetable, or veal stock; brown stock (from beef); milk; or tomato.

Thickening Agent—Thickening agents are used to give the base liquid a certain amount of viscosity, which allows the sauce to adhere to the food. Sauces can be thickened by a simple reduction of vinegar or cream (rapidly boiling to evaporate excessive liquid) or by the addition of starches (such as flour or cornstarch). Some sauces are emulsified (suspended as two unmixable substances) with egg yolks and butter, and other sauces are thickened through a puree of vegetables that gives a viscous consistency.

Additional Ingredients—The addition of seasoning and flavoring agents such as herbs, spices, fruit, and wine to the base sauces creates various derivatives known as secondary sauces.

Other Kinds of Sauces

With the popularity of world cuisine, sauces used in contemporary menus have expanded well beyond the classic sauces. The creative outlets for pan sauces, reduction sauces, salsas, vinaigrettes, and foams are endless. Here are samples of some of the more modern sauces that derive either from nouvelle cuisine or from other areas around the world:

☑ **Demi glace** (DEHM-ee glahs)—The base of many classic French sauces, demi glace derive from the reduction of espanole that can add a remarkable concentration of flavor.

☑ **Emulsified Sauces**—Some of the most popular sauces derive from this category of base sauce.

- *Egg based:* Hollandaise, Béarnaise.
- *Butter based:* Beurre blanc, compound butter, beurre noisette, and brown butter sauce.
- *Mayonnaise based:* Aioli or garlic Mayonnaise, tartar sauce, and remoulade sauce. Figure 5–6 shows an emulsified sauce and some of its necessary ingredients.

☑ **Reductions**—Simmering a liquid (stock, vinegar, wine, or cream) evaporates part of the water and leaves a concentrated flavor in a sauce-like consistency.

☑ **Glaze**—Similiar to a reduction, but concentrated further, a glaze is made by simmering a stock to evaporate the water (to about one-fourth of original volume of the stock) and concentrate the liquid and flavors within it.

☑ **Salsa, Relish, and Chutney**—These are a mixture of chopped vegetables or fruit with the addition of an acid such as vinegar or citrus that provides a sweet, sour, or spicy element. They can be made in varying degrees of spiciness and intensity of flavor. Typically, salsas are uncoooked; relishes and chutney often are cooked.

☑ **Pure Oils and Flavored Oils**—Many oils in their pure form, such as olive, peanut, and walnut oil, can provide a hint of additional flavor. It is also possible to create a more substantial flavored oil by adding flavor agents such as garlic and herbs to enhance the base oil.

☑ **Coulis and Purees**—Cooked or uncooked pureed vegetables or grains, these creations have a sauce-like consistency.

☑ **Broths or Jus**—These are unthickened, natural juice from the item being served (often meat or poultry).

☑ **Pan Sauces**—The base of a pan sauce is the *fond* (FAWN), or browned bits, clinging to the bottom of the pan after a food item has been sautéed. Once the food item has been removed from the pan, the pan is *deglazed* through the addition of a liquid (stock, water, or wine) while the concentrated fond is scraped in order to be dispersed into the liquid. The sauce can then be reduced (by evaporating the liquid) and thickened further or even enriched with the addition of butter or cream. Figure 5–7 shows the beginning stages of what eventually will be needed to create a pan sauce.

FIGURE 5–6 Emulsified sauce
(SGM/Stock Connection)

FIGURE 5–7 Deglazing
(Ian O'Leary © Dorling Kindersley)

Pairing Strategies for Sauces

Sauces, just like wine, are meant to enhance the dish or meal. However, in some situations, the sauce is the overriding component in pairing a wine. One of the defining questions is, "To what extent is the sauce an integral part of the dish?" Here are some suggestions for the times when it has been determined that a sauce is a major factor in a pairing decision:

1. Emulsified sauces are based in egg yolks, which yield a mouth-coating quality. Light- to medium-bodied white (or sparkling) wines with ample acidity can pair well and keep the palate fresh.

2. Béchamel and Velouté sauces are based in milk- or roux-thickened stock. Each one provides a heaviness and richness to a food item. A full-bodied white wine with adequate acidity or alcohol can mirror the body (and often flavors and texture) of the sauce, while the taste components of acidity and or alcohol can keep the palate fresh.

3. Brown sauces have a beefy richness to offer. In some cases, the sauce may be light and brothy; in others, it may be extremely thick and concentrateed. A medium- to full-bodied red wine can be effective, depending on the item the sauce will be used for. Often, a brown sauce is used on red meat or game, which would be able to hold up to these recommended wines.

4. Tomato-based sauces have ample acidity. It is best to mirror acidity in the food with that of the wine. Light- to medium-bodied red wines with sufficient acidity and subtle tannin can pair effectively.

> **THE ANALYTICAL APPROACH:**
>
> Principle #2
>
> **Connect bridge ingredients in food with flavors in the wine.**

After mirroring the body of both wine and food (see principle #1), the second principle involves finding a *bridge* ingredient or ingredients that the food and wine have in common. While bridges are not the most important matching considerations, paying attention to them can add an interesting dimension or validate the pairing experience.

Bridging Flavors

Bridge ingredients assist to connect the base ingredient (food type), cooking method, or sauce of a dish to a particular wine for a more effective pairing. Just as a bridge may create a connection between two bodies of land, a food-and-wine-pairing bridge uses the presence of certain ingredients in the food and wine to create a stronger association. Bridges can assist in linking complementary flavor components by mimicking or echoing an element found in both the wine and the food. Figure 5–8 illustrates how a bridge aroma and flavor are detected in both the wine and the food.

We begin by assessing the primary or even secondary flavors that are present in both the wine and the food. For example, when a primary flavor of herbs is evident in a food item, a wine that has some of those same herbal qualities may be paired with that item because they share a common bridge. However, it is important to stress that this is so, only assuming that the first principle of mirroring the body of the wine and food has been satisfied. Another example may include pairing a wine that has a buttery, creamy flavor and texture with a food item that has a buttery, creamy flavor.

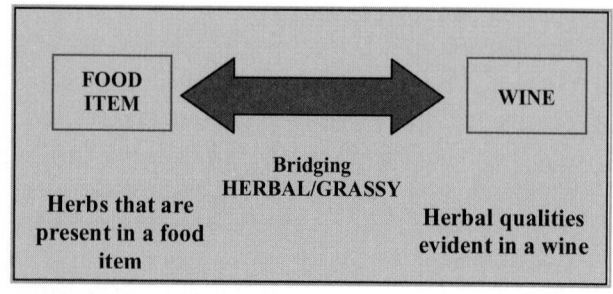

FIGURE 5–8 Bridging the ingredients in both the wine and food

(John Laloganes)

Pairing based on flavor alone doesn't guarantee a successful match, but it helps to ensure a more effective one. The goal is to find a component to play off of in order to create a bridge.

Example of the Bridging Approach

Following is an example of bridging ingredients in food with flavors in a wine:

Herbal Qualities

- **Food**—A lean fish placed in parchment paper with some fresh dill, lemon juice, and aromatic vegetables cooked en-papillote.
- **Wine**—Sauvignon Blanc sometimes has a recognizable grassy and herbal aroma and flavor associated with these seasonings.

An important reminder regarding principle #2, in order for a bridge to work, there need to be similar levels of body weight in the food as in the wine (as explained in principle #1). The Sauvignon Blanc often is considered a light- to medium-body, as the lean fish poached in its own juices, in essence, can be considered a light- to medium-body. The match can work without the bridge; however, the link makes it connect more effectively, providing a more complete dining experience.

Bridge Ingredient Categories

Pay attention to flavors, as they are considered accents to a dish. They can have a minor influence on the pairing; however, in a few cases, such as blackening spices or crusting of foods, they will have a major impact on the wine-and-food pairing. It can be helpful to think of flavors in terms of categories such as fruity, nutty, smoky, herbal, spicy, earthy, and meaty, as wines can sometimes have flavor categories that parallel these.

The following table shows particular flavors that may be detected by aroma or flavor within a wine and sometimes can be bridges, if used in the preparation of foods, to more effectively connect a wine and food:

CATEGORIES	EXAMPLES
Herbs/Spices	allspice, anise, basil, cilantro, dill, ginger, lemon grass, nutmeg, pepper, rosemary, mint, tarragon
Vegetables/Grains	beans, bell peppers, beets, corn, fennel, garlic, mushrooms, potatoes
Fruits	apples, bananas, cherries, coconut, figs, grapefruit, lemons, limes, lychee, mangoes, melons, oranges, peaches, pears, pineapples, plums
Dairy	butter, cream, milk
Nuts	almonds, hazelnuts, macadamia nuts, pecans, walnuts

Bridge Ingredient Possibilities

The following table does not present a complete list of bridge ingredients, but gives a small selection of potential possibilities, for purposes of illustration:

WHITE WINE	BRIDGE INGREDIENT POSSIBILITIES
Riesling	Fruits (raisins, pineapple, apricot, dried fruits), honey
Sauvignon Blanc	Herbs (dill, basil, oregano), vegetables (tomato, peppers)
Chardonnay	Nuts (pine-nuts, macadamia nuts, and almonds), dairy (cream and butter), vegetables (corn, potatoes)
RED WINE	**BRIDGE INGREDIENT POSSIBILITIES**
Pinot Noir	Vegetables/grains (garlic, beans, mushrooms, shallots, onions, bell pepper, mustard, fennel, lentils, potatoes)
Merlot	Fruits (dried cherries and cranberries)
Cabernet Sauvignon	Vegetables (black olives, mushrooms), herbs/spices (mustard, rosemary)

Each taste component affects how a wine is perceived on the palate, and the slightest variation in the intensity of these components can drastically alter the interactions that occur. The components can heighten or diminish a particular characteristic in the wine or the food.

Comparing or Contrasting Taste Components

Assess the primary taste components of the wine and the food. Wine may offer components such as sweetness (residual sugar), sourness (from acidity), bitterness (from tannin), and spiciness (from alcohol). Food may offer such components as sweetness, sourness, bitterness, creaminess, smokiness, spiciness, saltiness, and bitterness.

It is possible to select any one of the taste components to play off of that may make the pairing better. One of two approaches can be used. One is to compare the "like" qualities (the brother and sister approach) that are found in both the wine and the food. The other approach is to contrast (having "opposite" qualities) the *cat and dog* approach in the wine and the food. Either approach can act to intensify or diminish the sensation of taste components suitable to the preference of the diner.

Example of Both Approaches

Provided are examples of a comparison and a contrasting approach.

- **Comparison Approach**—An acidic red wine (such as Barbera or Sangiovese) is compared to an acidic tomato sauce. This approach of matching similar taste components of acid works to achieve a complementary match.
- **Contrasting Approach**—The acid in an acidic white wine (such as Sauvignon Blanc or Unoaked Chardonnay) contrasts with the fatness or richness of a cream sauce. This approach can add interest to a dish, while some taste components in the wine are matched against an opposite of one found in the food. Even though it is an approach of contrasting opposites, each component brings something to the other in order to achieve a complementary match. This approach can be used as a counterpoint to provide interest or to diminish or intensify a particular quality.

Sweet Wines

Sugar is present in grapes prior to fermentation, after which many wines are fermented dry, removing most perceptible sugar from the wine. Any unfermented sugar left over from fermentation is known as RS (residual sugar) and is perceived as fruit. The sweetness in wine with some perceptible residual sugar can suppress the components of bitterness (think of adding sugar to coffee), spiciness, and acidity (think of adding sugar to lemonade). The perception of sweetness can be affected by a variety of elements, such as acid, alcohol, salt, and tannin, in both wine and food.

Wine must be as sweet as or sweeter than a food item (such as dessert). If the food is sweeter than the wine, there is a tendency for the wine to taste dull and flat. When pairing sweet foods with a wine, try to keep the dish less sweet than the wine. If necessary, sweetness can be diminished by adding an acidic component such as citrus juice or vinegar or adding spices such as black pepper and chili powder. The following table identifies the effects of a sweet wine when paired with foods containing various components:

PAIRING WITH SWEET WINES	
EFFECTS OF SWEETNESS ARE HEIGHTENED WITH...	EFFECTS OF SWEETNESS ARE DIMINISHED WITH...
☑ Sweeter foods	☑ Salty foods
	☑ Spicy foods
	☑ Acidic foods
	☑ Tannic foods

High sugar levels are more associated with white wines, sparkling wines, dessert wines, many rosés, but, rarely, red wines. Following are some examples of wines that may occasionally have some varying levels of sweetness:

White Wine—Riesling, Gewürztraminer, Chenin Blanc, sparkling wines from Italy (Asti, Moscato di Asti, Prosecco), dessert wines. (See Chapter 11, "BUBBLES: Sparkling Wine" and Chapter 13, "NECTAR: Dessert Wines," for a detailed discussion.)
Rosé Wine—White Zinfandel, White Merlot, or, in general, some California rosé wines.
Red Wine—Sparkling wine from Italy (Brachetto and Lambrusco) and from Australia (Sparkling Shiraz), and varying dessert wines. (See Chapter 11, "BUBBLES: Sparkling Wine" and Chapter 13, "NECTAR: Dessert Wines," for a detailed discussion.)

Acidic Wines

Acid is fundamental to both a white wine's and a red wine's structure, making the wine taste crisp, fresh, and lively. Acid is perceived as sourness or tartness on the palate and causes salivation. Without an adequate level of acid, a wine is considered flabby or falls flat when paired with a food. Acidity has the ability to heighten or perk up flavors in food.

High-acid foods go well with crisp high-acid wines such as light- to medium-bodied whites, or light- to medium-bodied red with good acidity and low tannin. The following table identifies the effects of an acidic wine when paired with foods containing various components:

PAIRING WITH ACIDIC WINES	
EFFECTS OF ACID ARE COUNTERBALANCED WITH...	EFFECTS OF ACID ARE DIMINISHED WITH...
☑ Salty foods	☑ Salty foods
☑ Slightly sweet foods	☑ Sweet foods
☑ Fatty foods (from dairy fat)	
☑ Greasy/oily foods (from cooking methods)	

High acid levels are associated with white, rosé, and red wines from cooler climates, as well as with wines that either have been un-oaked or only lightly oaked. Examples of wines with ample acidity follow:

White Wine—Sauvignon Blanc, Pinot Gris, Pinot Grigio, Riesling, and most sparkling wine from around the world, particularly Champagne and Cava.
Rosé Wine—Most French or Spanish rosés.
Red Wine—Pinot Noir, Barbera, Gamay, Sangiovese, Dolcetto, and Cabernet Franc.

Tannic Wines

Tannin is a component that is fundamental to a red wine and can contribute to an increased level of body, weight, power, texture, and structure. Tannin is perceived as bitterness and causes a drying sensation.

High tannin in wine is subdued by the fat, protein, and heavy, chewy texture of meat. Meat that has been cooked to a rare, medium-rare, or medium degree of doneness is considered uncoagulated and has the ability to temper the tannin in a medium- to full-bodied red wine.

Meat that has been cooked medium well to well done is considered coagulated and does not temper tannin, but still has enough body and texture to pair well with a light- to medium-bodied red wine with low to medium tannin. The following table identifies the effects of a tannic wine when paired with foods containing various components:

PAIRING WITH TANNIC WINES	
EFFECTS OF TANNIN ARE HEIGHTENED WITH...	EFFECTS OF TANNIN ARE DIMINISHED WITH...
☑ Salty foods	☑ High protein foods
☑ Spicy foods	☑ Uncoagulated protein
☑ Tannic foods	☑ Fatty foods (animal fat)

Tannic levels are associated with red wines and are fairly undetectable in white wines. Examples of wines with moderate to high levels of tannin include the following:

Red Wine—Cabernet Sauvignon, Nebbiolo, Syrah, Grenache, Shiraz, Tempranillo, Zinfandel, Meriot, Cabernet Franc, and Sangiovese.

Fatty Foods

Fat adds richness, texture, mouth-feel, body, and weight to a dish. There are three basic types of fat: vegetable fat (olive oil, corn oil, peanut oil), dairy fat (cheese, butter, cream) and meat fat (beef, veal, pork, lamb). Fat can also be introduced from various cooking methods—primarily frying and sautéing—but it can be added as well in the form of a sauce. The following table identifies the effects of different kinds of fat and possible wine pairings:

PAIRING WITH FATTY FOODS
Vegetable fat–This type of fat contains mouth-coating qualities, but also a certain mineral flavor or other detectable flavor element. A white wine with substantial acidity or carbonation can counterbalance the oiliness, but bridge the flavor elements. These types of wines also work extremely well with fried foods because of the same ability to counter balance the fat and breading in the dish.
Dairy fat–This type of fat, rich and mouth coating, pairs well with full-bodied white wines that have significant weight, but also contain adequate alcohol or acid levels to counterbalance the richness.
Meat fat–This type of fat works best with a red wine that has substantial tannin. The tannin and fat can counterbalance and offset one another.

Salty/Smoky/Spicy/Highly Seasoned Foods (or SSSS)

Sometimes spices are a prominent factor in the flavor and texture of the dish. Spices can be categorized into three types: (1) sweet (cinnamon, allspice), (2) savory (curry, cumin), and (3) hot (curry, chili powder, horseradish, cayenne pepper). Heavy seasoning, spices or salts often take precedence over the type of food when a wine is chosen to match. These qualities can and often overpower food. Therefore, it may be best to match a wine to the cooking technique and spice level, instead of applying the typical pairing principle of matching a wine to the food type. The following table identifies the effects of salty, smoky, spicy and highly seasoned foods with various types of wine:

PAIRING WITH SALTY, SMOKY, SPICY AND HIGHLY SEASONED FOODS (SSSS)	
EFFECTS OF SSSS ARE HEIGHTENED WITH...	EFFECTS OF SSSS ARE DIMINISHED WITH...
☑ Oak-aging wine	☑ Residual sugar in wine
☑ High alcohol wine	☑ Acidity in wine
☑ Highly tannic wine	☑ Carbonation in wine
	☑ Fruit intensity in wine

White Wine—Youthful, acidic, fruity white wines with low to moderate alcohol, and with or without residual sugar, work most effectively. Examples are Sparkling wines, Rieslings, Chenin Blanc, Gewürztraminer, Pinot Grigio, and Pinot Gris.

Rosé Wine—Combines the fruitiness of a red wine with the crispness and lightness of a white wine. They are generally an appropriate warm-to-hot weather drinking option and work very well with full-flavored foods. spicy Asian, Latin American, or Cajun foods.

Red Wine—Young, acidic, fruity red wines with limited to no oak aging and with low alcohol and tannin work best. Examples are rosé, Pinot Noir, Gamay, Dolcetto, Tempranillo and Barbera.

OTHER TECHNIQUES USED TO ASSIST IN ACHIEVING AN EFFECTIVE WINE PAIRING

Food is easily adapted and altered by making minor adjustments to accommodate a wine pairing. There are many fine-tuning techniques that professional cooks use to build body, flavor, and texture into a food item. These methods can alter the appropriateness of a potential wine pairing. If a wine has been selected, applying these techniques can assist to connect a dish to a particular wine by either decreasing or building weight, body (or overall intensity) as well as flavors within the dish.

Adjusting food dishes, either intentionally or unintentionally, can alter a potential wine pairing. For example, linguine in a creamy Alfredo sauce is a simpler dish than sautéed jumbo shrimp, mushrooms, roasted red peppers, spinach, and spices with linguine in a creamy Alfredo sauce. Following are some possible adjustments that can be used to make a more cohesive match:

☑ **Skin On or Off**—Skin can be left on poultry (such as duck or chicken) to provide a heightened level of color, flavor, texture, and fat or taken off to lighten the intensity of a dish.

☑ **Bone In or Out**—Bones have a large amount of gelatine and flavor that contribute to the body of meat (porterhouse steak, pork chop, lamb chop), poultry (chicken), and seafood (finfish). Removing the bone or bones can slightly reduce the flavor and juiciness of a food item.

☑ **Combine Multiple Food Types**—Combining multiple foods can add dimension, change the flavor, and adjust the weight of the dish. For example, adding both sautéed shrimp and scallops to linguini pasta with olive oil and garlic alters the character of the dish.

☑ **Adjust Fat Content**—Leaving more external fat on a meat item adds richness and juiciness. Trimming away some external fat makes a food item leaner.

☑ **Adjust Cooking Method**—Altering a cooking method can be used to effectively match the intensity of a wine.

- ☑ **Alter the Type of Quantity of Sauce**—More or less sauce can adjust the weight or intensity of a dish.
- ☑ **Adding an Acid**—Squeezing a little lemon or vinegar over the food helps to liven the flavors and also may assist in bridging the flavor with the wine. In addition, the acid component in the food can be used to compare or contrast an acidic (or other) component found in a particular wine.
- ☑ **Using Infused Oil**—A splash of infused oil can heighten the flavors of any dish, from salads and soups to bread and pasta, and is great for sautéing or stir frying.
- ☑ **Dairy Fat**—Adding a pat of butter (or flavored butter) to melt over a finished food item can provide an additional bit of substance and weight and assist in bridging flavors that might be found in a particular wine. Finishing off a sauce or a risotto with a touch of cream can provide a similar effect.
- ☑ **Flavorful Poaching Liquids**—Using more flavorful liquids (wine, stock) than water when poaching can heighten the flavor of a dish.
- ☑ **Searing**—This is an important technique not only to seal the flavors and juices, but also to increase the flavors of meat prior to stewing, braising, or sautéing. Caramelization occurs on the surface and assists in adding complexity and in building aromas, flavors, and body in a food item.
- ☑ **Deglazing**—This method involves adding liquid to a pan over high heat in order to - remove and incorporate the dried brown bits left in the pan after the food item has been cooked. The liquid can be as simple as water or as complex as stock or wine.
- ☑ **Adjust Type of Fat**—Adjusting the type of fat (shortening, olive oil, vegetable oil, peanut oil) and what the item is coated in (batter or bread crumbs) prior to cooking will influence the flavor and intensity of the finished product. Also, a coating can cause a sauce to become absorbed into the food item, adding heightened flavor and richness.
- ☑ **Glazed or Crusted**—Food can be glazed or crusted with vinegar (balsamic vinegar) or wine (Madeira), condiments (honey, mustard, herbs) or bread crumbs. All of these coatings can act to heighten aromas, flavors, and the intensity of a dish.
- ☑ **Rubs**—A rub is a mixture of herbs and spices that are applied to an item, normally just prior to cooking or, in some cases, overnight. Since rubs lack liquid (as in marinades), a small amount can be extremely intense.
- ☑ **Marinade**—Marinading involves submerging a food item in a seasoned liquid (the marinade) of oil, acid, and flavorings for a short period. This method is used to tenderize a food item, and, more importantly, to flavor the product.
- ☑ **Brine**—This process involves submerging a food item in a ratio of salt and water (brine). It is used to enhance and season the interior of neutral flavored meats such as pork and poultry.

WINE AND FOOD PAIRING GUIDELINES

To achieve a happy marriage of wine and food, consider some general guidelines. These strategies have been preached for decades and certainly are useful to apply as loose, but reliable, guiding principles. Many of these guidelines follow the flow of the meal as each food course increases with intensity, body, and substance. An occasional palate cleanser (an intermezzo such as sorbet or a salad) may fall between a course or even each successive course. For example, many meals begin with an appetizer designed to be small and light so as not to overwhelm the palate, but instead to appease the hunger. Next, the soup or salad may follow, to provide another small source of nourishment and varying texture prior to the main event. Then the entrée—more substantial, heartier, and more filling—arrives. Finally, the dessert is consumed to provide satiety for the stomach and palate and to complete the dining experience.

Lighter Wines Before Heavier Wines

This approach runs parallel to the food courses—lighter foods before heavier foods. Most menus are designed to provide a diner with lighter courses first so as not to overwhelm the palate early in the dining process. Throughout the meal, the food courses increase in intensity, as do the beverages.

Dry Wines Before Sweet

This approach also runs parallel to the food courses—savory before sweet. A light, dry, crisp sparkling wine with an appetizer is a good example of a wine to serve with a beginning course. These kinds of wines cause salivation and do not overwhelm the palate too soon, whereas sweet wines tend to dull the palate and therefore are consumed at the end of the meal.

Seasonality, Occasion, and Mood (SOM)

There are certain moments, events, or times of year that can dictate a particular wine pairing.

Seasonality—Richer, heartier foods and beverages tend to be desired, sometimes unknowingly, with falling temperatures and crisp nights as fall and winter months approach. As fuller-bodied richer dishes are consumed, it is natural to pair richer, weightier wines that are compatible. Light, cool, and refreshing foods and beverages coordinate with rising temperatures, with long sunny days and warm evenings as the spring and summer months arrive.

Occasion—People drink different wines for different occasions. A customer might choose a wine with take-out food very differently than when dining at an upscale restaurant. A wine that might be appropriate for a summer barbecue could be quite different from wine that would be appropriate at a New Year's Eve festivity.

Not that people need a reason to drink other than for sheer enjoyment, but there is a certain correctness to selecting a particular type or style of wine for the given occasion.

Mood—This element is a free-for-all, as it really depends on the whim of the wine drinker. In some cases, the wine will be selected simply because a certain type or style of wine is desired or because a particular group of people may influence the decision. Sometimes, the time of day or day of week or amount of disposable income determines the choice of wine.

Regional Considerations

What would people drink if they found themselves in Burgundy, France? Local people usually drink the wines of their area with the cuisine of their region. Wine and food that evolve and grow together, go together. This guideline employs the classical approach to pairing wine and food.

Wine as a Main Ingredient

If a wine is incorporated within a dish, there is a natural partnership to pair the same or similar wine with the meal. This creates an obvious relationship between the wine and the food item; for example, when a Sauvignon Blanc is used as part of the sauce, it would seem appropriate to also serve it in a glass. The same care should be taken when using a wine in cooking as is taken with any other ingredients in the recipe. Most inexpensive wines (particularly the kind in jugs or bags) are low in alcohol, acid, and flavor. Therefore, an important philosophy to consider is, the dish will only be as good as the quality of the ingredients, including the wine.

FOUNDATIONS TO WINE AND FOOD PAIRING

NAME: _____ Score out of 20 points_____.

Use these questions to test your knowledge and understanding of the concepts presented in the chapter.

I. MULTIPLE CHOICE: Select the best possible answer from the options available.

1. A good guideline to follow when pairing wines with a food menu generally is

    a. Sweet wines are served before dry wines.

    b. Go from red to white wines.

    c. Progress from light- to full-bodied wines.

    d. Go from full- to light-bodied wines.

2. The first and foremost principle to follow when matching wine and food is to

    a. compare or contrast flavors.

    b. consider the mood, ambience, and occasion.

    c. contrast acidity with fat.

    d. balance the weight and intensity of the wine with the food.

3. A factor that can influence a food's weight and body is

    a. the cooking method.

    b. the sauce.

    c. the other ingredients (seasonings).

    d. all of the above.

    e. only answers a and b.

4. Which is a moist-heat cooking method?

    a. Grilling/broiling

    b. Smoking

    c. Deep Frying

    d. Poaching/Steaming

5. Coagulated protein (as in a pot roast) would pair best with

    a. Cabernet Sauvignon or Merlot.

    b. Merlot or Shiraz.

    c. Chardonnay or Sauvignon Blanc.

    d. Pinot Noir or Merlot.

6. Uncoagulated protein (as in a medium-rare T-bone steak) would pair best with

    a. Cabernet Sauvignon or Merlot.

    b. Pinot Noir or Merlot.

    c. Chardonnay or Pinot Noir.

    d. Riesling or Sauvignon Blanc.

7. A grilled wild king salmon would pair best with

    a. Cabernet Sauvignon or Merlot.

    b. Chardonnay or Sauvignon Blanc.

    c. Pinot Noir or Chardonnay.

    d. Sauvignon Blanc or Riesling.

8. Generally, medium-bodied acidic white wines can work well with

    a. acidic foods (lemon sauce).

    b. raw shellfish (oysters).

    c. light cream or butter sauce.

    d. all of the above.

    e. none of the above.

    f. only answers a and c.

9. Spicy foods have the ability to be paired with

    a. sweeter wines.

    b. fruity, low tannin wines.

    c. high-alcohol wines.

    d. all of the above.

    e. only answers a and b.

10. Fried foods have the ability to work well with

    a. sparkling wines.

    b. tannic red wines.

    c. high-alcohol red wines.

    d. fortified wines.

II. TRUE / FALSE: Circle the best possible answer.

11. A classic approach to wine and food pairing is where the food and wine have evolved together over a long period. **True / False**

12. The application of the analytical pairing approach can greatly increase the quality of a wine and food pairing. **True / False**

13. Generally, a wine's body should parallel that of the progression of the meal. **True / False**

14. Residual sugar in a wine can temper a moderately spicy food. **True / False**

15. Light-bodied red wines can pair effectively with coagulated protein. **True / False**

16. Light-bodied red wines go best with uncoagulated protein. **True / False**

17. Poached poultry and seafood work well with light- to medium-bodied acidic white wines. **True / False**

III. SHORT-ANSWER ESSAY / DISCUSSION QUESTIONS: Use a separate sheet of paper if necessary.

18. Provide some reasons that someone would pair wine with food.

19. Explain the difference between the classical pairing approach and the contemporary pairing approach.

20. Identify and describe the three principles of the analytical wine and food pairing approach.

FOUNDATIONS TO WINE AND FOOD PAIRING

ACTIVITY #1 FOOD TYPES

NAME _____

DIRECTIONS: Determine possible food types for each of the given Big Six grape varietals.

WHITE WINE VARIETALS	TYPICAL BODY AND WEIGHT	POSSIBLE FOOD TYPES
Riesling	Light-bodied	
Sauvignon Blanc	Medium-bodied	
Chardonnay	Full-bodied	

RED WINE VARIETALS	TYPICAL BODY AND WEIGHT	FOOD TYPE
Pinot Noir	Light-bodied	
Merlot	Medium-bodied	
Cabernet Sauvignon	Full-bodied	

FOUNDATIONS TO WINE AND FOOD PAIRING

ACTIVITY #2 PAIRING WINE TO FOOD TYPES AND COOKING METHODS

NAME _____

DIRECTIONS: Given a food type, expand on a possible cooking method for each and identify a possible wine pairing. Justify the reasoning.

FOOD TYPES	POSSIBLE COOKING METHOD	WINE JUSTIFICATION
Pork chop		
Salmon		
Oysters		
Whole chicken		
Chicken breast with skin		
Skinless chicken breast		
Beef stew meat		
Beef porterhouse		
Leg of lamb		
Risotto		

Unit 3
WINES OF THE NEW WORLD

"By prevailing over all obstacles and distractions, one may unfailingly arrive at his chosen goal or destination."

—*Christopher Columbus*

7

Wines of the United States and Canada

Throughout history...drought, inferno, world wars, depression and prohibition have all at one point attempted to either directly or indirectly handicap America's wine industry. But as of 2008, wine is produced commercially in all fifty states through 5,587 American wineries.

LEARNING OBJECTIVES

Upon completion of this chapter, the learner will be able to:

- Realize the significant wine producing areas within the United States and Canada.
- Understand U.S. labelling laws regarding grape, location, vintage, and vineyard.
- Comprehend the American viticulural area (AVA) concept.
- Recognize the most significant viticultural areas within the major wine-producing areas of the United States.
- Discern between the major grape varietals and styles of wine produced within each of the four significant wine-producing states.

UNITED STATES

Throughout history, drought, inferno, world wars, depression, and prohibition at one point have attempted to either directly or indirectly handicap America's wine industry. But as of 2008, wine was produced commercially in all fifty states through 5,587 American wineries, according to the Alcohol and Tobacco Tax and Trade Bureau (TTB). This is a dramatic increase; back in 1975, when the wine industry was in its adolescence, there were only 579 wineries throughout the United States.

The top four significant wine-producing states in America are California, Washington State, New York, and Oregon. In California alone, there are approximately 2,440 wineries that produce roughly 90% of all wine in America. There are also thriving wine industries in New York, with 271 wineries that manage 5% of U.S. production. Washington has 538 wineries, with 4% production, and Oregon, with 329 wineries, makes up less than 1% of the U.S. wine industry, in 2008, according to the TTB. Other states that produce a nominal amount of wine are not as well known outside their vicinity. These include Virginia, with 169, Texas, with 168 and Michigan, with 136 wineries.

American Viticultural Areas (AVA)

In 1978, the United States implemented *American viticultural areas*, or AVAs, as a way to set growing regions apart and to showcase their distinctions. These are unique grape-growing geographical areas, such as Napa Valley and Chalk Hill that have been officially designated as such by the TTB.

An AVA guarantees that, at a minimum, 85% of the grapes come from the location identified on the bottle. As of 2005, the TTB had recognized 170 AVAs throughout the United States. Lately, there have been an increasing number of sub-appellations designated to showcase even further distinction and specificity in a growing region. For example, there are approximately 14 sub-appellations within the larger Napa Valley.

American Labelling Information

Grape Name—To correctly label a wine with a grape name or varietal, the wine must contain at least 75% of that type. One significant exception to the 75% rule is that the state of Oregon requires a minimum of 90% for most varietals. States may always choose a stricter rule than the federal requirement, as in the case of Oregon, but never less.

Location—To identify a specific location or AVA on a wine label, at least 85% of the grapes must have come from that area.

If a wine is labelled with a broader country, state, county or multi county appellation on a label means that at least 75% of the grapes must have derived from the stated place of origin.

Vineyard—To identify an individual vineyard on a label, at least 95% of the grapes must have come from the vineyard specified on the label.

Vintage—If a vintage date is identified, then a minimum of 95% of the grapes within the bottle must have come from the year as specified on the label.

Marketing Terms—Terms such as *Reserve* and *Vintner's Reserve* are often used on U.S. labels. These terms do not have the legal meaning that they have in other countries, such as Italy or Spain. It is possible that the U.S. winemaker made a reserve or vintner's reserve with better-quality ingredients and production methods; however, there are no legal requirements to guarantee that this is so.

FIGURE 7–1 Map of California
(Thomas Moore)

CALIFORNIA

California produces the vast majority (approximately 90%) of wines in the United States and has grown from 150 wineries in 1960 to 2,440 in 2008 according to the TTB. In 2007, the state maintains over 480,000 acres of wine grapes and approximately 100 distinct *American viticultural areas* (AVAs) within California's five major wine-producing regions. Figure 7–1 shows a map of the significant wine regions in California.

The Famous Paris Wine Tasting of 1976

The Chardonnay and Cabernet Sauvignon grape varietals are historically significant to California, as they are the primary varietals that brought initial prestige and success to the state.

Up until 1976, France was generally regarded as the best producer of wines throughout the world. On May 24, 1976, everything changed. Nine of the most respected French wine judges participated in a 20-wine blind-tasting event held in Paris. Ten red wines were a mix of California Cabernet Sauvignons and red Bordeaux. In addition, a separate category of 10 white wines included a mix of California Chardonnay and white Burgundies.

The winners of first place for each category included a California red and white wine. The results caused a major uproar in France; to this day, many French people believe that the event was fixed. On the upside, this event encouraged the French to revisit their winemaking approach and make adjustments in order to remain competitive. Also, the results catapulted the United States to international fame as a world-class wine producer.

APPELLATIONS

The California climate is greatly influenced by the cool Pacific Ocean and the mountain ranges. Vineyards along the coast (and as far inland as 200 miles in some areas) are beneficially cooled from the ocean air. The impact of ocean waters creates ideal microclimates for grape growing in a way that sometimes reverses normal logic: For example, the farther north you travel in the North Coast wine region, the warmer it gets. Thus, the Napa Valley is warmer than many areas south of it, and some southern areas, such as the famed Carneros district of Sonoma County, are near the cooling influence of San Pablo Bay. The combination of these mesoclimates and microclimates, local soil types, and topography make the various wine regions of California ideal for growing an array of high-quality wine grapes.

California has roughly five primary wine-producing regions, with the *North Coast* and *Central Coast* known mostly for high quality. The Sierra Foothills, Central Valley, and Southern California regions are known mostly for quantity bulk production, with a few high-quality producers scattered throughout.

North Coast

North Coast is located in Northern California, just one hour's drive north of San Francisco. Its tradition goes back to the early nineteenth century in some of the oldest continuing vineyards in the country. The North Coast is recognized as the most prominent wine-producing region and contains some of the most successful AVAs in the United States.

The Winners of the 1976 Paris Wine Tasting

- **Stag's Leap Cabernet Sauvignon,** 1973 vintage, from the Stag's Leap AVA in California's Napa Valley, beat out four top Red Bordeaux, to win its category.
- **Chateaux Montelena Chardonnay,** 1973 vintage, from the Alexander Valley AVA in California's Sonoma County, beat out four top White Burgundies to win its category.

BERINGER VINEYARDS

Since 1876, Beringer has been one of the oldest Napa Valley wineries in continuous production. Even during Prohibition, the Beringer family was granted approval to produce wine and brandy for sacramental and medicinal puposes.

FIGURE 7–2 Welcome to Napa Valley
(CLAVER CARROLL/Photolibrary.com)

FIGURE 7–3 Chalk Hill Chardonnay label
(Chalk Hill Winery)

Napa Valley—This is California's preeminent wine production area and home of some 300-plus wineries. Napa is second only to Disneyland as the most visited American tourist destination, with over 4.7 million visitors annually. Napa Valley is 35 miles long and about 5 miles wide and is situated just the right distance inland from the cold northern Pacific Ocean. Hot, dry, sunny summer days (for ripeness development) and cool nights (for preservation of acidity) from the San Pablo Bay make Napa ideal for growing high-quality wine grapes.

Napa is most famous for high-quality (and some of the most expensive) Cabernet Sauvignon-based wines. In fact, about one-fifth of all vineyard acreage is devoted to Cabernet Sauvignon. Napa is also known for Chardonnay, Sauvignon Blanc, Merlot, and Zinfandel.

Napa Valley contains 14 different sub-appellations, or AVAs, including Atlas Peak, Howell Mountain, Oakville, Rutherford, Stags's Leap, part of Carneros, and others. Figure 7–2 identifies Napa Valley as the world's most famous wine growing region.

Sonoma County—Sonoma is a large appellation that is home to more than 250 wineries and 13 sub-AVA's, and growing. It is located west of Napa, closer to the ocean, with an overall cooler climate, but with a collection of microclimates that range from hot and dry to foggy and cool. Sonoma excels at Chardonnay, to which it has devoted to over one-fourth of vine acreage. But the vineyards of Sonoma County also produce quality Cabernet Sauvignon, Pinot Noir, Merlot, Zinfandel, and Sauvignon Blanc; and dozens of additional types of wine grapes can be found in this sprawling region.

Sonoma County contains 13 different sub-appellations, or AVAs, including: Alexander Valley, Chalk Hill, Dry Creek, Green Valley-Sonoma, Knights Valley, Russian River Valley, Sonoma Coast, Sonoma Mountain, Sonoma Valley, part of Carneros, and others. Figure 7–3 shows a Chardonnay label from the famous winery and appellation Chalk Hill.

Mendocino County—This is the northernmost wine-producing area and AVA in California's North Coast. It contains about 10 sub-AVAs. The most notable AVA is Anderson Valley, located near the Pacific Coast, which provides a cool, foggy climate that supports cool-climate grapes. Chardonnay, Pinot Noir, and Cabernet Sauvignon are the more dominate varietals.

Lake County—This AVA is north of Napa and east of Sonoma. It contains varying levels of altitude to make up for the lack of proximity to the ocean. The area features more temperature extremes between seasons and primarily focuses on warm-weather grapes such as Petite Syrah and Cabernet Sauvignon. Guenoc Valley is the largest AVA in Lake County and one of the older grape-growing areas in California.

Some Notable AVAs Throughout the North Coast

Alexander Valley—This large and densely planted AVA is located in the northern section of Sonoma County. Alexander Valley borders the Russian River, but experiences less fog and is located at higher elevations. The area is most noted for Cabernet Sauvignon, Chardonnay, Zinfandel, and Sauvignon Blanc.

FIGURE 7–4 Chalk Hill Vineyards and Cabernet Sauvignon
(Chalk Hill Winery)

Atlas Peak—This appellation is located in the southeast corner of Napa Valley. Atlas Peak takes its name from the highest point (about 2,600 feet) of the Vaca mountain range. The westward orientation of most vineyards provides maximum sun exposure. This, coupled with the gravelly and volcanic well-draining soil and high elevation, allows for a wide diurnal temperature range. This extreme in temperature range helps to preserve fresh fruit aromas and flavors, as well as acidity, in the grapes. Atlas Peak was originally planted with Sangiovese and Zinfandel, but now gives way to Cabernet Sauvignon, Merlot, and other Bordeaux-type varietals, in addition to Chardonnay and red and white Rhone-type varietals such as Syrah and Marsanne.

Carneros—This AVA is situated where the Napa and Sonoma Valleys meet in the south, just north of San Pablo Bay. The proximity to the bay yields a cooler maritime-type climate ideal for cool-climate grape varietals such as Pinot Noir and Chardonnay. Therefore, many of California's high-quality sparkling wine producers have been established there, including Domaine Carneros (by the French producer Tattinger) and Gloria Ferrer (by the Spanish producer Freixenet).

Chalk Hill—This Sonoma County AVA is a sub-appellation of the Russian River appellation. The name derives from its chalk-colored volcanic-ash soil, which promotes Chardonnay, Sauvignon Blanc, and Cabernet Sauvignon varietals. Figure 7–4 shows vineyards in the Chalk Hill AVA, as well as the Chalk Hill Cabernet Sauvignon.

Howell Mountain—This was Napa's first sub-AVA, with a small number of vine acres located in higher-elevation areas in the Vaca Mountains. Howell Mountain is most noted for producing Bordeaux varietals and Zinfandel.

Mount Veeder—This appellation encompasses 25 square miles of some of the steepest vineyards and most remote wineries in California. This viticultural area is located in the southeastern portion of the Mayacamas Mountains, which divide Napa and Sonoma Counties.

Oakville—An appellation located in the center of Napa Valley, Oakville contains many of Napa's prestigious wineries. It is positioned with the Mayacamas Mountains to the west and the Vaca range to the east. Oakville is famous for its gravelly well-drained soils, which contribute to well-structured Cabernet Sauvignons.

Russian River—This AVA is located in the northern section of Sonoma County. The climate of the Russian River is dramatically influenced by the cooling coastal-fog effect of the Pacific Ocean just a few miles to the west. The largely clay- and alluvial-based soils and cooler climate have allowed Pinot Noir and Chardonnay to become the signature varietals.

Rutherford— The majority of vines here are devoted to the premier grape of this appellation, Cabernet Sauvignon, with smaller amounts of Merlot and Zinfandel grown. The Cabernet is renowned for producing big structure; deep, complex fruit qualities; and richness and for expressing a terroir-like quality of "dirt and dust." Cabernets produced in Rutherford are known to have remarkable aging potential.

Spring Mountain—This Napa Valley AVA sits on steep terraces of the Mayacamas Mountains. It is dominated by the red varietals of Cabernet Sauvignon, Merlot, and Cabernet Franc. Chardonnay is the main white wine, with some plantings of Riesling and Viognier.

Stags Leap District—This Napa Valley AVA boasts volcanic soil, warm days that promote optimal ripening, and cool nights to maintain the grapes' acidity. The area is best suited to grow Cabernet Sauvignon and other Bordeaux varietals. Stags Leap District is one of the most historically significant of the AVAs, as it was Cabernet Sauvignon from Stags' Leap wine cellars that vanquished the top red Bordeaux's in the famous 1976 Paris tasting.

Central Coast

Central Coast is a large growing area along the Pacific Coast that extends from south of San Francisco to Santa Barbara. Over the last several years, California's Central Coast has matured into a region that produces world-class wines.

The Central Coast is a mega-AVA that includes many smaller sub-AVAs. The area is unofficially divided into northern and southern sections. Mountain ranges run throughout these areas in different directions, creating different pockets of microclimates that allow various grapes and styles of wine to be produced. The more common grape varietals are Chardonnay (with over half of the vineyard acreage), Pinot Noir, Viognier, Syrah, and Grenache.

Paso Robles—This area possesses a long growing season with a high diurnal range of temperatures between night and day—ideal for preserving a grape's acidity while still retaining its flavor development. Paso is known for Syrah, Zinfandel, and Cabernet Sauvignon grape varietals.

San Luis Obispo—A California wine region south of Paso Robles (although, technically, part of Paso Robles is located within San Luis Obispo County) and continuing south to Santa Barbara County, this large AVA produces many types of wine with varying quality levels. San Luis Obispo does grow the highest quantity of Syrah vines of all other California appellations.

Edna Valley—An appellation located south of San Luis Obispo, Edna Valley's location makes the region much cooler than surrounding growing regions and is ideal for growing Chardonnay and Pinot Noir.

Monterey County—This AVA is home to some of the best values in California wines.

Santa Ynez Valley—Located in Santa Barbara County, California, this AVA experiences cool ocean breezes that keep the valley temperate enough to grow world-class Pinot Noir, Chardonnay, and Syrah.

Santa Barbara—Located just south of San Luis Obispo, Santa Barbara is both a city and a county. Two of the main growing regions in Santa Barbara County are the Santa Maria and Santa Ynez valleys. Both of these valleys directly face the ocean, capturing the breezes that make these some of the coolest growing regions in California. For this reason, Pinot Noir, Chardonnay, and Syrah have done well. Other cool-climate varietals, such as Viognier and Riesling, thrive as well.

Santa Maria Valley—This is one of the cooler growing regions in California. Generally, the farther south in California you go, the warmer it gets. However, Santa Maria Valley is cooled by the Pacific Ocean, making it ideal for the cool-climate grapes that go into Pinot Noir and Chardonnay wines.

Sierra Foothills

Far to the east of the Pacific Ocean is home to California's original gold rush. Traditionally, this area is known for table grapes or low-quality inexpensive wine grapes. However, the Zinfandel grape varietal reigns supreme here, and new suitable grape varieties are slowly being planted as the region expands.

South Coast

This area is generally warm, with some spotty cooler areas, to produce wine grapes. One of the well-known appellations is in Temecula.

Central Valley

The Central Valley (also known as the San Joaquin) is a large, hot, fertile area that stretches almost 500 miles down the center of the state. San Joaquin is considered California's agricultural land, known for producing most of America's table grapes and raisins. The intense heat and sun overwhelms many grapevines, and production is mostly based on large quantities of grapes for mass-produced large wineries. The total acreage under wine grape cultivation in the Central Valley is massive and dwarfs all other California regions. The important appellations include Lodi and Woodbridge.

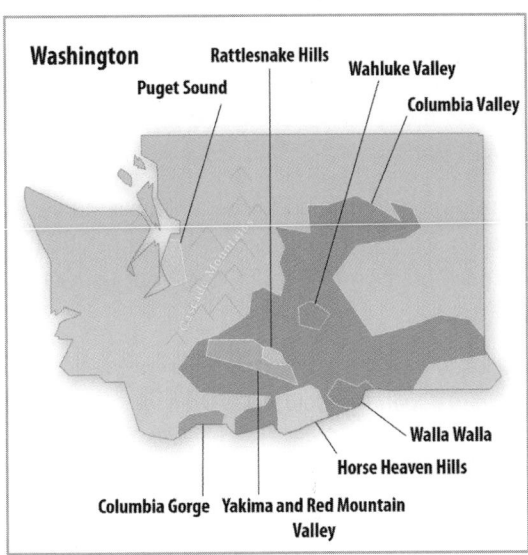

FIGURE 7–5 Map of Washington State
(Thomas Moore)

WASHINGTON STATE

Washington State is located in the northwest corner of the United States, just off the Pacific Ocean. According to the Washington Wine Commission, it's the nation's second-largest wine producer, with 31,000 acres of grapevines and over 530 wineries in 2007.

The climate offers sunny days, which allow the grapes to ripen through the long exposure to sunlight, and cool nights, which permit the grapes to maintain good acid profiles. Washington is significantly protected by the Cascade Mountains that cause a rain-shadow effect on the eastern side, which tends to be where the bulk of the wine regions are located. Figure 7–5 identifies the major wine-producing areas in Washington State.

The Varietals

Washington is a relatively youthful wine-producing region, with modern winemaking having begun in the 1960s with the emergence of Columbia Winery and Chateau Ste. Michelle. In the 1980s, Washington first established its reputation through the success of the Merlot grape varietal as its signature wine. Merlot eventually became the state's largest-selling red wine. As of 2007, Cabernet Sauvignon had surpassed Merlot, and Syrah had come in third for the most-planted grape varietal. Washington is also known for its white-wine grapes. Chardonnay, Riesling, Sauvignon Blanc, and Gewürztraminer are, in order, the top-producing white varietals.

APPELLATIONS

Washington maintains nine major viticultural areas, including Yakima (YAK-uh-maw) Valley, Walla Walla, Columbia Valley, Puget Sound, Red Mountain, Columbia Gorge, Horse Heaven Hills, Wahluke Slope, and Rattlesnake Hills.

Columbia Valley—Columbia Valley is the largest Washington wine region, with more than 17,000 vineyard acres that span from south-central Washington to Northern Oregon. The valley is protected from the Cascade Mountains, which act to shelter the region from the cool weather of the Pacific Ocean, making it one of the warmest growing areas in the Pacific Northwest. Columbia Valley's immense size yields several different types of subclimates that encourage various grapes to prosper. Thus, Columbia Valley Cabernet Sauvignon and Chardonnay grapes can fully ripen in most years. Other grapes such as Merlot, Sauvignon Blanc, Semillon, Chenin Blanc and Riesling also prosper in the long sunny days and chilly nights of the Columbia River Valley's growing season. The wines tend towards rich, ripe flavors with lively acidity.

Columbia Valley is considered an "umbrella" appellation, as it contains several smaller sub-appellations, including Walla Walla Valley, Yakima, Red Mountain, and the newer appellations of Wahluke Slope and Rattlesnake Hills.

Puget Sound—Washington's only official American viticultural area on the west side of the Cascade Mountain Range is Puget Sound. More than 45 wineries are based in the Puget Sound appellation, but only a few of them actually use locally grown grapes to make wine. Most wineries purchase grapes grown in the warmer, drier wine regions to the east of the Cascade Mountain range. Puget is a cool-climate region with a maritime climate. The large body of water of the Puget Sound basin moderates temperature extremes. Puget Sound specializes in cool-climate varieties such as Pinot Noir and the more adaptable Pinot Gris grape.

Yakima Valley—Yakima Valley is located in south-central Washington along the Yakima River. This area has a very diverse climate that allows for various grape varietals, such as Cabernet Sauvignon, Chardonnay, Syrah, and Merlot.

Walla Walla—Walla Walla is a remote wine region located in the southeast corner of Washington and extending slightly into Oregon. This region is one of the older established wine-producing areas in Washington, with a reputation for Merlot, Cabernet Sauvignon, and Syrah.

Columbia Gorge—This appellation is located in the southern section of Washington and extends into northern Oregon. Its vineyards span the Columbia River, which provides a moist, cooler climate.

NEW YORK STATE

New York State is located in the northeast corner of the United States just below Canada. According to the New York Wine and Grape Foundation, New York State is the nation's third largest wine producer with approximately 32,000 acres of grapevines in 2007. The evolution of quality wine from the Vitis vinifera vine species is emerging here, with the majority of the wines deriving from the lesser-quality-producing American grapevine species *Vitis labrusca*.

The Varietals

New York State is mostly known for its Riesling and Cabernet Franc varietals, which are the most widely planted varietals in the Finger Lakes AVA. New York State is also a noted producer of dessert wines and ice-wines, primarily from the white hybrid *Seyval Blanc* (say-vahl-BLAHNK) and *Vignoles* (VIN-yoal) varietals.

APPELLATIONS

New York State has four growing regions, but the majority (about 90%) of the wine is produced in the Finger Lakes AVA.

Finger Lakes

Finger Lakes Region is located in northern New York State partly between Manhattan and Niagara Falls and is home to more than 100 wineries. Finger Lakes appellation is about 300 miles northwest of New York city and sandwiched among four main lakes and sub-regions: *Cayuga* (kay-YOU-guh), *Canandaigua* (can-in-DAYG-wah), *Seneca* (SEN-uh-kuh), and *Keuka* (Q-kuh). The lakes make it possible to grow quality wine grapes in the otherwise cold, northerly climate by moderating the temperatures, which extends the growing season to allow grapes to fully ripen. The lakes also assist in keeping the ground from freezing in winter and so help improve the conditions for the vines.

Lake effect is a term used around the great lakes area and other large lakes in cool regions to describe the climatic influence on wine grapes. In the spring, the lakes' cooling effect (due to the cooler temperatures stored from the winter) retards the vines from budding until the spring frost is over. As the season progresses, the lakes store daytime heat, which lengthens the growing season. The water's heat retention delays frost that might damage vineyards in the fall. In winter, the lakes also cause heavy, moist snowfall, which blankets the vineyards, insulating and protecting the vines from the frigid air. The lake effect influences the environment for many miles inland from the water, creating a viticultural environment that would not otherwise exist in such a cool climate.

Long Island

The Long Island region also encompasses North Fork of Long Island and the Hamptons. The maritime climate of this region is moderate and helps provide an extended growing season.

Cabernet Sauvignon and Merlot are the most common red grapes grown here, while Chardonnay is the main white grape. While the wines have been steadily improving over the years, no wine from Long Island has gained any worldwide reputation as of yet.

OREGON

Oregon is located in the Pacific Northwest, nestled between Washington State to the north and California to the south. According to the Oregon Wine Board, Oregon is the nation's fourth-largest wine producer, with approximately 15,600 vineyard acres in 2007. It has been only within about the last 40 years that Oregon has been acknowledged as a world-class wine-producing state. Because most of the wineries are small in scale, an impressive 23% of total vineyards are dedicated to some form of sustainable winemaking. Figure 7–6 identifies Oregon's significant wine-growing areas.

The Varietals

Oregon has gained most of its fame from successfully growing cool-climate varietals such as Pinot Noir (one of the premiere producers in the world and the most-planted variety in Oregon) and Pinot Gris (the second-most-planted variety), but it also produces warm-climate varietals such as Cabernet Sauvignon and Merlot.

Labelling Laws

The local wine laws of Oregon tend to be a bit stricter than those of other U.S. states. Labelling must include a minimum of 90% of the grape varietal as listed on the label, but many wines often are 100% of the stated varietal. Due to potential ripeness issues, the only exception is Cabernet Sauvignon, which is allowed to be at least 75% in order to encourage blending if necessary.

Oregon's growing regions can be broken down into three AVAs that contain several smaller sub-AVAs.

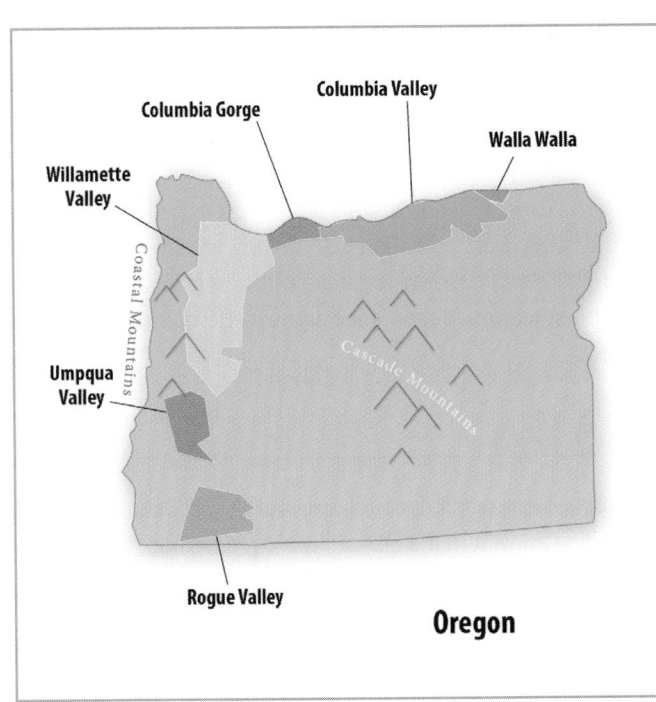

FIGURE 7–6 Map of Oregon
(Thomas Moore)

FIGURE 7–7 Adelsheim Pinot Noir label
(Adelsheim Winery)

APPELLATIONS

The winemaking regions are surrounded by natural barriers of the coastal range on the west, the Cascade Mountains on the south and east, and the Columbia River to the north.

Willamette Valley

Willamette (wuh-LAM-it) Valley is the largest AVA in Oregon (with over 10,000 acres of vines) and is named after the Willamette River that runs throughout the region. It boasts the majority (about 75%) of the state's wineries, with a concentration in the northern half.

The climate is relatively mild and moist, with warm, dry summers and cool, wet winters. The Cascade Mountains to the east and the coastal range to the west significantly influence and shelter the environment, creating a climate that somewhat mimics that of Alsace or Burgundy, France. The area tends to support cool-climate varietals such as Pinot Noir, Pinot Gris, Chardonnay, and Pinot Blanc.

The region has a large concentration of wineries and vineyards and contains six sub-appellations: *Chehalem Mountains, Dundee Hills, Eola-Amity Hills, McMinnville, Ribbon Ridge,* and *Yamhill-Carlton District*. Figure 7–7 shows an Oregon wine label from the Adelsheim Winery.

Eastern Oregon or Columbia Gorge

This AVA is known by both names and is located on both the Oregon and Washington sides of the Columbia River. The area is generally much warmer and drier than other Oregon appellations and supports such varietals as Cabernet, Merlot, and Syrah.

Southern Oregon

This area, with about 3,000 acres of vines, progresses from the southern point of Willamette Valley down to the California border. The climate is similar to Willamette, but is a bit warmer and drier because of the further southern influence.

Southern Oregon contains several major sub-appellations: *Applegate Valley, Red Hill Douglas County, Rogue Valley,* and *Umpqua (UMP-kwah) Valley*. Because of the region's warmer and drier climate, southern Oregon specializes in Bordeaux and Rhone grape varietals.

CANADA

Canada is not as large a producer of wine as it is a consumer. Canada is slowly moving away from the French hybrid grapes and making a serious effort to produce better-quality grapes from the more traditional international grape varieties. These newer wines have greater marketing potential and will continue to drive interest, particularly in the areas of southern British Columbia, with the Okanagan (oak-ah-NAH-gehn) Valley, and in Ontario, with the Niagara Peninsula. Figure 7–8 identifies the significant Canadian wine-growing areas within Ontario.

FIGURE 7–8 Map of Ontario
(Thomas Moore)

FIGURE 7–9 Frozen Vidal grapes
(Inniskillin Wines)

FIGURE 7–10 Inniskillin Ice wine label
(Inniskillin Wines)

The Varietals

Overall, Canada produces about 60% white wine (40% red wine), with Riesling leading the way. It also produces Chardonnay, Pinot Gris, Pinot Blanc and French hybrid varietals, and Vidal. Red wine varietals include Cabernet Franc, Cabernet Sauvignon, Merlot, Gamay Noir (also known as Gamay), Pinot Noir, and the French hybrid, Baco Noir.

Canada arguably is most known for its high-quality production of ice-wine. Grapes often are harvested in late December or January, yielding very small amounts of juice from each pressing of the frozen grapes. Common ice-wines are made from Riesling or Vidal grapes. Figure 7–9 shows frozen grapes on a vine.

APPELLATIONS

The Okanagan Valley and the Niagara Peninsula are the two prominent Canadian wine-producing areas. They are governed by the *Vintner's Quality Alliance*, or VQA, which is similar to other regulatory systems throughout Europe. The VQA is an appellation control system designed to authenticate the contents within the bottle through setting standards for viticulture and vinification practices.

Ontario

Ontario is Canada's largest wine-producing area, accounting for approximately 85% of production, with over 20,000 acres of grapevines. Ontario is considered a cool climate area similar to Germany or Burgundy, France. The VQA has recognized three viticultural areas, or VAs: Niagara Peninsula (the most significant of the three VAs), Lake Erie North Shore, and Pelee Island.

Niagara Peninsula

Niagara Peninsula is located in Ontario and most famous for its world-class *ice-wines*. For other grapes, the area is assisted by the lake effect from Lake Ontario in the North. The temperate climate allows for longer growing seasons by deterring damaging frosts, but the uneven ripening of red–wine grapes continues to make for huge vintage variations. Figure 7–10 depicts the famous ice-wine producer Inniskillin.

An increasing number of Pinot Noir, Cabernet Franc, Cabernet Sauvignon, and Merlot varietals are being produced, alongside Chardonnay and the more likely Riesling and Vidal Blanc grape varietals.

Okanagan Valley

Okanagan Valley is located just east of British Columbia, which is just north of Washington State. The valley is situated in a rain shadow between the coast and the Monashee mountain range. As of 2006, this area contained about 7,500 acres of vines and was the largest viticultural area in British Columbia. Okanagan Valley contains significant climate variations between its northern and southern sections.

In the north, the cold weather associated with Okanagan Valley is tempered by the lake effect. The northern section of the valley contains clay and gravel soil types. This area is most known for its Chardonnay, Pinot Noir, Riesling, and Pinot Blanc grape varietals.

In the southern section of Okanagan Valley is Canada's only desert, the northernmost tip of the Senora. Just as in the Columbia Valley, Washington, irrigation is the key to growing wine grapes. This southern end of the valley maintains a sandy soil type. The area is most known for its Cabernet Sauvignon, Merlot, and Syrah grape varietals.

WINES OF THE UNITED STATES AND CANADA

NAME: _____ Score out of 20 points_____.

Use these questions to test your knowledge and understanding of the concepts presented in the chapter.

I. MULTIPLE CHOICE: Select the best possible answer from the options available.

1. In the United States, if a vintage date is listed on a label, at least _____ of the grapes must have come from that year.

   a. 75%
   b. 85%
   c. 95%
   d. 100%

2. In the United States, if a specific vineyard is listed on a label, at least _____ of the grapes must come from that vineyard.

   a. 75%
   b. 85%
   c. 95%
   d. 100%

3. In the United States, if a specific AVA or location is listed on a label, at least _____ of the grapes must have come from that location.

   a. 75%
   b. 85%
   c. 95%
   d. 100%

4. In the United States, if a grape name is listed on a label, at least _____ of the grapes must come from the specified varietal.

   a. 75%
   b. 85%
   c. 95%
   d. 100%

II. TRUE/FALSE: Circle the best possible answer.

5. American wines are governed by the Vintner's Quality Alliance (VQA). **True / False**

6. California produces more wine than any other U.S. state. **True / False**

7. Ontario, Canada, produces the most wine in all of Canada. **True / False**

8. Columbia Valley is a significant grape-growing area in California. **True / False**

9. Napa Valley is a significant grape-growing area in Oregon. **True / False**

10. Willamette Valley is a significant grape-growing area in Oregon. **True / False**

11. On an American wine label, the terms *Reserve* and *Vintner's Reserve* have specific legal meanings. **True / False**

12. The North Coast region is known as one of the most famous wine regions in all of the United States. **True / False**

III. MATCHING: Connect the grape varietals below with the significant growing location. No answer may be duplicated.

LOCATIONS

13. _____ Significant red wine grape from Washington State.

14. _____ Significant white wine grape in Washington State.

15. _____ Significant red wine grape from California.

16. _____ Significant white wine grape from California.

17. _____ Significant red wine grape from New York State.

18. _____ Significant red wine grape from Oregon.

19. _____ Significant white wine grape from Oregon.

GRAPE VARIETALS

A. Pinot Gris

B. Pinot Noir

C. Riesling

D. Cabernet Franc

E. Cabernet Sauvignon

F. Chardonnay

G. Merlot

IV. SHORT-ANSWER ESSAY/DISCUSSION QUESTIONS: Use a separate sheet of paper if necessary.

20. As a newly hired beverage manager (whether for a restaurant or wine store), you noticed the wine selections are *all* Old World focused. How would you justify to the owner the need for incorporating New World wine selections?

PINOT NOIR
NABOTH'S VINEYARD
THE MILLTON VINEYARDS
1995
PRODUCE OF NEW ZEALAND
1998
PRODUCE OF NEW ZEALAND

8

Other New World Wine Countries

The most significant wine-producing countries of the New World include Argentina, Australia, Chile, New Zealand, and South Africa. These countries are perceived as dynamic, with enormous potential, and continue to gain immense popularity throughout the world. Overall, New World wines are reasonably priced and provide good value.

LEARNING OBJECTIVES

Upon completion of this chapter, the learner will be able to:

- Identify the significant wine-producing countries within the New World.
- Recognize the significant grape varietals and styles of wine produced within each New World wine-producing country.
- Recognize the most significant wine-producing appellations within the New World.

NEW WORLD

Since the early beginnings of winemaking, Europeans left their homelands to escape from political and religious injustice. A by-product of their flight was that they spread the influence of grapevine growing and winemaking around the globe. New societies came about through immigration, trade, exploration, and slavery routes as Europeans settled the New World countries. In various parts of the world, the immigrants wished to consume wine and other alcohol beverages that were comparable to those from their homelands back in Europe. Commodities markets for trading and selling products were created as a necessity as the settlers were faced with finding a source of earnings to support themselves. This led the immigrants to begin incorporating their knowledge and expertise of winemaking into the New World lands.

The most significant wine-producing countries of the New World are Argentina, Australia, Chile, New Zealand, and South Africa. These countries are perceived as dynamic, with enormous potential, and continue to gain immense popularity throughout the world. Overall, New World wines are reasonably priced and provide good value. New World wines use labelling practices similar to those of the United States, identifying the primary varietal, as opposed to labelling according to geography, as practiced by the Old World wineries.

In the Southern Hemisphere, the seasons are just the opposite of those in the Northern Hemisphere. Therefore, the autumn harvest occurs typically in the months of March and April, approximately six months earlier than the Northern Hemisphere harvest, in August and September. The term *flying winemakers* has become popular, as some winemakers (originally Australians) in the Southern Hemisphere have the luxury of working multiple vintages and contributing their skills and expertise as consultants to winemakers in the Northern Hemisphere. Some argue that this practice has led to a homogenization of wine and wine styles around the globe.

FIGURE 8–1 Map of Australia
(Thomas Moore)

AUSTRALIA

Australia maintains more than 1,300 wineries and 425,000 acres of vine. There are about 50 registered wine regions across Australia, and approximately 5 corporate-controlled companies make 75% of all the wine produced, which provides an economy of scale. These companies have also invested heavily in technology and mechanization, from vineyard to bottling, which contributes to the production of reasonably priced wines that offer great value. Australia has considerable success not only domestically, but also in the international market, due largely to the clever marketing approach of attaching playful characters and catchy names to the wine labels and selling wines at a desirable price point. Figure 8–1 identifies Australia's wine regions.

The Varietals

Australia produces wine from approximately 70 grape varietals, although most derive from only 5 key varietals (Chardonnay, Riesling, Semillon, Cabernet Sauvignon, and Shiraz). Shiraz was for a long time the predominant grape in Australia; now it rivals Chardonnay as the most widely planted grape variety, with more than 30,000 acres of vines. Semillon is the second most widely planted variety of white grapes, after Chardonnay.

Australian Wine Labelling

Australian wines are varietal based, similar to American wines. If wines are labelled by grape variety, at least 85% of the wine must be made from that grape. However, Australia has unique labelling requirements. If a wine comprises more than one variety and no single variety makes up 85%, then all varieties must be labelled in order of importance (by percentage used). For example, the label on a blend of Cabernet–Shiraz might state Cabernet 60% and Shiraz 40%.

If a place name is indicated on the label, then 85% of the grapes must have come from that region. Ninety-five percent of the grapes in vintage wines must have been harvested during the year listed on the label.

APPELLATIONS

Wine production in Australia is concentrated in cool valleys and coastal areas in the south or southwest.

Southern Australia

Adelaide Hills—This region contains several elevated vineyard sites and produces cool-climate varietals such as Riesling, Chardonnay, and Pinot Noir. Because of the large amount of these varietals (traditional grapes used to produce classic Champagne), these vineyards have been producing sparkling wine as well.

Clare Valley—Clustered near the city of Adelaide, this diverse region experiences both dry heat and cool sea wind. The vineyards are irrigated, because Clare Valley typically has the lowest rainfall of all the Australian wine regions. The cool higher-altitude vineyards allow the Riesling and Chardonnay grapes to ripen slowly throughout the growing season. Hearty reds such as Shiraz also are produced here.

Barossa Valley (bah-ROH-sah)—One of the most famous Australian wine regions and the first to become highly popular outside of Australia, the Barossa Valley has been producing wines longer than most other growing areas, with Shiraz vines dating back from the 1840s. The climate is ideal for growing legendary Australian Shiraz and other full-bodied red wines such as Cabernet Sauvignon and Grenache, as well as heartier whites.

Eden Valley—An area within Barossa Valley, but where the vineyards are at a higher elevation, Eden Valley boasts a cooler climate that is ideal for producing Rieslings.

McLaren Vale—The temperate maritime environment from the nearby ocean, coupled with rolling hills, creates a climate characterized by warm days and cool nights—perfect for maintaining the acidity balance that is vital for the rich, ripe fruit that is usually produced. The various microclimates of McLaren Vale allow many varieties to thrive, particularly Rhône varietals (Shiraz, Grenache, Mourvedre, Marsanne, and Viognier), but also Cabernet Sauvignon, Merlot, and Sauvignon Blanc.

Coonawarra—This is the most famous, highly recognized red wine district in Southern Australia, where vines were first planted in 1890. It is known primarily for its Shiraz and Cabernet Sauvignon, but also produces Chardonnay and Riesling. This key cool growing area is the home of the famous *Terra Rossa* soils (locally called "red earth"), which are composed of very old clay that is compressed until it resembles red brick. Figure 8–2 illustrates these famous soils.

FIGURE 8–2 Famous Terra Rossa soil
(RyMill Coonawarra)

Southeast Australia

Hunter Valley—Located about 100 miles northwest of Sydney, Hunter Valley is the most northerly of Australia's first-class vineyards. With long growing seasons, the area is traditionally known for its Shiraz and Semillon, but also produces a large amount of Cabernet Sauvignon and Chardonnay.

Yarra Valley—This is one of Australia's most picturesque and renowned wine regions, with its rolling, vine-covered slopes. A cool, inland region, Yarra Valley is known for the cultivation of Chardonnay and Pinot Noir. Cabernet Sauvignon and Shiraz also do well here.

Western Australia

Margaret River—Located in Western Australia, this area has perhaps the most maritime climate of any Australian wine district. It has a wide peninsula, around 60 miles cape-to-cape, and is bordered by the ocean on three sides. (Most Margaret River wineries lie only a few miles from the sea.) It produces a mere 2% of Australia's crush, yet represents around 20% of its premium bottled wines. It has excelled with varieties such as Cabernet Sauvignon and Semillon/Sauvignon Blanc, but Chardonnay has brought the most fame to this area.

Perth Hills—One of the newest and smallest wine-growing regions in Western Australia is Perth Hills. Many grapes are planted at higher and cooler altitudes here.

Swan District—This is the original wine district in Western Australia. Just north of the city of Perth, the Swan District is a very warm region and well suited for the fortified dessert wines.

NEW ZEALAND

FIGURE 8–3 Map of New Zealand
(Thomas Moore)

New Zealand is one of the southernmost wine-producing countries in the Southern Hemisphere. It comprises two large islands, called *North Island* and *South Island*, and a number of smaller islands. All of the islands are greatly influenced by the region's maritime climate, but still maintain a wide diversity in climate and terrain. New Zealand is a cool and damp environment, with cool nights even in the hot, sunny summers. This climate assists the grape varietals in maintaining their zesty acidity and fruit qualities. Figure 8–3 identifies New Zealand's wine regions.

The Varietals

New Zealand's success is a recent trend that has seen its greatest growth over the last 20 years, when it became one of the fastest-growing wine countries in the world. In 2006, New Zealand maintained over 57,000 acres of grapevines, dominated by 22,000 acres devoted to Sauvignon Blanc. Pinot Noir is the leading red wine varietal and trails Sauvignon Blanc in popularity. Chardonnay, Riesling, and Bordeaux varietals are other popular grapes found throughout New Zealand.

New Zealand is known mostly for wines that exude the pure personality of grape varietals. The pervasive use of stainless steel assists in preserving the grapes' acidity, the expression of the grapes' intensity, and the purity of the fruit. Oak aging is moderately applied in some areas, but, philosophically, doesn't overpower the expression of the grape's personality.

Screwcaps

A modern trend that New Zealand is noted for is the use of screw caps as the main closure to seal bottles of wine. This is a way to eliminate the concern of TCA, or cork taint. In addition, choosing the the screw cap is a natural progression for the winemaker, particularly if the wine has been stored in stainless steel prior to bottling. This practice supports the philosophy of pure essence of the fruit, youthfullness, and preservation of the acid qualities that oak aging and a cork would otherwise alter.

APPELLATIONS

North Island

Gisbourne—This region is located at the eastern tip of North Island. Gisbourne is coined the *Chardonnay Capital* of New Zealand because half of its vineyards are occupied by the Chardonnay varietal.

Hawke's Bay—Famous for its *Gimblett Gravels*, or rocky, stony soil, Hawke's Bay has been referred to as the *Bordeaux of New Zealand* because of the predominant Cabernet Sauvignon and Merlot- and Syrah-based wines.

Wellington—This area occupies the southern section of North Island, which includes the Wairarapa wine region. Martinborough, one of North Island's well-known subregions, is located within Wellington. Martinborough produces Sauvignon Blanc, but has become a leading Pinot Noir producer as well.

South Island

Nelson—This region is situated on the western side of the northern tip of South Island. Mountains to the west of the region provide a rain-shadow effect, while the coastline moderates the climate. Cool-climate grape types such as Chardonnay, Sauvignon Blanc, Riesling, and Pinot Noir thrive.

Marlborough—Possibly New Zealand's finest wine region and certainly the largest grape-growing area, Marlborough had over 29,000 acres of vineyards in 2006. Located on the northern end of South Island, Marlborough is a cool growing region with long, dry autumns that allow grapes to ripen. Sauvignon Blanc made the region well known, but it is Pinot Noir that is making great strides and has emerged as New Zealand's leading red grape varietal. Figure 8–4 shows a New Zealand vineyard.

Canterbury—A large wine region on South Island, Canterbury has many vineyards planted in white varieties, notably Riesling and Chardonnay.

Central Otago—This southernmost wine region in the world is characterized by varying levels of altitude. With a continental-type climate, Pinot Noir has become the leading varietal in Central Otago.

FIGURE 8–4 New Zealand vineyard
(Peter Bush © Dorling Kindersley)

ARGENTINA

Argentina is positioned in the heart of South America. Viticulture began during the Spanish colonization in the early 1500s and saw resurgence in the nineteenth century by a melting pot of European immigrants mostly from Spain, Germany, Italy, and France. In 2007 there were over 550,000 acres of vines, and until recently Argentina vintners were distributing most of their products domestically. Modern production techniques, greater vineyards

FIGURE 8–5 Map of
Argentina
(Thomas Moore)

planted at higher elevations (in some cases, above 4,000 feet), and an influx in interest and talent from abroad have all helped to reshape this South American wine region. As the popularity of New World wine has increased, Argentina has successfully increased its wine exports, gained greater fame, and become a key player in the world wine market. Figure 8–5 identifies Argentina's wine regions.

The Varietals

Argentina has gained a reputation over the past decade for its signature grape *Malbec*. Orginally from Southwest France, Malbec has prospered as both a blending grape and a standalone varietal. Other popular red grapes produced are Cabernet Sauvignon, Syrah, Merlot, and Tempranillo. Figure 8–6 shows Argentina's most significant grape varietal: Malbec.

White grape varietals are not as prevalent as red grapes, but a standout grape unique to Argentina is *Torrontes* (tohr-RAHN-tez). Other recognizable international varieties include Chardonnay, Chenin Blanc, Semillon, Sauvignon Blanc, and Viognier.

APPELLATIONS

Throughout Argentina, the environment varies dramatically from mountains to plateaus, deserts to wetlands, and glaciers to canyons. This diversity provides a vast array of varietals with optimal growing conditions. Although the country does not receive as much rainfall as other wine-growing countries, grape growers have set up elaborate systems of irrigation to ensure that their vineyards receive adequate water. Figure 8–7 shows a vineyard in Argentina.

Mendoza—This is the largest and most vital wine-growing region in Argentina (with over 80% of the country's plantings) and is also the largest wine-growing region in all of the Southern Hemisphere.

Red wines produced include large amounts of Malbec, Bonarda, and Cabernet Sauvignon, with lesser amounts of Merlot and Tempranillo. The vineyards in higher altitudes yield excellent white varietals such as Chardonnay, Chenin Blanc, Sauvignon Blanc, and Torrontes.

Uco Valley (OOH-co)—Located in the southwest part of Mendoza, with some of the highest elevation levels in all of Mendoza, the Uco Valley has the ideal climate conditions for varieties such as Semillon, Chenin Blanc, and Malbec.

San Juan—The second-largest production area in Argentina, San Juan contains a set of valleys with varying levels of elevation.

La Rioja—Dry and windy, La Rioja grows Malbec, Syrah, and Torrontes varietals.

Rio Negro and Neuquen—The Rio Negro region in southeast Argentina is just South of Mendoza. Wine production has been taking place there since the early 1900s. The climate is dry and warm and yields old-vine Malbecs and other reds. Neuquen borders Mendoza in the North and Rio Negro in the South and is a developing wine region producing a mix of white and red varietals.

Salta—This region is the northernmost wine-growing area and showcases the highest vineyards in all of Argentina, reaching as high as 10,000 feet above sea level. The most

FIGURE 8–6 Malbec grapes
(Wines of Argentina)

FIGURE 8–7 Vineyards in
Argentina
(Wines of Argentina)

planted white grape is Torrontes, while the most widely planted red grape varietal is Cabernet Sauvignon, with Tannat and Syrah as other significant grape varietals.

CHILE

Chile (CHEE-lay) is a long sliver of land located on the western coast of South America. It has a long history of winemaking dating back to the 1500s, but 1851 saw the arrival of French vine varieties. Chile has long been a country of isolation both geographically and climatically, with the Pacific Ocean to the west, the Andes Mountains to the east, and the Atacama Desert to the north. Since Chile has been free from the dictatorship of Augosto Pinochet over the past two decades, it has experienced an influx of foreign investment, particularly from Europe and the United States, which has assisted in modernizing the country's vineyards and wineries of Chile while broadening new markets. Chile's wine industry has been reshaped and has emerged from isolation with over 270,000 acres of vines. Figure 8–8 identifies Chile's wine regions.

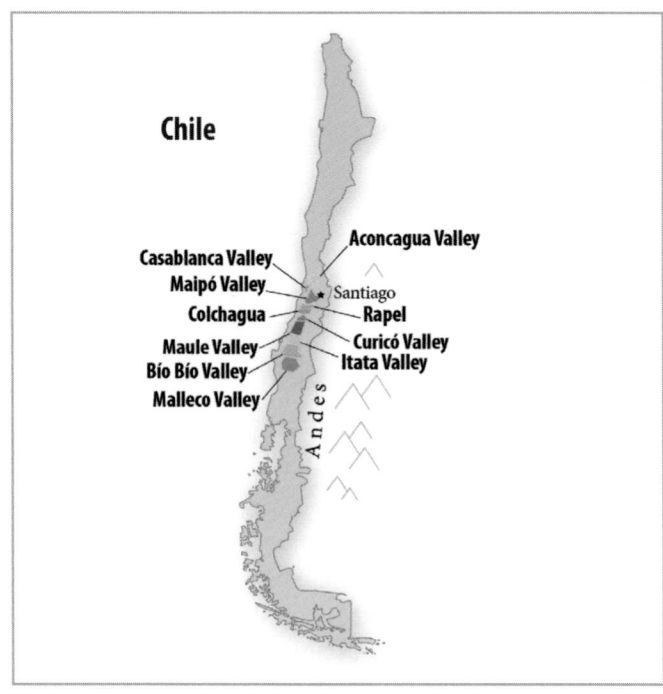

FIGURE 8–8 Map of Chile
(Thomas Moore)

The Varietals

Chile features a mild Mediterranean climate that is warm, sunny, and moderated by the cooling influence of the Pacific Ocean and the moisturizing influence of the Andes Mountains. Several grape varietals thrive in this environment, including Merlot, Cabernet Sauvignon, Syrah, Sauvignon Blanc, and Chardonnay. A unique aspect of Chile is the Carmenere grape varietal, which is similar to Merlot. It was recently rediscovered in Chile through the DNA fingerprinting process. For years, Carmenere was mislabeled as Merlot, until it was properly identified as a completely distinct grape varietal.

APPELLATIONS

Most of the premium rootstock in Chile was imported from France in the 1800s, just in time to avoid the disastrous infestation of the phylloxera pest, which had devastated a large number of the vineyards throughout Europe. Chile was one of the few wine-growing places spared destruction from phylloxera, and it remains home to some of the few remaining strains of original vines. It was a combination of Chile's sand-based soil (phylloxera doesn't thrive in sand) and geographic isolation from the rest of the world that prevented the devastation wrought on other vineyards.

Aconcagua (ah-KOHN-kah-gwah)

Aconcagua Valley—Located just north of the Central Valley, Aconcagua Valley has a warmer climate that supports red grapes such as Cabernet Sauvignon and Syrah.

Casablanca Valley—Located closer to the coast, Casablanca Valley enjoys a cooler climate that produces white wines—notably Sauvignon Blanc and Chardonnay, but also some Pinot Noir.

Central Valley

The main growing area in Chile is collectively known as the Central Valley, which produces the vast majority of wines. The climate is dry, and there is little risk of springtime frost. The proximity to the Andés Mountains helps to create a wide diurnal range between day and night temperatures. Central Valley comprises the most important subregions from north to south:

Maipó Valley (My-POH)—The Maipó region, located just south of Santiago, is one of Chile's renowned, long-established quality wine regions. Cabernet Sauvignon is the core of the region, but Merlot and Carmenere are also prominent.

Rapel Valley (RAH-pell)—A large growing area with diverse soil, Rapel Valley successfully grows Carmenère as a significant varietal. Colchagua is an important sub-region of Rapel Valley.

Curicó Valley—This is one of the cooler regions in Central Valley, due to the influence of the Pacific Ocean.

Maule Valley—Many vineyards are located in the valley and on the slopes of the coastal mountains. White varieties flourish, predominantly Sauvignon Blanc and Chardonnay, and many red varieties including Merlot, Cabernet Sauvignon, and Carmenère.

SOUTH AFRICA

South Africa's wine-growing areas are situated in the Southern Hemisphere, with a largely Mediterranean climate. According to the *South Africa Trade Group*, the country had over 255,000 acres of grapevines in 2007. The South African winemaking heritage goes back to the seventeenth century; however, it was not until the government deregulated the wine industry and emerged from the shadow of Apartheid in 1994 that a renaissance occurred, allowing South African winemakers to compete with the rest of the wine world. Figure 8–9 identifies South Africa's wine regions.

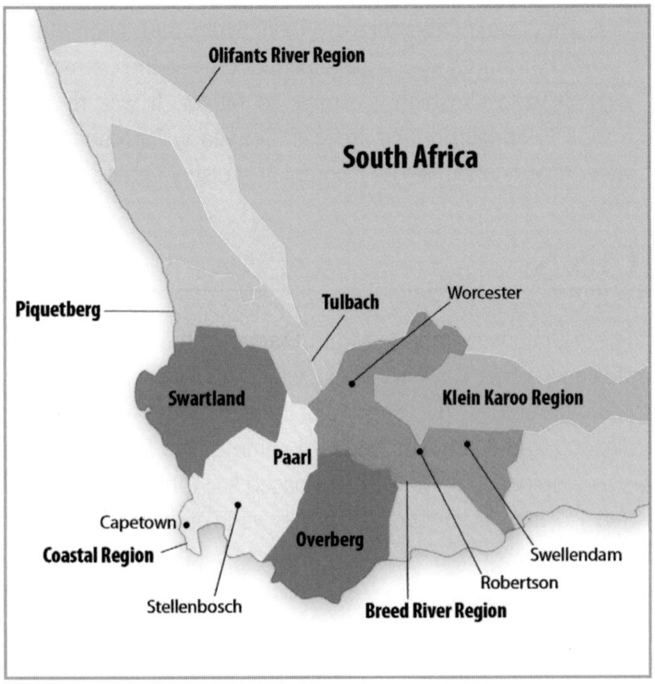

FIGURE 8–9 Map of South Africa

(Thomas Moore)

The Varietals

The climate associated with South Africa encourages a wide range of wine styles. Historically, Pinotage (a local grape that is a cross between Pinot Noir and Cinsault [SAN-soh]) had outperformed all other grape varietals. Now Cabernet Sauvignon has emerged as the leading South African varietal and currently surpasses all other red grapes. Syrah is the next major varietal, with the second-largest number of acres devoted to vines, followed by Merlot and then Pinotage.

White wine grapes include Chenin Blanc; known locally as *Steen,* it is the leading varietal of both white and red wine grapes. Chenin Blanc produces both dry and sweet styles. Other white wine varietals include Chardonnay, Sauvignon Blanc, and a small percentage of Viognier.

Over the last decade, producers have maintained a fairly rigorous uprooting and replanting process. This is largely due to the accessibility of new clones of existing varietals and a better understanding of site selection by the matching of the type of vine with a well-suited vineyard site.

Chardonnay is used for both table wine and sparkling wine. The South Africans produce a sparkling wine called *Méthode Cap Classique* by using the classic Champagne method of production.

APPELLATIONS

Depending on where the vineyard is located, it will be influenced by one of two oceans (Indian or Atlantic) that meet at the tip of South Africa and influence the vineyards by moderating the climate. South Africa has had the strictly legislated *Wines of Origin*, or WO, in place since 1973 to ensure the authenticity of its wines through the control of appellation areas.

The wine-producing areas are broken down into regions (the broadest-producing areas), then into district and wards (the smallest and most defined growing areas).

The four South African regions are Breed River Valley, Klein Karoo, Olifants River, and the Coastal Region. Most of the vineyards in South Africa are located in the southwest corner of the country called the Cape, or Coastal Region.

A wine that lists a name of a region, district, or ward on its label must contain 100% of grapes from that location. A wine is labelled according to its varietal (85% minimum as listed), similar to the European Union requirements.

Coastal Region

The Coastal Region is possibly the most recognized South African wine region throughout the world wine market. It contains many well-known districts and wards such as *Stellenbosch* (STELL-n-bahsh), *Paarl* (par-rl), and *Constantia* (kuhn-STAN-she-ah).

OTHER NEW WORLD WINE COUNTRIES

NAME: _____ Score out of 20 points_____.

Use these questions to test your knowledge and understanding of the concepts presented in the chapter.

I. MULTIPLE CHOICE: Select the best possible answer from the options available.

1. In Australia, if a wine comprises more than one grape and neither grape makes up at least 85%, then
    a. the grape that makes up the highest percentage is the only one which needs to be listed on the label.
    b. all grapes must be listed on the label.
    c. all grapes must be listed on the label in order of importance and by percentage.
    d. only one of the grapes needs to be listed, as determined by the winemaker.

2. Which New World country grows the most vines?
    a. New Zealand
    b. Argentina
    c. Chile
    d. Australia

3. Australia's Barossa Valley and Coonawara areas are best known for producing which grape?
    a. Chardonnay
    b. Merlot
    c. Riesling
    d. Shiraz

4. New Zealand's Marlborough area is best known for producing which grape?
    a. Chardonnay
    b. Merlot
    c. Riesling
    d. Sauvignon Blanc

5. The most significant wine region in Argentina is
    a. Salta.
    b. Rapel Valley.
    c. Mendoza.
    d. Margaret River.

II. TRUE / FALSE: Circle the best possible answer.

6. Most South African vineyards are located in the growing areas within the Coastal Region. **True / False**

7. All New Zealand producers use screw caps as closures for their wine bottles. **True / False**

8. In South Africa, another name for the Chenin Blanc grape varietals is *Steen*. **True / False**

III. MATCHING: In each of the following sentences, connect the grape varietal listed afterwards with the predominant location mentioned in the sentence: Answers may only be used once.

LOCATION

9. ____ significant white wine grape from New Zealand

10. ____ significant red wine grape from Australia

11. ____ significant white wine grape from Australia

12. ____ significant red wine grape grown in Argentina

13. ____ significant red wine grape from Chile

14. ____ significant red wine grape from South Africa

15. ____ significant red wine grape from New Zealand

16. ____ significant white wine grape from Chile

17. ____ significant white wine grape from Argentina.

18. ____ significant white wine grape from South Africa

GRAPE VARIETALS

A. Cabernet Sauvignon

B. Malbec

C. Chardonnay

D. Merlot

E. Sauvignon Blanc

F. Shiraz

G. Syrah

H. Pinot Noir

I. Chenin Blanc

J. Torrontes

IV. SHORT-ANSWER ESSAY / DISCUSSION QUESTIONS: Use a separate sheet of paper if necessary.

19. What is the philosophy behind the method, practiced by some New Zealand wine producers, of using screw caps to seal their wines?

20. Give a brief history explaining how New World wine countries started to produce wine.

Unit 4
WINES OF THE OLD WORLD

"Experience is the teacher of all things."

—*Julius Caesar*

OLD WORLD AND ITS NEW APPROACH

The major wine-producing countries associated with the Old World have been creating wine for thousands of years. Throughout the ages, the history of wine production has been entangled, on varying levels, with the political and sociological development of each country. Many of the bottle shapes, grape types, and styles of wine from the New World that have already been discussed in this text originated in the significant regions of France, Italy, Germany, or Spain.

The European Union (EU) was created just after World War II to bring peace, prosperity, solidarity, and stability to Europe. The EU is an economic and political partnership between 27 democratic European countries. The Union acts on a wide range of policies in order to benefit the member countries.

In the world of wine, the European Union organized a wine classification system consisting of two tiers, the bottom tier called *table wine* and the top tier called *quality wine*. The concept of the quality-wine level is based on a geographical-origin approach of wines produced from a specific place.

The EU has actively encouraged quality wine and discouraged the production of wines in the table wine category. In 2007, the EU and its member states agreed to uproot approximately 400,000 acres of grapevines in order to halt overproduction and government subsidies. This approach is being used to balance supply and demand, as well to encourage a focus on better-quality varietals and site selection.

9

Wines of France

French winemakers produce a variety of different wines in styles that may be a bit daunting to the novice wine drinker. However, by applying some generalizations on major varietals, regions, and appellations, it can become easier to solidify an understanding of French wines.

LEARNING OBJECTIVES

Upon completion of this chapter, the learner will be able to:

- Understand the significant wine-producing regions of France.
- Understand the French appellation control system and its levels of hierarchy.
- Know the major grape varietals and styles of wine produced within each of France's significant wine regions.
- Know the important subregions within Burgundy, Bordeaux, the Loire Valley, and Rhône.

FRANCE

France is one of the oldest wine-producing countries in Europe, with winemaking originating back to the sixth century B.C. It is also one of the largest producers and consumers of wine in the world. French wine has served as the standard of excellence of wine throughout the world for decades and is respected and often imitated by most major wine-producing countries.

The novice wine drinker may find that French wine selection can be intimidating, primarily because the labelling system is based largely on geography. Most French wines are labelled by the name of the place (which is registered and legally defined under French law) where the grapes are grown and the wine is made, rather than by major type of grape, as labelling is done in the New World. This is somewhat of a challenge for non-French speakers to have to read, understand, and pronounce French terminology, as well as to become educated in French geography and wine law.

French wines often are produced in a way that allows the expression of terroir to show through, with fewer overt fruit characteristics, and that allows the wine to gravitate toward more earth- and animal-oriented attributes. This wine paradigm associated with Old World France may not be as user friendly to the average wine drinker. For some, these expressions and attributes make French wines more dependent on consumption with food and less adaptable and drinkable by themselves, as many New World options are.

French winemakers produce a variety of different styles and types of wine. Applying some generalizations on major varietals, regions, and appellations makes it easier to solidify an understanding of French wines. The wine regions and appellations most commonly presented on American restaurant wine lists are outlined in this chapter. Figure 9–1 identifies the significant French wine regions.

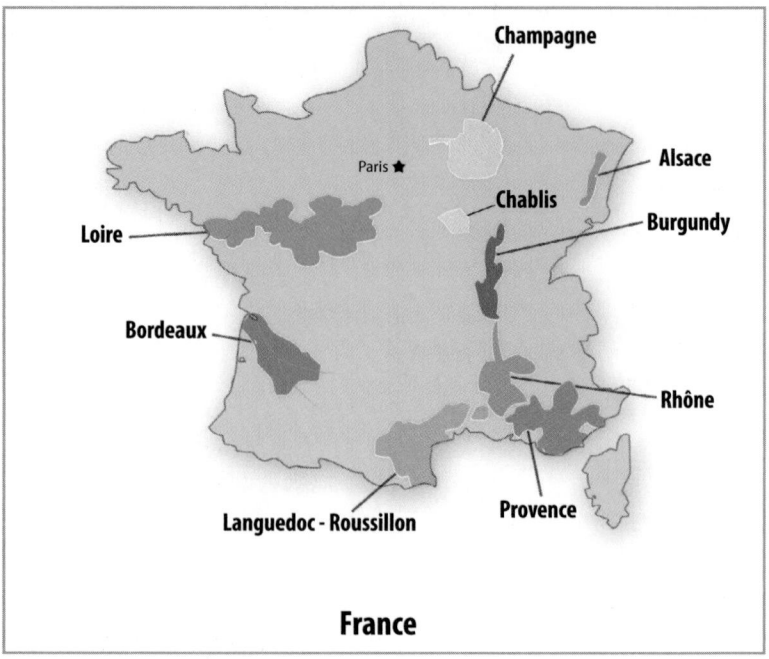

FIGURE 9–1 Map of France
(Thomas Moore)

An Introduction to French Wine

The regions of France can be divided into three broad areas on the basis of grape varietals and climate. Of course, these are generalizations, and there are obvious exceptions within each area. However, it can be helpful at this level of wine education to discuss the complexity of Old World wines more in generalities. There are seven significant wine regions in France that produce world-class wine. Each of these regions specializes in certain grape varieties for its wine, according to climate, soil, laws, local traditions, and so on.

1. The *northeastern* section of France (Champagne, Northern Burgundy, and Alsace) is subject to a continental climate that consists of four distinct seasons with short summers and harsh winters. This type of climate contributes to creating tart grapes with higher acid and the preservation of mineral qualities. The grapes produce low sugar and less ripe fruit, which ultimately yields a wine with lower alcohol content. Therefore, the technique of chaptalization (the addition of sugar to grape must) is frequently allowed in these regions according to appellation-controlled laws.

    Alsace (al-SASS)—This region produces mostly white wines from the Riesling, Gewürztraminer, Pinot Blanc, and Pinot Gris grapes. Alsace also produces sparkling wine and dessert wine.

    Burgundy (BER-gun-dee)—The Burgundy region produces both red and white wines. Red wine grape production is primarily from Pinot Noir and Gamay, while white wine production is from Chardonnay.

    Champagne (sham-PAYN)—Champagne is world famous for sparkling wines produced from varying blends of Pinot Noir, Pinot Meunier, and Chardonnay grape varietals. (This topic will be discussed in greater detail in Chapter 11, "BUBBLES: Sparkling Wine".)

2. The *western* section of France (Bordeaux and most of the Loire Valley) has a maritime climate of mild winters and cool summers, created from the moderating influence of the Atlantic Ocean.

    Bordeaux (bohr-DOH)—The Bordeaux region produces red and white wine and dessert wine. Red wine grapes are primarily blended in varying quantities of Cabernet Sauvignon, Merlot, Cabernet Franc, and others. White wines, whether dry table or sweet dessert wines, are produced primarily from varying quantities of Sauvignon Blanc and Semillon varietals.

    Loire (LWAHR) **Valley**—Loire produces mostly white wines, but also produces red wines, dessert wines, and sparkling wines. The white wines come primarily from Chenin Blanc and Sauvignon Blanc grapes and red wine dominated by the Cabernet Franc varietal.

3. The *midcentral* and *southern* sections of France maintain a Mediterranean climate. In hotter southern climates, grapes have less acid and higher sugar, which produces wine with higher alcohol levels, riper fruit and denser full-bodied wines.

    Rhône (ROHN) **Valley**—The Rhône Valley produces mostly red wines from Syrah, Grenache, and Mourvedre, with white wines produced from the Viognier grape.

    Languedonc-Roussillon (lahng-DAWK roos-see-YAWN) and **Provence** (praw-VAHNS)— In southern France, the majority of production is red wine from Syrah, Mourvedre, Grenache, and other varietals. In addition, produce some of France's most famous versions of fortified wine.

Useful French Wine Terms

-   **Barrique** (bah-REEK)—Often refers to a barrel that holds approximately 60 gallons, used in Bordeaux
-   **Blanc** (BLAHNK)—White wine

- **Cépage** (say-PAHZH)—Vine or grape variety
- **Château** (shah-TOH)—Often refers to a wine estate located on the land of the vineyard
- **Clos** (KLOH)—The term originally used in Burgundy to mean an enclosed vineyard
- **Côte** (KOHT) or **Coteaux** (koh-TOH)—Often refers to a slope or hillside
- **Cru** (KROO)—Refers to a ranking of a vineyard or estate; may also represent vineyard areas that are known for producing exceptional wines
- **Domaine** (doh-MAYN)—The term often used in Burgundy to refer to a single vineyard estate that may or may not derive from the location in which the grapes were grown
- **Piéce** (pee-YES)—Often refers to a barrel that holds approximately 60 gallons, used in Burgundy
- **Rouge** (ROOZH)—Red wine
- **Vendage** (vahn-DAHZH)—Grape harvest or vintage

THE FRENCH CLASSIFICATION SYSTEM

Created in 1935, the *Institut National des Appellations d'Origine* (an-stee-TYOO nah-syaw-NAHL dayz ah-pehl-lah-SYOHN daw-ree-ZHEEN), or INAO, is officially authorized to regulate the French wine industry according to standards that safeguard not only the consumer from fraud, but also the winemaker from unfair competition. The INAO guarantees that all appellation-controlled (AC) products hold to a rigorous set of standards. The creation of the AC system was designed to allow the consumer to distinguish between a wine with a simple name of origin and a fine wine with a "controlled" name of origin.

French wine is truly rooted in *terroir-based* laws, meaning that the wine has to be produced from specific appellations with permitted grape varieties, in suitable soils, and following defined procedures for viticulture and vinification. The French wine system is hierarchical, and theoretically, the wines should be better the higher they are up the rung, but in practice it doesn't necessarily work that way. The classification system defines four levels with varying quality standards. Figure 9–2 illustrates the French wine classification system.

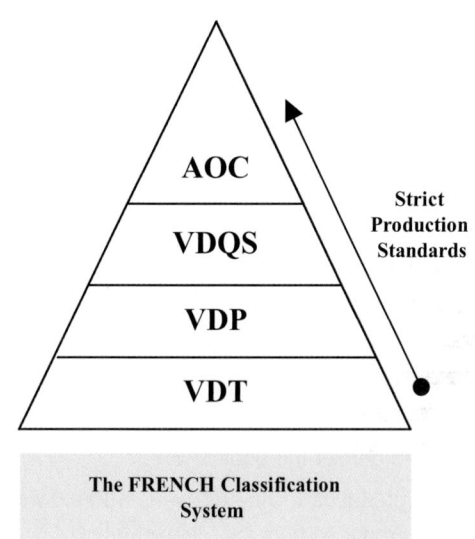

FIGURE 9–2 **French wine classification system**
(John Laloganes)

Appellation d'Origine Controlée (ah-pehl-lah-SYAHN daw-ree-JEEN kawn-traw-LAY) **(AOC or AC)**

AOC wines are held to the highest standard of the classification levels within the classification system. Vineyard growing areas, yields, varietals, blends of varietals, and alcohol content are highly regulated. In addition, all wines must be bottled within the region. The designation and regulations apply to all wines made from grapes grown in a designated AOC area of production.

Some AOC wines are further classified into *Grand Cru, Premier Cru,* or other designation. Each AOC has its own unique system of classification to determine this additional designation.

Vins Delimites de Qualite Superieur (van deh-lee-mee-TAY kah-lee-TAY soopehr-YUR) **(VDQS)**

Classified under a minor level of production with less strict, but similar, standards to the AOC level, VDQS wines hold great promise and are striving for recognition by the INAO for promotion to the AOC level. They can be thought of as virtually an AOC-in-waiting, or in transition, until they have a proven track record of consistent quality.

Vins de Pays (van-duh pay-ee) **(VDP)**

The vins de pays are regional wines whose broader growing area and grape varietal may be listed on the label. But the restrictions are more lenient than they are for wines at the previous two levels.

Vins de Table (van-duh-tab) **(VDT)**

The vins de table classification is at the lowest level with the loosest quality standards. These wines can be produced from grapes grown anywhere in France, with no regard for the level of yield per vine. The European Union actively discourages the production of wine at this level, and the vins de table classification is a declining category. These wines are most often consumed locally or used for distillation.

ALSACE

Alsace is a region located in the northeastern area of France, close to the German border east of the *Vosges* (vohzh) Mountains. Its location keeps this wine region relatively isolated from the rest of France. For many centuries, France and Germany had fought over the land of Alsace, which was ruled by Germany several times. The region's architecture, language, and grape varieties reflect this influence. Figure 9–3 identifies Alsace, France.

The Varietals

Alsace maintains some 35,000 acres of grapevines and is the largest producer of the nation's white wine (about 95%). With its vast soil types and cool, dry, and sunny climate, Alsace supports a variety of different white wine grapes. The Alsatians use the same grape varietals as the Germans, but, unlike the Germans who often leave varying amounts of residual sugar in the wines, the Alsatians ferment them mostly or even completely dry. It has been said, "Alsace uses German grapes, but makes them into a French style."

FIGURE 9–3 Map of Alsace
(Thomas Moore)

The primary grapes of Alsace are Riesling, Gewürztraminer, Pinot Gris, Muscat, and Pinot Blanc. Arguably the greatest wines of the region come from the Riesling varietal, and Gewürztraminer follows a close second.

APPELLATIONS

The region of Alsace contains two wine-specific areas: the *Bas-Rhin* (bahs-rine) and *Haut-Rhin* (oht-rine). Bas Rhin is located in the north and maintains a wetter, cooler climate. Many of the average-quality wines, or *edelzwicker* (ed-del-zvik-her, which means "blended wines"), derive from this location.

In the south, the Haut Rhin sustains many high-quality vineyards. They are often perched in the foothills of the Vosges Mountains. The mountains and nearby forests protect the area, creating a rain-shadow effect, which results in little rainfall and prolonged sun exposure to allow the grapes to ripen longer and gain maximum flavor development.

The minimum alcohol requirement of an Alsatian wine is 8.5%, but many are often much higher. In order to achieve a typical 12%–14% alcohol content, the wines can be chaptalized (the addition of sugar to grape must), because the region's cool climate may not always allow the grapes to produce enough sugar on their own.

FIGURE 9–4 Riesling Schlossberg Alsace Grand Cru
(Domaine Weinbach)

Alsace Grand Cru

Alsace Grand Cru require strict grape-growing and wine-making methods allowing four select kinds of grapes (Riesling, Gewürztztraminer, Pinot Gris, and Muscat) from designated vineyards (although there are a few minor exceptions). Currently, 51 named vineyards are entitled to use the term *Grand Cru* (though many producers who earned the ranking choose not to use it because of a disagreement over the merit of the classification system). Figure 9–4 shows an Alsatian wine label from the famous Domaine Weinbach.

Bottle Shape and Labelling

Due to the German influence, most Alsatian wines are bottled in the typical German bottle. Alsace is also an AOC wine region that is allowed to label its wines by the grape name. When the wines are labelled with a grape name, 100% of the wine is made from the corresponding varietal.

Other Wines

The norm in Alsace is to produce dry white wines; however, a small amount of red and rosé wine is made from the Pinot Noir varietal. Alsace winemakers also produce small amounts of sweet and sparkling wine.

The terms *vendage tardive* (vahn-DAHZH tahr-DEEV), which is French for "late harvest," and *selection de grains nobles* (made from Botrytis Cinerea) are used to represent the dessert wine produced in Alsace. These wines can be made only from the permitted Grand Cru grape varieties. Figure 9–5 shows a Vendage Tardive Alsace Grand Cru wine label from the famous Domaine Weinbach.

Alsace also produces *Crémant d'Alsace*, a sparkling wine made from the local grapes, mainly from Pinot Blanc, but also from Chardonnay, Riesling, Pinot Gris, or Pinot Noir. Alsatian sparkling is made in the traditional bottle-fermented method, which is the same method used in the production of Champagne.

FIGURE 9–5 Vendage Tardive Alsace Grand Cru
(Domaine Weinbach)

LOIRE VALLEY

The Loire Valley is one of the world's greatest white wine regions. The Loire River extends the length of the Loire Valley, from far west of the Atlantic Ocean, inward some 634 miles through central France. With over 125,000 acres of vines, Loire produces various styles of wine, such as sparkling wine, dry table wine, off-dry table wine, and sweet dessert wine.

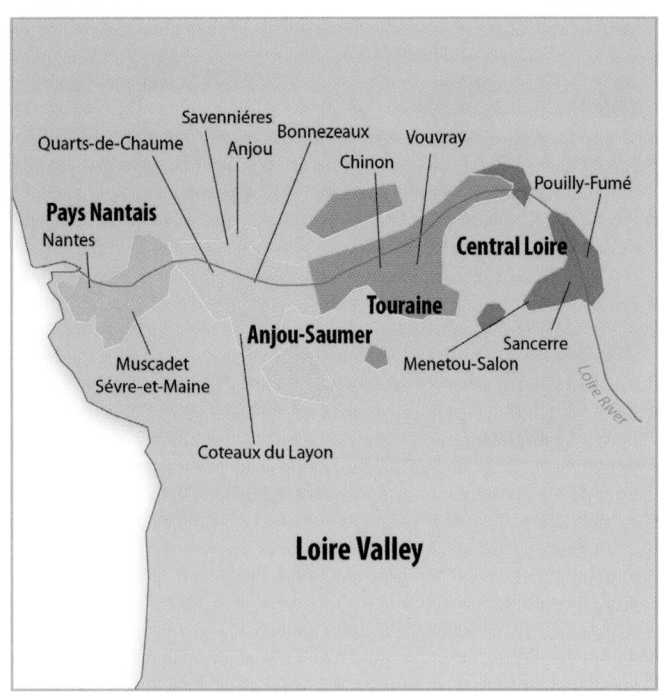

FIGURE 9–6 Map of Loire Valley
(Thomas Moore)

Figure 9–6 identifies the Loire Valley, France, and the significant wine regions.

Without the same level of prestige as that shared by other French wine regions, Loire has worked creatively to find notable ways to be recognized by the consumer. Some Loire winemakers have turned to organic or biodynamic farming and winemaking in order to add distinctiveness and marketability to their products. Nicolas Joly, a flourishing winemaker in the Loire, has often been referred to as "the father of biodynamics."

The Varietals

Loire is mostly known for its white wine grapes, Chenin Blanc, Sauvignon Blanc, and Muscadet, known locally as *Melon de Bourgogne* (meh-lohn duh boor-GAWN-yuh). But it also produces red wine from Cabernet Franc and Gamay varietals.

Wines are almost always unblended and are typically unoaked or lightly oaked. The philosophy of winemaking is to showcase the true nature of the grape, yielding its expression of terroir.

APPELLATIONS

The Loire Valley is divided into four main regions. Beginning at the east end heading west, they are (1) Central Loire, (2) Touraine, (3) Anjou-Saumer, and (4) Pays Nantais.

Central Loire—Unblended Sauvignon Blanc reaches its finest expression in the districts of *Sancerre* (sahn-SEHR) and *Pouilly-Fumé* (poo-YEE few-MAY). When Sauvignon Blanc is grown in this area, it is known as Blanc Fumé because of the smoky, or flintlike, aromas it possesses. Typically, Sancerre tends to be leaner than Pouilly-Fumé, but wines exhibit high acidity, with elements of mineral characteristics.

Other production areas of this region include *Menetou-Salon* (meh-neh-TOO sah-LOHN), *Quincy* (kan-SEE), and *Reuilly* (reuh-YEE), which produce other Sauvignon Blanc–based wines. Central Loire also produces red and rosé wines in Sancerre made from Pinot Noir and Gamay varietals. Figure 9–7 shows a Sancerre wine label.

Touraine (too-REHN)—The climate of Touraine offers good conditions for the cultivation of red and white wines. The best red wines are made from Cabernet Franc or Gamay in the distinguished production areas of *Chinon* (she-NYOHN) and *Bourgueil* (boor-GUH-yuh).

The most celebrated white wine in Touraine belongs to the *Vouvray* (voo-VRAY) appellation. Wines from Vouvray are produced from Chenin Blanc and made into many styles, from dry to sweet, from grapes affected by Botrytis Cinerea, as well as sparkling wines known as *Crémant d'Loire* (kray-mahn).

Anjou-Saumer (ahn-ZHOO soh-MYOOR)—The wine area of Anjou-Saumer produces a variety of styles. White wine is the most recognized, made from Chenin Blanc and produced in a dry style into a wine called *Savennières* (sa-veh-NYEHR).

Anjou-Saumer is also a famous area for the production of sweet wines. In favorable years, the development of Botrytis Cinerea produces a rich, luscious, concentrated flavor in the grapes. The best sweet wines are from the appellations of *Quarts de Chaume* (kahr duh SHOHM), *Bonnezeaux* (bawn-ZOH), and *Coteaux de Layon* (koh-toh deu leh-YAWN).

FIGURE 9–7 Bottle of Sancerre
(Kim Sayer © Dorling Kindersley)

Rosé d'Anjou (roh-ZAY dahn-ZHOO) and *Cabernet d'Anjou* (KA-behr-nay dahn-ZHOO) are pink wines produced from various red grapes such as Cabernet Franc, Malbec, Cabernet Sauvignon, and Gamay.

The Loire Valley's sparkling wine *Crémant de Loire* (kray-MAHN day LWAHR) is also produced in the Saumur area by the classic bottle-fermented method. These wines are made from Chenin Blanc, Chardonnay, or Cabernet Franc grapes.

Pays Nantais (pay-ee nahn-tay)—Located near the Atlantic Coast, Pays Nantais produces a prominent light dry white wine, sometimes with a light spritz, called *Muscadet* (muse-kah-DAY). Muscadet is named for the grape used to produce it rather than for its place of origin. Locally, the grape is called *Melon de Bourgogne* (meh-lohn duh boor-GAWN-yuh).

The best representation of this wine comes from the *Muscadet de Sèvre-et-Maine* area. Many producers age the wine on its lees by a method called Muscadet sur lie, which improves the wine by increasing the complexity and creating a full body.

BORDEAUX

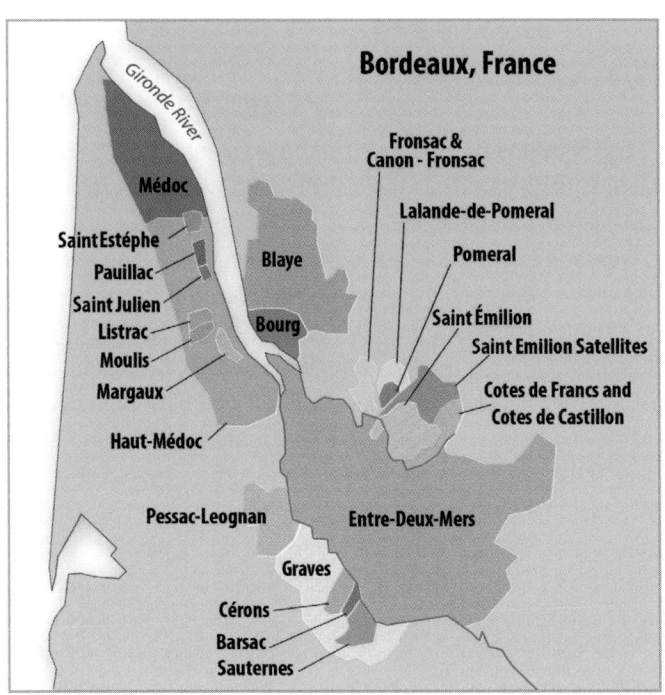

FIGURE 9–8 Map of Bordeaux
(Thomas Moore)

The Bordeaux region, located in western France, is naturally divided by the *Gironde* (zhee-RAWND) estuary and the *Garonne* (gah-RAHWN) and *Dordogne* Rivers into three broad zones with distinct geographical conditions. These zones form a left bank, a right bank, and an area between the banks to cover over 300,000 areas of vines. A variety of soils and maritime climate assist to provide wines with their unique character and connection to the land upon which their grapes are grown. Figure 9–8 identifies Bordeaux, France, and the major wine-producing areas.

This region produces some of the world's finest and most famous red, white, and dessert wines. *Bordeaux* has become synonymous with *quality* and *prestige* and is the source of the *chateau* concept (the French word for "castle," which has come to mean "wine estate"). Many of the world's most sought-after wines come from this region.

There are some everyday wines (vins de pays and vins de table) produced in the various locations of Bordeaux. The majority of the wines in the region are considered the best in the world and carry the *Premier Cru* designation. Wines in Bordeaux can be grouped into three appellation levels:

1. **Regional**—Bordeaux or labelled under a proprietary name, from a very generic, large appellation.
2. **District**—The district where the grapes were grown, such as Médoc or Entre-Deux-Mers. A fairly generic, but more specific, appellation designation than "regional."
3. **Village**—Where the vineyards are located, such as *Margaux* (mahr-GO), from a very specific point of appellation.

The "1855" Classification

In addition to their AOC rating, Bordeaux's thousands of acres are classified by the estate or chateau to which they belong. In 1855, several local wine merchants were commissioned by the Bordeaux Chamber of Commerce to group, or rank, the best estates (as opposed to

Burgundy, where they rank the vineyards) of Bordeaux for the upcoming World's Fair. Figure 9–9 shows a Chateau Lafite Rothschild wine bottle.

The ranking took into account the sales history of Médoc chateaux since 1755. The top 61 estates were categorized into five different classes, or levels, in descending order of quality from the highest growth, or cru, called first crus, down through the fifth cru. This ranking became known as the famous "1855 classification." Only one significant change has occurred (believed to be politically based) in the classification: the elevation of Château Mouton Rothschild from second growth to first growth in 1973.

The Varietals

Bordeaux is mostly known for its long-lived ageable red and dessert wines and, to a lesser extent, its dry white wine. Bordeaux wines are almost always blended from varying amounts of the following possible grapes:

> **White Bordeaux or Dessert Wine:** (1) Sauvignon Blanc, (2) Semillon, and (3) Muscadet (in small amounts)
> **Red Bordeaux:** Primarily from (1) Cabernet Sauvignon, (2) Merlot, (3) Cabernet Franc, and (4) others in smaller amounts (Petit Verdot, Malbec, and Carmenere)

APPELLATIONS

The Bordeaux wine region is distinguished by its defining *Gironde* (zhee-RAHWN) estuary, which naturally separates the area into a left bank and a right bank. Within this region are numerous AOC districts and villages, but the six most significant growing areas are Médoc/Haut-Médoc, Graves, Pessac-Léognan, Sauternes/Barsac, St Émilion, and Pomerol.

On the *Left Bank,* or west side, of the river, the gravelly soil is mixed with pebbles and sand due to its proximity to the Atlantic Ocean and clay farther away. This area enjoys slightly warmer air temperatures, and the soil remains warmer as well. These factors allow for more slowly developing Cabernet Sauvignon grapes to reach optimal ripeness. The vines are old, strong, and hearty, and they produce wines with enormous power and aging potential. The notable appellations are as follows:

Médoc (may-DAWK)—Wines from Médoc are red, primarily from Cabernet Sauvignon, Merlot, Malbec, Cabernet Franc, and Petite Verdot. The wines are full bodied and tannic when young and more balanced and elegant when matured. Significant village appellations from Médoc and, more specifically, surrounded by the Haut Médoc, include *Saint-Estèphe* (san teh-STEHF), *Pauillac* (poh-YAK), *Saint Julien* (san zhoo-LYAN), *Listrac* (lees-TRAHK), *Moulis* (moo-LEE), and *Margaux* (mahr-GOH).

Pessac-Léognan (peh-SAK leh-oh-NYAHN) and *Graves* (GRAHV)—These areas produce some red wines, but most of the region is famous for its dry whites and the sweet wines from the areas of *Sauternes* (soh-TEHRN) and *Barsac* (BAHR-sak). Red wines from Pessac Léognan have a powerful bouquet, and white Bordeaux typically is made as well. The red wines of Graves are basically equivalent to those in the Médoc. But generally, reds contain slightly lower amounts of Cabernet Sauvignon and higher amounts of Merlot, compared with the wines of the northern appellations.

In the southern section of Graves, some of the most famous sweet wines in the world can be found in *Sauternes* and surrounding areas of *Barsac, Bommes* (BOME), *Fargues* (far-GAY), and *Preignac* (pray-NYACK). Sweet wine production is particularly sensitive to climate influences. Most of these areas are clustered in areas prominent in autumn mists, on high-mineral-content soils. The sweet white wines are made with noble rot, also called *Botrytis Cinerea*, a desirable mold that pervades the grapes. The two most notable sweet

FIGURE 9–9 Chateau Lafite Rothschild—Pauillac
(SGM/Stock Connection)

wine producers are *Chateau d'Yquem* (shah-TOE dee-kehm) in Sauternes and *Chateau Climens* (sha-TOE klee-men) in Barsac.

On the *Right Bank,* cool air and soil temperatures from higher concentrations of wet, compact clay and limestone soil coordinate with faster-maturing Merlot and Cabernet Franc, which are more suited for these conditions. The wines are approachable and young (with some notable exceptions), compared with those of the Left Bank. The prominent appellations are as follows:

Pomerol (POAM-ehr-all) and *Saint-Émilion* (sahn-eh-meel-YOHN)—These districts produce only red wines and are focused primarily on Merlot and Cabernet Franc, with lesser amounts of Cabernet Sauvignon and Malbec. Pomerol tends to be more structured than Saint Émilion. Notable in Saint-Émilion are *Chateau Ausone* (shah-TOE ow-zo-ney) and *Cheval Blanc* (shuh-VAHL blohng), two of the greatest wines of the region.

Unlike the Médoc's 1855 classification, Saint-Émilion reclassifies its wines every decade. The first classification officially took place in 1955. More recent reclassifications occurred in 1996 and 2006. Saint Émilion historically revises its list, or *crus,* of its top châteauxs every 10 years to keep the region dynamic and competitive, particularly at the top levels. The 2006 classification is in a current state of flux. A handful of winemakers who had their wines demoted from the classification brought charges against the system. The courts have instilled a three-year holding period to revert all wines back to the previous 1996 classification until the case can be resolved.

The estates of Pomerol have never been officially classified as the other wine-growing areas have. Instead, the reputation of each producer is generally known and trusted.

In the *middle*—Between the Left and Right Banks is the large *Entre-Duex-Mers* (ahn-truh duh MERR) district. This district focuses on dry white wines made from the traditional Bordeaux white wine varietals.

BURGUNDY

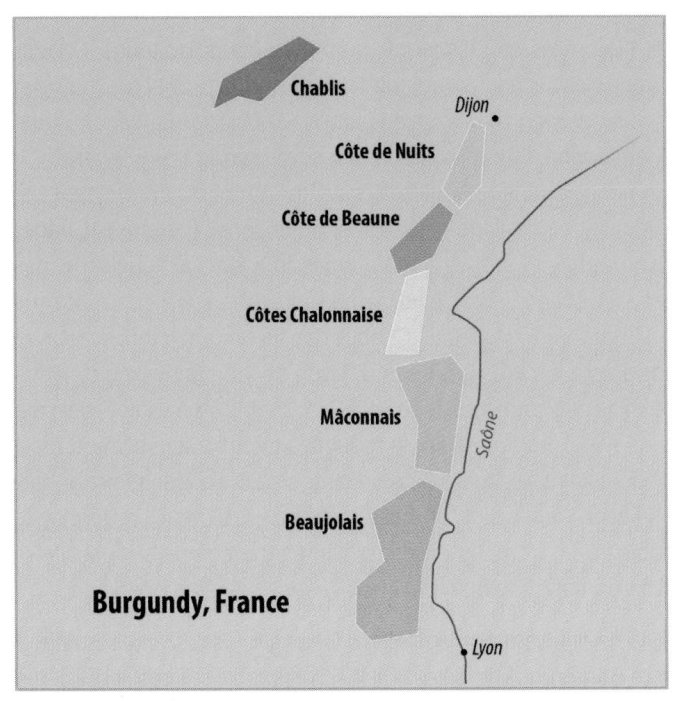

FIGURE 9–10 Map of Burgundy
(Thomas Moore)

Burgundy is one of the world's most famous wine-growing areas, located in Eastern France, southeast of Paris. Burgundy stretches from Dijon to Lyon, and the region is divided into five districts: Chablis, Côte d'Or (broken down into the Côte de Nuits and Côte de Beaune), Côte Chalonnaise, Mâconnais, and Beaujolais. The region consists of approximately 60,000 acres of vines that comprise over 100 Appellations d' Origine Controlee (AOC), or legally-defined producing areas—about twice as many as in Bordeaux. Figure 9–10 identifies the major wine regions of Burgundy, France.

Classification of Burgundian Wines

The combination of the end of the French Revolution in 1799 and the creation of the *Napoleonic Code* in 1804 removed the church from the vineyards and established that all heirs, regardless of age or gender, would share equal inheritance. This law has resulted in numerous individuals owning part of the famous vineyards in the Burgundy region. Historically, this movement led many vineyard owners to merely sell off their grapes to *négociants,* who would ferment and bottle their own wine. The situation is quite different from that in Bordeaux, where a single family or corporation owns each chateau.

In Burgundy, as in the rest of France, wines go by the name of the place they come from. In many ways, Burgundy is the most intensive *terroir*-oriented French wine region. In 1861, Burgundy classified its vineyards (in contrast to Bordeaux, which classified its estates). The top 33 Burgundy vineyards are classified as *Grand Crus*, and 570 are ranked second best, or *Premier Crus*. The vineyards are ranked according to several quality levels identified by level of specificity and quality of the appellation:

1. **Regional Wines,** or those labelled ***Bourgogne*** (BOR-gun-YAY)—These are made from grapes grown anywhere in the Burgundy region.
2. **Village**—These are wines with a hint of their origin (for example, Gevrey Chambertin or Puligny Montrachet). The village level can be thought of as a subregion.
3. **Premier Crus**—This labelling means "first-growth vineyards"; sometimes the term *1er Cru* may appear. The Premier crus are identified by the village name (for example, Gevrey-Chambertin), followed by the vineyard name, such as Clos Saint Jacque.
4. **Grand Cru**—Great-growth vineyards are wines that come from the best vineyards made in this region and are identified by the vineyard name alone (for example, Chambertin).

The Varietals

Burgundy maintains a continental climate that is best suited for cool-climate varietals such as Pinot Noir (known as Red Burgundy) and Chardonnay (known as White Burgundy). Farther south into Beaujolais, the soil and climate change and support a lesser-known Burgundian varietal known as Gamay.

APPELLATIONS

Chablis (shah-BLEE)—This is one of the five subregions and the northernmost part of Burgundy. It is located about 90 miles southwest of Paris (two hours by train). Chablis areas are ranked as one of four classifications ranging from *Grand Cru Chablis*, the most coveted, to *Premier Cru Chablis*, *Village Chablis*, and, finally, *Petit Chablis*, which is the most basic and simple of Chablis wines. Chablis is home to seven grand cru vineyards.

CHABLIS GRAND CRU VINEYARDS

1. Blanchot (blahn-SHOH)
2. Bougros (boo-GROH)
3. Grenouille (gruh-noo-yuh)
4. Les Clos (lay-KLOH)
5. Les Preuses (lay-PREWZ)
6. Valmur (vahl-MEWR)
7. Vaudesir (voh-day-ZEER)

About 100 years ago, American winemakers borrowed the French name *Chablis* to label their nondescript low-quality white wine. For some Americans, therefore, Chablis went on to mean inexpensive, slightly sweet wine that comes in a box, although this has changed over the last decade. Authentic Chablis is named after the town central to the region that specializes in the Chardonnay varietals. Chablis has its unique interpretation of Chardonnay, as it often yields a style of citrus aroma and flavor, dry and fairly acidic, with a flinty, mineral style (because of its clay and limestone soils). In Chablis, the wine is delicate in aroma and flavor; therefore, most producers apply reductive techniques in which most wines are fermented and aged in stainless steel vats or in large, older wooden tanks or barrels that impart a subtle oak flavor. Application of these techniques allows Chardonnay to truly express itself. The Chablis style, in many cases, is almost the complete opposite of Californian and Australian Chardonnay, in which the liberal use of oak aging pervades.

Côte d'Or (koht-d-OR)—The vineyards of the Côte d'Or begin just 30 miles south of Dijon at the northern section of Burgundy. The Côte d'Or (hills of gold) produces some of the best Pinot Noir and Chardonnay in the world. The region is further divided into the *Côte de Nuits* (koht duh NWEE) in the north and *Côte de Beaune* (koht duh BOHN) in the south.

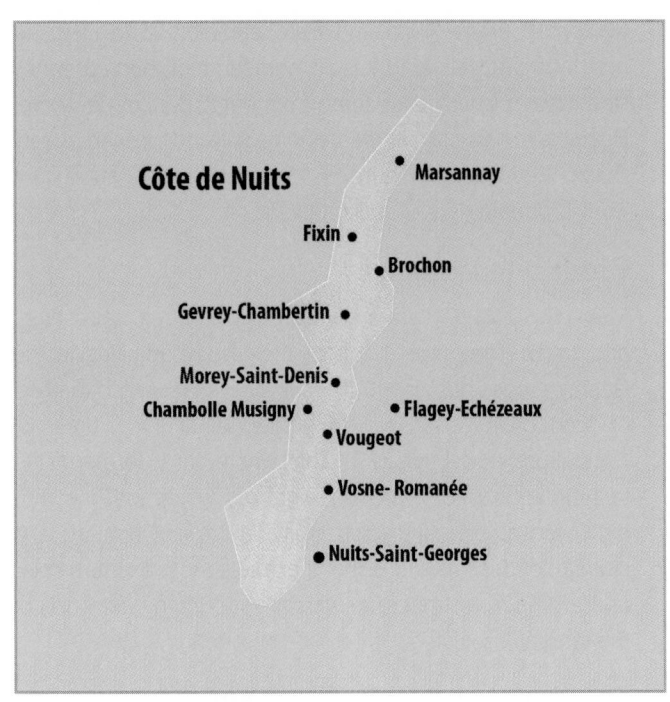

FIGURE 9–11 Map of Côte de Nuits
(Thomas Moore)

Côte de Nuits contains the highest-quality (firmest, longest lived) red Burgundy, but a small amount of excellent white Burgundy as well. It contains 24 out of the 25 red grand cru appellations.

Important Côte de Nuits villages that are surrounded by famous vineyards are as follows:: *Gevrey-Chambertin* (j hev-ray shahm-behr-TAN), *Morey-Saint-Denis* (maw-ree san duh-NEE), *Chambolle-Musigny* (shawm-bohl moo-sih-NYEE), *Vougeot* (voo-ZHOH), *Vosne-Romanée* (vohn raw-mah-NAY), and Nuits-Saint-George (nwee-san-ZHORZH). Figure 9–11 identifies the significant villages in Côte de Nuits.

Côte de Beaune (koht duh Bohn)—The Côte de Beaune area is located in the south of Côte d'Or and is considered the heart of White Burgundy country. This area is more diverse, offering great reds, but even greater legendary whites with a broader range of character and quality.

Important Côte de Beaune villages that are surrounded by famous vineyards are as follows: *Aloxe-Corton* (ah-lohx-kor-TAWN), *Beaune* (BONE), *Pommard* (pohm-MAHR), *Volnay* (vohl-NAY), *Meursault* (mehr-SO), *Puligny-Montrachet* (poo-lee-NYEE mohn-rah-SHAY), and *Chassagne-Montrachet* (shah-SAHN-nyah moan-rah-SHAY). Figure 9–12 identifies the significant villages in Côte de Beaune.

Côte Chalonnaise (koht shahl-oh-NEZ)—This subregion offers reasonably priced wines derived from Pinot Noir or Chardonnay. The wines can be compared to the wines produced from the Côte d'Or, but in minor-league versions. Some of the more notable wines from Chalonnaise consist mostly of grapes grown in vineyards on slopes or at higher elevation, from a collection of four smaller subdistricts: *Rully* (ru-YEE), *Mercury* (mer-cure-AY), *Givry* (gee-VREE), and *Montagny* (mon-tah-NYEE).

Mâconnaise (mah-kawn-NEH)—This large grape-growing area takes its name from the town of Macon (mah-KAWN). The climate becomes highly differentiated from the northern section of Burgundy and tends to produce less quality-oriented versions of Burgundian wines, but offers many affordable options.

White wine mostly made from Chardonnay or Aligoté yields the majority of production. Reds and rosés are made from the Pinot Noir and/or Gamay grapes. Several regional wines are produced, but also a few quality village wines, with their own appellations, such as *Pouilly Fuissé* (poo-YEE fwee-SAY) and *Saint Véran* (sahn-vay-RAHN). Both are known for producing Chardonnay wines of comparable style.

Beaujolais (BOE-zjoh-lay)—This region grows primarily the Gamay grapes (98%) rather than the Pinot Noir or Chardonnay grapes as in the rest of Burgundy. Beaujolais is located in the southern region of Burgundy. It is broken into

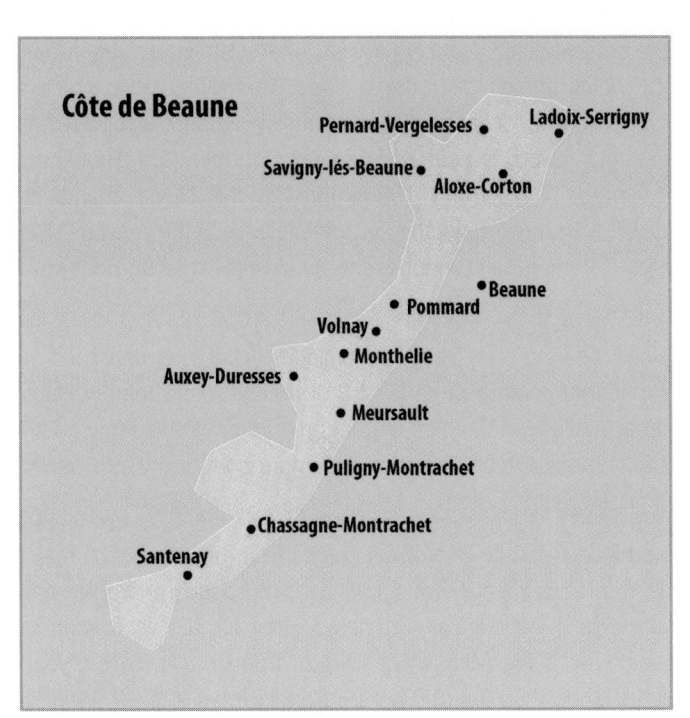

FIGURE 9–12 Map of Côte de Beaune
(Thomas Moore)

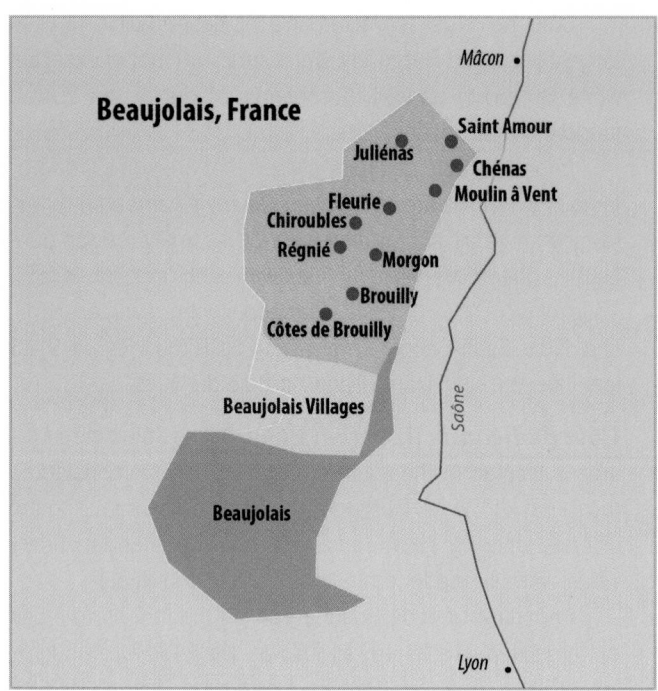

FIGURE 9–13 Map of Beaujolais
(Thomas Moore)

two broad areas: Haut and Bas Beaujolais. The Haut, or northern part, has granite soils and some of the best wines (the *crus* of Beaujolais) come from here. Bas, or southern, Beaujolais has clay and limestone soils for lesser quality (basic Beaujolais). Figure 9–13 identifies the significant wine-producing areas in Beaujolais.

Production Process

Many Beaujolais wines are inexpensive, young, refreshing, and fruity. They owe much of their fruity qualities to the Gamay grape, but also to the *carbonic maceration* method of production (discussed in greater detail in Chapter 3, "Viticulture and Enology"). This whole-berry fermentation technique is used to produce light red wines with low tannin, intense color, and fresh, fruity flavors and aromas. The strength of this method is that it extracts the maximum color and aroma from the grape without introducing as much of the tannin associated with other red wines.

Locations and Classifications

The 12 appellations of the region are divided into three categories, or levels of quality: Beaujolais (with Beaujolais Nouveau), Beaujolais Village, and the Crus of Beaujolais.

Beaujolais—The Gamay grapes produced here are grown in the southernmost region called Bas-Beaujolais. They produce very simple, flowery, and fruity wines that must be drunk young, as they are not intended for keeping.

Beaujolais Nouveau—The Gamay grapes produced are within the basic category and consist of about 50% of Beaujolais production. Young wines are produced in the Beaujolais region of France from the current year's Gamay harvest. After grapes have been harvested, they are fermented by the carbonic maceration method. The fermentation process takes about three to four days. The wine, only about nine weeks old when it is released, is full of the fresh, lively aromas and flavors of pear, cherries, and bubble gum. Beaujolais Nouveau shot to popularity in the 1970s and 1980s through the clever marketing approach of promoting the urge to "Come and get the first wine release of the season". The creator and promoter, Georges Duboeuf, still produces the most popular of all Beaujolais Nouveau wines.

Beaujolais-Villages—Wines bearing the Beaujolais-Villages label are restricted to being made from Gamay grapes that come from at least 2 of the 39 communes in Haut-Beaujolais and account for about a 25% of the total annual production of this region. Due to the better growing conditions, these are better wines with more complexity and depth. They can be kept from one to a few years.

Crus of Beaujolais—The highest-quality Beaujolais comes from one of the 10 major vineyard regions called *crus*. Each cru creates wine with its own special character and dimensions of aroma and flavor. The crus historically are named after villages with romantic-sounding names, such as Fleurie and Saint-Amour. The crus include *Brouilly* (BREW-yee), *Chenas* (shay-NAH), *Chiroubles* (shee-ROOB-luh), *Cote De Brouilly* (coat duh BREW-yee), *Fleurie* (FLUR-ee), *Julienas* (ZJOO-lee-ay-nah), *Morgan* (mor-GAHN), *Moulin à Vent* (MOO-lan ah vahn), *Régnié* (reh-N'YAY), and *Saint Amour* (sant ah-MOOR).

RHÔNE VALLEY

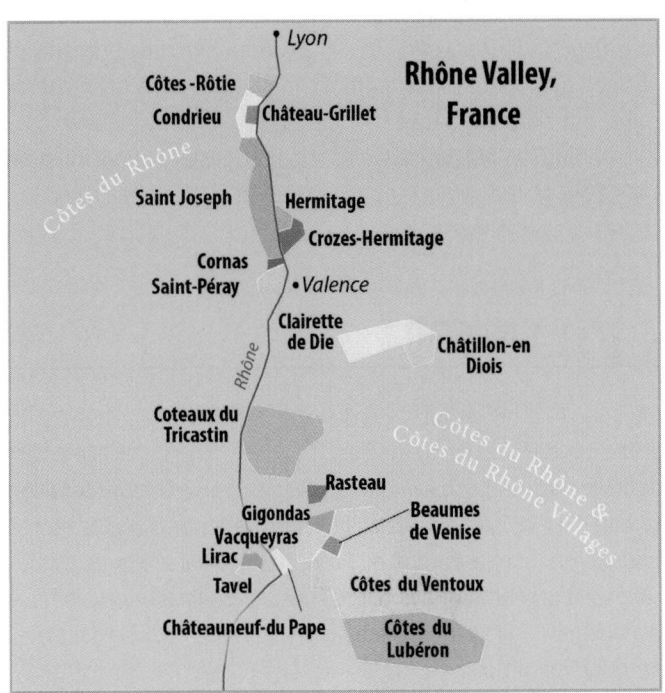

FIGURE 9–14 Map of Rhône Valley
(Thomas Moore)

Rhône is located in the southeast section of France, south of the Burgundy region. It is separated into two areas: the Northern Rhône and the Southern Rhône. While they both receive ample sunshine, the two are vastly different. The Northern Rhône terraine is steep and cooler, whereas the Southern Rhône is flatter, sunny, and warmer. The Rhône River runs southward for 120 miles through the valley, extending its way through vineyards. Nearly all Rhône wines are red (about 91%), followed by rosés and whites. Figure 9–14 shows the significant appellations in the Rhône Valley.

APPELLATIONS

Northern Rhône

Northern Rhône ranges from Lyon to the village of Valence. This northern section maintains a semi-continental climate and produces predominately single-variety red wines from *Syrah*, with small amounts of white wines from *Viognier* and others.

The classic wines of the northern Rhône reds are based on the Syrah grape in the renowned areas of *Côte Rôtie* (koht roh-TEE), *Hermitage* (her-mee-TAHZH), *Saint Joseph* (san zhoh-ZEHF), and *Crozes-Hermitage* (krawz her-mee-TAHZH). They can be cellared for as long as Bordeaux and sometimes continue to improve for decades.

White wines are based on a blend of *Viognier*, *Rousanne* (roo-SAHN), and *Marsanne* (mar-SAHN) grape varietals. Some of the red wine producers in the north use small amounts of these varietals to add fragrance and soften tannins in their wines.

The famous (but very rare) white wines of the region are from *Condrieu* (kawn-DREE-yuh), *Chateau Grillet* (sha-TOH gree-YEH), and *Saint-Péray* (san pay-REH).

Southern Rhône

Southern Rhône extends southward toward Avignon. The red wines of the southern Rhône tend to be blends of grapes dominated by Grenache, with smaller amounts of up to a dozen other red and white varieties. Some of the allowable blending varietals include Mourvèdre (moor-VEH-druh), Cinsault (SAN-soh), and Syrah.

Wines from anywhere in the northern or southern Rhône region can be labelled *Cotes-du-Rhône* (koht deu ROHN) or *Cotes du Rhône-Village* (coat-duh-RONE-vee-LAHJ). These are blended wines (with up to 13 permitted grape varieties) from anywhere in the region, but with a predominant Grenache base.

The most famous red wine appellation from the southern section is *Châteauneuf-du-Pape* (shah-toh-nuhf-doo-PAHP), or CDP. Predominantly, CDP is a red wine (a small amount of white wine can also be found) that is always blended, usually from a possible 13 different grapes, but dominated by Grenache, then Syrah, with smaller amounts of Mourvèdre, Cinsault, and others.

Châteauneuf-du-Pape means "Pope's new castle" and was named after the relocation of the Italian papal court to the French Rhone city, Avignon, in the fourteenth century to house the first French pope (Pope Clement V). Figure 9–15 depicts very old vines with rocky, stony soil.

FIGURE 9–15 Very old vines image
(Christophe Delorme)

Gigondas (zhee-gawn-DAH) is another southern Rhône appellation where Grenache with Syrah or Mourvèdre predominates, possibly along with a little of the 10 other allowable varietals.

Tavel (ta-VEHL) and *Lirac* (Lee-RACK) produce some of the most complex-tasting pink (or "rosé," as they say in French) wines in the world. This is a careful blending primarily of Grenache-based wine with a small amount of Cinsaut grapes that undergo partial maceration to gain pink color from the red-skinned grapes. According to French wine law, rosé wines may not be made from blending red and white wines together; instead, they must be made from the partial maceration of red wine grapes. Rosés of Tavel often produce medium-bodied wines with refreshing acid levels.

SOUTHERN FRANCE

Located in Southern France, these wine regions border the Mediterranean Sea with Languedoc-Roussillon to the west and Provence to the east. Southern France, is like a vast sea of drinkable, inexpensive, historical, and somewhat rustic wines. Languedoc-Roussillon is an enormous growing area with over 750,000 acres of vines; Provence has 50,000 acres of vines. Collectively, they produce about one-third of all French wine, but are largely categorized as either Vins de Table (DT) or Vins de Pays (DP). These classification levels have been somewhat appealing because they allow the winemakers the freedom to be quite creative and adaptable in their production processes.

APPELLATIONS

The Mediterranean climate is a key to the character of the grapes and wines of these regions. While it is hot and dry, with plenty of sunshine, the grape varieties planted must be quite hardy. When harvested, the grapes will be very ripe due to the existing climate.

Languedoc (lahng-DAWK)

The Languedoc wine region is the most extensive in France and represents 40% of the total France vineyard area. It produces the majority of France's table wines and Vin de Pays wines.

Languedoc produces about 90% of red table wine, with traditional varietals consisting of Carignan, Cinsaut, Grenache, Mourvèdre, Cabernet Sauvignon, and Merlot. The region is gradually losing its bulk-wine image, as many producers are incorporating greater amounts of the fashionable Syrah and Cabernet.

Coteaux de Languedoc—This large appellation contains several smaller wine-producing areas. Notable AOC appellations in Languedoc include *Corbieres* (coor-bee-EHR), *Fitou* (fit-OOH) and *Minervois* (mee-nehr-VWAH). Primarily, these red-wine-producing areas use partial carbonic maceration to preserve fruit and lessen the effects of tannin.

Roussillon (roo-see-YAWN)

Roussillon produces the majority of France's *Vin Doux Naturels* (or VDNs). VDNs are made by the addition of grape brandy to the wine during the fermentation process. The brandy kills the yeast activity and preserves the remaining sugar, yielding a sweet, fortified wine.

Two notable AOC appellations in Roussillon are *Côtes du Roussillon Village* and *Collioure* (kol-yoor).

Some Vin Doux Naturels (VDN) in southern France are *Banyuls* (bahn-YULES) and *Banyuls Grand Cru*. The latter is an appellation close to the Spanish border that produces France's famous red and white wine Vin Doux Naturels. The red wine is based on a minimum 50% Grenache, with the Grand Cru requiring 75%. *Maury* (moh-REE) produces both rosé and red Vin Doux Naturel from Grenache. *Rivesaltes* (reev-ZALT) produces red wine, mainly from Grenache, or white Vin Doux Naturel's from Muscat.

Provence (praw-VAHNSS)

The Provence region begins where the Rhône Valley has ended. Vineyards travel on hillsides and on flatlands exposed to extensive sunlight. Provence produces about half of the rosé wine made in France, and a majority of the wine made in Provence is rosé. The grapes predominately used in this region include Syrah, Grenache, Mourvèdre, Cinsault, and others.

Some AOC appellations in Provence are as follows:

Côtes de Provence (koht duh praw-VAHNSS)—Côtes de Provence is the largest area, a wide area covering the French Riviera from the cities of Marseille to Nice. This area is best known for its production of rosé wines, but red wines are also appealing, as they keep improving in quality.

Bandol (ban-DOAL)—Bandol is one of the best red wines from Provence. Mourvèdre grape is a strong base that contributes body and spice to any Bandol.

Bellet (behl-LAY)—This appellation maintains some of the smallest production (about 80 acres of vines) of wines throughout France, but offers whites, rosés, and red wines.

WINES OF FRANCE

NAME: _____ Score out of 20 points_____.

Use these questions to test your knowledge and understanding of the concepts presented in the chapter.

I. MULTIPLE CHOICE: Select the best possible answer from the options available.

1. The Côte d'Or is divided into
   a. Dijon and Lyon.
   b. Côte Chalonnaise and Mâconnaise.
   c. Côte de Nuits and Côte de Buenne.
   d. Médoc and Haut Médoc.

2. The best quality appellations in Beaujolais are designated as
   a. Beaujolais Nouveau.
   b. Gamay Beaujolais.
   c. Beaujolais Village.
   d. Crus of Beaujolais.

3. The most significant red wine grape in Northern Rhône is
   a. Gamay.
   b. Syrah.
   c. Cabernet Sauvignon.
   d. Grenache.

4. In the Loire Valley, the appellations of Sancerre and Pouilly-Fume are most famous for their white wine produced from which grape?
   a. Chardonnay
   b. Chenin Blanc
   c. Riesling
   d. Sauvignon Blanc

5. Sauternes is most famous for what style of wine?
   a. Dry white wine
   b. Dry red wine
   c. Sweet white wine
   d. Sweet red wine

6. The top rated vineyard in Burgundy is
   a. Grand cru.
   b. Clos.
   c. Commune.
   d. Premier crus.

7. The famous 1855 classification categorized the wines mostly of
   a. Médoc.
   b. Graves.
   c. Pomerol.
   d. Saint Émilion.

8. Alsace is unique in that it is the only AOC wine region that labels its wines with the
   a. vintage date.
   b. location.
   c. producer.
   d. varietal.

II. TRUE / FALSE: Circle the best possible answer.

9. Wines from Bordeaux are almost always blends. **True / False**

10. Burgundy is home of the famous Left and Right Banks. **True / False**

11. Alsace is known for its crisp, dry white wines. **True / False**

12. A white or red burgundy will come from anywhere in Burgundy. **True / False**

13. Chablis is known for producing full-bodied oaky Chardonnay. **True / False**

14. The Loire Valley is known for producing all different styles of wine, including dry white and red wines, dessert wines, and sparkling wines. **True / False**

15. Right Bank Bordeaux specializes in Merlot-dominated red wines. **True / False**

16. Beaujolais wines are generally made in a fruity, low-tannin style. **True / False**

17. Southern France collectively produces a large amount of Vins de Table (DT) or Vins de Pays (DP). **True / False**

18. Northern Rhône is noted for producing white and sparkling wines. **True / False**

19. The red wines of the southern Rhône tend to be blends of grapes dominated by Grenache, with smaller amounts of up to a dozen other red and white varieties. **True / False**

III. SHORT ANSWER ESSAY / DISCUSSION QUESTIONS: Use a separate sheet of paper if necessary.

20. Identify some reasons that can make French wine intimidating and challenging for the novice to the intermediate wine drinker.

10

Other Old World Wine Countries

Along with France, the countries of Italy, Germany, and Spain have nurtured and developed many of the vines and winemaking techniques that have formed the foundation of wine culture and enjoyment throughout the world.

LEARNING OBJECTIVES

Upon completion of this chapter, the learner will be able to:

- Understand the wine classification systems associated with Italy, Germany, and Spain.
- Comprehend the meaning of significant label terminology associated with Italy, Germany, and Spain.
- Discover Italy's, Germany's, and Spain's most significant wine regions with their corresponding grape varietals and wines.

ITALIAN WINES

FIGURE 10–1 Map of Italy
(Thomas Moore)

Inhabitants of Italy have been making wine for thousands of years. Today, Italy is one of the largest producers of wine in the world and yet, as a country, is only three-fourths the size of California. Italy is well suited for the vineyard, with over 80% of the land being mountains or hilly and having close proximity to the ocean. Figure 10–1 identifies Italy's 18 (out of 20) significant wine regions.

The vineyards throughout Italy have vastly different soils, altitudes, grape varieties, and climates. Italy's span is as far north as the Alps (bordering Austria, Switzerland, and France), which have a cool, alpine, continental climate, to the warmth of Southern Sicily (near North Africa), which has more of a Mediterranean-type climate. Overall, the soils can vary from volcanic, to limestone (or tufa), to clay.

There are over one million vineyards, 94 provinces, and 8,090 communes throughout Italy's 20 major wine-growing regions. Italy is one vast vineyard that produces a variety of grapes of both international and indigenous types. It has been noted that Italy has well over 400 authorized grape varieties. The abundance of grapes contributes to a huge range of flavor and style options, but also to confusion on the international markets.

Wine is produced throughout Italy, but many of the finest, best quality, and most prestigious wines come from the northern half. *Piedmont* is in the northwest, *Tuscany* is in the north–central, and *Veneto, Trentino* and *Alto-Adige* are the three regions in the northeast part (called Tre Venezie) of Italy.

In Italy, the culture of food and wine are inseparable. The wine and food have evolved together over thousands of years. An important feature that stands out in Italian wine is the preservation of the grapes' high acidity, with no excessive overt fruit or oak, making them very compatible with food.

Useful Italian Wine Label Terms

- **Bianco** (bee-ahn-koh)—"White," as in white wine in Italian.
- **Classico** (KLAH-see-ko)—The designation on a wine label indicating that the grapes and wine come from the original classic growing area rather than the expanded zone. Example: Chianti Classico as opposed to Chianti Rufina.
- **Passito** (pah-SEE-toh)—A dry or sweet wine made from partially dried grapes.
- **Ripasso** (ree-PAH-so)—A winemaking technique that allows a wine to remain in contact with the lees from a previous passito wine through re-fermentation.
- **Riserva** (Rih-ZERVA)—The designation on a wine label indicating that the wine has additional barrel aging, but the duration of aging varies by region. Example: Three years for Chianti Riserva, but five years for Barolo or Brunello Riserva.
- **Rosso** (RAWH-soh)—"Red," as in red wine in Italian.
- **Superiore** (soo-payr-YOH-reh)—The designation on a label indicating that the wine has a slightly higher alcohol content.
- **Vendemmia** (vayn-DAYM-myah)—Vintage or grape harvest.
- **Vino** (VEE-noh)—"Wine," in Italian.

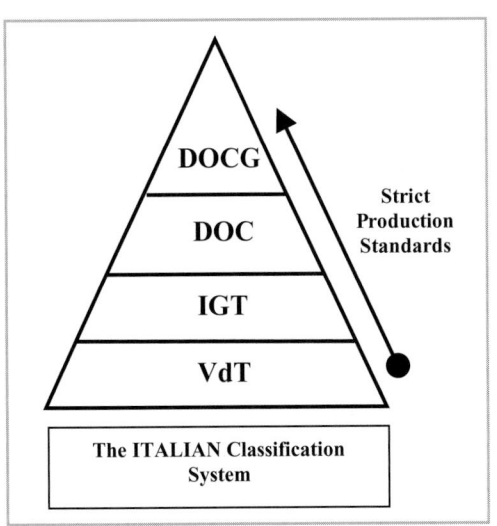

FIGURE 10-2 Italian wine classification
(John Laloganes)

Italian Classification System

Italy adopted a comprehensive, nationwide, regulatory quality-control system in 1963. The purpose of the Italian system is to regulate the production of wine, protect the defined wine zones, and guarantee the authenticity and consistency of style by defining boundaries, maximum yields, grape varieties, and production methods. Each wine-producing area is governed by the laws according to its quality level as granted by the Italian government.

The system was loosely modeled after the French AOC system; however, the Italian system has been highly criticized for its overgenerous awarding of high classification levels to wine areas that, arguably, are not necessarily deserving of it. Figure 10–2 illustrates the Italian wine classification system.

1. Denominazione d'Origine Controllata e Garantita (DOCG) (deh-NOH-mee-nah-SYAW-neh dee oh-REE-jee-neh con-traw-LAH-tah eh gah-rahn-TEE-tah)—Wines classified in this manner are produced according to the strictest standards of any of the other classification levels. Vineyard growing areas, yields, varietals, blends of varietals, and alcohol content are highly regulated.

The designation and regulations apply to all wines made from grapes grown in a designated region and must be approved by a government tasting panel. All wines at this category are given an identifiable paper strip just below the lip of each wine bottle.

There are approximately 32 DOCGs throughout Italy. On the left-hand side there is a list of the first wines granted the DOCG classification.

2. Denominazione d'Origine Controllata (DOC) (deh-NOH-mee-nah-TSYAW-neh dee oh-REE-jeh-neh con-traw-LAH-tah)—The second-highest classification level in the Italian system, this level requires that wines be produced with specific grape varietals in delimited geographical areas, by defined methods and quality standards in grape growing and wine production. There are approximately 350 DOCs throughout Italy.

3. Indicazione Geografica Tipica (IGT) (in-dee-kat-tsee-OH-nay jay-o-GRAF-ee-cah TEE-pee-cah)—This category was introduced in 1992 as a solution to the strict limited allowance for experimentation being required in the upper two levels of the Italian classification system. At this level, grape varietals can be identified on the label; however, specific places of origin are not allowed.

The regulations under this Italian quality level are often called the *Goria laws*, in reference to the Prime Minister Giovanni Goria. He designed this level to encourage Italian wine producers to still create wine within the existence of the Italian wine law system, yet have some flexibility to experiment. Some of Italy's most famous and prestigious wines are found at this level. *Sassicaia* (sahs-ih-KY-yah) and *Tignaello* (tig-ny-YEHL-low) are two examples.

4. Vino da Tavola (VdT) (VEE-no dah TAH-voh-lah)—The VdT designation is positioned at the lowest level, with the greatest amount of freedom. The producers are not allowed to label the grape varietal or specific location.

First Five Wine Areas Granted the Prestigious DOCG Classification

1. **Barolo** (bah-ROAL-oh)
2. **Barbaresco** (bah-BAHR-es-co)
3. **Chianti** (key-AHN-tee)
4. **Vino Nobile di Montepulcianocino** (VEE-no NO-bee-lay dee-MOHN-tay-POOL-chee-AHN-oh-CHEE-no)
5. **Brunello di Montalcino** (BROO-nel-oh dee MOHN-tahl-CHEE-no)

Major Wine-Producing Areas

Italy can be divided into four major wine areas, each containing several regions (communes), subregions (provinces), and appellations (zones) known for certain wines or features:

1. **Northwest Italy**—Sparkling wines and firmly structured red wines from indigenous grapes such as Barbera, Dolcetto, and Nebbiolo.

2. **Northeast Italy**—Mainly single-varietal white wines, often of French or German origin. However, there are some famous expressions of blended indigenous grape varietals and bold red wines from indigenous grape varietals (Corvina, Molinara, and Rondinella) made through the recioto process.
3. **Central Italy**—Premier red wines usually dominated by the Sangiovese grape varietal.
4. **Southern Italy and the Islands**—Rustic red wines made from a mix of different indigenous grape varietals, such as Aglianico, Primitivo, and others. In addition, the fortified wine Marsala is made in Southern Italy.

Northwest Italy

Northwest Italy encompasses the wine-producing areas of Piedmont, Lombardy, Liguria, and Emilia-Romagna.

Piedmont (PEED-mawnt)—Piedmont is located in Northwest Italy and remains one of the two greatest wine regions in the country. It has a high number of DOCGs, and while it is home to remarkable red wines, it also produces a range of wines (whites and sparklings) that are usually labelled with the varietal names and are frequently of great quality. The most important wine zones are centered near the towns of Asti and Alba.

Nebbiolo (neh-b'YOH-loh)   Barolo and Barbaresco are the two most famous and important appellations. The wines of the Nebbiolo grape ("nebbia" in Italian means "fog," and the grapes are so named because of the fog that rolls into the region) are intense, powerful, and, often, lightly colored wines. The common aromas and flavors include prune, tar, licorice, black cherry, and dried flowers. This grape is quite temperamental, low yielding, and late ripening. It also requires long aging to tame its fierce tannins. Even though Barolo and Barbaresco are made from the same grape, the grapes are grown in different microclimates and are processed differently. By law, Barolo must be aged a minimum of three years (at least two years spent in a barrel), and five years with a minimum increase in .5% of alcohol if labelled as a riserva. Barbaresco is aged two years (at least one year spent in a barrel), and four years with a minimum increase in .5% of alcohol if labelled as a riserva.

Other Good Nebbiolo-Based Wines—*Gattinara* (gah-tee-NAH-rah) and *Ghemme* (gehm-MEH) are both located in Northern Piedmont and offer reasonably priced alternatives to Barolo and Barbaresco. In Gattinara, the Nebbiolo grape is known locally as *Spanna* (spahn-NUH).

Other Wines Produced in Piedmont—Piedmont makes other very interesting red wines, and younger winemakers are experimenting with new oak barrels and other New World techniques.

Barbera (bar-BEHR-ah)   Along with Sangiovese, Barbera is the most widely planted grape in Italy. Barbera is significant in the towns of *Alba* (AHL-bah), *Asti* (AH-stee), and *Monferrato* (mohn-fayr-RAH-toh). The wines are labelled with the grape name first, followed by the growing area. For example, *Barbera d'Asti* is a wine produced from the Barbera grape derived from the town of Asti.

Dolcetto (dohl-CHET-toe)   This red wine grape varietal is significant in the town of Alba, where the wine is known as Dolcetto d'Alba. Similar to Barbera, the wine is labelled by grape name, followed by the growing area. For example, *Dolcetto d'Alba* is a wine produced from the Dolcetto grape that derived from the town of Alba.

Brachetto (brah-KAY-toh)   Brachetto is a red grape that makes either red table wine or the more common sparkling wine. It is most famous as a *frizzante* (lightly carbonated) red sparkling wine found as *Brachetto d'Acqui* (dah-KWEE) in the southeast portion of Piedmont.

White Wines Produced in Piedmont—The red wine in Piedmont seems to get all of the international attention; however, some appealing white and sparkling wines from local indigenous grapes can be found. The three most famous local white wine grapes are as follows:

Arneis (ahr-NAYZ), from the Roero area; *Cortese* (kohr-TAY-zee), from Gavi (also known as *Cortese di Gavi*; and *Moscato* (mo-SKAHT-oh), from Asti. Moscato (the local term for Muscat) is used to produce the very popular sparkling wines *Asti Spumante* (ahs-tee spoo-MAHN-tee) and *Moscato d'Asti* (moss-CAH-toe duh-AHS-tee). (The subject of the sparkling wines of Piedmont is expanded on in Chapter 11, "BUBBLES: Sparkling Wine.")

Lombardy (LOM-barh-dee)—Lombardy is located in Northern Italy near the Swiss border. This region contains two significant DOCG areas that it is most celebrated for: *Franciacorta* (frahn-chah-KOR-tah) and *Valtellina* (vahl-teh-LEE-nah). Franciacorta is noted for white wines from Pinot Bianco (the local term for Pinot Blanc) and spumante (the Italian term for "sparkling wine"). Valtellina is noted for its red wines, dominated by *Chiavennasca* (KEE-ah-VENN-eh-scah), the local term for the Nebbiolo grape.

Liguria (lee-GOOR-ee-ah)—The Liguria region stretches along the Mediterranean from the French border of Provence down toward Tuscany. Unofficially known as *the Italian Riviera*, Liguria is possibly more famous for its resort area than its wine.

Emilia-Romagna (eh-MEE-lyah raw-MAH-nyah)—Emilia-Romagna is located in North Central Italy just north of Tuscany. This region is home of the famous red frothy sparkling wine *Lambrusco* (lam-BROO-sko), also named after its grape. It has a red-cherrylike aroma and a flavor that is lightly sparkling and, usually, sweet; however, dry versions are made as well.

In Emilia-Romagna, the capital city is Bologna, the center of gastronomic activity, which is widely recognized for its foods such as Parmesan cheese and Parma hams.

Northeastern Italy

Northeastern Italy encompasses the wine-producing areas of Veneto, Friuli-Venezia Giulia, and Trentino Alto-Adige.

Veneto (VEH-neh-toh)   The Veneto is an extensive region of Northeastern Italy that borders Austria and Yugoslavia and includes the towns of Venice and Verona.

Soave (SWAH-vay)   This dry white wine, made from primarily the *Garganega* (gahr-gah-NEH-gah) varietal, is occasionally blended with a small amount of the Trebbiano grape. *Soave Classico* comes from the smaller, more defined, and original Soave-producing area.

Valpolicella (vahl-paw-lee-CHEHL-lah)   This wine is made from a blend of three indigenous grapes: *Corvina* (kor-VEEN-uh), *Rondinella* (rahn-dun-EHL-luh), and *Molinara* (mo-lin-ahr-uh). It is a fruity, medium- to full-bodied red wine with moderate tannins and aromas suggestive of cherries, chocolate, and a hint of almond.

Bardolino (bahr-doh-LEE-noh)   This wine is made with the same blend of grapes as Valpolicella, yet is a lighter-bodied version occasionally served chilled.

Recioto della Valpolicella (reh-CHAW-toh deh-lah vahl-paw-lee-CHEHL-lah) or **Recioto della Valpolicella Amarone** (am-ah-ROH-neh)   This wine is made from the same blend of grapes as in Valpolicella, but the grapes have been partially dried prior to fermentation. Drying the grapes prior to fermentation is known as the *passimento process* and is a technique that is used to increase the body and mouth feel of the wine.

As the wine goes through fermentation, if the yeast stops leaving residual sugar, the wine is a Recioto della Valpolicella, or simply, Recioto. If the yeast consumes all the grape sugar, yielding a bold, dry wine with relatively high alcohol of 15%–16%, the wine is referred to as Recioto della Valpolicella Amarone, or simply, Amarone.

Prosecco (praw-SEHK-koh)   Prosecco is produced in the northeastern part of Italy's Veneto region. It is a sparkling wine made from the grape of the same name. The charmant, or bulk, method is used to create the carbonation. The degree of effervescence is often indicated on the bottle, by either the term *spumante* (spoo-MAHN-tay), which indicates standard bubbles; *frizzante* (FRIZZ-zahn-tay), meaning light effervescence; or *frizzantino* (FRIZZ-zanh-tee-noh), signifying wine that is slightly sparkling.

Trentino-Alto-Adige (trehn-TEE-noh AHL-toh AH-dee-jay)—Trentino-Alto-Adige is Italy's northermost region and borders Germany, Austria, and Switzerland. Trentino-Alto-Adige is split into two provinces: (1) *Trentino*, around the city of Trento to the south and influenced by Italy, and (2) *Alto Adige*, around the city of Bolzano to the north (known as the South Tyrol), with a prominent German and Austrian influence.

The climate of Trentino-Alto-Adige is perfect for a variety of cool-weather white wine grapes, notably Chardonnay, Pinot Grigio, and Pinot Bianco, as well as sparkling wines. Farther south in the Trentino region, Cabernets and Merlots also do well.

The Alto-Adige, because of its history, is bilingual, and the German and Austrian influence is sometimes reflected on the selected grapes and the wine label. Many of the vineyards are located on steep hillsides, emphasizing quality. Approximately half of all wines produced in this area are given the DOC status (the highest number of DOCs of any Italian region).

Friulli-Venezia Giulia (free-OO-lee veh-NEHT-zee-ah JOO-lee-ah)—*Friulli*, as this wine region is called, is located in the northeast corner of Italy. It is known primarily for high-quality white wine varietals such as Pinot Grigio, Pinot Bianco, and also the red wine varietal Merlot. Wines usually are labelled according to their grape varietal.

Central Italy

This location encompasses the wine-producing areas of Tuscany, Marche, Umbria, Latium, and Abruzzi.

Tuscany (TUHS-kuh-nee)—The Tuscany region, located in Central Italy, is the home of the most famous of all Italian wine, *Chianti*. Most wines from Tuscany are red and based primarily on the Sangiovese grape, which is predominant throughout this region. Some of the most famous wines (named after their place), where Sangiovese is the principle varietal, are as follows: Chianti, Brunello (a clone of Sangiovese) di Montalcino, Vino Nobile di Montepulciano, and Carmignano. Also, Tuscany grows some Cabernet Sauvignon and Malvasia, which is the local white wine grape.

Chianti (kee-AHN-tee)   Chianti is a large wine zone located in Tuscany around the medieval cities of Florence and Sienna. The region of Chianti has been recognizable since the Middle Ages and is still currently the most famous.

Chianti is made primarily from the red sangiovese grape and historically has been made with smaller amounts of the white grape *Trebbiano* (treh-bee-AHN-oh) or *Malvasia*

(MAHL-vah-see-uh) varietals to lighten the wine. Most often, Chianti consists of between 75% and 100% Sangiovese and can be blended with up to 20% of Cabernet Sauvignon and/or Merlot.

Chianti is produced in one of the eight distinct, adjacent zones surrounded by the original core area *Chianti Classico* (KLAHS-see-koh). The zones are very similar to subdivisions within a neighborhood, with the most famous called *Chianti Classico* and *Chianti Rufina* (roo-FEEN-ah), which are commonly seen on labels and sold in restaurants and wine shops.

Chianti Classico is the most famous region in Tuscany because it is one of the first zones of Chianti, having been identified in 1716 and expanded in 1932. *Classicos* are made with good length, body, and complexity. If a bottle is labelled *Riserva*, it must have at least 12.5% alcohol and be aged for a minimum of three years and three months. Riservas are more full bodied than a typical Chianti Classico, often worthy of aging for years, and typically rank among the best red wines of Italy. A comparable (though slightly lighter) type of Chianti Classico is *Chianti Rufina* (key-ahn-tee roo-FEEN-ah).

Other Chianti districts include *Chianti Montalbano* (mahn-tehl-BAH-noh), *Chianti Colli Fiorentini* (KAWL-lee fee-or-ehn-TEE-nee), *Chianti Colli Senesi* (KAWL-lee sehn-AY-zee), *Chianti Colline Pisane* (KAWL-leen-ay pee-ZAH-nay), *Chianti Colli Aretini* (KAWL-lee Ahr-ehn-TEE-nee), and *Chianti Montespertoli* (mohnt-ehs-PEHR-tohl-ee). A wine produced from any of these subdistricts can be labelled by the specific name or can simply go by *Chianti*.

Super Tuscan Wine—One of the most revolutionary movements and defining moments in Italian wine history came from the rise of the *Super Tuscan Wines*, an unofficial name given to a certain category of wines. Officially, these wines fall under the Italian wine classification system at the IGT level. The wines were declassified from their DOCG status because they are made from non-traditional blends of the local Sangiovese grape, with varying amounts of international grapes such as Cabernet Sauvignon, Cabernet Franc, Syrah, or Merlot. The explosion of Super Tuscans was an obvious sign of innovation in Tuscany. The orginal and most notable wines are Sassicaia and Tignaello.

Sassicaia (sahs-see-KAH-yah)   A Cabernet-Sauvignon-based red wine with varying amounts of the local Sangiovese varietal. This wine has forever changed the landscape of Italian wines. Even though it originally was declassified (because the laws at the time did not permit the use of Cabernet Sauvignon) and given the lowest classification of VdT, it was one of the most expensive and critically acclaimed wines of Italy.

Tignanello (tee-nyah-NELL-oh)   Made in the Chianti region, Tignanello is named after the Tignanello vineyard operated by the well-known Antinori organization. Like Sassicaia, Tignanello had broken tradition and the legally allowable blending of grape varietals since its inception in 1971.

DOCG Chianti Alternatives—South of the Chianti zone is the town of Montalcino, which has become famous for its *Brunello di Montalcino* (broo-NELL-o dee mawn-tahl-CHEE-noh). The sloped vineyards are devoted entirely to the Sangiovese grape, known locally as *Brunello*. Brunellos produce rich and bold wines that have the ability to age for decades because of Montalcino's warm climate and quality-oriented growing and production methods. These wines are required to be aged for four years (with a minimum of two years in oak barrels), or five years for Riserva.

Rosso di Montalcino (RAWS-soh dee mawn-tahl-CHEE-noh)   A lighter version of Brunello di Montalcino, this wine is made from the same grapes from lesser vineyards and requires less aging, as it is intended to be consumed in its youth while waiting for the Brunello di Montalcino wines to evolve.

Vino Nobile di Montepulciano (VEE-noh NAW-bee-lay dee mawn-teh-pool-CHAH-noh)   This is an Italian red wine from the Tuscany region made from the *Prugnolo* (proo-NYO-loh) grape (the local term for Sangiovese). It is produceed in and around the town of Montepulciano.

Carmignano (car-mee-NYAH noh)   This is a small growing area just outside Florence. Its wine must be made from predominant Sangioves with between 10% and 20% of Cabernet Sauvignon and Cabernet Franc.

MARCHE (MAHR-kay)—Marche is an Italian wine region that is best known for its white wine produced from the *Verdicchio* (vehr-DEEK-kyoh) grape. It is a simple, dry white wine.

UMBRIA (OOM-bree-uh)—Located in Central Italy, Umbria is known for a mix of red and white wines primarily made from local grapes. The white wine *Orvieto* (ohr-vee-YAY-toh) is made primarily from Trebianno grapes, and the red wine *Sagrantino di Montefalco* is made from Sagrantino and Torgiano grapes.

LATIUM (LAH-tyum)—The Latium region is located on the western coast of Central Italy. It produces inexpensive, neutral white wine from the *Frascati* (frahs-KAHT-ee) area, made from the Trebbiano and Mavasia grapes.

ABRUZZI (ah-BROOD-dzee)—Abruzzi is located east of Rome on the coast of the Adriatic Sea. The main grape variety used for white wines is the Trebbiano (otherwise known as *Ugni Blanc* in France). Montepulciano is the main grape, followed by Sangiovese for red and rosé wines. *Montepulciano d'Abruzzo* (mawn-tay-pool-CHAH-noh dah-BROOD-dzoh) is made from the Montepulciano grape.

Southern Italy and the Islands

This region encompasses the wine-producing areas of Campania, Puglia, Basilicata, Sicily, and Sardinia.

Campania (kahm-PAH-nyah)—Campania is located near Naples along the eastern coast of Southern Italy. The most well known wine is from the area of *Taurasi* (tow-RAH-zee), produced with mostly the red wine grape *Aglianico* (ah-LYAH-nee-koh). This grape is sometimes called *Barolo of the South,* as it is known for its boldness, as is Barolo from the Piedmont region.

Basilicata (bah-zee-lee-KAH-tah)—Basilicata is located in Southern Italy. The notable wines are produced from the red wine grape Aglianico.

Puglia (POOL-yuh)—Puglia is located in the southeast section (the "heel") of Italy. The primary red grapes are Primitivo (the local name for the Zinfandel grape) and Negroamaro.

Sicily (SIHS-uh-lee)—Sicily is an island off the coast of Southern Italy and is one of the oldest most historic wine-producing regions in the world. Yet this region suffers in comparison with the wine quality of Northern Italy. Besides the region's economic disadvantages, the grape varietals are often obscure and the wines are not well publicized.

Nero d'Avola (neh-ROH dah-voe-lah), the most widely planted grape, historically has been used in blending, but is being featured more as a stand-alone varietal. More recently, this grape is being blended with the international varietals Merlot and Cabernet Sauvignon.

Sicily is historically known most for *Marsala* (mahr-SAH-lah), Italy's most famous fortified wine. Today, it is often relegated to the kitchen.

Sardinia (sahr-DIHN-ee-uh)—This island off the coast of Italy historically has been known for its Cannonau (cahn-AH-now) (otherwise known as Grenache in France and the U.S.) based red wines. Cannonau typically makes fleshy, heady, very fruity wines in their youth. They tend to age rapidly, showing tawny colors and being prone to oxidation or maderization after only a relatively short time in the bottle.

GERMAN WINE

FIGURE 10–3 Map of Germany

(Thomas Moore)

Germany is located in the heart of Europe and borders Denmark, Poland, the Czech Republic, Austria, Switzerland, France, Luxembourg, Belgium, and the Netherlands. It is one of the northernmost (and coolest) wine-producing countries in Europe. As a result, most of the 13 wine regions, or *Anbaugebiete* (AHN-bough-geh-BEET-eh), are concentrated in the southwestern part of Germany. Figure 10–3 is a map identifying the significant wine-growing regions of Germany.

Useful German Wine Label

Terms

- **Anbaugebiete** (AHN-bough-geh-BEET-eh)—Wine region
- **Einzellage** (INE-tsuh-lah-guh)—Vineyard
- **Halbtrocken** (HALP-trawk-en)—An off-dry wine that never contains more than 18 grams of residual sugar per liter
- **Rotwein** (RAWT-vine)—Red wine
- **Trocken** (TRAWK-en)—A dry wine without perceptible residual sweetness. The wine never contains more than 9 grams of residual sugar per liter.
- **Wein** (VINE)—Wine
- **Weinberg** (VINE-behrk)—Vineyard
- **Weingut** (VINE-goot)—Wine estate
- **Weiss** (VICE)—White
- **Weissherbst** (VICE-hehrbst)—Rosé wine

German Classification System

The wine laws of Germany establish four levels of classification for their wines, starting with the strictest level of standards first. Figure 10–4 illustrates the German wine classification system.

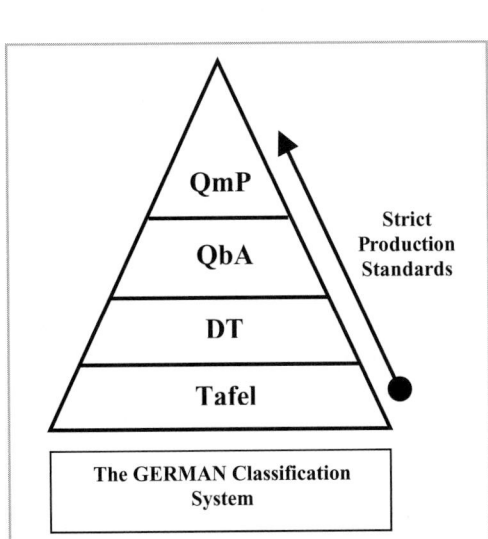

FIGURE 10–4 German wine classification

1. **Qualitätswein mit prädikat** (kvah-lee-TAYTS-vine meet PRAY-dee-kaht)—Often referred to as the *prädikat wines* or QmP for short, these wines make up the top level of German wine classification. The term "Qualitätswein mit prädikat" translates to "quality wine with special attributes." The growing of grapes and production of wine are held to a specific set of standards based upon the particular growing region. The wine must be made from its own natural grape sugar (with no chaptalization) or with the addition of the *süssreserve* (ZOOSS-ray-ZEHR-veh).

2. **Qualitätswein Bestimmter Anbaugebiete** (or QbA) (kvah-lee-TAYTS-vine buh-SHTIMM-ter AHN-bow-gah-BEET-eh)—This term translates to "quality wine." Wine that is classified into this category has come from one of the 13 approved wine regions and from approved grapes. The wine must have a minimum of 7.5% alcohol, and the winemakers are allowed to chaptalize their wines in order to increase sugar content.

3. **Deutscher Tafelwein** (DOY-cher TAH-fel-vine)—This wine is consumed mostly locally and is seldom exported. A wine labelled *Deutscher Tafelwein* (DTW) is a table wine of German origin.

4. Tafelwein (tah-fel-vine)—The lowest of the quality levels, with the least restrictions. If a wine is labelled simply as *tafelwein,* it may not be of German origin.

The Sussreserve

The way that the Germans devised to maintain some sweetness in their wine is known as the *süssreserve*. This method involves fermenting the wines fully dry, with low alcohol and high acid. Before fermentation, a small quantity of unfermented juice is held back. Later, this juice will be blended into the dry wine in order to adjust and balance the acid-to-sweetness ratio.

Label Indicators of Grape Ripeness

The grapes obtain greater ripeness by being harvested later (because they spend a longer time in the sun). These ripeness levels directly determine the natural sweetness of the grapes and the ultimate cost of the wine. At the prädikat quality level, all grapes must develop their own natural sugar content throughout the growing process, and no wine is allowed to be chaptalized, but the sussreserve is acceptable.

The sugar levels in the wine are ranked according to the *Oechsle* (UHX-leh) method at harvest. This method was devised by Christian Ferdinand Oechsle. The oechsle system maintains separate ripeness standards, depending on grape variety and region. The higher the ripeness of the grapes, the higher the wine will be categorized. The level will also translate to a wine that has a fuller body (from greater sugar) and higher concentration. The categories do not reflect whether the wine is sweet or dry; ultimately, the winemaker decides the style of the wine according to when fermentation is halted.

A wine eventually will be a sweeter style if the fermentation is interrupted before all sugar is converted into alcohol, therefore leaving residual sugar in the wine. If the fermentation continues until little or no sugar is left, the wine will be dry. Grapes for dessert wines (the Auslese level and above) have so much natural sugar that they often will not ferment completely (because most yeast strains die off at around 15% alcohol) and residual sugar (sweetness) will remain.

Generally speaking, the riper the grape or classification, the sweeter, more concentrated, and more expensive the wine will be. At the lower ripeness or sugar content level of the grapes, beginning at the Kabinett level, and as the grapes contain more sugar, they are placed in different categories, ascending toward the highest level of a TBA level. Figure 10–5 shows the graduating staircase of grape ripeness for the prädikat level of German wines.

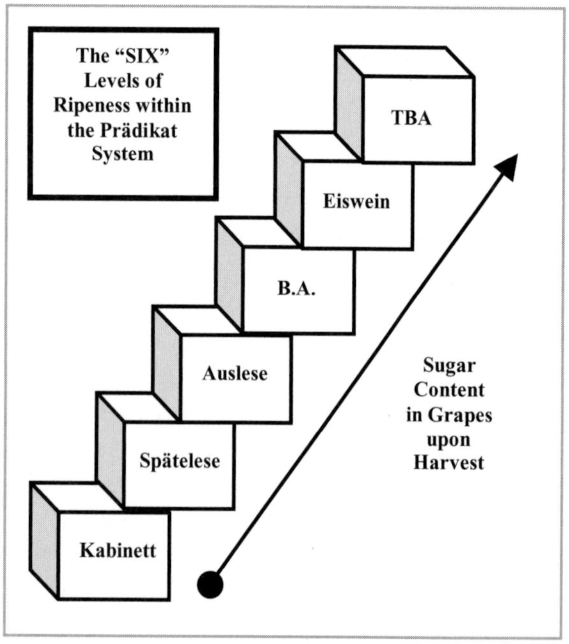

Kabinett (kah-bih-NEHT)—Usually light (low alcohol that often hovers around 8.5% or 9%), these dry-to-sweet wines are made of grapes ripened at normal harvest. They usually have a delicate stucture and contain some minerality. Kabinetts often contain high malic acids, leaving an aroma and taste of tart green apples. They sometimes are spritzy with tiny bubbles from a touch of undissolved CO_2.

Spätlese (SHPAYT-lay-zuh)—These are *late harvest* wines made from very ripe grapes picked after the normal harvest. The later harvest lets the grapes dry and ripen on sunny autumn days, which increases the intensity of the fruit and the flavors. These wines are intense in flavor and concentration, which makes them compatible with richer food.

FIGURE 10–5 "Prädikat" Ripeness Scale
(John Laloganes)

Spätlese wines can range from dry to sweet. A good indication is the level of alcohol. If the alcohol is higher, the wine may be drier. If the alcohol is lower, there is a greater chance that the wine has considerable residual sugar.

Auslese (OWS-lay-zuh)—*Select picking* refers to selective hand harvesting of extremely ripe bunches of grapes, often with a touch of noble rot (called *Edelfaule* (ay-duhl-FOY-luh) in German). These wines are intense in bouquet and taste and usually are sweet (although dry versions can also be found).

Beerenauslese (BA) (BEHR-ehn-OWS-lay-zuh)—BA is the German term for *select berries* that have been hand picked. BA is a rich, sweet dessert wine made of overripe, shriveled berries that are almost always affected by noble rot. The noble rot causes the water content in the grape to diminish and, therefore, all the flavors to be concentrated.

Eiswein (ICE-vine)—These wines are of at least BA sweetness intensity and have been made from grapes harvested and pressed while frozen. This is a unique wine with a highly concentrated aroma and intense fruit, acidity, and sweetness.

The production of Eiswein involves freezing the grapes on the vine at 32°F well into the winter time. During the process, the water inside the grapes freezes, but not the other components, of which sugar is the largest. When the grapes are crushed, the frozen water is not pressed out, but only the luscious, viscous, sugary nectar of the grape juice. Through this process, the water has been extracted from the juice, which doubles in sugar and acid and is highly concentrated in flavor.

Trockenbeerenauslese (TBA) (TRAWK-uhn-BEHR-en-OWS-lay-zuh)—TBA is the German term for *dry select berries* that are harvested individually. TBA berries have been affected with *Botrytis cinerea*, a fungus that causes them to dry up on the vine. These wines are rich, sweet, luscious, and honeylike in flavor and aroma.

The Varietals

Germany is located in the far northerly climate for grape growing. Because of the cool continental climate (except in small pockets), red wine grapes do not flourish to the degree that white wine grapes do. Therefore, the majority of wine produced derives from white wine varietals, predominately Riesling. Other white wine grapes include: *Müller-Thurgau* (MOO-lehr TOOR-gow), *Silvaner* (sihl-VAH-ner), Kerner, Gewürztraminer, *Grauburgunder* (GROUW-buhr-gunder) or Rulander (otherwise known as Pinot Gris), and *Weissburgunder* (VICE-buhr-goon-dair) (also known as Pinot Blanc) all prevalent grape varietals found throughout Germany.

A small fraction of red wine grapes are grown in Germany. The most notable is the up-and-coming *Spätburgunder* (SHPAYT-buhr-gunder) (also known as Pinot Noir), leading the way for red grapes.

Germany's marginal climate has led winemakers to cross-breed many grapes. Some reasons crosses are created is to allow the grapes to become late budding or early ripening, produce a higher yield, or of better disease resistance. Some popular German crosses and hybrids include Kerner, Muller-Thurgau, and many more white and red varietals.

Appellations

Many of the famous vineyards are established along the Mosel and Rhine Rivers and their tributaries. The tempering influence of the rivers allows high-quality wine grapes to grow this far north. Germany's unique microclimate creates a long growing season that allows the flavors within the grapes to mature slowly, the sugars to develop, and, yet, the acids to remain high. The harvest may take several weeks because the grapes rarely ripen in unison and therefore are harvested at different times.

FIGURE 10–6 Vineyards of the Mosel
(German Wine Institute)

Mosel-Saar-Ruwer (MOH-zel sahr ROO-vayr)— The Mosel-Saar-Ruwer arguably is Germany's most famous wine-growing region. The Mosel River is the spine of the Mosel-Saar-Ruwer wine region, and the vineyards extend along the two small tributaries, the *Saar* and the *Ruwer*. The grapes are grown on steep hillsides (sometimes on 70-degree inclines) along the steep river banks. The Mosel region is widely known for its unique *slate* soil type that imparts a distinctive taste ranging from fruity to earthy, or *flinty*, sometimes with a hint of effervescence. Figure 10–6 shows the Mosel-Saar-Ruwer growing area.

The wines of the Mosel-Saar-Ruwer are nearly all from the Riesling grape, which makes a range of products, from light, richly fragrant wines to famous honeyed dessert wines. All of them are united by crisp acidity and generally low alcohol content. Other good wines are made from Gewürztraminer, Pinot Gris, Pinot Noir, Sylvaner, Müller-Thurgau, and several other grapes.

While some of the wines from the famous vineyards of the middle Mosel district can come with very high price tags, the best values often are from the upper and lower regions that lay claim to some excellent wines at fairly reasonable prices.

Rheingau (RINE-gauw)—Rheingau is arguably the second most famous wine-growing region in Germany and home to some of the world's oldest wine-growing families. According to the Wines of Germany trade group, of the small amount of vineyards that Rheingau maintains (7,500 acres), about 80% of it is ranked at the QmP level. This makes Rheingau more focused on overall quality than any other German wine region.

The region of Rheingau is one long hillside moving from east to west. The fairly flat, dimpled landscape evolves into progressively steep slopes bordered by the Taunus forest to the north and the Rhine river to the south. The southern-facing exposure, moisture from the river, the large amount of clay in the soil, and the Mediterranean-type climate combine to produce densely rich-flavored wines.

The popularity of this region's wines has driven prices upward; however, good values are still to be found if one seeks out the smaller producers. The main grapes are from the Riesling grape varietal, which yields elegant wines with a fruity aroma, pronounced acidity, and concentrated flavor. In addition to Riesling, a small amount of red wine is produced from the Spätburgunder varietal.

Vineyard Classification

Since 1994, the Rheingau was the first German region to have a semi-official vineyard classification, drawn up by the Charta (KART-ah) organization and the Verband Deutscher Pradikats (VdP Rheingau).

The best sites are allowed to carry the designation *Erstes Gewächs* (AYR-stess GUH-vehks), or first-growth vineyards. The use of this designation is optional, and the wine has to meet several criteria, such as the following: The wine must be made in dry style or at least in an Auslese, the grapes must be hand picked, and traditional techniques of winemaking must be used.

Rheinhessen (RINE-hehs-uhn)—Deep within a valley of gently rolling hills, bordered by the Nahe and Rhine Rivers, lies the region of Rheinhessen. This is the largest German wine-growing region, with over 63,000 acres of vines. In this land of varying climates and geography, many different types of grapes, both red and white varieties, are planted, producing wine that is delicately fragrant and fuller bodied than wine of the other regions, because Rheinhessen maintains a slightly warmer climate.

The rolling hills, varied soils, and favorable climate make it possible to grow many different grape varieties, both red and white. Silvaner is the predominant grape.

Rheinhessen is the birthplace of *Liebfraumilch* (LEEB-Frouw-MILCH), originally made from grapes grown in vineyards surrounding the Liebfrauenkirche. This wine is one of Germany's biggest exports to the United Kingdom and the United States. Liebfraumilch can originate from any of four wine regions: Nahe, Rheingau, Rheinhessen, or Faultz. The grape is dominately Muller Thurgau, and the wine is engineered to be sweet, with no true sense of place or personality.

Rheinhessen wines are often characterized as being soft, fragrant, medium-bodied, mild in acidity, and easy to drink.

Pfalz (FAHLTS) (Formerly known as Rheinpfalz)—Bordered by Rheinhessen on the north and France on the south and west, Pfalz is Germany's second-largest wine region in acreage, but often has the largest crop of all. Pfalz is second only to the Mosel in acreage planted with the Riesling grape. Here, it yields wines of substance and finesse, with a less sharp acidity than in Mosel.

The region boasts many small producers whose commitment to quality is beginning to renew the region's reputation for producing excellent wines. It has recently begun a trend back toward low-yielding high-quality vines.

Baden (BAH-den)—In this southernmost wine region of Germany, the famed *Black Forest* region of Baden is Germany's third-largest wine region, with over 65% of the wines ranked at the QmP level of quality. It is primarily a long, slim strip of vineyards nestled between the hills of the Black Forest and the Rhine River.

Baden's different soil types (gravel, limestone, and clay, to volcanic stone), combined with its warm climate, contribute to its multitude of different grape varieties. Nearly half of the vineyards are planted with Burgunder (Pinot) varieties:

Nahe (NAH-huh)—The Nahe River lends its name to one of Germany's dynamic wine regions. Bordered by Mosel to the west and Rheingau to the north, Nahe has diverse soils of slate, sandstone, clay, and loam. The region recently underwent a classification of its top vineyards. The designation given to the best sites is *Grosses Gewichs*, meaning "great growth." The wines given this designation must (1) come from the designated vineyard, (2) be of the Riesling grape varietal, (3) be made from grapes picked when the level of ripeness is high, and (4) be aged on the lees.

SPAIN

Spain has a long history of winemaking, possibly reaching as far back as 3,000 years. This country maintains more vineyards than any other country in the world, yet is only the third-largest wine producer (after Italy and France). This disparity exists because of the overall dry, warm air that reduces vineyard yields. Ever since the 1980s, Spain has been undergoing an economic revolution and has been in the process of rediscovering itself economically, culturally, and socially. Spain's renaissance has influenced technology in the vineyards, the winery, and the overall wine quality. New producers and labels are appearing annually, and great strides in quality and consistency are being made throughout the country. Figure 10–7 identifies Spain's significant wine-growing areas.

FIGURE 10–7 Map of Spain
(Thomas Moore)

Spain is located just south of the *Pyrenees* (pear-ah-nees) *Mountains* and contains two significant rivers, the Ebro and Duero, which maintain vineyards along their banks.

Traditionally, Spain has distinguished itself mostly for its red wines from *Rioja* (ree-OH-hah); fortified *sherry* wines from Andalusia (ahn-dah-loose-EE-yah); and *Cava* (CAH-vah), Spain's sparkling wine primarily from Penedes (pay-NAY-dayss) in the Catalonia/Barcelona area. More recently, the world is becoming aware of Spain's vast offering of every wine option imaginable due to its diverse climate and varying soil types. In addition to Spanish sparkling and fortified wine, Spain produces ranges of light crisp whites, to full-bodied whites and fruity rosés, to full-bodied red wines and more.

Local grape varietals such as Tempranillo and Garnacha (otherwise known as Grenache) are used predominantly for the red wines. Tempranillo is the most significant grape grown throughout Spain. It appears on many of the DO's/DOCa's by different names, showing many different expressions based on location.

The Spaniards classically have maintained a fondness for older, aged wines. Since the 1980s, groups of young, maverick winemakers have contributed an influx of new, more contemporary philosophies about, and techniques for, grape growing and winemaking. It appears that Spanish producers carry on two philosophies: The traditionalists practice longer oak barrel aging, where the emphasis is on oxidative qualities within the wine. The other perspective is one associated with the modernist style. This style emphasizes less aging and greater preservation of fruit.

Useful Spanish Wine Label

Term

- **Blanco** (BLAHNG-koh)—Refers to a white wine
- **Bodega** (boh-DAY-gah)—A generic term for a Spanish winery or wine cellar
- **Cosecha** (koh-say-chah)—Harvest or vintage
- **Doble Pasta** (DOH-blay PAHSS-tah)—A wine made with the addtion of grape skins to a fermenting wine. This technique adds heightened structure and body to a wine. Doble Pasta is similar to Italy's ripasso method.
- **Generoso** (heh-neh-ROH-soh)—A dry or sweet wine with high alcohol of 15% or more.
- **Pago** (PAH-go)—A classification created in 2003 to represent a single vineyard estate that performs all grape growing, winemaking, and bottling on the premises
- **Rancio** (RAHN-thyoh)—A fortified wine that has been deliberately oxidized or maderized
- **Rosado** (roe-SAH-do)—Refers to a rosé wine, made by allowing the juice to have only brief contact with the skin of the red wine grapes
- **Tinto** (TEEN-toe)—Referring to a red wine
- **Vendimia** (vayn-DEE-myah)—Vintage or grape harvest
- **Vino Joven** (VEE-no HOE-ven)—Young wine

Spanish Classification System

The Spanish government's Instituto Nacional de Denominaciones de Origen (INDO) (equivalent to France's INAO) guarantees the authenticity of its wine by designating each with a

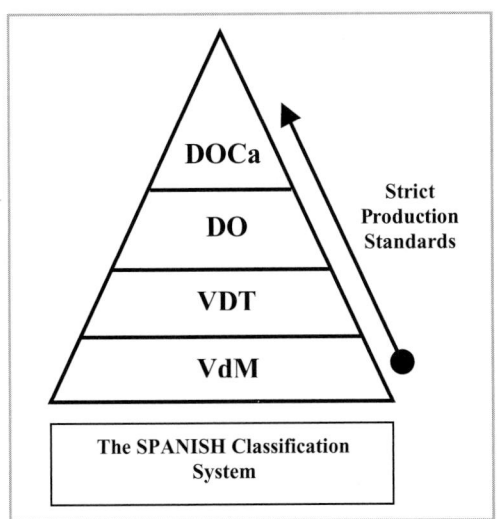

FIGURE 10–8 Spanish wine classification system

(John Laloganes)

region classification. The system is similar to those of France, Italy, and Germany, which divides the wine into two levels: quality wines and table wines.

The *quality wines* are required to maintain stricter standards and are equivalent to France's AOC and VDQS. The quality wines are classified according to a DO or a DOCa, in which each one is overseen by a *consejo regulador* (cohn-SAY-ho ray-goo-lah-DOOR), or administrative body. These agents ensure that each bodega acts in accordance with the individual DO quality requirements such as yield per hectare, aging requirements, and so on. Each individual consejo regulador within each DO/DOCa region issues *contraetiquetas* (con-trah-ett-ee-kAY-tahs), or back labels, as a stamp of approval.

At the *table wine* level, the standards are much looser and allow for more freedom with grape growing and winemaking. The table wine levels are comparible to France's Vin de Pays classification. Figure 10–8 illustrates the Spanish wine classification system.

Denominacion de Origen Calificada (DOCa) (deh-naw-mee-nah-THYON deh aw-REE-hen kah-lee-fee-KAH-dah)   This category is designed for winemakers that have a long, established track record of producing quality wines. Wines deserving this designation are produced in particular geographical areas by defined methods and quality standards in grape and wine production. As of 2008, there are 2 DOCas throughout Spain. The first DOCa was granted to the Rioja area in 1991 and Priorat in 2004.

Denominacion de Origen (DO) (deh-naw-mee-nah-THYON deh aw-REE-hen)   This category is the second level down from the DOCa. Wines are required to be produced in particular geographical areas according to defined methods and quality standards in grape and wine production. As of 2008, there are 65 DOs throughout Spain and constantly growing.

Vino de la Tierra (VdT) (VEE-noh day lah TYEHR-ah)   These are country wines with a hint of local origin. Their producers are allowed to use regional geographical names on the label.

Vino de Mesa (VdM) (VEE-noh day MAY-sah)   This is ordinary table wine made in bulk production from grapes that originate in a wide variety of regions. There is no designated vintage or location of origin identified on the label.

Major Wine-Producing Areas

As of 2008, there are 67 DOs and DOCas throughout Spain, and the number is constantly growing. Listed next are some significant DOs and DOCas that are becoming more available and popular in the marketplace.

Northwest Spain

Galicia (gah-LEE-thee-ah) and the Basque Country

Galicia is also known as *Green Spain*, which makes reference to its cool and misty climate with lush vegetation. Galicia's DOs include Rias Biaxes, Ribeiro, Ribeira Sacra, and Valdeorras, among others.

Most of Galicia's DOs rely heavily on indigenous white wine grapes, such as Albarino, Treixadura, Loureira, and Torrontes.

Rias Baixas (REE-ahs BY-shehs)—Rias Baixas is located in the northwest corner of Spain, just above Portugal. The cool, moist, maritime climate lends itself to aromatic white wine varieties. Eleven grape varietals are allowed in this DO, but about 90% of plantings are devoted to the Albariño (ahl-bah-REE-nyoh) grape varietals. This thick-skinned white wine grape is grown throughout Galicia and also is the dominant varietal in *Vinho Verde* wine, produced in neighboring Portugal.

Basque Country (Bask)—Basque Country is primarily known for producing a youthful, white, fresh wine known as Txakolina (Cha-co-LEE-nah). It is produced from an indigenous, aromatic, white wine varietal, Hondarribi Zuri (hahn-dur-ah-bee zoowr-ee), which comprises the majority of the plantings.

Northeast Spain

(The Mediterranean Coast)

Penedès (pay-nay-DESS)—This area is located in Catalonia, just south of Barcelona. Penedès produces both red and white wines, but is mainly known for being the region where *Cava* was first created.

Cava (meaning "underground cellar") is the term used to represent Spanish sparkling wine. Cava has been made on a large scale since 1872 and has since been required to be produced in the same way that classic sparkling Champagne is made. Cava wines can be made by several approved DOs throughout Spain, but Penèdes remains at the forefront, contributing about 90% of cava production.

Most Cava is produced from the trilogy of indigenous grapes: *Macabeo* (mah-kah-BEH-oh), also known as Viura; *Xarel-lo* (sah-REHL-lyoh); and *Parellada* (par-eh-LYAH-duh). Chardonnay is also allowed to be blended in, but has been done so in small quantities. Outside of Catalonia, many Cavas use Macabeo as the dominant or even the sole grape in the wine. (Cava is discussed in greater detail in Chapter 11, "BUBBLES: Sparkling Wine.")

Costers Del Segre (koh-stehr del SEH-gray)—An increasingly wide range of wines is produced in this burgeoning DO. It showcases whites, rosés, and reds made from a mix of different grape varietals and sparkling wines made from Chardonnay.

Priorat (pree-oh-RAHT)—Priorat has a long history of winemaking, but has just begun to prosper, having gained DOCa status only in 2004. The area is of volcanic origin, which gives its *llicorella* (lyee-cor-EL-yah) soils unique features of reflecting and conserving the heat.

The influx of talented winemakers into Priorat brings a contemporary approach to wine production. The agable red wines often are dominated by Garnacha or blended with varying amounts of Carignan.

Jumilla (hoo-MEEL-lyah)—Monstrell (known as Mourvédre outside of Spain) is the dominant varietal, with over 85% of the plantings.

Duero River Valley

Castilla and León

Rueda (roo-AID-ah)—This area is home to Spanish white wines made primarily from *Verdejo* (vehr-DAY-ho), with smaller amounts of *Viura* (vee-YURE-ah), known as *Macabeo* in Catalonia and Sauvignon Blanc grape varietals. These wines often are made from single varietals, but are sometimes blended with each other.

Rueda also produces sparkling wine known as *Rueda Espumoso*, which must be made with varying percentages of the white grape varietal, Verdejo. Some traditional bodegas continue to produce oxidized Rancio and Generosos wines.

Cigales (see-GAHL-ess)—The Cigales DO produces many *rosado*, or rosé, wines from Tempranillo (known as Tinta del País) and Gamacha grapes. Some red wines are also produced by carbonic maceration. There are currently many experimental plantings occurring with several international varietals under vines such as Cabernet Sauvignon, Merlot, and Sauvignon Blanc.

Ribera del Duero (ree-BEHRR-ah del DWAY-rroh)—This DO is one of the most reputable wine regions of Spain, located north of Madrid and west of Rioja and situated along the Duero river. The region is best known for producing wines based on Tempranillo (also known as Tinta del País or Tinto Fino)—red wines that must contain a minimum of 75% of the varietal—with the liberal use of French oak.

The wines are fruity, with high preservation of acid, allowing for early consumption, but also are capable of aging into Gran Reservas. Permitted grapes include several international varietals such as Cabernet Sauvignon, Malbec, and Merlot.

Ribera del Duero is the home of some of Spain's most expensive and prestigious wines from the bodega *Vega Sicilia* (VAY-gah see-THEE-lyah). Created in 1864 from Bordeaux vines and French winemaking methods, this wine is unique and one of the most expensive wines produced in Spain, with a philosophy comparable to that of the Super Tuscans of Italy. This wine blends mostly the local Tempranillo grape with smaller amounts of the international Cabernet Sauvignon.

North Central Spain

(Ebro River Valley)

Rioja (ree-OH-hah)—This DOCa takes its name from the river *Rio Oja* and is located in north-central Spain between mountain ranges and along the path of the Ebro River. Rioja is one of the leading Spanish wine regions, most famous for its production of red wines. It remains the most recognizable of all Spanish wine-producing areas.

Rioja was the first Spanish wine region to receive the highest quality designation DOCa, in 1991, for consistent quality and authenticity of its wines.

A typical red Rioja is a blended wine made primarily from *Tempranillo*, with varying amounts of *Garnacha* and smaller amounts of *Graciano* (grah-thee-AH-no) and *Mazuelo* (mah-THWAY-low) (known as Carignan outside of Spain).

The Rioja wine region is divided into three distinct subregions: *Rioja Alta* (AHL-tah), *Rioja Alavesa* (ahl-lah-VACE-ah), and *Rioja Baja* (BAH-hah). These subregions are quite different in that they consist of varying levels of altitude, climate, and soil types.

- Rioja Alta is relatively dry, with high elevation. (*Alta* or *Alto* means "tall" in Spanish.)
- Rioja Alavesa has the highest elevation and is known for its chalky soil.
- Rioja Baja is the hottest and driest area of Rioja, with heavy stone soils. It is also the lowest in elevation; hence, it has the nickname *baja*, which means "low" in Spanish.

Classically, Rioja wines have been created from a blend of grapes from all three subregions, although single-vineyard wines have been gaining popularity as a way to illustrate their unique terroir differences. Figure 10-9 shows a bottle of Rioja.

Rioja also produces a lesser-known white wine that often consists predominately of Viura and, possibly, with varying amount of Malvasia and Garnacha Blanca. It is common to enhance the white Rioja with a touch of oak aging.

Navarra (na-VAHR-rah)—This winemaking region, located in northern Spain, was once known only for its rosé wines. Increasingly, red wines of note have been coming out of this region.

FIGURE 10-9 Marques de Caceres Rioja label

(© Dorling Kindersley)

Southern Spain

Andalucía—Jerez (heh-RAYTH)—Jerez is located in southeast Spain. The formal demarcated area was established in 1933 and was Spain's first Do. (Jerez is discussed in greater detail in Chapter 12, "BOLD: Fortified Wine.")

Aging Standards

Traditionally, the Spanish winemakers (more specifically, those in Rioja) have been loyal to the long aging periods required of their wines. They classically have not released wines until the wines were ready to drink. It was a way to differentiate themselves from Bordeaux, France, whose philosophy is to release wine early, which requires that the wine be cellared for an extended period before being consumed.

The Quality Wines are given aging categories that describe the durations of their aging period, as established by each DO and DOCa.

The styles range from youthful Joven, which have no aging requirements, to Crianza, Reserva, and Gran Reserva. Many of the old-school winemakers are obsessed with aging their wine. The labelling of age is purely voluntary, but also very traditional.

Vino Joven (Ho-vehn) Vino Joven wines, translated as "young wines," are intended for early consumption and have no—or, at most, minimal—wood aging requirements. The period of aging is always shorter than that legally established for Crianza wines.

Vino de Crianza (Kree-AHN-thah) Vino de Crianza wines are any DOCa or DO red wines that have been aged a minimum of 24 months, at least 6 months of which were in a barrel. The appellation areas of Rioja, Navarra, and Ribera Del Duero require 12 months in wood. White and rosé wines labelled as a Crianza must be aged for one year, at least six months of which are in wood.

Vino de Reserva (ree-SEHR-vah) Vino de Reserva wines are any DO or DOCa red wines that have been aged a minimum of three years, one year of which was in wood. White and rosé wines labelled as Reserva must be aged two years, six months of which are in wood.

Vino Gran Reserva (GRAHN ree-SEHR-vah) Vino Gran Reserva wines are any DO or DOCa red wines that have been aged a minimum of five years, of which at least one-and-a-half years were in barrels. The appellation areas of Rioja, Navarra, and Ribera Del Duero require a minimum of two years in wood. White and rosé wines labelled as Gran Reserva must be aged four years, at least six months of which were in wood.

The following chart identifies and summarizes each category's aging requirements:

SPAIN'S AGING REQUIREMENTS		
AGING CATEGORIES	**WHITE / ROSÉ WINE**	**RED WINE**
Crianza	At least 6 months in oak with a total aging of 1 year	At least 6 months (1 year for selected areas) in oak with a total aging of at least 2 years
Reserva	At least 6 months in oak with a total aging of at least 2 years	At least 1 year in oak with a total aging of at least 3 years
Gran Reserva	At least 6 months in oak with a total aging of at least 4 years	At least 1½ years (2 years for selected areas) in oak with a total aging of at least 5 years

OTHER OLD WORLD WINE COUNTRIES

NAME: _____ Score out of 30 points_____.

Use these questions to test your knowledge and understanding of the concepts presented in the chapter.

I. MULTIPLE CHOICE: Select the best possible answer from the options available.

1. The term *classico* refers to wine

   a. made in an old-fashioned style.
   b. made in the original production area.
   c. made to taste like an old vintage.
   d. made at least 10 years before released.

2. In Italy, the term *riserva* means

   a. the same period of aging for all wine.
   b. no legal requirement.
   c. that the wine has been aged with no restrictions.
   d. different things, depending on the appellation.

3. Barbaresco and Barolo are made from which grape?

   a. Dolcetto
   b. Sangiovese
   c. Pinot Grigio
   d. Nebbiolo

4. Barolo is considered

   a. medium-bodied and sweet.
   b. full-bodied, tannic, and robust.
   c. light- to medium-bodied.
   d. poor quality.

5. The most significant red wine grape found in Tuscany is

   a. Sangiovese.
   b. Nebbiolo.
   c. Barbera.
   d. Cabernet Sauvignon.

6. Super Tuscans often are created from a combination of the local Sangiovese and

   a. Riesling.
   b. Cabernet Sauvignon.
   c. Pinot Noir.
   d. Shiraz.

7. In German, *trocken* means

   a. ripe.
   b. acidity.
   c. dry.
   d. sweet.

8. The unique soil of the Mosel is

   a. chalk.
   b. slate.
   c. granite.
   d. clay.

9. The most significant grape varietal in Rioja, Spain, is

   a. Sangiovese.
   b. Riesling.
   c. Tempranillo.
   d. Garnacha.

II. TRUE / FALSE: Circle the best possible answer.

10. Chianti Rufina is generally better than Chianti Classico. **True / False**

11. The Trentino-Alto-Adige region in Italy is known for its Pinot Grigio. **True / False**

12. The Spanish historically have been in love with aging their wines for extended periods. **True / False**

III. MATCHING: Match the Old World country on the right with the wine region on the left.

13. _____ Priorat

14. _____ Piedmont

15. _____ Rheingau   A. Germany

16. _____ Mosel   B. Italy

17. _____ Rioja   C. Spain

18. _____ Veneto

19. _____ Chianti

20. _____ Trentino-Alto-Adige

21. _____ Tuscany

IV. MATCHING: Using the number 1 (lowest) through 6 (highest), place the German ripeness categories in order of lowest to highest sugar content upon harvest.

22. ____ Trockenbeerenauslese (TBA)   25. ____ Auslese

23. ____ Kabinett   26. ____ Spätlese

24. ____ Eiswein   27. ____ Beerenauslese (BA)

V. MATCHING: Connect each wine with its primary grape varietal.

28. ____ Chianti   A. Sangiovese

29. ____ Rioja   B. Tempranillo

30. ____ Barolo   C. Nebbiolo

Unit 5
OTHER TYPES OF WINE

"We do not grow absolutely, chronologically. We grow sometimes in one dimension, and not in another; unevenly. We grow partially. We are relative. We are mature in one realm, childish in another. The past, present, and future mingle and pull us backward, forward, or fix us in the present. We are made up of layers, cells, constellations."

—Anais Nin

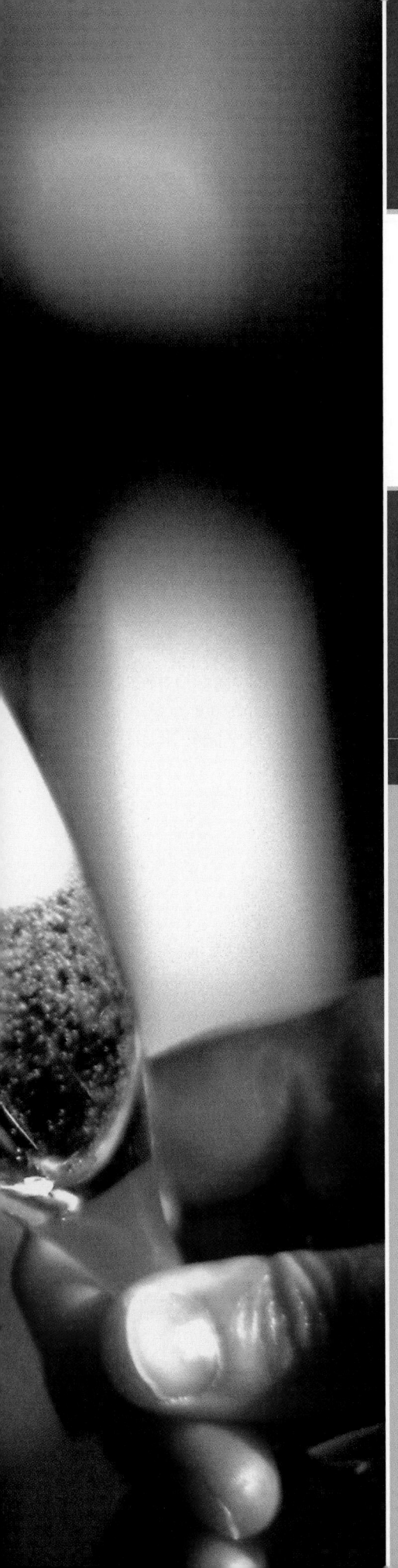

11

BUBBLES:
Sparkling Wine

Sparkling wines are created in nearly every major wine-producing country. They can be found in a wide range of styles (from delicate to powerful, simple to complex, and dry to sweet), quality levels, and price points; but the most historic, prestigious, and reputable type of sparkling wine is Champagne.

LEARNING OBJECTIVES

Upon completion of this chapter, the learner will be able to:

- Explain the process of sparkling-wine production.
- Distinguish between bottle fermentation, transfer method, tank method, and méthode rural.
- Identify the two major styles of sparkling wine and potential food matches for each.
- Provide several strategies for pairing sparkling wine with food types.
- Identify several significant sparkling-wine-producing countries and other regions around the world.

BUBBLES: SPARKLING WINE

Sparkling wine is a generic term used to identify any table wine with the addition of its distinguishable effervescence, or CO_2. Along with climate and type of grapes, the method of incorporating the bubbles is one of the most important defining quality factors in what separates a poor-to-average-quality sparkling wine from an excellent one.

Sparkling wines are created in nearly every major wine-producing country. They can be found in a wide range of styles (from delicate to powerful, simple to complex, and dry to sweet), quality levels, and price points; but the most historic, prestigious, and reputable type of sparkling wine is Champagne. The terms *sparkling wine* and *Champagne* are often used interchangeably; however, although they can be similar, they actually are quite different. All Champagne is sparkling wine, though not all sparkling wine is Champagne. By understanding Champagne and how it is produced, we can understand almost all other sparkling wine in the world.

Champagne

Champagne is both a region and a type of wine. To be specific, Champagne is a sparkling wine that derives from the Champagne region of France and is made according to stringent AOC laws. Champagne in some form (not how we know the sparkling wine to be today), has been made for over 300 years.

The Location

The wines come from the northernmost vineyards in France, about 90 miles northeast of Paris. The most prestigious Champagne houses and vineyards are located near and/or within the city of *Rheims* (REEMZ) and the town of *Epernay* (ey-perh-NEH). Figure 11–1 identifies the Champagne region of France.

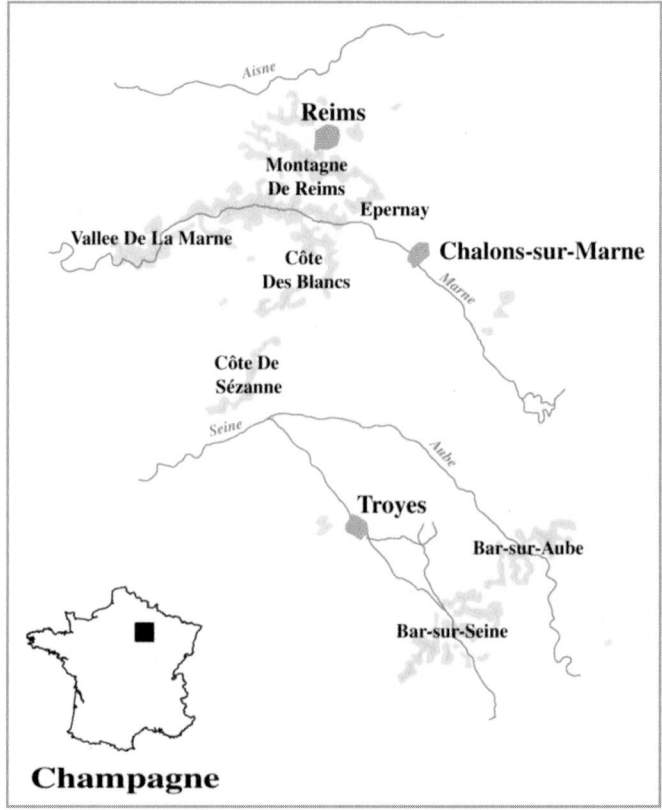

FIGURE 11–1 Map of Champagne
(Hoke Harden, CSW, CSS, Brown-Forman Corporation)

FIGURE 11-2 Chalk subsoil and roots of the vine
(Collection CIVC. Photographer: FION Alain)

The cold northerly climate and chalky soil (supposedly 60 feet deep in some areas) contribute to making the distinctive, crisp, and minerally taste of Champagne. The climate is so inconsistent that most Champagne (the wine, approximately 75%) is *nonvintage,* meaning that it is blended from multiple years in order to balance out quality variations to achieve a certain *house style* that is duplicated with every bottle. Figure 11-2 depicts Champagne's chalky soils.

Grape Varietals

Several different grapes can be used to produce a sparkling wine, but they often share a characteristic in common: substantial acidity. In Champagne, only three grape varieties are permitted for use in the Champagne blend:

1. **Chardonnay** is derived primarily from the areas of *Côte Des Blancs* (coat day BLANHG) and *Côte De Sézanne* (coat du say-ZAHN). This grape lends considerable acidity to the wine. When blended in higher amounts or as a solo varietal in the sparkling wine *Blanc de Blanc*, it produces a lean and crisp light-bodied wine. Figure 11-3 shows a cluster of the Chardonnay grapes.
2. **Pinot Noir** is found in the *Montagne de Reims* (mawn-TAH-nyuh) growing area. This grape provides considerable body and some fruit qualities to the wine. When blended in higher amounts or as a solo varietal (often with Pinot Meunier) in the sparkling wine *Blanc de Noir,* it produces a fuller-bodied, fruitier wine with some noticeable tannin. Figure 11-4 shows a cluster of the Pinot Noir grapes.
3. **Pinot Meunier** (muh-NYAY) is primarily from the *Vallee De La Marne* (vah-LAY duh lah MARN) area. This grape provides considerable fruitiness and some structure of tannin to the wine. Figure 11-5 shows a cluster of the Pinot Meunier grapes.

FIGURE 11-3 Close-up of a cluster of Chardonnay grapes
(Collection CIVC. Photographer: CORNU Alain)

FIGURE 11-4 Close-up of a cluster of Pinot Noir grapes
(Collection CIVC. Photographer: CORNU Alain)

FIGURE 11-5 Close-up of a cluster of Pinot Meunier grapes
(Collection CIVC. Photographer: CORNU Alain)

Production of Champagne or Other High-Quality Sparkling Wine

Winemakers can produce sparkling wine of excellent quality largely by using the classic *Champagne method* of production, known as *méthode champenoise* (may-TOAD

FIGURE 11–6 Harvest time in Champagne: porter of small picking baskets (full of Chardonnay clusters)

(Collection CIVC. Photographer: HADENGUE FREDERIC)

FIGURE 11–7 Harvest time in Champagne: basket full of Chardonnay clusters

(Collection CIVC. Photographer: HADENGUE FREDERIC)

cham-pen-WAHZ), or *MC method*. This production method creates a secondary fermentation within the bottle to create the carbon dioxide (CO_2).

Any producer of sparkling wine around the world may choose to use the classic Champagne method, but Champagne is one of the few sparkling wines that *must* use this technique. The steps outlined next are required in order to produce all Champagne. Producers around the world who choose to create high-quality sparkling wines in the style of Champagne generally will mimic these steps.

1. Harvest—The grapes are harvested early (typically in late September), to maintain their high, crisp, acid levels and low sugar content. Since Champagne undergoes two separate fermentations, grapes are harvested with low sugar levels in order to achieve lower amounts of initial alcohol. The first fermentation creates the initial base wine (basically, a table wine at this point), and the second fermentation produces and traps the carbon dioxide. Figure 11–6 shows a harvest taking place in Champagne. Figure 11–7 depicts a basket of Chardonnay grapes after being picked from the vine.

2. Pressing—Grapes are pressed gently with a wide device to prevent excess time traveling through skins, in order to limit juice and skin contact. The juice is then placed into stainless steel tanks where the first fermentation takes place in order to create the base wine.

The first pressing of juice, or *free run*, goes into the highest-quality sparkling wine; it is the only juice allowed in vintage Champagne. The second pressing, or *taille* (tail), goes into reserve for nonvintage Champagne.

3. First Fermentation—The first fermentation creates a *base wine* (known as vin clair) that is characteristically dry and acidic and near 10%–11% alcohol content. All Champagne and high-quality sparkling wine producers reserve some of this base wine for future vintages of their *house style* in the nonvintage wine they reproduce year after year. Figure 11–8 shows some stainless steel vats used for the first fermentation.

4. Blending—The *Cuvée Assemblage* (coo-VAY ah-sahm-BLAHZH) is a blending of multiple base wines from various years (often, dozens of different wines) to create a desired, consistent, house style. In a vintage year, a smaller percentage of reserve base wines can be blended. These wines may be aged in stainless steel tanks, wood barrels, or

FIGURE 11–8 Stainless steel vats for first fermentation
(Collection CIVC. Photographer: CORNU Alain)

FIGURE 11–9 Assembling
(Collection CIVC. Photographer: VISUEL IMPACT)

a combination of the two. Figure 11–9 shows several separate vin clairs being prepared for taste testing.

5. Second Fermentation (Incorporating the Carbonation)—This is a strictly controlled process called *Méthode Champenoise* that *must* be used to make all Champagne. It also may be used to make all other high-quality sparkling wines throughout the world.

The blended base wine is now bottled and combined with a dose of sugar and yeast, *Liqueur de Tirage* (lick-KYOOR duh tee-RAHZH), in order to induce a secondary fermentation. Through the secondary fermentation, a greater degree of alcohol (totaling around 12%) will be produced, along with carbon dioxide. The carbon dioxide will be trapped and create the characteristic bubble formation associated with sparkling wine. With the MC method, the sediment or dead yeast cells eventually will be removed, without the wine ever leaving its original bottle.

Champagne uses the labelling terminology, Méthode Champenoise to indicate the high quality production method. Other high-quality sparkling wine producers may use the identical production method, but may use alternative terminology. If the bottle lists *Traditional Method, Classic Method, Fermented in this Bottle,* or *Methodo Classico,* it is made by the Champagne method.

Alternative Methods of Incorporating Carbonation

There are other methods of incorporating carbonation into a sparkling wine, though Champagne is not allowed to use any of them. These alternative methods will dramatically influence the cost, labor, and style of a sparkling wine.

Transfer Method—This technique starts out as the traditional method of obtaining the complex aromas and flavors associated with Champagne. However, the entire contents of the bottle are emptied into a large pressurized tank for bulk clarification and transferred back into a bottle. This method increases efficiency and reduces production costs.

The transfer method is a great alternative to the Méthode Champenoise process because it has an advantage of producing a secondary fermentation within the bottle, which contributes some of the same complex flavors. But its disadvantage is that the resulting wine is slightly less intense, with shorter-lived bubbles.

If a sparkling wine is created in this manner, the label will state, *Bottle Fermented* or *Fermented in Bottle*. Note the distinction between the Champenoise method term "Fermented in *this* bottle" versus the transfer method's phrase "Fermented in *the* bottle." This latter terminology indicates that the wine has left its original bottle to be clarified of its sediment.

Charmat or **Tank Method**—The Charmat or Tank Method is a mass-producing technique in which the base wine undergoes secondary fermentation in a pressurized tank, or *autoclave* (AW-toh-klayv). After fermentation, the wine is filtered, sweetened, and bottled, all under pressure.

This method is inexpensive and is intended for wines that are not meant for long aging; therefore, it creates a light, easy-to-drink fruit-forward style of wine. Some of these types of wine may have varying amounts of residual sugar yielding a sweeter wine. Many sparkling wines are produced in this manner, including Sekt (Germany) and Asti, Moscato d'Ast, Prosecco, and Brachetto (Italy), as well as inexpensive sparkling wines around the world.

Pump Method—The pump method incorporates carbon dioxide (CO_2) into the base wine as it is being bottled. This method is similar to the creation of soda pop and is an inexpensive method often associated with producing a low-quality fruit-style sparkling wine.

Méthode Rural—By the *méthode rural*, the wine is bottled prior to completion of the first fermentation. The result is lighter, softer sparkle remaining in the wine, with a slight residual sugar. Asti, Moscato, and Prosecco may be made in this manner.

6. Aging—At this stage, the bottles are cellared and inverted into racks (called *pupîtres*) (pew-PEE-truhs) at a 45° angle in order to encourage the yeast to travel toward the neck of the bottle for eventual removal. The wine is stored a minimum of 15 months for nonvintage, and at least 3 years for vintage Champagne. Figure 11–10 identifies Champagne being cellared.

During this period of aging, yeast cells break down into what are known as *lees* and undergo the process of *autolysis* (aw-TAHL-uh-sihss). This decomposition of yeast cells

FIGURE 11–10 Champagne cellar with wooden racks called "pupîtres"
(Collection CIVC. Photographer: CORNU Alain)

FIGURE 11–11 Remuage Pupîtres
(Collection CIVC. Photographer: PIPER HEIDSIECK)

FIGURE 11–12 The sediment in the bottle neck (dégorgement)
(Collection CIVC. Photographer: JONKER JAN)

causes chemical changes that contribute a creamy texture and a toasty, complex aroma and taste. Autolysis contributes significantly to the character of a longer-aged sparkling wine, compared with a shorter-aged or non-aged sparkling wine.

7. Remuage (Reh-moo-ajh)—Remuage is a long, tedious hand-crafting process that takes place during aging. Over a period of six to eight weeks, each day the bottles are given a gentle shake, or *riddled,* a quarter turn in order to allow gravity to pull the lees toward the neck of the bottle. This step allows for the eventual removal of sediment without the wine being emptied from its bottle. Traditionally, the remuage was done by hand, but increasingly it is now being carried out in large, mechanized racks (known as gyro-palettes) in order to increase efficiency and decrease the labor expense. Figure 11–11 shows this more modern gyro-palette version of remuage.

8. Dégorgement (day-gorge-MAWN)—This is the process of removing the sediment (or lees) from the neck of the bottle. The neck of the bottle is dipped into an icy brine or glycol solution, which creates a small, frozen ice plug that contains the sediment. The bottle is placed upright, and the cap (or temporary cork) is taken off. Due to the internal pressure of the wine, the ice plug with the sediment shoots out of the bottle. At this point, the wine is completely dry, with no sugar remaining. Figure 11–12 shows the yeast sediment in the neck of the bottle.

9. Dosage (doh-ZAHJ)—Dosage is the sweetening syrup, or the *dosage d'expédition* (a mixture of sugar and wine), added to the wine to adjust the desired degree of sweetness and replenish the small amount of wine lost during dégorgement.

10. Bottling/Corking—Sparkling wines are distinguishing by their effervescence, or CO_2, which creates pressure within the bottle. This pressure is equivalent to 5–6 atmospheres or

FIGURE 11–13 Aging after disgorgement
(Collection CIVC. Photographer: CORNU Alain)

80–120 lbs per square inch (psi), approximately two to three times the pressure of a car tire. The carbonation is more stable at cold temperatures and unstable at room temperature. Due to the level of pressure, the sparkling wine bottle is made with thicker glass than that of other wine bottles. Each bottle also contains a *punt end*, or indentation, in the bottom of the bottle to help stabilize and secure the bottle. Figure 11–13 shows bottles being aged after disgorgement.

The bottle is sealed with a cork secured with a wire muzzle. Then the bottle is returned to the cellars for several months before being labelled for shipping.

Other Sparkling Wines

Champagne is made from a blend or, *cuvée,* of three grape varietals: Pinot Noir, Pinot Meunier, and Chardonnay. Most sparkling-wine-producing areas have the freedom to incorporate varietals that are appropriate (or indigenous) to their place of origin and to the desired style of the finished product. However, many high-quality California producers will duplicate (in a respectful way) the style of Champagne and incorporate the same or similar varietals.

France—Sparkling wine made outside the Champagne region is referred to as *Crémant* (kray-MAHN), such as *Crémant d'Alsace*, meaning a sparkling wine from the Alsace region of France. Many of the French (non Champagne) sparkling wines utilize local grapes associated with that region.

Spain—Spain is the largest producer of sparkling wine in the world. The Spanish sparkling wine *Cava* can be made in several authorized locations throughout Spain, but the vast majority (about 95%) is made in Catalonia. Cava typically uses three local grapes (completely different from those which Champagne uses) indigenous to Spain called *Macabeo* (mah-kah-BEH-oh), *Xarel-lo* (sah-REHL-yoh), and *Parellada* (par-eh-LYAH-duh). These grapes tend to be preferred by most producers, but currently there is experimentation with the addition of some classic Champagne-type grapes in the blend. Cava offers a good transition from Champagne to American sparkling, with reasonably priced wines and high minerality.

Italy—Mostly indigenous grapes are used to produce Italy's sparkling wines. *Asti* and *Moscato d'Asti* are produced from the Muscat grape, *Brachetto d'Aqui* (brah-KET-toe) is made from the *Brachetto* grape, and *Prosecco* (praw-ZEHK-koh) is produced in the Veneto from the *Prosecco* grape.

The generic term for sparkling wine in Italy is *spumante*, but the term has a dual meaning because it also can refer to a sparkling wine with a normal level of carbonation. The term *frizzante* (free-DZAHN-tay) is used to distinguish a sparkling wine with a less pronounced, softer sparkle and *frizzantino,* (free-DZAHN-tee-noe) indicate slight sparkling.

FIGURE 11–14 Champagne cellar
(Collection CIVC. Photographer: HADENGUE FREDERIC)

Nonvintages (NV or Multivintage)—A nonvintage is produced by most Champagne houses and all sparkling wine producers around the world. Nonvintage sparkling wine will not indicate a year on the label, because it is made from a blend of several cuvees from different years. These wines are made to achieve a *house style* that remains consistent in quality and taste from year to year. Nonvintage Champagne is released at least 15 months after harvest and often consumed within 5 years from harvest.

Vintage Champagne—Vintage Champagne indicates that a minimum of 95% of the grapes from the current year's harvest are within the bottle, though not every year is declared a *vintage*. The wine is released at least three years after harvest, after it has gained depth and complexity through the aging process. Vintage Champagne has the ability to be cellared for several years after purchasing, and even up to a decade before consumption. Vintage Champagne is expensive and considered to be prestigious. It is priced almost three times (and often even higher) more than nonvintage. Figure 11–14 shows a Champagne cellar, where the bottles rest until being released.

Blanc de Blanc—Blanc de Blanc roughly translates to "white from white." It is made from 100% Chardonnay (or other white wine grapes outside Champagne). The color is pale and light, and the wine has a certain delicate, lean, yet crisp style.

Blanc de Noir—Blanc de Noir roughly translates to "white from black." It is made from 100% Pinot Noir and/or Pinot Meunier grapes. The blend de Noir style is full bodied compared with Blanc de Blanc and traditional Champagne blend. The wine is likely to contain some perceptible levels of tannin and possibly a tinge of pink color because of the juice contact with black skins.

Pétillant (pay-tee-YAWN)—This sparkling wine contains less carbonation (around 3.6 atmospheres) than normal sparkling wines. Pétillant wines have less sugar added for the secondary fermentation, producing less gas pressure in the finished wine. This process can be comparable to the Italian *frizzante*.

Tête de Cuvée (tet duh koo-VAY)—An unofficial term, this often refers to a superior quality selection to identify a producer's best or most prestigious wine.

Dom Pérignon

Dom Pérignon (dohng pay-ree-NYOHNG), one of the most famous brands of Champagne, is named after an eighteenth century Benedictine monk. The monk is known to have perfected the blending of different grapes and created a durable bottle to withstand the carbonation present in sparkling wine. To the dismay of many, Dom Perignon is not responsible for creating Champagne (it happened quite by accident), but certainly, his contributions are numerous.

Dom Pérignon as a brand was launched in 1921 by *Moët et Chandon* (moh-eht ay shahng-DAWNG) as their premium level. It is similar to *Laurent-Perrier's* (loh-RAHNG peh-ree-ay) *Grand Siècle, Roederer's* (ROH-duh-rer) *Cristal,* and *Taittinger's* (tate-teen-ZHEHR) *Comtes de Champagne.*

Dom Pérignon is a *single-vineyard* wine made only from grapes in a single, exceptional year.

"Champagne" Used in Other Ways

In the past, the term *Champagne* in the United States has been used as a generic term to capitalize on the fame of the official and authentic Champagne. When the term is used in America or anywhere else that is not Champagne, it does not relate to place of origin, as it does in France. In 1927, representatives from Champagne asked countries to sign a treaty not to call sparkling wine *Champagne*. Most countries eventually agreed, except for the United States. The term *Champagne* is sometimes still used, and labels may read, "California Champagne" or "champagne" (with a small "c," which indicates that the wine does not originate from the authentic place). Beware of producers using this terminology; the products often are low-quality versions that resemble the Champagne style very little.

STYLES OF SPARKLING WINE

For simplicity, the vast world of sparkling wines can be understood better when the wines are categorized according to style. Two broad styles of sparkling wine are (1) complex and (2) fruit. Not every sparkling wine fits neatly into one of these categories, but some wines have more characteristics in common with one grouping than with the other.

Body of Sparkling Wine

Either style of sparkling wine can allow for various kinds of body. These styles can describe wines that range from delicate and light bodied (Blanc de Blanc) to bold and full bodied (Blanc de Noir) and from dry to sweet. The grapes and proportion of grape varietals, climate the grapes grew in, and winemaking techniques will largely affect the body.

STYLE #1 – Complex Style Sparkling Wine

A complex style sparkling wine is a sparkling wine that expresses the primary character of the grapes, but, more importantly, the complexity of the secondary winemaking techniques associated with bottle fermentation, oak aging, malo-lactic fermentation, and aging on the lees.

Aromas/Flavors—These include yeasty (brioche, biscuit), citrus fruit (lemon), tree (apple), bakeshop sauces (honey, vanilla, butterscotch, cream, butter), bakeshop nuts (toast, hazelnut, almond, popcorn).

> **Location**—Some of the best and most noted places include France (Champagne, Loire), Spain (Penedes, Catalonia), and California (Carneros, Napa, Sonoma).
>
> **Types**—Complex style sparkling wines include Blanc de Blanc, Nonvintage and Vintage Champagne, Cava from Spain, and high-quality sparkling wine from the United States.

STYLE #2 – Fruit Style Sparkling Wine

This style of sparkling wine expresses the primary character of the grapes. It characterizes a fairly straightforward, simple type of wine that preserves primary fruit qualities. Some of these types of wine have varying levels of residual sugar that results in a sweet wine.

Aromas/Flavors—These include fruit tree and candied (white peach, pear, apricot, watermelon, green apple, strawberry, Jolly Rancher), nuts, taffy, bubble gum, cream soda, cotton candy, and gummy bears.

> **Location**—Some of the best and most noted places include Germany, Italy (Piedmont, Veneto), California (Napa and Sonoma), and Australia.
>
> **Types**—Fruit sparklings include Asti and *Moscato di Asti* (from the Muscat grape), *Brachetto* from Italy's Piedmont region, *Prosecco* from Italy's Veneto region, *rosé* sparkling, *Sparkling Shiraz*, *Blanc de Noir*, and some inexpensive sparkling wines found throughout the world.

Pairing Strategies for Sparkling Wine

Overall, sparkling wines have several attributes that allow them to be one of the most adaptable types of wine to partner successfully with various types of food. Sparkling is a type of wine that works for most occasions, with or without food.

The combination of these factors (as identified on the left-hand side of the page) allows sparkling wines more successfully to partner with food than any other wine. Sparkling wine even has the ability to pair with so-called difficult ingredients and foods such as smoky, fried, spicy, salty, sweet, and mouth-coating food items such as chocolate and cheese.

1. **Complex Style Sparkling Wine**—This wine is often at the *brut* dryness level and contains enough richness to partner with cooked and smoked fish, white truffle risotto, steak tartare, beef carpachio, and cheese (soft, rind ripened, semi-soft, and hard cheeses).

   Blanc de Blanc—These sparkling wines pair best with lighter, delicate food items and preparations such as assorted canapés, stuffed mushrooms, caviar, shrimp, raw shellfish, ceviche, and sushi. This style of sparkling wine contains generous acidity and effervescence that together stimulate the appetite and cleanse the palate.

   Vintage Champagne—This sparkling wine is made from a single, optimal season, from grapes of greater concentration, distinction, and a longer required aging period. These factors create a wine that is distinctive and rich on the palate and that pairs with bold foods (lobster, poultry with skin-on, grana or other heavily aged type cheeses) and preparation methods (roasting, broiling and grilling), with rich sauces (butter, milk and emulsified).

WHY SPARKLING WINE IS A VERSATILE FOOD PAIRING PARTNER

☑ It maintains lower alcohol than most wines.

☑ It contains ample acidity and effervescence that work together for more interesting sensations on the palate.

☑ Its ability to produce various styles, from dry, to sweet and light, to full bodied, accommodates various types of food.

FIGURE 11–15 Pouring of Champagne into a flute"
(Collection CIVC; Photographer: LECOMTE Jean-Marie)

2. **Fruit Style Sparkling Wine**—These wines are fruit forward (and, in some cases, contain residual sugar) and act to counterbalance the distinctive ingredients used in each cuisine. Fruit styles can partner well with cuisines that occasionally have spicy or pungent ingredients. Examples are Asian (which encompasses Chinese, Thai, Vietnamese, Japanese, and more) and African cuisine. This style of sparkling wine also pairs excellently with custard, fruit, and chocolate-based desserts.

   Blanc de Noir—This sparkling wine can pair with heavier, bolder food items and preparations methods. Blanc de Noirs contain fruity aroma and fuller body, with slight tannin from the higher proportion of Pinot Noir and/or Pinot Meunier grapes in the wine.

   Rosé—These sparkling are made from either a combination of red and white base wines or through the maceration process of red grapes bleeding some colored juice into the wine. Because of the higher proportion of influence of red wine grapes, Rosé sparkling offer a greater fruit aroma and flavor.

Serving and Tasting Suggestions

There are some definite signs that help determine whether one has chosen a low- or a high-quality sparkling wine. Some of the reasons may be associated with different methods of production or service techniques. Following is a list of visible signs that should be taken note of. Figure 11–15 depicts the pouring of a Champagne into a proper glass (the flute) that allows a sparkling wine to best express itself.

☑ **Chilled**—Ensure that sparkling wine is well chilled (40–45°F), as chilling wine will accentuate its crisp acidity and preserve bubble life.

☑ **Pouring**—When pouring the sparkling wine into a glass, always proceed slowly so as not to create excessive foam, or *mousse*, in the glass. The mousse is the formation of bubbles that form on the surface of a glass after the sparkling wine has been poured. Any excess mousse will cause early dissipation of bubbles.

☑ **Size of Bubbles**—The degree of mousse refers to the way the bubbles of CO_2 feel in the mouth. A poor mousse may be described as coarse (large bubbles) and short lived, whereas a good mousse may be described as full, creamy, and fine, made up of numerous very fine CO_2 bubbles. The MC and transfer production methods have the ability to create a more condensed, finer bubble through fermentation in a tightly enclosed space.

FIGURE 11–16 A glass of sparkling wine with a proper mousse

(Collection CIVC. Photographer: LECOMTE Jean-Marie)

☑ **Rate of Flow of Bubbles**—The MC and transfer production methods create a mousse that flows a bit more slowly and methodically than mousses created by other production methods.

☑ **Tasting**—When tasting, it is not necessary to swirl the wine in the glass, because the carbonation will assist to transport aroma and flavor molecules toward the surface of the glass and into the nose and palate. Excessive movement will cause the bubbles to dissipate prematurely. Figure 11–16 shows a glass of sparkling wine with a proper mousse.

COMPARISION OF COMPLEX STYLE VERSUS FRUIT STYLE SPARKLING WINE			
	Complex Style *Classic (Champagne)*	**Complex Style** *(High-quality Champagne impersonators)*	**Fruit Style**
VARIOUS NAMES and TYPES	Champagne (Vintage or Nonvintage), Blanc de Blanc, Blanc de Noir	Sparkling Wine, Cava, Blanc de Blanc, Blanc de Noir	Brachetto, Prosecco, Asti, Moscato d'Asti, Rosé, Sparkling Shiraz
Grapes Used	Permitted varietals include Chardonnay, Pinot Noir, and Pinot Meunier. They can be used individually or blended in various quantities.	Can use any grapes, but often respectfully imitate Champagne by using Chardonnay and Pinot Noir. Sometimes, completely different grapes may be used, but ones with qualities similar to the traditional grapes contribute.	Brachetto uses Brachetto grapes, Asti; Moscato d'Asti uses Moscato (or Muscat) grapes; and Sparkling Shiraz uses Shiraz.
Production Methods	Méthode Champenoise	Traditional method or transfer method	Tank Method Pump Method Méthode Rural
Aging	Longer aging produces more complexity due to effects of autolysis. Nonvintage – Minimum of 15 months Vintage – Minimum of 36 Months	No requirements, but often several months (in some cases, years) of aging. Cava requires aging a minimum of 9 months and 18 months for Reservas	Aging is typically avoided, because it would contribute undesirable complexity and mask fruit aromas and flavors.
Aromas/Flavor Emphasis	Secondary complexity from winemaking techniques	Secondary complexity from winemaking techniques	Primary fruit with fresh youthful taste
Bubble Perception	Small, less aggressive bubbles with a smoother mouth-feel	Small, less aggressive bubbles with a smoother mouth-feel	A bit larger, more aggressive bubbles with a fresh mouth-feel

BUBBLES: SPARKLING WINE

NAME: _____ Score out of 20 points_____.

Use these questions to test your knowledge and understanding of the concepts presented in the chapter.

I. MULTIPLE CHOICE: Select the best possible answer from the options available.

1. The soils in the best Champagne vineyards contain

   a. clay.
   b. gravel.
   c. chalk.
   d. sand.

2. Frizzante is an Italian sparkling wine that has

   a. normal sparkle.
   b. heavier sparkle.
   c. less sparkle.
   d. no sparkle.

3. Brut style of sparkling wine is

   a. dry.
   b. very dry.
   c. slightly dry.
   d. sweet.

4. Two styles of sparkling wine are

   a. smoky and sweet.
   b. salty and fruity.
   c. complex and fruity.
   d. complex and simple.

5. The process of collecting the yeast in the neck of the bottle during the Champagne production process is known as

   a. disgorging.
   b. remuage.
   c. dosage.
   d. riddling.

6. After the yeast is removed in the Champagne process, sugar is added to the wine to adjust dryness/sweetness. This is known as

   a. disgorging.
   b. remuage.
   c. dosage.
   d. riddling.

7. Champagne is allowed to use any or all of the permitted three grape varietals, including Chardonnay, Pinot Noir, and

   a. Pinot Gris.
   b. Pinot Blanc.
   c. Pinot Grigio.
   d. Pinot Meunier.

8. Descriptive aroma/flavor terms for complex sparkling wine would least likely include

   a. yeasty.
   b. creamy.
   c. nutty.
   d. fruity.

9. Descriptive aroma/flavor terms for simple sparkling wine would least likely include

   a. yeasty.
   b. berries.
   c. bubble gum.
   d. taffy.

10. Disgorgement is

    a. the process of cleaning the bottle before use.

    b. the process of cleaning the barrels before use.

    c. the process of removing dead yeast cells from a bottle of sparkling wine.

    d. the process of removing the grape skins from the wine after fermentation.

II. TRUE / FALSE: Circle the best possible answer.

11. The majority of Champagne is a blended wine that is aged several years in order to achieve a certain *house style*. **True / False**

12. *Blanc de Noir* sparkling wine roughly translates to a white wine made from black grapes. **True / False**

13. *Cava* is the name given to the most important type of sparkling wine made in Spain. **True / False**

14. The *MC* method is the name used for the production method to make sparkling wine in Champagne, France. **True / False**

15. It is important to swirl the sparkling wine in the glass in order to release its aroma. **True / False**

16. Lighter sparkling wine (Blanc de Blanc) can work best with more robust food items and heavier, weightier sparkling wines (Blanc de Noir) can pair better with more delicate food items. **True / False**

III. SHORT-ANSWER ESSAY/DISCUSSION QUESTIONS: Use a separate sheet of paper if necessary.

17. List and describe three reasons that Champagne is a unique type of sparkling wine. Explain the statement, "All Champagne is sparkling wine, but not all sparkling wine is Champagne."

18. Identify two examples of complex sparkling wines and two examples of fruit-driven sparkling wines.

19. Explain how, in Champagne and other high-quality sparkling wines, the dead yeast cells are removed from the bottle.

20. Identify at least two pairing strategies for sparkling wine. Why is sparkling wine considered to be one of the most adaptable food-friendly wines?

APPENDIX

WINE GLOSSARY: From A to Z

A

acetaldehyde (ass-ah-TAHL-duh-hide)—A compound that causes a wine to have oxidized qualities, caused by the unintentional and undesirable effect of oxygen.

acetic acid—Wines contain several types of acid, but acetic acid has the odor and taste of vinegar. If this acid is present at more than minimal levels, the wine would be considered faulty.

acidity—Present in all grapes and therefore all wines. Perceived as sourness and causing salivation on the palate, acidity is extremely important in determining the structure, shape, and life span (or backbone) of all wines, but particularly of white wines. Good acid levels make a wine crisp and refreshing, and prolong the aftertaste. Acidity also helps to preserve a wine, allowing it to be aged. Wines that are low in acidity are often described as tasting flat or flabby.

adaptation—A temporary loss in the ability to perceive an aroma, a flavor, or a taste.

aeration—The deliberate choice of incorporating oxygen into a wine, allowing it to "breathe" in order to soften the tannins and allowing the aromas and flavors to open up and integrate with one another. Young red wines benefit most from aeration, which is accomplished by decanting or by swirling the wine in a glass.

aftertaste—Also called the "finish," this is the taste that remains in the mouth after the wine is swallowed. A really great wine will have a long, complex, lingering aftertaste. The amount of aftertaste can be associated with how concentrated the wine is.

aging—The process of storing wine in either inert (stainless steel, concrete, etc.) or oxidative (oak, chestnut, etc.) containers in order to preserve or contribute additional flavors and allow the components of the wine to integrate.

alcohol—Derived from the fermentation of grape sugars by yeast, alcohol, affects the weight, strength, and overall personality of a wine. In U.S. table wines, the law allows a 1.5% variation from the level identified on the label.

alluvial—Highly fertile (said of soil). Alluvial soil is often located near rivers, floodplains of rivers, or the foothills of mountains.

american oak—Along with French oak, American oak is the most widely used wood in the world to build barrels in which to age wine. Because they contribute strong, intense elements of coconut, vanilla, etc., aroma and flavor to the wine, American oak barrels are most often used to age red wines. American oak varies with the forest and state of its origin.

American Viticultural Area (AVA)—A distinctive grape-growing geographical area, such as Napa Valley and Sonoma Valley, that has been officially designated by the Alcohol and Tobacco Tax and Trade Bureau (TTB). An AVA guarantees that, at a minimum, 85% (with some exceptions) of the grapes came from the location identified on the bottle.

amphora (ahm-FOR-uh)—A two-handled Greek vase with a swelled belly, narrow neck, and large mouth. Historically, an amphora was often used to transport wine or oil.

analytical approach—A methodical three-step approach to pairing wine and food. The method involves (1) mirroring the body and weight (or overall intensity) of the wine and the food to ensure that neither one overwhelms the other, (2) connecting bridge ingredients in the food with flavors in the wine, and (3) comparing or contrasting taste components between the wine and the food on the basis of the desired emphasis of the match.

antioxidants—These have recently been linked to reducing the risk of heart disease and certain types of cancer. Antioxidants have compounds in them that inhibit the formation of cancer cells and reduce the buildup of fat cells in the arteries.

anthocyanins—The name of the pigment found in red grape skins that provides the color to the finished wine.

appellation—A geographic designation of the place where a wine's grapes were grown, such as Napa Valley, Chianti, and Bordeaux. The regulations vary in coverage from country to country and region to region. The French and Italians also regulate what grapes can be grown where, winemaking methods, yields, etc. In America, the appellation references where the grapes were grown and does not specify grape-growing or winemaking methods.

Appellation d'Origine Contrôlée (AOC or AC) (ah-pehl-lah-SYAHN daw-ree-JEEN kawn-traw-LAY)—French term for "controlled appellation of origin" and refers to wine, cheese, butter, etc. The designation is given and controlled by the French governmental agency Institut National des Appellations d' Origine (INAO), and it guarantees that the products to which it pertains have been held to a set of rigorous standards. The appellation d'origine contrôlée is the foremost category in the French system and ensures the quality of a wine and that the wine meet quality criteria in several growing and production steps.

aroma—The scent of a wine; frequently used interchangeably with the word *bouquet*. Smelling the wine on the outside, as opposed to the inside. Some tasters apply the term *aroma* only to the fruit-like natural smells of a wine and refer to the more complex smells of bottle- or barrel-aged wines as *bouquet*.

aromatic—A wine-tasting term used to describe a wine that is highly fragrant.

astringent—The dry, mouth-puckering sensation caused by wines (usually young reds) that are high in tannin. Sometimes astringency can be appealing in a wine and favorably complement food. Astringency tends to decline with bottle age.

auslese (OWS-lay-zuh)—German for "select picking"; refers to the selective hand harvesting of extremely ripe bunches of grapes, often with a touch of noble rot (called *Edelfaule* in German).

autolysis (aw-TAHL-uh-sihss)—The process of decomposing dead yeast cells. Gives Champagne and other high-quality sparkling wines their distinctive character that occurs throughout the aging process.

B

backbone—Often used to describe wines with good acidity and structure.

balance—Describes a wine with harmonious components, in reference to the balance of acids, tannins, fruit, sweetness, and alcohol. Typicity (tih-PISS-it-ee) must also be considered in defining what the balance is for a particular varietal.

balthazar—A very large bottle that holds 16 standard bottles.

barrel aging—The length of time a wine spends in a barrel before being bottled. Barrel aging allows the wine to be exposed to the slow passage of oxygen and a small amount of evaporation, influencing the personality of the wine in several ways. Tannin in red wine softens; white wines become richer and more full bodied. Aging can add aromas and flavors of vanilla, spice, tobacco and wood.

barrel fermented—Indicates a wine that has been fermented in barrels. Will increase the wine's body and add complexity, texture, and flavor, but not to the degree that barrel aging will provide.

barrique (bah-REEK)—Barrel for fermenting or aging that holds approximately 60 gallons; used in Bordeaux.

Beerenauslese (BA) (BEHR-ehn-OWS-lay-zuh)—The German term for select berries that have been handpicked. BA is a rich, sweet dessert wine made of overripe, shriveled berries that are almost always affected by noble rot.

bianco (bee-ahn-koh)—Italian for "white," as in white wine.

big six grapes—Grapes from which Riesling, Sauvignon Blanc, Chardonnay, Pinot Noir, Merlot, and Cabernet Sauvignon wines are made. These grapes are arguably the most noble, as they are adaptable and produced around the world.

biodynamics—Philosophical viewpoint asserting that the land is a living system and vineyards are an ecological self-sustaining whole.

bitter—A sensation that may be caused by tannin. Slight bitterness in a wine may be a desirable trait; however, "overbitterness" is considered a fault and characterizes a poorly made wine.

blanc (BLAHNK)—French for "white," as in white wine.

blanc de blancs (BLAHNK duh BLAHNK)—Translates to "white from white," or a white wine made from white grapes. Most often used to describe sparkling wines made from Chardonnay or other white wine varietals.

blanc de noirs (BLAHNK duh NWAR)—Translates to "white from red," or a white wine made from red grapes. Most often used to describe sparkling wines made from Pinot Noir and Pinot Meunier or other red wine varietals.

blanco (BLAHNG-koh)—Spanish for "white," as in white wine.

blind tasting—A wine tasting that is conducted with no knowledge of the grape varieties or origins of the wine on the part of the tasters. In a double-blind tasting, the taster has no information about what he or she is sampling.

bodega (boh-DAY-gah)—A generic term for a Spanish winery or wine cellar.

body—Body is the feeling of a wine's viscosity, weight, or fullness in the mouth. It is usually the result of extract, alcohol content, or residual sugar. Wines are often described as light bodied, medium bodied, or full bodied, a spectrum comparable to skim milk vs. 2% milk vs. whole milk.

botrytis cinerea (boh-TRI-tis sihn-EAR-ee-uh)—Also called noble rot, a beneficial mold that may grow on wine grapes, causing them to dehydrate and shrivel resulting in the remaining juice becoming highly concentrated. This desired condition yields the honeyed richness of many classic dessert wines such as Sauternes, Trockenbeerenauslese, and Tokaji.

bottled by—Indicates the winery or group that bottled the wine, but did not necessarily grow, pick, or ferment the grapes.

bouillie bordelaise (Bwee-YEE Bor-duh-LEZZ)—An antifungal solution consisting of copper sulfate, lime, and water. Historically, commonly used in Bordeaux, France.

bouquet—The secondary smells of a wine. The term is used to refer to the addition of odors associated with winemaking methods, such as the odor of barrel-aged wine, which includes complexities beyond the fruit aromas.

breathing—Allowing a wine to come into contact with some oxygen for a short time. Breathing allows the components of the wine to integrate and is typically done when the bottle of wine is opened and the wine is poured into the glass.

brettanomyces (breht-tan-uh-MY-sees)—Often referred to as brett, a spoilage yeast that can grow on grapes and affect a wine during processing. Brett can add a horse-saddle aroma and flavor to a wine.

brilliant—A wine of high clarity. Highly filtered wines will always be brilliant—yet the process of filtration can strip some of the personality from a wine.

brix—A system used to measure the sugar content in grapes and wine. Brix at the time of harvest is normally in the range from 20° to 25°. After fermentation, brix can indicate how sweet a wine is as a measure of its residual sugar.

brut (BROOT)—Used in reference to sparkling wine; indicates that the style is dry.

buttery—Describes a rich wine with an aroma, flavor and texture like that of melted butter. Often referring to Chardonnay and often is the result of malolactic fermentation.

C

canopy—The foliage (leaves) that is produced from the grapevine.

canopy management—The practice of adjusting or positioning a vine's leaves, shoots, and fruit as the vine grows, in order to gain such beneficial advantages as increased exposure to sunlight and movement of air.

cap—The thick layer of skin, stems, and seeds that collects at the top of the tank during the fermentation of red wine.

capsule—The metal or plastic material that covers the cork and top of a wine bottle. Now used for decorative purposes, the capsule originally functioned as a means of protecting corks in old cellars from being attacked by insects. The capsule also limited moisture loss and mold growth.

carbonic maceration—Also called "whole-berry fermentation," the process of intracellular fermentation of whole grapes that allows the carbon dioxide which is produced to eliminate all oxygen. This fermentation technique is used to produce fruity, red wines with low tannin and an intense color. Often associated with Beaujolais wines.

cava—Spain's sparkling wine made by the traditional French method. Cava is produced mainly in the Catalonia–Barcelona area of Spain. The traditional méthode champenoise must be used.

cépage (say-PAHZH)—Vine or grape variety.

chaptalization (shap-tuh-luh-ZAY-shuhn)—The addition of sugar to grape juice before fermentation has been completed, in order to achieve a desired alcohol content with the finished wine. Chaptalization is common in cooler northern Europe, such as Burgundy, where grapes have to struggle to fully ripen, and is not allowed in warmer regions, such as Rhône.

charmat (shar-MAH)—Also known as tank or bulk process, this is an inexpensive way to create carbonation and limit complexity in sparkling wine. The wine undergoes secondary fermentation in a stainless steel pressurized tank, which results in coarse, large bubbles and simpler fruit flavors.

chateau (shah-TOH)—Often refers to a wine estate located on the land of the vineyard. In Bordeaux, a winery that has vineyards and that produces and bottles its own wine. This is the equivalent of the American terminology *estate bottled*.

chewy—Describes full-bodied, sometimes tannic wines.

claret—Historically, a British term used for red wines from Bordeaux.

clarity—A wine-tasting term used to indicate a wine's freedom from particles.

classico (KLAHS-see-koh)—A term used in Italy to signify the original or classic vineyard zone before an area was expanded.

clean—Otherwise known as healthy. A wine that is absent of any foreign and unpleasant odor and taste.

clone—A reproduction of a vine with distinctive traits of its parent vine. Usually produced through cuttings or grafting from the original vine, but may also arise through natural evolution.

clos (KLOH)—The term originally used in Burgundy to mean an enclosed vineyard.

condensed tannin—The tannin that is present in skins—particularly, the tannin found in seeds and stems; also referred to as unripe tannin because of its ability to taste bitter on the palate, especially if the grapes were harvested too early.

cooper—A barrel producer.

corked—Describes a faulty wine that smells and tastes similar to a musty basement or a wet newspaper or cardboard. Caused by a cork made defective by 2,4,6-trichloranisole (try-klor-ANN-iss-sahl), or TCA.

côte (KOHT) or **coteaux** (koh-TOH)—French term that refers to a slope or hillside.

coulure (coo-LYUR)—Condition that may occur when a flower has been improperly pollinated, resulting in insufficient fruit set and causing berries to abort or fall off the clusters.

crémant (kray-MAHN)—A term used to describe French sparkling wine made outside of the Champagne region, but employing the méthode Champenoise in its production.

crianza (kree-AHN-thah)—A Spanish wine-aging classification for any DOCa or DO. Applied to red wines aged a minimum of 24 months, at least 6 months of which were in a barrel. The appellation areas of Rioja, Navarra, and Ribera del Duero require 12 months in wood. White and rosé wines labeled Crianza must be aged for one year, at least six months of which are in wood.

criadera (kree-ah-DEHR-ah)—Spanish term that translates to nursery. Referring to a young wine used in the production of Sherry.

crisp—Wine-tasting term that denotes a desirable feature in white wines. The term indicates that the wine is firm and refreshing, meaning that it has adequate or ample acidity.

cross-pollination—Pollination that occurs between two different grapes of the same vine species, either naturally through evolution or intentionally within a vine nursery.

cru (KROO)—French term for rank or level (often translated as *growth*), used to define the hierarchy of vineyards within appellations. In Burgundy, France, the highest quality wines are given the Grand Cru term, and in Bordeaux they are called Premiere Crus.

crush—Usually late August, September, or October in the Northern Hemisphere, when grapes are harvested and crushed. In the Southern Hemisphere, the crush is usually in late February, March, or April.

crushing—The most common technique for extracting the juice from grapes, particularly in red wine.

crust—The name applied to sediment that forms in the bottom and sides of a wine bottle. Crust is commonly found in Vintage Ports or unfiltered or aged red table wine.

cuvée (koo-VAY)—An unregulated term that some wineries use to indicate a special blend or reserve batch of wine of various grapes or vintages blended together.

D

decanter—A glass vessel into which wine is decanted.

decanting—A technique used with either old red wines to remove sediment or young red wines to allow oxygen to soften the components. Decanting involves slowly pouring wine from the bottle into another container (typically a decanter) in order to separate the liquid from the sediment. The procedure also may be used to aerate the wine in order to soften the tannin and allow the wine to open up and the aromas and flavors to integrate.

dégorgement (day-gorge-MAWN)—French term for disgorging the removal of collected yeast that has settled in the neck of the bottle during Champagne production.

demi-sec (DEHM-ee SEK)—Literally "half dry," though, when referring to sparkling wines, it indicates a medium sweetness.

Denominación de origen (DO) (deh-naw-mee-nah-THYON deh aw-REE-hen)—The second-highest quality wine level of wines from Spain. DO requires that wines which are produced in particular geographical areas use defined methods and quality standards in their grape and wine production. As of 2008, there are 65 DO's that have been awarded this designation.

Denominación de Origen Calificada (DOCa) (deh-naw-mee-nah-THYON deh aw-REE-hen kah-lee-fee-KAH-dah)—The highest quality wine level of wines from Spain. DOCa requires that wines which are produced in particular geographical areas use defined methods and quality standards in their grape and wine production. As of 2008, only two DO's have been awarded the coveted DOCa designation.

Denominazione d'Origine Controllata (DOC) (deh-noh-mee-nah-TSYAW-neh dee oh-REE-jeh-neh con-traw-LAH-tah)—The second-highest quality level of wines from Italy. DOC requires that wines which are produced in particular geographical areas use defined methods and quality standards in their grape and wine production.

Denominazione d'Origine Controllata e Garantita (DOCG) (deh-NOH-mee-nah-SYAW-neh dee oh-REE-jee-neh con-traw-LAH-tah eh gah-rahn-TEE-tah)—The highest quality wine level of wines from Italy. DOCG requires that wines which are produced in particular geographical areas use defined methods and quality standards in their grape and wine production.

depth/deep—Wine-tasting term indicating a wine's intensity, complexity, and concentration, or aromas, flavors, and/or color.

dessert wine—Any type of wine that is sweet.

diacetyl (die-ASS-ih-tahl)—A chemical by-product of malolactic fermentation that adds a buttery aroma and flavor.

distillation—The process of heating a fermented mixture to separate the water by causing the alcohol to vaporize and then recondense with a higher strength and greater purity, whereupon it may be referred to as a spirit. The most common type of spirit used in fortified wine is brandy, which is made from grapes.

domaine (doh-MAYN)—French term for estate or property. Often used in Burgundy, France, where it refers to a single property that may or may not be made up of several vineyards from different locations.

dosage (doh-ZAHJ)—Denotes the addition of a small amount of wine and sugar to top off and adjust the sweetness of a bottle of sparkling wine.

doux (DOO)—French term for "sweet."

dry—A wine with no perceptible level of sweetness.

E

earthy—Used to describe an aroma of soil or mushrooms.

edelfäule (ay-duhl-FOY-luh)—German term for "noble rot."

eiswein (ICE-vyn)—A German term for "ice-wine," a wine made from grapes that are harvested and pressed while frozen. The juice that is released is highly concentrated, fruity, acidic, and sweet.

elegant—A wine-tasting term that describes a beautiful, well-balanced wine.

enology (ee-NAHL-uh-jee)—Also spelled *oenology*. The science and study of winemaking.

enophile (EE-nuh-file)—Someone who enjoys and appreciates fine wine, also spelled *oenophile*.

esters—Compounds produced from the reaction between alcohol and acids. They may contribute to complexity in the smell of a wine. Esters contribute many of the fruit aromas in a wine, such as pineapple, strawberry, cinnamon, and apple.

extra-dry—The equivalent of semi-dry, a term used to describe sparkling wines that are not as dry as Brut.

extract—The components and concentration of a wine that contribute to its body, flavor, and color.

F

fat—A wine-tasting term that describes the mouth feel of wines that are full bodied because the wine is either high in alcohol, oak aged, or high in sugar. Most late-harvest dessert wines are luscious and fat.

fermentation—The process by which yeast metabolizes grape sugars, producing ethyl alcohol, carbon dioxide, heat, and other by-products that affect the aroma and flavor of wine.

field blend—It used to be a common practice to intersperse complementary grapevines in a vineyard; when all the grapes are harvested together, the resulting wine is often referred to as a field blend.

fill level—The amount of wine in a bottle that is gauged by its height in the bottle.

filtering—A clarification process done to wine before it is bottled. The purpose of filtering is to remove sediment, grape skins, dead yeast, etc., from the wine. However, it is increasingly being minimized (or avoided whenever possible) because the greater the degree of filtering, the more flavors and character are stripped from the wine. Many wineries are using the more labor-intensive, old-fashioned practices of fining or racking to clarify wines these days.

fining (FINE-ing)—A clarification process done to wine before it is bottled. A traditional technique for clarifying wines by adding egg whites or bentonite (clay) to barrels of wine. These agents cause the particles and sediment to slowly sink to the bottom of the cask, where the material is then removed. Fining is considered a less intrusive process for clarifying wines than filtering.

finish—Sometimes referred to as the *persistence*, it's the lasting impression, or aftertaste, of a wine on the palate after the wine has been spit out or swallowed. A long, complex finish is generally desirable, though it ultimately depends on the typicity of a grape varietal.

flat—Also called "flabby." A wine-tasting term that is often used to describe white wines that are low in, or lacking acidity and to describe red wines that are low in, or lacking, acidity and tannin. Sometimes said of a wine that has been open for too long and lost its vibrancy. Also may be applied to a sparkling wine that has lost its carbonation.

flavonoids—A group of chemical compounds found in grape seeds, stems, and skins that contribute color, aromas, flavors, and antioxidant benefits.

flavor—The word used to describe the process of smelling the wine on the inside as the wine aromas are forced up the nasal passages.

flight—A grouping of several (often three to four) small portions of different wines that have been selected for some comparision or for contrasting purposes.

flinty—A stone or mineral-like aroma or flavor character used to describe a wine.

flor (FLOOR)—In reference to Spanish Sherry, these are the live yeast cells that naturally develop on certain wines after they have been fermented. Flor contributes aromas and flavors, but also acts to preserve the wine from oxygen while it is barrel aged.

floral—A wine that has aromas or flavors of flowers.

flowering—A term used in the vineyard to reference when small flowers begin to appear on the vine. They occur typically about 2½ months after bud break.

flute (FLOOT)—A tall, slender stemmed glass that is ideal for drinking sparkling wine.

fortified added—A category of wine in which table wine is the base, with added alcohol (in the form of a distilled spirit—often an unaged brandy). Fortified wine typically contains between 15% and 22% alcohol, and it is possible to have white or red options that can be made into wines that are dry, sweet, or somewhere in between. Port, Sherry, and Madeira are the most common fortified wines.

free-run juice—The initial juice released from the grapes once they have been pressed or crushed. Generally, the initial juice is considered to be of the best quality, because it has less contact with seeds and stems that may cause bitterness.

French oak—The classic wood for wine barrels that imparts flavors of vanilla, cedar, or other spices. The oak from different French forests lends slightly different characteristics to the wine and is therefore named for the forest region from which it was harvested.

French paradox—In the 1980s, medical studies found a paradox in that French people who have a fatter diet also have a low incidence of heart disease. The study found that the higher amounts of wine consumed by the French lowered health risks. The study concluded that people who consume moderate amounts of red wine are less likely than nondrinkers to suffer from cardiovascular disease. This finding led Americans to increase their consumption of red wine.

frizzante (free-DZAHN-tay)—An Italian term for slightly sparkling wine. Equivalent to the French term *Petillant*.

fruit set—A term used in the vineyard to identify when the grapevine flowers evolve into tiny green grape berries.

full body—Said of a wine that is high in extract, alcohol, or sugar. Can be compared to the weight or viscosity of whole milk.

G

geographically based—Applied to European wine labels, this concept simply refers to wines that are produced from strictly regulated areas of the wine-growing country.

geographic indicators—Australia's term for appellation, geographic indicators are that country's control system of identifying where the grapes are grown. Australian winemakers are required to maintain a minimum of 85% of a grape varietal from the location identified on the label.

glycerin—A by-product of fermentation that is most noticeable in wines with a higher alcohol content and in late-harvested wines, giving a smooth, fuller tactile impression.

gönci (GOON-ts)—The traditional 136-liter containers or barrels in which Tokay wines are created.

grafting—A technique used in the vineyard whereby a vine is secured to a different vine or rootstock. Grafting is often used to attach *vinifera* cuttings to American *lubrusca* rootstock that is *phylloxera* resistant.

grand cru—Literally, "great site" in France, this term refers to top-tier vineyards and their wines. In Burgundy, this term denotes the highest classification of vineyard.

Gran Reserva (GRAHN ree-SEHR-vah)—Spanish wine classification indicating the time of aging. Gran Reserva wines are any DO or DOCa red wines that have been aged a minimum of five years, of which at least one-and-a-half years were spent in barrels. The appellation areas of Rioja, Navarra, and Ribera del Duero require a minimum of two years in wood. White and rosé wines labeled as Gran Reserva must be aged four years, at least six months of which were in wood.

grappa (GRAHP-pah)—Also known as *marc* in France. An Italian spirit distilled from the remains of the grape skins, seeds, and stems. These remains are also known as pomace (PUHM-ess).

grassy—A wine having aromas and flavors of grass or fresh hay.

H

halbtrocken (HALP-trawk-en)—German term for "half-dry," meaning that the wine is semi-sweet.

hang time—Delay in harvesting grapes, with the expectation of increasing flavor development. This practice produces very ripe fruit that yields a "jammy" quality in the finished wine.

heavy soil—Soil with a high ratio of clay with high water retention and nutrients. Tends to be colder than other types of soil.

hectare—A measure used in Europe to represent the size of vineyards or regions. 1 hectare is equal to approximately 2.47 acres.

herbaceous—A wine having aromas and flavors of fresh herbs or grass.

horizontal tasting—An evaluation of wines from a single grape variety from different locations, from a single region, etc.

hot—A wine that is high in alcohol and that causes a burning sensation in the back of the throat.

house style—Nonvintage wines (which are blends of multiple vintages) allow vintners to create a "house style" by blending for consistency and distinctive, recognizable aromas and flavors year after year. For example, Champagne producers create a house style with their nonvintage Champagne.

house wine—A wine offered by the glass in a restaurant, often as an inexpensive option, but sometimes found in several price tiers.

hue—The shade of color of a wine.

hybrid grapes—Grapes created from cross-pollinating two different vine species, such as American vine (to obtain hardiness) and European vine (to obtain complexity) varieties.

hydrogen sulfide—Chemical responsible for the off-odor of rotten eggs in a wine.

hydrolyzable tannin—The type of tannin extracted through oak barrels and often referred to as ripe tannin, as it benefits by softening from aeration during the aging process.

I

ice-wine—A sweet dessert wine made from grapes that have been frozen on the vine or in freezers. Because the grapes are pressed while frozen, they release the sweet concentrated juice and leave behind the frozen, slushy water content. An ice-wine is called an Eiswein in Germany.

Indicazione Geografica Tipica (IGT) (in-dee-kat-tsee-OH-nay jay-o-GRAF-eecah TEE-pee-cah)—This category of wine was introduced in 1992 as a solution to the strict limited allowance for experimentation required in the upper two levels of the Italian classification system.

inert aging—The process of storing wine in a container that prevents the passage of oxygen, therefore preserving the wine's natural aromas and flavors. An example of such a container is a stainless steel or concrete container.

Institut Nationale des Appellations d'Origine (INAO) (an-stee-TYOO nah-syaw-NAHL dayz ah-pehl-lah-SYOHN daw-ree-ZHEEN)—The French governmental agency responsible for establishing and enforcing standards for the Appellation d' Origine Controlée system.

isinglass (Izing-Glas)—Used as a fining agent, this is a type of gelatin that comes from the bladder of fish.

J

jeroboam (jer-ah-BOME)—A large bottle that holds the equivalent of six regular bottles. However, with respect to sparkling wine, a Jeroboam holds four standard bottles of wine.

joven (HO-vehn)—Spanish term for *young*. A Spanish wine made with no or very little aging.

jug wine—An inexpensive generic wine that is of low quality. Often uses the place names of high-quality French wine regions and may be sold in 1-liter or 1.5-liter packaging.

K

kabinett (kah-bih-NEHT)—The lowest of the QMP levels indicating that the grapes from which a wine is made have been picked at normal harvest time with a standard sugar content of 17–21%.

L

lactic acid—An acid produced in high levels after a wine has undergone malolactic fermentation. This acid has an influence on the style of the wine by producing a softer, milky-type acid.

lake effect—Term used around the U.S. Great Lakes area and other large lakes in cool regions to describe the climatic influence on wine grapes. The lake effect retards early budding in the spring and allows for a longer growing season with a later harvest in the fall.

late harvest—Refers to wines made from grapes picked later than the normal harvest time and therefore with a higher sugar content (24% or above). Most late-harvest wines contain some residual sugar and would be appropriate for or with dessert.

late-bottled vintage port (LBV)—LBVs are an increasingly popular category of Port that is similar to, but less expensive than, Vintage Ports. LBVs spend an extra three to four years aging in a barrel before being bottled, which makes them more mature and easy to drink than Vintage Ports from the same year. Some LBVs are filtered before bottling; those labeled "Tradition" are unfiltered and will deposit sediment with further aging.

leathery—Said of a red wine that is rich with tannin.

lees—Sediment and dead yeast cells found in a barrel or tank during and after fermentation. "Sur Lie" is the French term for a wine left on the lees and denotes a winemaking technique used to increase complexities in the aromas and flavors during the aging process.

legs—The tears or sheets of wine that slide down the sides of the glass after it has been swirled. The more pronounced legs indicate a wine that has a higher alcohol or sugar content. Generally, the slower the flow and the more defined the legs are on the side of the glass, the fuller bodied is the wine.

light—Characterized by a low degree of alcohol and/or body.

light soil—Soil with a high ratio of sand with low water retention and low maintenance of nutrients.

Liqueur de Tirage (lick-KYOOR duh tee-RAHZH)—In Champagne, a blended base wine bottled and combined with a dose of sugar and yeast in order to induce a secondary fermentation. Through the secondary fermentation, a greater degree of alcohol (totaling around 13%) is produced, along with carbon dioxide.

loam soil—A mix of clay, silt, sand, and organic matter. Considered fertile and drains well.

M

maceration—The contact time between the grape skins (and sometimes stems) and the wine prior to and during the fermentation process in order to extract greater color, tannin, aroma, and flavor.

macroclimate—The general or broad climate in a large area such as Napa Valley or Champagne.

maderized—Said of a wine showing evidence of oxidation, including a brownish color and a bad Madeira-like flavor. Maderization is acceptable for certain types of wine, such as Madeira and Gran Reserva Rioja.

magnum—A bottle that holds two standard-size wine bottles.

malic acid—An acid found in large amounts in wine grapes and in some finished wines. Malic acid is responsible for producing a crisp, fresh feel and is also found in fruits such as apples.

malmsey (MAH'M-zee)—The richest and sweetest type of Madeira wine made from the Malvasia grape (though called Malmsey on the island of Madeira).

malolactic fermentation (ML)—Secondary fermentation (actually, a biochemical reaction) that converts the malic acid (fruit acids) in a wine to softer lactic acid (milk acids), so that the wine becomes softer, rounder, and more complex. Total acidity is also reduced. Most red wines go through this process, and so do some white wines, particularly Chardonnay.

mature—Ready to drink. All of the wine's components are in harmony.

meritage (MEHR-ih-tihj)—A term created by California wineries for Bordeaux-style red and white blended wines. A meritage wine must be made with two or more classic Bordeaux grape varietals. Producers may label the wines with the term *Meritage* or may use a proprietary name if they choose. Examples of wines that fall into this category include Opus One and Joseph Phelp's Insignia.

mesoclimate—The climate in a small area such as a vineyard or a portion of a vineyard.

méthode champenoise (may-TOAD cham-pen-WAHZ)—The traditional method for making Champagne and other high-quality sparkling wine. The method induces a secondary fermentation and traps the carbon dioxide within the original bottle. It is an expensive, labor-intensive process.

methuselah—The equivalent of eight standard bottles.

microclimate—The climate in a very small area, such as a row of vines within a vineyard.

micro-oxygenization—A winemaking technique that introduces the deliberate passage of a small amount of oxygen into the wine as it is being aged.

mildew—There are two main types of fungi that can cause damage within the vineyard. *Downy mildew* is associated with wet, humid growing areas. *Powdery mildew* (also called *odium*) is found in dry climates. Both can be treated with copper sulfate sprays.

millerandage (mill-lehr-AHN-dahj)—Condition in which grape bunches contain berries of varying sizes and maturity levels, causing a lower quality of wine.

mise en bouteille au chateau (meez ahn boo-TAY oh shah-TOE)—French term for *bottled at the winery*.

mousse (MOOSE)—A French term associated with the "foam" on the surface of a sparkling wine.

must—The unfermented juice of grapes before it is turned into wine.

N

nebuchadnezzar—A giant wine bottle holding the equivalent of 20 standard bottles.

negociant—A wine merchant who buys grapes or already fermented wines and then ages, blends, bottles, and ships them under their own label. Many famous French wine companies (particularly in Burgundy and the Rhône), such as Jadot, Duboeuf, and Drouhin, make wines from vineyards they do not own and thus are negociants.

noble rot—Also called *Botrytis cinerea*, a beneficial mold that may grow on wine grapes, causing them to dehydrate and shrivel resulting in the remaining juice becoming very concentrated. This desired condition yields the honey-like richness of many classic dessert wines, such as Sauternes, Trockenbeerenauslese, and Tokaji.

non-vintage (NV)—Said of a wine blended from multiple harvests; nonvintage wines are particularly common in sparkling wines, Sherries, and Ports. Blending allows the winemaker to create an individual "house" style that can be fairly consistent from bottle to bottle, year after year.

nose—The broadest term for the bouquet and aroma of a wine. The smell of a wine.

nouveau—A tradition started in Beaujolais, France, where a red wine is quickly fermented and then bottled and released within about eight weeks from harvest. Nouveau (or new) wines should be consumed within months of release.

O

oaky/oak—Describes the aroma or taste character of a wine that has interacted with an oak barrel. Most of the world's greatest red wines (and many of the world's greatest whites) are aged in wood before bottling and show some vanilla-spice-toast character and complexity contributed through the wine's interaction with oak.

Oechsle (UHX-leh)—A German method of measuring sugar content in unfermented grape juice.

off-dry—Said of a slightly sweet wine in which sugar is slightly perceptible.

old vines—"Vieille vines" in French. A wine made from old grapevines. Theoretically, old vines should produce better fruit, but they also yield less quantity.

oxidation—The chemical reaction whereby a wine is unintentionally exposed or overexposed to oxygen, causing the wine to become spoiled.

oxidative aging—The process of storing wine in a container that allows the slow passage of oxygen over time, therefore causing the wine's aromas and flavors to be enhanced. Oxidative aging can occur in oak or chestnut wood barrels.

oxidized—Said of a wine that has lost its freshness from exposure to oxygen, similar to an apple turning brown and losing its flavor once the skin is peeled. Oxidation causes chemical changes and deterioration that alters the colors, aromas, and flavors of wines. Oxidized wines are also referred to as "maderized." Using a wine preserver (which blankets the wine with inert gas and prevents contact with oxygen) can lessen or prevent oxidation. Oxidation is desired in certain types of wine, such as Madeira.

P

passito (pah-SEE-toh)—An Italian method of laying grapes on mats or hanging them to partially dry for weeks to several months. This process, which evaporates water content and concentrates flavors and sugar content, can produce a dry or sweet wine, depending upon when fermentation has ended.

peak—The time when a wine is meant to be drunk; the time when it attains its smoothest, fullest, most well balanced flavors and components. This time can vary from a few months for Nouveau or some white wines to decades for a Vintage Port or Red Bordeaux.

performance factors—Combination of aspects (color, aroma, flavor, acid, alcohol, tannin, body level, and so on) that cumulatively create the distinctive personality of a particular grape varietal. Performance factors can be used to identify the defining elements of a particular grape as it has been produced around the world by various viticulture and winemaking techniques.

pétillant (pay-tee-YAWN)—French term for slightly sparkling. Equivalent to the Italian term, frizzante.

phenolics—Chemical compounds found in grape skins and seeds and extracted from oak barrels. Phenolics are responsible for the tannins, color pigments, and flavor compounds in wine.

phenolic ripeness—Otherwise known as flavor ripeness, represented by a group of compounds that contribute color, aroma, flavor, and tannin to a grape. This kind of ripeness allows the tannins to become softer as the growing season progresses. Phenolic ripeness often trails sugar ripeness, but is important for allowing the maximum flavor of the grape to be obtained.

phylloxera (fil-LOX-er-uh)—The name of an insect that attacks and devastates the roots of grapevines. It spread from America to Europe in the 1860s and destroyed the vineyards of France, after which it spread elsewhere. Most of the world's vineyards are now grafted on American rootstock, which is more resistant to Phylloxera.

pièce (pee-YES)—Often refers to a barrel for aging or fermentation that holds approximately 60 gallons; used in Burgundy.

pierce's disease—A disease caused by a bacterium that is transferred through its insect host (the glassy-winged sharpshooter) and that kills the grapevine.

polymerize (PUH-lym-err-ize)—To separate or fall out of a liquid solution and form a sediment. Over time, a red wine's tannin (in combination with color pigment) will polymerize in the wine bottle.

pomace (PUHM-ess)—The solid remains left over after pressing grapes to extract juice. Pomace consists of the skins, seeds, stems, and remaining pulp of the grape. These remains may be fermented and distilled to create grappa.

prädikatswein (preh-dih-KAHTS-vine)—The highest quality category for wine made in Austria.

premier cru—This French labeling means "first-growth vineyards"; sometimes the term "1er Cru" may appear. In Burgundy the term denotes the second-best classified vineyard, but in Bordeuax it's the highest ranking of a classified estate.

press wine—The juice extracted after the initial pressing of white wine grapes and after fermentation for red wine grapes. Press wine has more color and, often, more tannins than free-run juice. Winemakers may blend a portion of press wine with the free-run juice for backbone.

private reserve—A term used to indicate a producer's best offering. Private Reserve has no legal definition and is applied to everything from $10 to $200 bottles of wine.

prohibition—A time in America when it was illegal to produce, transport, sell, and consume alcohol (with some exceptions, such as alcohol for sacramental purposes). Prohibition lasted from 1920 to 1933.

pruning—A viticultural practice of cutting back grapevines and related foliage in order to concentrate the vines' energies into the remaining grapes to make a high-quality crop.

pulp—The soft, succulent part on the inside of the grape, where the juice, acid, sugar, and flavor can be found. Approximately 75% of a grape by weight, pulp plays a major role in providing acid (which is present in the juice) and is pivotal in giving both red and white wine good structure.

pumping over—The aggressive process of pumping and circulating the juice of the grape (with a giant hose) over the cap during fermentation. Commonly used in Bordeaux in order to extract maximum color, juice, and tannin from grape skins.

punching down—The gentle process of pushing the cap (skins, seeds, and stems) down into the wine as it ferments. Commonly used in Burgundy.

punt—The indentation found in the bottom of most wine bottles and which is especially important in sparkling wine bottles, where it acts to strengthen the bottle.

pupître (pew-PEE-truh)—A French term for the "A-frame" rack in which bottles are placed for riddling for the production of Champagne.

puttonyos (PUH-tohn-yosh)—Name of the basket in Hungary which holds the aszú berries that were mashed into a sweetened paste.

Q

qualitätswein (kvah-lee-TAYTS-vine)—Term representing middle-quality wines in both Germany and Austria.

qualitätswein mit prädikat (QmP) (kvah-lee-TAYTS-vine meet PRAY-dee-kaht)—Term representing the highest quality wines in the German classification system. There are six subcategories within the QmP system, ranked in ascending order according to their sugar content upon harvest: kabinett, Spätlese, Auslese, Beerenauslese, Eiswein, and Trockenbeerenauslese.

R

racking—The practice of transfering wine from one container to another to rid the wine of sediment by leaving the sediment behind in the first container. Racking is essentially decanting on a grand scale by moving a wine from barrel to barrel. Racking is more labor intensive, but less disturbing to the wine, than filtration.

recioto (reh-CHAW-toh)—An Italian wine (speciality of the Veneto) made by the Passito method. If the wine is left with residual sugar, it is known as Recioto. If the wine is fermented dry, it is known as Amarone.

rehoboam—A large (rah-moo-ajh) bottle equivalent to six regular bottles.

remuage (reh-moo-ajh)—French term for riddling—that is, the process of shaking the Champagne bottles to encourage the lees to move towards the neck of the bottle.

reserva (ray-SEHR-vah)—A Spanish wine classification indicating the time of aging. Reserva wines are any DO or DOCa red wines that have been aged a minimum of three years, one year of which was in wood. White and rosé wines labeled as Reserva must be aged two years, six months of which are in wood.

reserve—This term may be found on American wine bottles and may mean a winery's top-of-the-line wine, but has no legal definition. It is used mostly for marketing purposes.

residual sugar—A measurement of the amount of grape sugar remaining in a wine after fermentation. Dry wines have little or no residual sugar (0.1–0.2%), whereas dessert wines contain as much residual sugar as 28–30%.

resveratrol (rez-VEHR-ah-trawl)—One of the phenolic compounds found in high amounts within grape skins and that have beneficial affects on cholesterol levels and prevention against certain kinds of cancer.

retronasal passage—Passageway connecting the throat with the nose and that enables a person to detect a wine's flavors inside the mouth.

riddling—The process of placing Champagne bottles upside down in a rack, in which they are shaken over a period of several weeks. The shaking allows the lees to collect at the neck of the bottle in order to eventually be discarded.

ripasso (ree-PAH-so)—A winemaking technique common in Italy that allows a wine to remain in contact with the lees from a previous passito wine through re-fermentation.

riserva (Rih-ZERVA)—Italian designation on a wine label indicating that the wine has additional barrel aging, but that the duration of aging varies by region.

robust—Full bodied, intense.

rosado (roe-SAH-do)—In Spanish, refers to a rosé wine, made by allowing the juice to have only brief contact with the skin of the red wine grapes.

rosé—French term for pink. Rosé wines range in color from pink to salmon and are made from red wine grapes through limited skin contact in order to extract only a slight amount of color. Sometimes, a small amount of red wine may be added instead.

rosso (RAWH-soh)—Italian for "red," as in red wine.

rotwein (RAWT-vine)—German for "red wine."

rouge (ROOZH)—French for "red," as in red wine.

round—Describes a smooth, well-balanced wine.

S

saignée (san-YAY)—A method of producing wine that allows some of the color from red grape skins to bleed into the fermenting juice, creating a pinkish color.

salmanazar—A large bottle that holds the equivalent of 12 regular bottles.

sediment—The color pigments and tannins that form together and naturally separate out from a red wine as it ages. The wine is removed from the sediment through the decanting process.

seeds and stems—Seeds are found on the inside, and stems are found on the outside, of a grape, and both may contribute a bitter component if crushed or used in excess. Stems and seeds contribute approximately 5% of the grape by weight.

sekt (ZEKT)—A German sparkling wine.

skin—That part of the grape found on the outside and in which reside the tannin, flavor, and color. Making up approximately 20% of the grape by weight, skin has an even greater influence on the style and structure of a red wine, which are achieved when the skins are allowed to ferment with the juice.

skin contact—The process of macerating the skins and grape juice together in order to extract flavor, tannin, and color.

solera system (soh-LEH-rah)—An intricate blending system used in Spain to produce Sherry.

sommelier (saw-muh-LYAY)—A French term for a wine steward. This individual is responsible for managing the wine program, which may include ordering and storing the wine, educating staff, making wine recommendations, and serving wines to customers. Sommeliers are often hired by fine-dining restaurants, but the term has been increasingly applied to wine experts in all forums (wine bars, retail stores, etc.) where wine is sold.

sparkling wine—A category of wine in which table wine is the base, with large amounts of CO_2 added for carbonation. Sparkling wine typically contains between 10% and 13% alcohol.

Spätlese (SHPAYT-lay-zuh)—The second ranking of the QMP levels, Spätlese indicates that the grapes have been picked after normal harvest and with a sugar content of 19–23% by weight.

spritzy—A pleasant, light sparkling sensation (sometimes found in young wines) caused by a slight secondary fermentation or the addition of carbon dioxide.

spumante—Italian term for sparkling wine with regular or standard levels of carbonation.

stainless steel aging—Method used primarily for white aromatic wines whose primary flavors and crisp acidity need to be preserved. Stainless steel doesn't truly age the wine; rather, it preserves the wine and prevents the passage of oxygen that would otherwise alter the wine's personality.

stemmy—Green, astringent character of wines fermented too long with the grape stems.

sticky—Australian term referencing a sweet dessert wine.

still wine—A term that applies to any wine that is not sparkling.

structure—A wine's texture, mouth feel, and balance.

struggling vine philosophy—Philosophical viewpoint which theorizes that the farther a vine's roots must dig to find nutrients, the fewer, but better quality, grapes will be produced, with thicker skins and more concentrated flavor.

sulfur dioxide—Sulfites are a derivative of sulfur and a natural by-product of fermentation. Most wines naturally contain very low levels of sulfites. However, winemakers have added sulfites to wine for hundreds of years to clean and sterilize equipment and barrels, to kill off bacteria, and to prevent browning and possible spoilage. Sulfur is also sometimes sprayed in a vineyard to prevent disease and pests. Under U.S. law, any wine with sulfites higher than 10 ppm must state "contains sulfites" on the label.

Super Tuscan—An unofficial name originally given to wines from Tuscany that are made from international varieties such as Cabernet Sauvignon or Merlot, rather than primarily local varieties such as Sangiovese. Because they are made outside the traditional Tuscan winemaking practices, these wines are labeled with the lower quality classification within Italy's system.

superiore (soo-payr-YOH-reh)—The Italian label designating a wine as having a slightly higher alcohol content.

sur lie (soor LEE)—A French term which indicates that a wine was aged "on the lees" (on sediment consisting mainly of dead yeast cells and small grape particles). This process is a normal procedure for fermenting red wines; Burgundian winemakers discovered that it often added complexity to their Chardonnays, and now the process is used in many white wines from around the world.

süssreserve (ZOOSS-ray-ZEHR-veh)—Winemaking method that involves fermenting the wines fully dry, with low alcohol and high acid. Before fermentation, a small quantity of unfermented juice is held back. Later, this juice will be blended into the dry wine in order to adjust and balance the acid-to-sweetness ratio.

T

table wine—This category of wine gets its name because it is made to be drunk at the table with meals. The alcoholic content of table wine generally is between 8% and 15%. Table wines are white, pink, or red wines that can be dry, sweet, or somewhere in between.

tannin—A natural chemical compound found in grape skins (mostly of red wine grapes), seeds, and stems, but also in oak barrels. Tannins produce an astringent, mouth-puckering sensation. Tannins are common in most fine young red wines and help form natural preservatives that allow wines to develop and age. Tannins soften in time, either naturally or with exposure to oxygen.

tartrates—Natural, harmless crystals that look like shards of glass and often form in a barrel, bottle, or cork. They may occur from the tartaric acids present in a wine if the wine gets very cold. Upon serving a wine, it would be proper practice to decant it if it shows evidence of tartrate crystals.

TCA—An acronym for 2, 4, 6-trichloroanisole (try-clore-AN-iss-all), a chemical that has a wet-cardboard odor and flavor commonly associated with tainted cork.

terroir (tehr-WHAR)—French term that encompasses all the environmental factors that affect the grapevine, such as the interactions among soil, climate, topography, and grape variety within a specific vineyard.

tête de cuvée (tet duh koo-VAY)—French term for a Champagne producer's best bottling.

thin—Lacking body; often used to describe a wine that tastes diluted.

tinto (TEEN-to)—Spanish for "red wine."

tirage (tee-RAHZH)—Method whereby, in Champagne production, the blended base wine is given a dose of sugar and yeast in order to induce a secondary fermentation.

toasty—A flavor imparted by oak barrels.

transfer process—The sparkling wine production process whereby the wine is removed from the bottle, transferred to a pressurized tank for filtering, and then rebottled.

trellis—An artificial support used to hold and train grapevines to grow off the ground.

trocken—German word meaning *dry*.

U

ullage (UHL-ihj)—The air space in the bottle between the top of the wine and the bottom of the cork.

V

varietal—A specific grape variety. Also denotes a wine made mostly or entirely from one grape variety.

varietal based—A concept applied to most non-European wine labels. The term simply refers to the grape variety used to make the wine.

varietal character—Sometimes referred to as "typicity," the varietal character identifies the aromas, flavors, and taste sensations typical of a particular grape variety.

vegetal—A word applied to wines that smell or taste like plants or green vegetables.

vendage (vahn-DAHZH)—Grape harvest or vintage.

vendage tardive—A French term for "late harvest."

véraison (vehr-ray-ZOHN)—Natural process whereby, near the middle to end of summer, the green berries begin to change color and become recognizable as grapes.

vin de pays—The name translates to "country wine." This is the third level of quality classification in the French wine laws. Varietals are allowed to be mentioned on the labels. These wines are predominant in the south of France.

vineyard—A grape-growing area that ranges in size.

viniculture—The science of growing wine grapes and making wine.

vino (VEE-noh)—"Wine" in Italian.

Vino da Tavola (VdT) (VEE-no dah TAH-voh-lah)—Lowest level designation of wine, with the greatest amount of freedom. The producers are not allowed to cite the grape varietal or specific location on the label.

vintage—Term that refers both to the year the grapes from which a certain wine was made were harvested and to the wine made from those grapes. To place a vintage on the label, most wine-producing regions now require that at least 95% of the wine contain grapes harvested from only that year. Historically, some wine regions were lax in requiring that vintage dates be accurate. Wines that are blended from more than one harvest are called non-vintage wines.

vintage ports—These wines are created from grapes deriving from a single year. The wine is bottled within 2½ years of the vintage and spends most of its life evolving within a bottle.

vintner—Wine producer or winery proprietor.

viticulture—The science or study of grape growing.

vitis vinifera—The classic European grapevine species most responsible for producing the world's best wines, including Pinot Noir, Chardonnay, Cabernets, etc.

W

wein (VINE)—German for "wine."

weiss (VICE)—German for "white."

weissherbst (VICE-hehrbst)—German for "rosé" (wine).

wood-barrel aging—A centuries-old tradition that uses wood vessels to store and age most red wines and many full-bodied white wines. The industry standard is to use French or American oak as the preferred wood. Oak from other places, such as Slovenian oak, is sometimes still used. In the past, different wine regions have used different kinds of wood, such as mahogany, chestnut, and pine.

world cuisine—In the broadest sense, food that has been created in present-day times and that may incorporate a combination of modern or classical practices, ingredients, and techniques.

Y

yeast—Important microorganisms that cause fermentation by converting sugar to alcohol. The predominant wine yeast, *Saccharomyces* (sack-row-MY-ceese) *cerevisiae*, is the same microorganism that ferments beer and makes bread rise. Two categories of yeast are cultured yeast and wild yeast.

INDEX